ISLAM : GENDER JUSTICE

ISLAM
GENDER JUSTICE
Muslims Gender Discrimination

ASGHAR ALI ENGINEER

GYAN

Islam : Gender Justice–Muslims Gender Discrimination

ISBN : 978-81-212-1176-5

Published in 2013 in India by
Gyan Publishing House
23, Main Ansari Road, Daryaganj,
New Delhi - 110002
Phones : 23282060, 23261060
Fax : (011) 23285914

E-mail: books@gyanbooks.com
website: gyanbooks.com

Laser Type Setting : Rajender Vashist, Delhi
Printed at : Chawla Offset Printers, Delhi

Contents

Preface

This book contains essays on Muslim Personal Laws and gender justice written from time to time and some of which were published in *Dawn* newspaper, Karachi as a monthly column. It was thought necessary to collect these essays in the book form as these essays were widely discussed on various forums including on inter-net and are of permanent value. Gender justice is becoming increasingly important in all religious, caste and ethnic communities, particularly among Muslims as people feel Islam does not do justice to women and suppresses their rights.

Islam does no injustice to women at all. It is perception, not reality. Islam is the first religion in the world, if we go by the Qur'anic pronouncements on gender issue to have given them well-defined rights and even made them equal to man. Then the question arises why women are so lagging behind in Islamic countries and appear to be subordinated to men? It is obviously due to patriarchal culture. And since Muslim societies are generally lagging behind in economic and educational development, patriarchy in these countries remains strong and finds justification under the garb of distorted interpretations and other medieval texts which came into existence during that period to assert superiority of men over women.

However, some well known Islamic scholars tried to reform situation and advocated reforms in personal laws, especially after encounter with colonialism 19th century onwards. I have also attempted critique of Muslim personal laws known as Shari'ah laws and tried to restore Qur'anic spirit of gender justice. Some of the essays have been written on certain gender issues, fatwas etc. and some essays have been written on reformers like Maulavi Mumtaz Ali Khan and others.

It is hoped these essays will dispel many misunderstandings both among Muslims as well as non-Muslims about gender issues in Islam. If it happens this book would have served its purpose.

Asghar Ali Engineer

Introduction

ANTI-ISLAM FILM AND REACTION IN THE MUSLIM WORLD

A Coptic American, extreme right winger and Islam hater made an anti-Islam film and put it on internet. Its reaction was very violent in the Muslim world beginning with Libya wherein an American ambassador Christopher Steve along with four other consulate staff was killed in violent demonstration. It was followed by violent demonstrations in Egypt, Yemen, and other places. Saudi Arabia which normally remains officially silent also had to strongly protest on Government level.

Of course some countries like Indonesia, Malaysia and others remained comparatively peaceful though signs of unrest are there in these countries too. In other words the countries covered by Arab Spring were mostly affected. And on this occasion a private agency in Iran once again renewed the prize offer (with increased amount of 3.3 million dollar) on Rushdie's head.

Rushdie of course reacted characteristically by saying that blasphemy should be one's right. It is difficult to say what shape this renewed offer on Rushdie's head will take. It may remain only a formal announcement. It seems difficult that it would become a raging controversy as it did when Ayatollah Khomeini had declared price on Rushdie's head. Politically it was very different context.

Ayatollah Khomeini then was a great hero for the Muslim youth as he had declared America a great Satan (*Shaytan-e-buzurg*) and America all over the Muslim world then was seen as an evil incarnate who had tried to stop an Islamic revolution and Rushdie was seen as a western agent who had, in the name of human rights, insulted the Prophet of Islam thus trying to weaken Islamic revolution. One cannot expect that kind of reaction from the Muslim youth anymore.

But as for the anti-Islamic film *Innocent Muslims* there is a different political context (i.e. the Arab Spring), no less significant than Islamic revolution of Iran. The only difference is that Iranian revolution was actively opposed by America whereas Arab Spring was seen as favourable by

American rulers under the pretext of bringing in democracy to the Arab world.

In Libya America and NATO forces had played an active role in overthrowing Gaddafi who had played an anti-American role throughout his life except perhaps during the last phase when he had tried to reconcile with Western powers. In Syria too America, like Libya, is interested in what it chooses to call 'regime change'. Needless to say both in Libya and Syria America had not played so innocent a role as it would like the world to believe.

Today both in Libya and Syria Al-Qaeda has become hyper-active but even at the cost of making al-Qaeda quite active, America's priority is to destroy Gaddafi and Bashar al-Assad, the old enemies of America and the only obstacles in total domination of Middle East by America. Both of them have been anti-Israel too and with their elimination, America will be free to promote its interest in the area.

For al-Qaeda too it suits well as both Bashar al-Assad and Gaddafi have been enemies being revolutionaries and seen as anti-Islamic forces by them (i.e. al-Qaeda) Thus both the regimes, ironically, are seen as enemies both by America and al-Qaeda. Thus the violent demonstrations against the film are result of number of factors. What is to be understood is that these demonstrations are less Islamic and more for down to earth factors – political, economic and sociological.

The media, especially western media, is portraying these demonstrations as purely a violent religious act, act of fanaticism particularly because it is Islamic. It is not so simple as the media is portraying it. First of all we must reckon with the oil factor. America's sole interest in this region is neither Islam, nor democracy, nor dictatorship, for that matter. It is oil, pure and simple.

There is as yet no alternative to oil and most of the oil resources of the world are in this region. America wants to maintain its grip on this region at any cost. The first danger it smelt in the region was the Islamic revolution of Iran. U.S. was exceptionally hostile to Iranian revolution. Not because it was Islamic revolution; it was because Iran was emerging as challenge to American leadership in the region. It was equally hostile to Fatimi's democratic revolution in early fifties of the last century and to undo that revolution it had used Ayatollah's against the Fatimi's secular democratic revolution.

After the then Iranian revolution of 1950s number of left-oriented regimes emerged in Middle East i.e. Iraqi and Syrian (Baath Party-led revolution) and Libyan Revolution in 1969, apart from Jamal Abd al-Nassir's Young Officers' coup in Egypt in mid-fifties. Nasser's revolution was no less dangerous than that of Iranian revolution in 1979. It nationalized Suez Canal and France,

Britain and Israel invaded Egypt morally supported by USA. It was Soviet Union which threatened these powers and made them retreat.

The Arab Spring, was also seen similarly an opportunity by America to intervene and do away with 'enemies' like Gaddafi and Bashar al-Assad. But like before, it is not as simple as America thinks. The demonstrations are aimed politically against American interests in the region. Of course it is utterly foolish to make such film which has been described as 'idiotic' or utterly simplistic.

It is true the American regime, much less the people, had anything to do with making of the film and so one wonders why kill its ambassador and consular staff or why demonstrate against America. These demonstrations do not mean that people put responsibility of the film on America. It clearly means that they have utterly hostile feelings towards American domination and repeated interference in the region. They want America to get out of the region.

Unfortunately America does not want to learn lessons. After Libya it rushed to the aid of rebel not for its love of democracy in Syria but for its hatred of the enemy i.e. Bashar al-Assad. America is fully aware of the fact that al-Qaeda is trying to capture the rebel forces. But it thinks Bashar al-Assad is much greater enemy and it can take care of al-Qaeda later. Let not America think that the rebels in Syria would feel grateful to America after success of rebellion. These rebels too carry anti-American feelings hidden in their hearts and when time comes they will manifest it as it happened in Libya.

Many moderate Muslim intellectuals are saying that moderates should speak out against violent demonstrations. I fully agree with this viewpoint. We must oppose violence anywhere and in whatever form. Moreover it is not people of America who are to be blamed for events like anti-Islamic film. It is after all small number of right wingers who are compulsive haters of Islam.

Also, people of America like any other people of the world, are manipulated by the powerful media to think that American foreign policy is right in the Middle Eastern region. For them the principles, and not the interests, play role in framing these policies. Also, hatred is not the right answer for hatred. As a Muslim and as a Gandhian I think love and understanding is the right answer.

To prevent such violent demonstrations the Imams should play creative role in Friday sermons. They should explain to Muslims what are Islamic values and why they should desist from such demonstrations. Also, as a value we oppose US policies, not America or American people. American principles are as great as any other principles. Among those principles are freedom of expression and freedom to follow ones dictates of conscience. There can be no compromise of that.

But this is possible only when our Imams are highly educated and capable of analyzing facts as they are. The kinds of Imams we have are illiterate in matters other than Islamic Shari'ah and Islamic theology. Imams play very significant role in lives of Muslims, especially in Asian and African countries. Muslim intellectuals and moderate Muslims should see to it that Imams should not only be Islamically educated but also in other matters as they influence Muslim thinking on socio-political matters through their sermons on Friday.

The Muslim media also has to play highly responsible role in such matters. We see that Muslim media also, like Imams of the mosques, play to the gallery. Today we are living in the age of democracy and in democracy media plays very important role. We know western media too does not play responsible role. On one hand it displays deeply rooted prejudices and on the other, it guards the interests of multi-national corporations.

But if we believe in Islamic values of justice and peace we have to suppress our anger and display more patience failing which "Islam stands for peace" will become mere rhetoric and such display of violence on all such occasions does show it is mere rhetoric. As good Muslims we should go beyond mere rhetoric and show in action that we stand for justice and peace.

Asghar Ali Engineer
Centre for Study of Society and Secularism
Mumbai.

1

Religion and Muslim Women

Issues in Islamic Feminism

Is there anything like Islamic feminism? Most of the Islamists maintain such a term is contradiction in terms. For them feminism is against teachings of Islam. It is a western phenomenon and those women who are westernised and want to stick to Islam in name only. They dismiss this phenomenon with contempt. However, this attitude is more because of strong influence on their minds of conservative Islam. The conservative *ulama* insist on assigning women position subservient to men. Wives, according to them, should accept authority of their husbands.

A deeper examination of Qur'anic verses makes it clear that it firmly upholds dignity of women as that of men. It does not discriminate between two sexes. In fact it was social environment in which Shari'ah formulations were made that affected Islamists' viewpoint about women rather than the Qur'anic teachings. Today's social environment is radically different and women awareness of their rights has increased phenomenally.

There is nothing wrong in revisiting Shari'ah formulations regarding women today and attempt to reformulate issues in the light of contemporary social milieu. After all the great Imams themselves had formulated issues in respect of women's legal and moral status in medieval milieu. Only condition is such reformulation or rethinking should be in the light of the Qur'an.

One should not be scared of the word feminism as our '*ulama* tend to be. After all feminism is all about women's rights. The Qur'an is so much concerned about women's rights that it will not be wrong to say the Qur'an preached feminism for the first time in the world and the Prophet was the first feminist. One should not shy away from the new terms. Obviously feminism is not an old Shari 'ah term. But new terms can always be adopted. After all the term human rights does not exist in shari'ah but today the term like 'Islamic human rights' is freely being used. Why then not 'Islamic feminism'?

What is Feminism?

Feminism is nothing but a discourse on women's rights in modern context. For all these centuries women were treated as subordinate to men. And this was thought to be quite natural. Women were confined to home and hearth and were not allowed any public role in general though there might have been some exceptions. Generally, they did not even acquire education. A woman who could perform domestic chores with expertise was considered excellent in marriage market. She could become an ideal wife.

So her maximum achievement was limited to domestic field. She had no independent personality of her own. She was extension either of her father, brother or husband. She could be consulted but could not take decision herself. Decision was ultimately taken by father, brother or husband. Even if she did, she could be overruled. She had no right to earn her own living. It was thought against family pride that wife earns. This was interpreted as husband's inability to maintain his wife. Even if a wife could earn she was prevented from doing so. Even today many husbands to be, stipulate condition that their prospective wives will give up the job after marriage.

All this is slowly changing in the modern society. Literacy has become universal. Even most orthodox families now send their daughters to schools and colleges. In fact, certain statistics clearly show that more girls are graduating than boys even among backward Muslim communities in India. Recently on my visit to Kolhapur in Maharashtra, I discovered that among very poor and backward caste Muslims (mostly baghbans ? a backward caste among Muslims in Maharashtra) there are girls who have done post-graduation in science and humanities whereas there is not a single boy who has achieved so much in the field of education.

Earlier primary education was considered more than enough. And coeducation was considered 'sin'. Today Muslim girls are going for coeducation without any hesitation. We have to remember that society is not static. Unfortunately, our *'ulama*, dyed in the wool orthodox, think society is static and any change is unacceptable. They have frozen society to early Islamic period i.e., eighth and ninth centuries A.D.

Ulama's attitude may be frozen, Muslims' attitude is not. Most of them are accepting changes and adjusting themselves keeping their Islamic conscience intact. All changes are not bad or un-Islamic, those un-Islamic could be surely rejected. Feminist discourse, as we will show, is not unacceptable to one who cares for ones Islamic conscience. Every knowledgeable Muslim has right to decide, there being no priesthood or church in Islam. Even a *fatwa* by most learned *alim* could be rejected by a Muslim who does not agree with his opinion. Of course, there are less informed Muslims who might consider these *fatwas* as binding.

However, with increased awareness and sources of knowledge available such less informed Muslims are also decreasing in number. It is also important to note that the *'ulama* are accepting modern technology when it suits them. For example, today Internet and e-mail networks are being used by the 'ulama to spread orthodoxy. But it is not going to consolidate orthodox positions in the long run. As Marshal McLuhan, an American sociologist put it in 1970s 'media is the message'. The modern media being used by orthodox 'ulama cannot but be influenced by the modernity of the medium which will impact their minds for change in attitudes.

The *Ulama* are also accepting divorce through SMS, which, Islamically speaking, is most unjust and un-Islamic but in keeping with the orthodoxy and medieval ethos. Any modern technology, which can perpetuate orthodoxy, is acceptable but not those values, which uphold the real Qur'anic spirit of justice.

The modern feminist discourse is based on justice. Suppression of women's rights is gross injustice and hence feminism rejects it. All serious students of Qur'an very well know that justice forms core value of Qur'an. Anything unjust is *zulm* (oppression, wrong doing) in the Qur'anic terminology. How then the feminist discourse in this respect can be construed as 'un-Islamic'?

Today, it is considered for woman a fundamental right to acquire education. Is not acquisition of Islamic education an Islamic right? The Prophet (PBUH) made it obligatory both for men and women to acquire knowledge (talabul 'ilm faridatun 'ala kulli muslimin wa *muslimatin* ? Acquisition of knowledge is obligatory on every Muslim man and Muslim woman). Still the orthodox Muslim society strongly resisted providing education to their womenfolk for several centuries. How 'Islamic' was their stand, which was perpetuated in the name of Islam?

Could campaign for modern education for Muslim women become an issue of Islamic feminism? Today, even in bastion of orthodoxy like Saudi Arabia women graduates are more than fifty per cent. And it is not only in religious education but in modern university education. Saudi society needs female teachers and doctors. But the Saudi women are no more confined to these fields alone. They are going now for aviation training, business management training and so on. Although the Saudi women are still far behind their sisters in other fields in other Muslim countries but change is more than perceptible. It is inevitable.

The Qur'an also does nowhere restrict knowledge to men alone. In fact *'ilm* (knowledge) is most central to Qur'anic teachings. *Allah* is also repeatedly described in Qur'an as knower and urges upon all Muslim men and women to acquire knowledge. It was male dominated Muslim society, which restricted knowledge to men and deprived women of their fundamental right to acquire knowledge.

Islamic and Western Feminism

One must of course make distinction between western and Islamic feminism. Western feminism today has been heavily influenced by its consumer culture. And in consumer culture instant gratification is central and values quite marginal. Islamic feminism, on the other hand, is based on values and these values are quite central. For example, women are not consumable commodities and their bodies cannot be commercialised.

In Western feminist discourse, women are owners of their bodies implying that they are free to let their bodies be used for any purpose, including commercial purpose, if they so decide. Thus they are free to allow their semi-nude bodies for commercial ads, or even for free sex. Thus they have unrestricted rights over their bodies, not circumscribed by any values.

These women can even opt for what is called 'live-in' relationship without any formal marriage. They can also opt for adulterous relationship as owners of their bodies. This is just not acceptable as far as Islamic feminism is concerned. It does not mean they are not owners of their bodies. Of course they are but subject to certain fundamental values prescribed by the Qur'an.

These values are prioritised over ownership of the body. Freedom without values and sense of responsibility becomes licentiousness. Hence all human bodies including those of men are subject to fundamental values. One cannot, for example, use ones body freely for sex without marriage. Sex for mere pleasure cannot form part of Islamic feminism. Sex primarily is for perpetuating human species and this can best be done through marriage and family. For perpetuating human species institution of marriage plays very important role. In western feminism family has lost its relevance and a woman is entitled to sexual pleasure for pleasure's sake. Sexual pleasure is not the tool for raising family but an end in its self.

In Islamic feminism sexual pleasure is a tool, not an end. Islam, it is important to note, does not deny women right to sexual pleasure though it does not reduce it to an end itself. Some Muslims go for female circumcision to deprive her of sexual pleasure. It is more of tribal custom than any religious injunction. Most of the Muslims do not accept female circumcision. It is unjust to deprive her of that. Islamic shari'ah also clearly lays down that if a man hides his impotency from his bride at the time of marriage and she discovers it after marriage, she is fully entitled to divorce on that ground. This itself clearly shows that she is entitled to sexual pleasure along with raising family.

A woman is owner of her body subject to, as pointed out before, some value-based conditions. She, for example, cannot be compelled for sex, if she is unwilling. She fully controls her body. Sex in marriage also has to be with consent of both the partners. Islamic feminism, however, may not go as far as admitting of 'marital rape', as in western feminism. But that does not mean husband has absolute rights over his wife's body. Husband's rights are also subject to certain value-based conditions.

A woman, according to the Qur'an, posses full dignity, as much as a man has and forced sex will be obviously violation of this dignity. But since violation of dignity cannot be equated with marital rape it cannot be punished. A Muslim man has to desist from violation of his wife's dignity.

One can however, quote the Qur'anic verse 2:223 that women are like tilth and go to your tilth when you like and send (good) beforehand for yourselves? Some feminists might maintain that this verse goes against her dignity as she is like her ploughing field and he can go to his field when he likes. First, this verse should be read along with the preceding one i.e. verse 222 which prohibits man to go near her when she is undergoing her period and also instructs man to go near her as *Allah* has commanded and *Allah* has commanded to respect her dignity.

Secondly, woman being field for man only means she conceives after man's seed is implanted into her womb. It is she who conceives and rears children. In many religious traditions earth is likened to mother as earth grows food to sustain human beings. Similarly woman has been likened to field as she conceives and produces children to perpetuate human species. It in no way detracts from her dignity. On the other hand, it enhances her respect in our eyes. One has to properly understand the context in which it has been said.

The verse 4:34 is also controversial in this respect as this verse has been grossly misunderstood and implies that woman is subordinate to man and goes against feminist concept. We have discussed this verse and every word in it elsewhere and this is not the place to discuss it here again. This verse also should be read along with 33:35 and if read both together will not create any misunderstanding. The verse 33:35 clearly establishes Islamic feminist point of view that a woman is equal in every respect to man. She is not a wee bit inferior to him. There is no question of her being subordinate to man, much less, his property.

No Qur'anic *verse* should be read in isolation and this is precisely what the orthodox 'ulama do. They highlight one verse and suppress the other, in keeping with their prejudices against women. The prejudiced view regarding women 'they are inferior, they are created for serving men and it is their Islamic duty to obey their husbands' are not on account of Islam but on account of the social ethos they are surrounded with.

Need for Islamic Feminism

Why use the term Islamic feminism? What is its need? Before we answer this question let us answer their question, 'why feminist movement arose in the west?' When women were educated and their awareness of equality with men found no response in the society and they found themselves subordinated to men, an aggressive feminist movement arose. Women found that they do not have even right to property and they have not been enfranchised in many western countries they reacted strongly. Women in Europe got right to property as late as 1930. Neither they could be elected to high political offices, nor could they become peers to men in higher corporate structures, they began to demand their rights.

Some extremist feminists even began to burn bras as they thought they were being reduced to sexual dolls. But later on feminists developed more balanced viewpoint. However, women continue to be object of lust and in all commercial ads their semi-nude images are used seriously violating their dignity. Though due to pressures of feminist movement, women's position has improved quite a bit, still it is far from being ideal. Still in most of the western countries women are not elected to high political offices. For the first time in British political history Margret Thatcher became Prime Minister and for the first time in German history a woman has been elected a chancellor.

In the USA, still a woman has to become vice-president, let alone President. Even in France, a woman has yet to become the President. But their situation is, however, fast improving thanks to the feminist movement. Now more and more women are getting elected as legislators in several European countries. In Sweden, more than 40 per cent parliamentarians are women.

In Muslim countries, situation of women is really despicable. In Saudi Arabia they are not allowed to vote (municipal elections were held in some Saudi Arabian cities) and not allowed to even drive. In Kuwait women won right to vote recently after a prolonged struggle. In several Muslim countries like Egypt, Jordan, Pakistan etc. they are killed in the name of family honour if they try to marry a man of their choice or even found talking to some male friend. All major decisions are taken by men even in family matters and they cannot play any public role. In these countries, they are even denied right to education and are forced to veil themselves.

There is an urgent need for Islamic feminist movement. Islam has given them rights like right to marry, right to divorce, right to own property, right to earn their own living, right to education and right to inherit. Unfortunately, all these Islamic rights are being denied to them by the Muslim society. In the West, there was no concept of these right until early 20th century. In Islam, these rights existed all along but women were not allowed to avail of them by the conservative male-dominated society.

Unfortunately, Muslim women have to struggle hard to win the rights their religion has given them and denied by their men. Some time ago the leading Islamic seminary in Deoband issued a *fatwa* that Muslim women cannot contest elections but modified later by saying they have not observe veil while campaigning. It is also to be noted that there is no concept of veil in the Qur'an, there is only the concept of dignified dressing. However, men everywhere are forcing veil on women. The Qur'anic verse 24:31 makes it very clear that what should be displayed should be displayed.

The Islamic feminist discourse has to articulate all these rights given to women by the Qur'an and if there happens to be any grey area it has to be subjected to fresh interpretation in the light of contemporary developments. The Islamic feminist discourse does not deviate from the Qur'anic rights but does not, at the same time accept male point of view in interpreting the Qur'an. Women must not only acquire Qur'anic scholarship but should also display courage in reinterpreting Qur'anic verses relating to women and develop a Qur'anic feminist narrative.

Such Islamic feminist discourse is inevitable. But there are formidable obstacles on this way. Modern educated women have no knowledge of Qur'an and *hadith* and what is worse, no interest in acquiring such scholarship. Those who have been educated in Islamic *madrasas* are too conservative to ever attempt such a bold interpretation. They have been brought up in traditional Islamic discourse.

However, it is high time some Muslim women volunteer to acquire deeper Islamic scholarship, mastery over Qur'anic Arabic and launch Islamic feminist movement. Marriage in Islam is not a subordinate relationship between man and woman but an equal partnership. Both being party to mutual obligations. She cannot be divorced arbitrarily as is the practice today. Marriage has been described by the Qur'an as 'strong bond' (4:21) which one cannot break at husband's whim.

Also Islamic feminist discourse should empower women to make their choice whether they want a child or not on grounds of health, family size and economic capability. A man cannot force woman to go on bearing children, as she is much more than a child-bearing machine. An Islamic feminist discourse has to be a necessary choice for women.

Thus it will be seen from above that Islamic feminist discourse is not only justified but is essential to empower her to achieve full human dignity accorded her by the Qur'an.

Women's Rights in Islam

The question of women's rights in Islam has become more pertinent in our time because literacy and higher education have significantly increased among women, as have urbanisation and the pressures exerted by it.

Women are no longer prepared to accept their position as 'the second sex', as the French feminist Simone de Beauvoir put it in the last century. Women today are very conscious of their rights and they rightfully demand gender parity in all fields.

Muslim women are far behind their counterparts in other world communities; they are more subjugated to men's will than women in other faith-traditions. Muslim women arguably suffer more because of Sharia rules whose interpretation is projected as 'divine' and 'immutable' which it is not. This illusion persists among Muslims (men and women) perhaps only because Sharia is based on the *Qur'an* and *hadith.*

What many people realise is that Sharia, though based on the *Qur'an* and *hadith*, is in fact based on the interpretation of the *Qur'an* (and *hadith*), and interpretation is human while the Qur'anic text is divine. This human interpretation of the divine text has all along been done by men and hardly by any women. Even when some women attempted it, the overwhelming authority has been that of men. I meet many women educated in women's *madressahs* today, who fully justify all such interpreted Sharia rules and accept their secondary position in society.

This situation can be balanced perhaps if more women scholars interpreted the Qur'an. The Qur'an indeed gives equal rights to women unambiguously (2:228). Thus, when women interpret the Qur'an from their perspective, they would benefit from the rights given to them by the *Holy Book*. In some cases problems also arise because Qur'anic verses have been interpreted in the light of certain *ahadith*; *ahadith* also need to be critically examined.

The science of *hadith* was developed by the *muhaddessin* (those who specialise in the science of *hadith*), which entirely depends on the narrator. The authenticity of a *hadith* depends on the character of narrator, not on his/her intellectual capacity or ideological position towards women. Also, in some cases even if a *hadith* apparently contradicts a Qur'anic formulation it may be accepted as long as it fulfils other criteria. Thus, it will be seen that *riwayat* (narration of text) is held as more important than dirayat (i.e. intellectual criterion) by traditional theologians.

This is precisely why the Qur'an was perhaps so interpreted in a male-dominated and feudal society to subject women to men's overriding authority. The Qur'anic positions and unambiguous formulations for equality of men and women were, considerably diluted in such formulations. One of the key values of the Qur'an, namely, *adl* (justice), became secondary when it came to women's rights.

Qura'nic verses on polygamy or *nushuz* (rebellion by women, 4:34) were so interpreted, especially with the help of *ahadith*, that their real meaning and intent were lost and social ethos prevailed over divine intent. Even the verses on *talaq* (divorce) were interpreted by some to justify triple divorce in one sitting. Thus, the verses on polygamy and divorce were so interpreted to subject woman to man's overriding authority.

There is a great need for women theologians in Islam who can read and interpret the Qur'an. Some men like Maulavi Mumtaz Ali Khan, who was one of the colleagues of Sir Syed Ahmed Khan, did excellent work in the 19th century to advocate gender–equality, based on his interpretation of Islam. His book '*Huququn Niswan*' is an excellent work published in early 1890s. Another such theologian in the 20th century was Maulana Umar Ahmad Usmani, who was a graduate from Darul Uloom (before he migrated to Pakistan), and a great advocate of gender equality. He named his book – quite significantly – 'Fiqh al-Qur'an' because his understanding of the Qur'an is not based on *hadith* literature; he depends for his formulations only on the Qur'an.

Recently, some women scholars were making efforts to understand the Qur'an from their own perspective. Fatima Mernissi of Morocco and Amina Wudud and others have done excellent work interpreting the Qur'an from independent scholarly perspectives. Also, from the US, one scholar, Laleh Bakhtiar, has translated the Qur'an into English from a feminist perspective. She calls it 'inclusive' as against others exclusive. But all this is not sufficient though quite important. More women theologians should come forward and interpret the Qur'an. It is not easy to challenge the corpus of literature on the Qur'an for the last 1,300-1,400 years. This is necessary to restore to women the rights they lost to men under a feudal social ethos.

The writer is an Islamic scholar and heads the Centre for Study of Society and Secularism, Mumbai.

Qur'an, Women and *Hadith*

Qur'an indeed had ushered in a revolution as far as women's rights were concerned. Women hardly enjoyed any rights before Islam neither in marriage, divorce no inheritance. She was thought to be totally dependent on father, husband or brother and had no individual existence. Qur'an straight away gave her distinct individual legal personality. Women did not enjoy such status anywhere in the world. In fact even philosophers like Aristotle thought women and animals had no soul.

This revolutionary approach to women's distinct individuality was hardly acceptable to the Arab society. Arabs were, by and large, a patriarchal society and wanted to keep women under their thumb. But after Islam became a national religion for Arabs they could not have easily denied what the Qur'an gave to women. Thus they found a via media of *hadith* and thousands of *ahadith* came into existence quite derogatory of women and taking away from women what Qur'an had given them.

Thus women, by the time Umayyads took over political power, again lost their equality given by Qur'an and after Islam spread to Iran and parts of Roman empires influences of feudal culture overpowered thinking of Islamic jurists and that further eroded women's status. Now she was again confined to home and it became her duty to obey her husband and not to go pour of home without his permission. According to one *hadith* the Prophet (PBUH) said that if *sajda* were permissible to man I would have ordered her to perform *sahda* before her husband. Such *ahadith* are thrown on her face to make her subjugated to her husband.

On the basis of some *ahadith* of doubtful origin she was even denied right to enter mosque. She was given untrammeled right by the Qur'an to enter into marriage contract herself and without her consent no marriage could be valid. But the jurists opined that even her silence amounted to her consent and even if she cries it should be taken as her consent because she is crying as she would be separated from her parents.

Thus we see that the conservative patriarchal society had its deep imprint on the minds of Islamic jurists and what is more unfortunate is that *Ulama* subsequently developed the doctrine of *taqlid* (blind imitation) and almost forbade *ijtihad* or fresh thinking about what was formulated more than 1200 years ago. Not only this, the *Ulama* also did not allow women to follow provisions of another school, if it benefited them.

Thus women following Hanafi school could not benefit from any provision in *Maliki* school, if it was more beneficial to them. These four schools in Sunni Islam i.e. *hanafi, Shafi'i, Maliki* and *Hanbali* were product of human thinking and human interpretation of Qur'anic pronouncements and hence by no stretch of imagination could be 'divine' or immutable but these schools acquired almost divine status and common Muslims thought the laws framed by these respective jurists are immutable.

I am not saying here that we should completely reject entire corpus of *ahadith* but what I am proposing is that we must rigorously screen all *ahadith*, including those from *Sihah Sitta* i.e. the six authentic collections and reject those which directly contradict Qur'anic pronouncements. In other words Qur'an must have precedence over *hadith* and we will have to develop new science of *Usul al-Fiqh* i.e. principles of jurisprudence.

According to this, first we will have to fix what are basic principles culled from Qur'an which must be applied for framing any law pertaining to marriage, divorce, inheritance, custody of children etc. For example doctrine of justice *'adl* is very fundamental to Qur'an. No law framed which contradicts this doctrine can be admissible. The Qur'an itself has applied this doctrine say in case of polygamy very rigorously and declares if you fear you cannot do justice, then marry one!

Unfortunately our jurists almost, if not completely, ignored it and four wives became more fundamental than justice. And they also ignored that this verse (4:3) was revealed to do justice to widows and orphans and to protect their properties. It did not apply to marrying any women but only widows and orphans to ensure protection of their properties.

Our jurists even incorporated many pre-Islamic customary practices (*'aadat*) and they too became part of Islamic law. Thus triple divorce in one sitting which was strictly banned by the Prophet (PBUH) also became part of Shari'ah law and today thousands of women in India are victims of this arbitrary law. And the Qur'anic right of *khul'a* and according to one authentic *hadith*, Prophet (PBUH) made it her absolute right, was subjected to husband's prior consent and now husbands use this 'right' to consent to persecute their wives.

Many more examples could be given but for now these are enough to demonstrate and to urge that there is great need to restore Qur'anic rights to our women and to re-claim individuality and dignity accorded to women by Qur'an.

Muslim Women Versus Maulavis

I recently,read two different reports, one in a leading English daily and the other in an Urdu daily from north India. The English daily carried through its reporters interviews with young *Madrasa* girls from Kerala. Though *madrasa* authorities have strictly banned press from talking to madrasa girls. It is interesting to note that these *madrasa* girls have aspirations of their own.

One *madrasa* girl, 15 years old said 'I want to become – pilot', the other of similar age said, 'I wish to become a doctor and third girl said I want to become an IAS (Indian Administrative Service) officer. Most of the other girls also showed similar aspirations to achieve something and be something in life.

The other report in the Urdu daily reported a speech by Maulana Shamsuddin Chaturvedi of a Barelvi school who while tying *Dastar-e-Fazilat* (Turban of Merit) on students who had completed memorising the Qur'an, that Islam is a complete code of life and that we must observe its teachings meticulously in our lives and not allow our women outside home and make them observe veil.

"*Áurten ghar ki zeenat hain*" (women are pride of our homes) and they should not venture out of homes. It has brought about decline of Muslims. Unlike our ancestors, we do not observe teachings of Islam. We dishonour our families by allowing women to become lax in their morals. The sum and substance of his exhortation was that Muslims should exercise strict control over their women.

What does this contrast show? What Muslim women want and what our 'ulama desire. It clearly shows that our ulama live in the world of their own. And what is ironical is that the 'ulama do not even live in the ideal world of Islam. They live in the world of Islam created by medieval mindset. This is precisely the world in which the Taliban also live and that is why they persecute, harass and even kill those women who want to achieve something in this world.

Just before I read these reports, I was surrounded by some Hindu women who worked among Muslim women for their uplift in Bihar and asked me why Islam puts so many restrictions on women and why Muslims can divorce their wives by pronouncing the word *talaq* thrice? I began to explain to these women that it is not teaching of the Qur'an but some Muslims use controversial *ahadith* to allow triple divorce or put restrictions on women.

Two Urdu journalists who had come to interview me, were also sitting by my side. When I used the word 'controversial *ahadith*, they became angry and began arguing with me whose Islam are you talking about? It is your Islam, not real Islam. These Urdu journalists apparently were 'educated' and yet had similar attitude as our 'ulama have.

Our institute is conducting these days interviews of noted '*ulama* in order to codify Shari'ah laws pertaining to marriage, divorce, inheritance etc. as they are applied today very loosely in India. When they are asked about codifying rules for regulating polygamy, most of them maintain it cannot be regulated as men have 'right' to marry up to four wives without even consulting first wife, or wives, if there are more than one.

This is necessary, they maintain, to check prostitution. Qur'an, does not even indirectly justify polygamy on such grounds. When we point out the verse on polygamy was revealed after battle of *Uhud* in which 10 per cent of Muslim males were killed and it was meant for taking care of widows and orphans, not to check prostitution, they say it is your own invention.

Some of them showed ignorance of the verse :129 which says you cannot do justice to more than one wife, even if you desire and do not leave first wife suspended (*mu'allaqatan*) and said man has unrestricted right to marry four wives. No doubt it is these traditional '*ulama* for whom tradition, *hadith*-based Islam is more important that Qur'anic Islam which accords equal status to women.

There is thus an urgent need to reeducate our 'ulama in real Islam so that Muslim women can breathe easy and be able to realise their rights on which we spend so much of our oratorical skills but then go on to deny them these rights in practice. Thus one of the real *jihads*, among others, is to struggle for women's rights so concretely and precisely spelled out by the Qur'an.

Islam no more can be practised the way it was practised during the medieval ages. Modern Islam either has to be in conformity with the Qur'an, the revealed scripture of *Allah*, or we will face serious problems and end up producing Taliban like Islam.

Maulvi Mumtaz Ali–A 19th Century Advocate of Women's Rights

It is generally thought that movement for women's rights began with western educated people and in 19th century. But very few people know about Maulavi Mumtaz Ali Khan, a traditional '*alim*, product of Darul 'Uloom Deoband who was very enthusiastic supporters of gender equality. There are two things to be noted here: one, he was a traditional '*alim* and was not under the influence of western thought and two, he was advocating gender equality purely on the basis of Islamic traditional sources i.e., Qur'an and *hadith*.

The Maulavi was enthusiastic supporter of women's rights and was one of the colleagues of Sir Syed. However, Sir Syed had lot of troubles on his hand due to his campaign for a modern educational institution for north Indian Muslims. He was facing stiff resistance from orthodox 'ulama and did not want more trouble and so he advised Mumtaz Ali Khan not to publish his book *'Huququn Niswan'* the manuscript of which he showed to the Syed. However, the Maulavi was very enthusiastic about women's rights and wanted to educate Muslim men and women and went ahead with its publication.

Huququn Niswan, I dare say without any exaggeration, is like charter of rights for Muslim women. Mumtaz Ali Khan proves from Qur'an through his interpretations of relevant Qur'anic verses that men and women have equal rights and that women have no authority over women, as believed by Muslim men. This book, because of its advocacy of women's rights, soon went into oblivion and was not available.

I obtained its copy from a US library and published it. It must be read by all Muslim women to get duly armed with Qur'anic arguments to fight for their case. He had married to a woman who was not educated but he not only educated her but also made her editor of a women's magazine which had become quite popular in those days. This magazine, besides educating women in their rights also made them aware of contemporary events, especially socio-cultural.

Maulavi sahib's arguments were quite ingenious based on his interpretation of Qur'anic verses. He took all traditional arguments by which men asserted their superiority over women. He called such superiority as *mardon ki jhuti fazilat* (false superiority of men). For example, men usually argued that if women were equal to men why *Allah* did not grace any woman with (*nubuwwat*) prophethood?

Mumtaz Ali Khan gives quite an ingenious reply to this argument. He says according to tradition there have been one lakh and twenty four thousand prophets and we know names of only about a dozen prophets. How can then we say there were no women prophets at all unless we know all the names. Similarly, his reply to the argument that why women are half the witness, if they are equal to men, his argument is as follows:

The Qur'an itself does not say that women are half witness but only recommends that in financial transaction have two women and one man if two men are not available. This, according to Mumtaz Ali, is a privilege for women rather than any stigma as two women have been recommended because often women have certain problems like menstruation or pregnancy and cannot go to the court to bear witness. Such privilege is not available to men. Thus according to Maulavi sahib, it is a privilege, not a stigma for women.

He also refutes the argument that *Allah* first created adam and then eve and hence adam has superiority over Eve. Mumtaz Ali Khan also refutes this argument and says these are stories taken by commentators of Qur'an from Christian and Jewish sources and Qur'an itself does not say adam was created first and then eye for his comfort and company. From Qur'an one can not prove who was created first and who was created later.

Similarly, the argument about permissibility of four marriages simultaneously is also effectively refuted as he says there is no clarity in the verse (4:3) whether it allows four wives simultaneously, or one after the other or divorcing one and marrying second and so on. According to him four wives simultaneously is not the intention of the Qur'an for which he gives elaborate arguments.

In any case, it is a most interesting book with alternate interpretations of Qur'anic verses as far as women's rights are concerned. One can say it is first feminist interpretation of Qur'an in the Indian subcontinent as early as ninteenth century.

Islamic Feminism

Often people object to the term feminism as being a western terminology. One *Maulana*, when invited to speak in a workshop of this title refused to come as feminism is un-Islamic. Is the use of this terminology objectionable from Islamic viewpoint? Not at all. In fact Islam is the first religion which systematically empowered women when women was considered as totally subservient to man. There was no concept of her being an independent entity and enjoying equal right with dignity.

What is feminism? Nothing but women's movement to empower her and to consider her full human being and not mere second sex as 'Simon de Bouire called her. Thus we see in western countries until early part of 20th century she did not enjoy an independent status. It was only after 30s of twentieth century, that she won equal status legally and various western countries passed the laws to this effect. Yet patriarchy is looming large on her in these countries.

Though Qur'an empowered her and gave equal status but Muslims were far from ready to accept gender equality. The Arab culture was too patriarchal to accept equality. Many *ahadith* were readied to scale down her status and she, in most of the Islamic societies became dependent entity and Qur'anic formulations were so interpreted as to make her subordinate to men. One *hadith* even said that if *sajdah* (prostration) were permitted before human beings, she would have been asked to prostrate before husband.

This is totally contradictory to the Qur'an but who cares. It is patriarchy which influences our laws, not Qur'an. In fact when it comes to patriarchy it prevails over the Qur'an. Either Qur'anic formulations were disregarded or so interpreted as to conform them to patriarchy, Now time has come to understand the real spirit of the Qur'an. But Islamic world still does not seem to be ready. What is worse due to poverty and ignorance Muslim women themselves are not aware of their Qur'anic rights. A campaign has to be launched to make women aware of these rights.

Another important question is what is the difference between Islamic and western feminism or is there any difference at all. If we go by definition of feminism as an ideology of empowerment of women, there is no difference. However, historically speaking Muslim women lost the rights they had due, mainly, to feudalisation of Islam dominated by patriarchal values, in the west. On the other hand, women had no rights and but won through great deal of struggle and this struggle came to be known as 'feminism' i.e., women's empowerment.

But there are significant differences also between Islamic and western feminism. Islamic feminism is based on certain non-negotiable values i.e. equality with honour and dignity. Freedom has certain Islamic responsibility whereas, in the west freedom tends to degenerate into licentiousness, though not in law but certainly in social and cultural practices. In western culture, sexual freedom has become a matter of women's right and sex has become matter of enjoyment and lost its sanctity as an instrument of procreation.

Though Qur'an does not prescribe *hijab* or *niqab* (covering whole body with a loose garment and face as well) as generally thought but does lay down certain strict norms for sexual behaviour. Both man and woman have right to sexual gratification (a woman has as much right to sexual gratification as man) but within marital framework. There is no concept of freedom for extramarital sex in any form. Sex is permissible only with marital framework. Sex, as far as Islam is concerned, is not mere enjoyment but an act for procreation and hence has sanctity.

It is important here to emphasise that in a patriarchal society men decided the norms of sexual behaviour. It was theorized that man has greater urge for sex and hence he needs multiple wives and woman tends to be passive and hence has to be content with one. This is not true as far as Qur'an is concerned. Qur'an's approach is very different. It is not greater or lesser degree of sexual urge which necessitates multiple or monogamous marriage.

Whole emphasis is on monogamous marriage (in both the Qur'anic verses i.e. 4:3 and 4:129). Multiple marriages were permitted only to take care of widows and orphans and not for greater sexual urge and the verse 4:129 gives the norm of monogamy and not to leave first wife in suspension or neglected. Thus as far as Qur'an is concerned sexual gratification is a non-negotiable right for both man woman. And hence a divorcee and a widow are also permitted to marry and gratify their sexual urge.

Also, in western capitalist countries women's dignity has been compromised and she has been reduced to a commodity to be exploited. Her semi-naked postures and her sexuality is exploited commercially and unabashedly. It is totally against the concept of woman's honour and dignity. Unfortunately, western feminists do not consider this as objectionable but accept it as part of woman's freedom. A few even advocate prostitution as woman's right to earn her bread.

This is against the concept of Islamic feminism as while sanctioning sexual gratification as much right of woman as that of man, it prohibits extra-marital sexual liaison and on one hand upholds dignity and honour of woman and on the other, exalts sex on the level of sanctity and restricts it for procreation.. Thus it would be seen that discourse of Islamic feminism, while having something in common with modern western feminism, it also significantly differs from it. Islamic feminists have to observe certain norms which modern western feminists are not obliged to.

On Women's Right in Islam

In the contemporary world, rights of women in general and those of Muslim women, in particular, has become quite an important issue. Our institute is strongly committed to gender equality and we have been doing whatever we can by way of research, writings, awareness workshops etc. to promote Muslim women's rights within Islamic framework. I have tried to write, as it is my priority area, on practically every aspect of this subject.

Recent *fatwas* and controversies about women's rights in Islam have once again raised this controversial issue in media as well as in academic and Islamic circles. Also, in European countries *hijab* or face veil is being banned by some countries and has attracted adverse attention in media. Our stock reaction is western media is hostile to Islam (which is largely true) but never examine issues involved critically, much less take practical measures.

In terms of *fiqh* (jurisprudence) in general, and in the area of personal laws (*ahwal al-shakhsiyah*) in particular, has become stagnant and fatwas are issued on the basis of certain juristic texts evolved during early centuries of Islam. Whenever any question is asked pertaining to women's rights, our *Ulama* take resort to these juristic texts and issue their ruling without taking real context and problem into account.

When some who stand for women's rights differ, they are accused of being western feminists or Muslims only in name. This is so painful and disturbing. When some Muslim women themselves try to acquire Qur'anic scholarship and study of sunnah, they too stand accused of being anti-Islam distorting Islamic laws. Unfortunately, some people holding university degrees are also indulging in such accusations as they are disturbed by changes.

Once, I was invited by the law faculty of Aligarh Muslim University to deliver an extension lecture on "Rights of Women in Islam" which was also being attended by many female students of law and other faculties. I spoke on the subject only with reference to Qur'an and *sunnah* to prove that both men and women enjoy equal rights in all the fields of active life.

To my shock and embarrassment of audience, a lecturer in law stood up and said, 'sir, you have forgotten to say that men should also get pregnant and produce children' I told him politely please address this question to *allah*, not to me. This is how many educated who teach in universities, think. Even these educated men and women too are totally ignorant of how Islamic jurisprudence evolved over a couple of centuries and consider it as divine and immutable.

When one stresses importance of ijtihad in Islam the stock reply is there is no one qualified to do it and some argue the doors of *ijtihad* have been closed after sack of Baghdad in 1258. Now we have to conserve whatever has been inherited. First, the question arises who closed the door of *ijtihad*? Is there any central authority in Islam to pronounce such a closure? This is simply not true.

There are very complex reasons for *Ulama* shunning their duty to do ijtihad. One has to go into these reasons. Another thing I would like to stress is that the Islamic process of jurisprudence has been one of the most dynamic one for few centuries and was based on a central Qur'anic value of justice. I can say there have been few attempts in human history to undertake such law making enterprise with justice being so central to it.

Ijtihad was the very spirit of the whole project. As long as Islam was confined to the Arab Peninsula, the questions faced by jurists were relatively simple. Also, all companions of the Prophet were around and there was hardly much difficulty in solving the problem. But once Islam began to spread speedily in non-Arab parts of the world with vastly different cultures, customs and traditions, complexity of problems increased.

Also, add to this the fact that companions of the Prophet were also not around after two generations and then even followers of these companions and followers of followers of these companions also gradually vanished leaving a great gap. It is then that great jurists with the spirit of ijtihad appear on the scene and try to tackle new problems which were arising. New tools like *qiyas* and *ijma'* (analogical reasoning and consensus among *Ulama'*) were invented which clearly made it human enterprise.

Here we are more concerned with the question of women's rights in this process of legislation. Since Islam was a great liberation movement for whole of humanity and especially weaker sections of society, women could not have remained unaffected. The widows, the divorcees, the slave girls and orphans were great sufferers among them. Widows were treated with contempt as in India. Also, there were no written laws in a tribal society. Everything either depended on customs and oral traditions or on arbitrary behaviour of the powerful.

There are many instances in which some men had as many as eight or ten wives. The eldest son after father's death could even take his step mothers (except his own mother) as his wives and have sex with them. Also, to have daughters was considered as a matter of shame. The Qur'an has described it as follows: "And when the birth of a daughter is announced to one of them his face becomes black and he is full of wrath. He hides himself from the people because of the evil of what is announced to him, Shall he keep it with disgrace or bury it (alive) in the dust? (16:58-59)

How ashamed these pre-Islamic Arabs felt when daughter was born and in most of the cases buried it alive. And see how Qur'an elevated their status to that of equality with men and empowered them with all the rights- individual dignity, right to marry man of her choice, right to stipulate conditions for marriage, right to divorce (*khula'*), right to inherit, right to her own earnings and right to property. In short her status was raised from chattel to full human being with all the rights.

It was not short of any revolution. Then the Prophet himself married a widow and fathered all the daughters and loved them more than one would love ones sons. He was especially attached to his youngest daughter Fatima and would even stand up when she entered his house. There is a chapter in *Qur'an al-Nisa'* (The Women) but no chapter like *al-Rijal* (men).

There are several verses in the Qur'an which emphasisethat men and women would be equally rewarded and no discrimination would be made. Thus we find in the Qur'an, "So their Lord accepted their prayer, (saying): I will not suffer the work of any worker among you to be lost whether male or female, the one of you being from the other." (3:194). And also see verse 33:35 if there is any doubt in any ones mind about equality in matters of reward and punishment for both men and women.

Then important question is why this was not reflected in practice and in the process of legislation and schools of *Shari'ah* or different *madhahib*? This is the key question and we would like to throw light on this question. It is on understanding this question that lies the way to bring about necessary changes in the status of Muslim women today and to restore it to the one accorded her by the Qur'an.

Before we discuss this, I would like to say that even the Islamic jurisprudence as it obtains today is not, and could not be, oblivious of justice as a value though in some cases justice did become secondary. Certain pronouncements of the Qur'an are so clear that the Shari'ah law could not ignore them. But then there is another problem that of social values, customs and traditions which further mar the spirit of justice.

One or two examples should suffice. Let us take, for example, the question of child marriage. Since marriage is a contract in Islam, a daughter could not enter into a contract and hence her marriage guardian (often father) entered into the contract on her behalf. But then as a child she cannot authoriseher father to do so.

Hence the *Hanafi* school provided for her to accept or annul her marriage. This right is called *khiyar* al-bulugh i.e. option of puberty. However, in Muslim society child marriage remained but option of puberty was lost. Once father married off his daughter how can she refute it? It becomes the question of izzat (honor). Thus social customs become more important than Shari'ah provisions

Many more examples can be multiplied. In certain Muslim communities like *Memons* for example, women did not inherit and instead Hindu customary law applied to them until 1937 Shari'at Act came into existence. Even today ground situation is very different from what has been provided for in *Shari'at* law. Also, half-literate village *imams* and panchayats enforce customary laws in the name of Islam and media passes them off as Islamic provisions.

Thus it would be seen that in most of the cases there are complex problems and interactions between Islamic provisions, social customs, tribal practices and patriarchal values. To legitimise these practices, Islamic *Shari'ah* is wrongly invoked and irony is that our *Ulama* keep silent knowing fully well it is not Islamic. Even if they oppose, it is so discrete that it has hardly any impact on the society. They fear public reaction.

In fact many scholars have repeatedly pointed out that one must distinguish between fiqh and shari'ah. *Fiqh* is nothing but an attempt to understand a problem, to know it and it has to be a continuous process as new situations and new problems keep on arising. Shari'ah is the final product whereas fiqh is a process, a tool and a means. We should also keep in mind that the great imams struggled to find solutions to various problems they encountered in their own times and geographical locations.

Imam Abu Hanifa, for example, lived in Iraq which was a confluence of Arab and non-Arab cultures. Kufa, where he lived, was basically a military camp and had a large number of mawalis (clients of various tribes) from various countries conquered by Muslims. They had their own customs, traditions and social values and used to approach the *Imom* with their problems.

Thus the conquered countries also caste their shadow over the process of *fiqh*. Here the question of face veil becomes important. Is face veil Qur'anic or part of Prophet's (PBUH) sunnah? Of course there are differences of opinion. But Qur'an certainly does not specify face veil but only says do not display your *zeenah* (i.e. bodily charms and adornments) publicly

Face veil, in all probability came from non-Arab feudal culture of Persia and Sassanid empires. Recently, in a conference in Vienna of 100 *imams* and religious advisors from 40 countries concluded that Islam does not make it a requirement for women to wear face veils. After all, they concluded, face veil is nowhere mentioned in the Qur'an, nor is there a Qur'anic injunction to cover the face.

Even in *hadith* there is no unanimity of face veil having been clearly mandated. Some scholars say it is some maintain there is no such mandate.

Some say only hair should be covered. But all agree that women cannot cover their faces while offering five times prayers or performing *hajj*. Thus both while offering prayers and performing hajj women cannot cover their faces. And *hajj* is performed along with thousands of men.

Mohammad Marmaduke Pickthall, a British convert to Islam and translator of Qur'an in English observes in his lecture delivered in 1925, "The Relation of the Sexes", that the veiling of face by women was "not originally an Islamic custom. It was prevalent in many cities of the East before the coming of Islam, but not in cities of Arabia. "Muslim leaders adopted the face veil for their women, he said, "when they entered the cities of Syria, Mesopotamia, Persia and Egypt. It was once a concession to the prevailing custom and was a protection for their women from misunderstanding by peoples accustomed to associate unveiled faces with loose character…it has nothing to do with the religion of Islam, and for practical reasons, it has never been adopted by great majority of Muslim women."

However, slowly, as feudal culture became the norm face veil struck its roots and slowly Islamic theological resources were used to make it appear Qur'anic and part of sunnah. There is one interesting example. Mu'awiyah was appointed governor of Syria during 2nd Caliph Hazrat Umar's time. Hazrat Umar was very strict in following simple way of life. When he was told that Muawiyah sits on a throne and others stand on both sides of throne with folded hands, Umar was furious and sent a letter to Muawiyah asking his explanation.

Muawiyah wrote to him, 'if I do not do here no one will follow my orders as Syria has been governed by Roman emperors for centuries and they are used to this way of governance'. Umar did not object thereafter. And then of course Caliphate was itself transformed into *mulukiyyat* i.e. kingdom and kingdom also accepted as Islamic. Thus it will be seen that foreign influences work on legal system and before we understand becomes our way of life and we accept them as legitimate.

Islamic jurisprudence could not remain uninfluenced by such influences and since the body of Shari'ah developed over a period of three centuries and Islamic jurists (*fuqaha*) worked on developing it in far off centers like Mecca-Madina, Iraq, Egypt and Spain, how can we say that cultures in these great Islamic centres did not influence thinking of these great jurists.

It is said that during these centuries there were more than 100 different schools of law of which not more than four survived in *Sunni* Islam. It is because independent thinkers and jurists used their intellectual powers to comprehend different problems and find solution and, there being no church and priesthood in Islam, freedom to think and comprehend problem for oneself was no problem. And if they could find some followers, their school of thought also persisted.

In fact no one shut doors of *ijtihad* at any point of time but once these four schools of jurisprudence found large number of followers and others did not survive, others were discouraged to develop more such schools. The Shi'ah Islam, on the other hand, retained the institution of ijtihad by independent *mujtahids* (those who do ijtihad) as twelth *Imam* went into seclusion and there was no one from the Family of the Prophet (PBUH) to guide the process of jurisprudence.

The Ismailis, on the other hand, perfected their own school under the guidance of 14th Imam Mu'iz in the form of book called Da'im *al-Islam* around 10th century and is followed ever since. There has been no further development in the *Isma'ili* school ever since. Besides that there are other minor schools like Zahiri School or *Ibadi* but followed by small number of people. Also, the Nizari Isma'ilis headed by Aga Khan today believed that one of their Imams Hasan *'ala zikrihi al-Salam* suspended application of *Shari'ah* law and said there was no need to follow any formal *Shari'ah* law as such.

Now the need to trace this brief history of development of Shari'ah law is to show that the rigidity with which we follow it today is uncalled for and, leaving apart *'ibadat* (matters of spiritual worship) we have to rethink in all other social, legal and criminal matters as far as Shari'ah law is concerned. Muslims have accepted many changes in these matters throughout Islamic world.

Indian Muslims themselves accepted many changes when the British Government suspended application of Islamic criminal law and introduced their own criminal code which was translated into Urdu by Maulavi Nazir Ahmed and was given title of Shamsul *Ulama* (Sun of the Islamic theologians) for his services. No one objected to it. But main problem arises when it comes to personal laws involving marriage, divorce, inheritance etc.

Why this resistance? Mainly because of question of women's rights is concerned in these matters and our society in general and conservative *Ulama* who come from the same society, in particular, are not prepared to concede gender equality which is so clearly pronounced by the Qur'an and suppressed consequently by patriarchal social influences. This was realized by many *Ulama* who had open mind and tried to rectify situation.

During colonial period some Islamic thinkers under the influence of modernity tried to rethink and reformulate Shari'ah provisions. Muhammad Abduh of Egypt who rose to be grand Mufti of Egypt showed great courage in re-thinking. Here in India, thinkers like Sir Syed, Maulavi Mumtaz Ali Khan and Maulavi Chiragh Ali did great work of *ijtihad* which again shows doors of ijtihad were never closed by any one. What is needed is courage and bold thinking going directly to Qur'anic values and Prophet's *sunnah* in conformity with the Qur'an rather than resorting to plethora of controversial *ahadith.*

Today, there has been complete transformation of concept of women's rights, their empowerment and their social role. Gender is nothing but social construction, not natural in origin. However, Islamic theologians refuse to accept changing concepts of gender and its social construction and still think women should perform domestic role and should not go out and do what men have been doing.

What they talk of *Shar'i hudud* (limits) is nothing Qur'anic in it but the gender role evolved during medieval ages and sanctified as Shar'i requirement. During the Prophet's time women played revolutionary role and liberated themselves from men's slavery and became harbingers of Islamic revolution. They, however, lost out to feudal patriarchal values again when Islam spread to areas where Sassanid and Roman Byzantine empires were well entrenched and feudal values were firmly rooted.

Today, though oil in the Middle East has put wealth in the hands of Arab ruling classes but it will take a while for thorough social transformation to take place. The rest of Islamic world is still grappling with the fundamental questions of poverty and illiteracy from Algeria to Egypt to South and South East Asia (except Malaysia) to Indonesia and the Philippines. Add to this the anti-Islamic propaganda of western media always attacking Islam and Muslims and US-Israel aggression which gives rise to political Islam reviving itself in reaction. And revival of traditional Shari'ah becomes an important agenda of political Islam. Still many Muslim intellectuals are engaging themselves with women's question.

Women's Day and Muslim Women

March 8 is celebrated throughout the world as women's day and 2012 it happened to be hundred year and so specially significant. However, one did not see much enthusiasm about this day in Muslim countries except some women, aware of this day, demonstrated. They do not betony support from government or even from society as a whole. That year thousands of Egyptian women gathered in Tahriri square with great enthusiasm but far from getting any support they were attacked. It was very shocking indeed.

Again the media and many activists will blame Islam for this. But it is not true. In fact I would like to reiterate that Islam has given equal rights both to men and women in clearly and unambiguously pronounced words. However, this was far ahead of its time and patriarchal society was not prepared to accept it anyway and rather than contradicting the Qur'an, which they could not dare do, they resorted to producing a*hadith* (pl. of hadith) which totally contradicting Qur'an and also formulated a doctrine that *ahadith* are extension of Qur'an and as much bound on Muslims as Qur'an itself.

This did the trick and Muslim men in patriarchal society could do what they could not do by directly flouting the Qur'an. It is human nature that even if you accept in theory something as Divine injunction and yet, it goes against your age old socio-cultural practices or against your interests, you would flout it through other means. If all Muslims had followed Qur'an injunctions and values, ignoring their own socio-cultural practices, the world would have been very different in post-Islamic revolution.

But it never happens and women's question is one of the most delicate questions. In patriarchal society men would never concede equality of rights to women thus foregoing their dominance over women. In western countries we see equality of rights, at least on paper, if not rigorously in practice, it did not happen in a day. The fact that a women's day had to be observed indicates the struggle women had to wage in those countries and for years.

Until 30s of the last century (i.e. 20th century) women in western countries hardly enjoyed equal rights. Even in communist countries like the Soviet Union, despite belief in gender equality, women were subjugated and had to carry double burden of working outside and inside home. When I visited Soviet Union in nineties of last century and asked to women activists, I came to know how, despite equal rights, they faced all sorts of discrimination and had to be content with inferior position.

This is not justification of what is going on in Islamic countries. It is only explanation of why it is happening. Things are changing in Islamic countries too but women in these countries have to struggle hard and have to face formidable challenges. The greatest obstacles for them are poverty, illiteracy, lack of awareness and theocracy, in that order. These are no ordinary challenges.

Poverty and illiteracy is a result of broad pro-capitalist and market-oriented policies and we do not wish to comment about. These are very different kinds of challenges. However, I would like to discuss theological and socio-cultural challenges which are no less formidable. Unfortunately, the theocrats have driven deep into the minds of Muslims that the Shari'ah laws are divine and not a dot or comma can be changed. Not that theocrats believe this doctrine of immutability; they do not want to forgo their own domination and some even feel insecure that overwhelming socio-cultural milieu would go against any change

The fear of isolation is very real for religious leaders especially in view of the fact that their rivals may take advantage of the same. I had a dialogue with the chief mufti of Saharanpur, (a town which is centre of Islamic learning in India) on validity of triple divorce in one sitting. He not only conceded the fact that it is un-Islamic and must be abolished forthwith. However, he was afraid of taking any public stand saying I would be isolated and no other ulama would support me.

Many *Ulama* belonging to new generation feel the need for change, especially those who, after completing their theological courses, go to modern secular educational institutions for degree courses. However, overwhelming majority of *Ulama* are very orthodox, extremely backward in outlook and resist any suggestion for change. Some of them, though not all, believe that shari'ah laws cannot be changed or that no one in our times is qualified enough to do *ijtihad* (re-interpreting or re-thinking).

What is worse it is men who always do theologising though, in Islam there is no such restriction at all. Men and women are equally entitled to theologise or be faqih i.e. understand issues and formulate shari'ah laws. But in patriarchal society men never allowed women to theologise or be faqih. Ironical though, most of the a*hadith* have been narrated by *Hazrat 'Aishah*, the wife of the Prophet (PBUH) In history of Islam there have been several women who have been learned scholars of Islam but not even one who founded any Shari'ah school.

Another problem is that Islamic societies never experienced modernisation from below. It is ruling classes, rich and powerful who modernized themselves and in some cases they introduced modernisation from above and coerced poor and illiterate masses to accept modernisation. In former case masses were left out high and dry anyway and in later case masses refused to accept modernisation as there lives were immersed in age old traditions and feel no need for change.

In all Muslim countries ruling classes have been enjoying benefits of modernity and their women escape ordinary laws. However, in some Islamic countries like Tunisia, Morocco and Iran during Shah's time, Turkey and others, modernity was imposed from above forcing women to give up *hijab*, wear mini-skirts and other western dresses etc. and there was upheaval in the society in many cases.

In some cases like Iran, the ruler (i.e. the *Shah*) was overthrown and in countries like Turkey coercion had to be used to enforce modernity. There are also countries like Pakistan, Jordan etc. where traditional Islamic laws were codified to reduce its arbitrary nature and to improve lives of Muslim women.

The first requirement to bring about real and acceptable change is to provide universal education comprising all secular subjects. It greatly helps create proper understanding issues and also enables women to know what is going on in the world and around them. In Kerala, India, due to high literacy rate among Muslim women, family planning has gone up to 64 per cent as compared to average 35 per cent. It is a great change.

Secondly, there has to be awareness campaign for rights of Muslim women and difference between what Qur'an says and what is found in

Shari'ah laws and reasons for these differences. Since our Institute of Islamic Studies conducts such awareness workshops for Muslim women, we have seen how awareness makes all the difference. The notion that Shari'ah law is immutable is removed from their mind.

Such awareness can be created even among women who are either not literate or have gone through only initial stages of literacy but being educated helps a lot in any case. It is also our experience that victims among them (i.e. divorces or those who had to live with co-wives or were deprived of their just right to inheritance etc.) are quick to comprehend and ready to work for enlightenment of other women.

It should also be noted that condemnation of Shari'ah law helps a little in bringing about change. Women like Taslima Nasreen or Hirsi Ali and others have only strengthened conservative forces and further increased problems of Muslim women. What is needed is to understand different factors involved in preventing change and try and remove these difficulties. It is not Shari'ah law which is to be primarily blamed, it is socio-cultural attitudes which stand to be blamed.

And it is not easy to change socio-cultural attitudes which have been around us for centuries. It will take at least few decades that too if there is constant movement to change these attitudes and I must say, to end on hopeful note, change is coming. With modern education spreading even countries like Saudi Arabia where women are most oppressed, change is coming and women are demanding equal rights.

Islam, Women and Gender Justice

It is generally thought that Islam treats women unfairly and gender justice is not possible within Islamic law known as the Shari'ah law. This assertion is partly true and partly untrue. True as far as the existing shari'ah laws are concerned. Untrue, as the existing laws were codified during 2nd and 3rd centuries of Islam when general perspective of women's rights was very different from today's perspective. The Qur'anic verses which are quite fundamental to the Islamic law, were interpreted so as to be in conformity with the views about gender rights prevailing then.

It is important to note that scriptural injunctions are always mediated through prevailing social ethos. Also, and it is more fundamental to framing of laws based on scriptures, scriptures both reflect the given situation and also transcend it. There cannot be any scripture - revealed or otherwise - which is uni-dimensional i.e. it reflects only given situation. Every scripture tries to go beyond what is given and it faces stiff opposition from those who loses out if the transcendental perspectives are spelled out and enforced. The scriptures condemn prevailing social malaise and provide a new vision. Those who benefit from the new vision embrace the new faith. Those who lose oppose it tooth and nail. But, the vested interests and those who want to perpetuate the old order have their own strategies. Soon they find ways and means to hijack new religion to their own benefit. This is done in number of ways: (1) They capture political power and religion becomes part of political establishment and loses its initial revolutionary thrust as it is appropriated by the ruling classes; (2) they convert religion itself into an establishment and a power-structure develops around it. Religion is then used more for distribution of favours than for spiritual enrichment; (3) intellectual resources are used to restore *status quo ante* and this is done chiefly by interpreting the scriptures in a way which will rob it of its transcendental thrust. Thus a theology is developed which is supportive of status quo. One must distinguish between what scriptural pronouncements are and what theology is woven around it. Scriptural pronouncements are divinely inspired and hence transcendental and theological formulations are human and hence often contradict divine intentions. Scriptural pronouncements are an option for the weaker sections whereas theological formulations are weapons in the hands of powerful interests. It is therefore necessary that theological formulations be continuously challenged by scriptural pronouncements. One must strive to build up creative tension between theological and scriptural. While scripture remains immutable with its transcendental spirit, theology must change facing new challenges and newly emergent situations.

Those who oppose any change in theological formulations and shari'ah laws are those who lose their dominant position and the priesthood who monopolise theology and religion for them is instrumental in promoting their interests rather than spiritual source of inner enrichment. The priesthood, monopolising theology, project it as divine and immutable. The run of the mill faithful understanding of religion is mediated through the priesthood and hence they are made to believe that theology as formulated by them or their predecessors is divine and hence immutable. Any change will amount to changing the divine will.

In Islam, it is common belief that the shari'ah is divine and hence immutable. Whenever any measures for gender justice are proposed one meets with this stock argument. It is important to note that shari'ah, though undoubtedly based on the Holy Qur'an, is a human endeavour to understand the divine will. It is an approach to, rather than divine will itself. The priesthood i.e. the community of '*ulama*' projects it as a divine end itself and hence refuse to admit any change. The Shari'ah is divine has become a commonly accepted position. Thus what was thought of women's rights during the early period of Islamic history has come to be the final and immutable. Even to think of, much less changing it, is interfering with the divine, and hence an unpardonable sin.

As pointed out above, there is a big gap between the scriptural i.e. the Qur'anic pronouncements, and, Shari'ah formulations. While the Qur'anic pronouncements are purely transcendental in spirit, the Shari'ah formulations have been influenced by human situation as well as human thinking on all related issues. Women were in subordinate position in the patriarchal societies and this subordinate relationship came to be reflected in the Shari'ah laws relating to her rights. The transcendental divine spirit was conveniently ignored and the prevailing situation was rationalised through contextual Qur'anic pronouncements. As pointed out above, there is always a creative tension between what is and what ought to be in scriptures. However, this tension is often resolved in favour of the prevalent rather than the emergent and prevalent is eternalised by rationalising certain divine pronouncements.

On the Methodology of Creating Islamic Legal Structure

If we want to effect necessary changes in the Shari'ah laws, it is important to understand the methodology of creating of Islamic legal structure. The Islamic legal corpus is known as Shari'ah. As Shari'ah is, after all, a human approach to divine will as reflected through the scripture i.e. the holy Qur'an, it is not uniform but has several variants. In the *Sunni* Islam itself there are four different schools of jurisprudence i.e. Hanafi, Shafi'i, *Hanbali* and *Maliki*. Besides these schools there is what is known as the Zahiri school. Also, there are several schools in the Shi'ah Islam as well. The Ja'fari or the Ithna 'Ashari School, the Isma'ili school and the Zaidi school.

The Sunni Islam bases Shari'ah - besides the Qur'an - on *Sunna* (i.e. the sayings and doings of the Holy Prophet), *qiyas* (analogy) and finally ijma' (consensus). However, except the Qur'an, the remaining three sources i.e. *Sunna*, *qiyas* and *ijma*' are controversial. Some *ahadith* (sayings of the Prophet) are acceptable by some while they are rejected by others. Some a*hadith* are considered weak (*da'if*) and some of doubtful origin and some outright forgeries. Also, qiyas, analogical reasoning varies from jurist to jurist. There is controversy about ijma' as well. The crucial question is whose ijma'? Of the jurists and the '*Ulama* or of the entire community? Also, has ijma' ever been possible? Have all '*Ulama*, let alone the entire community, ever developed consensus on any issue? There are hardly any instances of this nature in the history of Islamic jurisprudence. Thus it will be seen that except the Qur'an which is divine and there are no textual differences about it, the three other fundamental sources i.e. *Sunna*, *qiyas* and *ijma*' are human and hence controversial. It is also important to point out here that about the Prophet's pronouncements i.e. a*hadith* there is controversy whether they be considered as divine or human. The *Ahl-e-Hadith* (i.e. the followers of *Hadith*) consider *hadith* as divine like the Qur'an while many others do not give it that status and consider it as human and hence not eternal.

The Shi'i jurisprudence (Shari'ah) is based on the Qur'an and the pronouncements of the Prophet as reported by Imams i.e. the male descendants of the Prophet's daughter Hazrat Fatima and her husband 'Ali. The Qur'an as interpreted by these Imams is considered as the only right interpretation, every other interpretation is considered as mere conjecture or opinion (ra'i). And tafsir bi'r ra'i (i.e. Qur'anic interpretation or exegesis through human opinion) is rejected outright in the Shi'a Islam. But there is controversy in the Shi'ah Islam as to who is rightfully appointed *imam*. The *Ithna 'Asharis* (twelvers), the Isma'ilis (also referred to as seveners), Zaidis, the Qaramitas and the Alavids, all mutually differ on this issue. All these sects have Imams of their own and consider others as not rightfully appointed and hence have no legitimacy. Also, the juridical pronouncements of these *imams* differ from each other even on matters of principles, at times.

Thus had it been immutable the Shari'ah would not have differed from one school to the other and from sect to sect. The Qur'an, being divine, does not differ and is immutable. It admits no change. However, its interpretation differs from sect to sect and from one school to the other. Thus the Qur'an is divine and its interpretations are human and what is human admits of change. The Shari'ah, being based on human interpretations of divine word, can, and does admit change. What was thought to be just in respect of women's rights in medieval ages, is no longer so. The idea of justice also changes with changing consciousness and what is just in one age may not necessarily be just in the other. We will throw more light on this aspect little later. It is in fact very important aspect as far as the Qur'anic concept of law is concerned.

One of the important sources of the Shari'ah law is *hadith* or *Sunna*. As pointed out above, this too is not above controversy. There are two types of controversies about this seminal source of Islamic law: (1) whether *hadith* is divine or human and (2) whether it is authentic, weak or forged. The Qur'an is unanimously accepted as divine and there is no controversy bout it. Also, its contents are also accepted with unanimity and without any controversy. No one maintains that this or that verse of the Qur'an is unauthentic, or added later, or of doubtful origin. But it is not so as far as *hadith* literature is concerned. There are several *ahadith* which are controversial. Either they are considered of doubtful origin or weak or outright forgery. It is said that Imam Abu Hanifa, the founder of the Hanafi School of law, accepted only 17 *ahadith* as true and authentic and yet he used many more while giving his juridical opinions.

There are Muslims who maintain that *ahadith* are divine like the Qur'an. They believe that the Qur'anic verse "Nor does he speak out of desire. it is naught but revelation that is revealed" (53:3-4) applies to the Prophet's all pronouncements including his ahadith. These Muslims believe that *ahadith* too, are divine and hence above any human controversy. Thus this source of Shari`ah also becomes equally divine for them. However, there is no unanimity about it. Not only that *hadith* is not believed to be divine by large sections of Muslims, it is not above controversy as to its origin. Imam Bukhari, one of the greatest collectors of *ahadith*, is said to have collected more than six hundred thousand a*hadith* of which he accepted only four thousand and rejected others as of doubtful origin or outright forgeries. This clearly shows how some interested people were producing *hadith* literature to serve their own ends. Unfortunately, many of these a*hadith* went into juridical formulations in general, and about women, in particular. These formulations reflect the prejudices and dominant thinking of the time rather than the Qur'anic principles. These formulations, therefore, cannot be treated above change.

Also, there is yet another problem about *hadith* literature. And this problem remains, even if *hadith* literature is treated as divine and immutable. The Qur'an which is unanimously held to be divine by all Muslims contain many pronouncements which are directly related to the then prevailing Arab social structure. These pronouncements also reflect the social norms or social problems as they existed then. These pronouncements cannot be of universal application in other societies and cultures. We would like to cite examples. There was a practice called *zihar* among Arabs. It is mentioned in 33:4 and 58:2-3 . It was a practice among Arabs to declare their wives like their mothers and abandon them. Thus in verse 33:4 the Qur'an says, "*Allah* has not made for any man two hearts within him; nor has He made your wives whom you desert by *Zihar*, your mothers..." Edward William Lane defines *Zihar* in his Arabic-English Lexicon as husband telling his wife thou art to me as the back of my mother. In verse 2 of Chapter 58 the Qur'an says, "Those of you who put away their wives by calling them their mothers - they are not their mothers. None are their mothers save those who give them birth, and they utter indeed a hateful word and a lie..." And in verse 3 of the same chapter it is said, "And those who put away their wives by calling them their mothers, then go back on that which they said, must free a captive before they touch one another. To this you are exhorted..."

From above two verses we come to know that Arabs used to desert their wives calling them like the back of their mothers and some used to go back on that vow and would like to touch their wives again. The Qur'an prescribed that they free a captive (i.e. a slave) before breaking their vow. Now this practice was unique to the Arab society of that time. We do not find such practices in other societies. Also, today there is no institution of slavery. it has already been abolished. If an Arab today pronounces *Zihar* on his wife and wants to take back his vow there are no slaves available to free. Thus such verses in the Qur'an should be treated as contextual i.e. revealed in the context of that society and are no more valid as social practices have changed. Similarly, the institution of slavery is no more. There are several pronouncements about slaves and slavery in the holy Qur'an but they are no longer applicable as the institution itself does not exist any more. But in Shari'ah as formulated in the 2nd and 3rd century *Hijrah* (Islamic Calendar) these practices prevailed and hence elaborate laws were made by the jurists based on Qur'an or *hadith*. But they are totally irrelevant today. Thus the proposition that Shari'ah laws are immutable is not maintainable.

The Qur'anic verses thus should be divided into two categories namely (1) contextual and (2) normative. The normative pronouncements of the Qur'an are eternal and while re-thinking issues in Islamic Shari'ah, particularly pertaining to women's rights the normative pronouncements will have precedence over the contextual. But during the early centuries contextual often had precedence over normative and it was quite normal then. And hence these formulations became widely acceptable in that society. These laws were thought to be normative then and hence struck deeper roots in society as well as in hearts and minds of the people as well and came to acquire status of immutability with the passage of time.

Thus even if *hadith* is accepted as divine its contextuality will have to be kept in mind. It is also said, and rightly so, that the Prophet explained the Qur'anic verses through his words and deeds and who knew the meaning and import of the Qur'anic verses better than the Prophet. Quite true. But the question of contextuality remains. The holy Prophet, while dealing with the given society, could not have gone beyond its context in explaining and practising the Qur'anic pronouncements. Again it can best be illustrated with an example of women's status in that society. While explaining the cause of revelation of the Qur'anic verse 4:34, all classical commentators like Tabari, Fakhruddin Razi and others maintain that the Prophet allowed a woman (daughter of his companion) right to retaliate against her husband who had unjustly slapped her but, in view of the prevailing social ethos it laid to unrest among the men and Qur'an reversed the Prophet's decision. This once again shows that the question of contextuality is very important and highly relevant in all judicial pronouncements be they those of the Prophet or other Islamic jurists.

Another example is this respect is that of *milk-e-yamin* i.e. legitimising sexual relations with a slave girl. There is near unanimity among the Islamic jurists that it is permissible to have sexual relations with slave girls and that the Prophet himself had such relations with a Coptic Christian slave girl. The modernists and some other commentators of course challenge this formulation and maintain that the Prophet had married her. But Maulana Maududi, one of the contemporary Islamic thinkers and founder of the *Jam'at-e-Islami*, maintains in his commentary on the Qur'an (*Tafhim al Qur'an*) that the

Prophet had relations with the slave-girl without marrying her. Most of the eminent medieval jurists concur with this. But if this view that sexual relations with a slave-girl is permissible is accepted the contemporary society would not approve of it. Thus the Prophet's *Sunna* cannot be seen out of its social context.

There were four great jurists in *Sunni* Islam who founded four different schools of jurisprudence. All four differ from each other on many issues. Much has been written on causes of these differences. But the modern scholars maintain that one important reason was their differing social situations. Imam Hanbal and Imam Malik lived in Madina and thus were quite close to social ethos of that society in which the Prophet himself lived. They were closer in their juridical formulations to what the Prophet said and did in that society. Imam Shafi'i and Imam Abu Hanifa, on the other, lived in Egypt and Iraq respectively which were confluences of many cultures and thus were unorthodox in their methodology in arriving at juridical opinions. While Imam Malik and Hanbal mainly relied on *Hadith*, Imam Sahfi'i and Abu Hanifa used qiyas and *ijma'* more liberally, apart from *Hadith*. Thus while the former two Imam's formulations were closer to Arab practices in Mecca and Madina, the latter two Imam's formulations had been largely influenced by other practices as well. This clearly shows that Shari'ah is influenced by human situations and can incorporate situational changes. The Arab *'adat* (the Arab customary law) also became integral part of the Shari'ah law. Thus the then prevailing opinions about women in the Arab society greatly influenced the Shari'ah laws pertaining to women. The Arab *'adat* cannot certainly be considered divine injunctions and hence immutable. In fact the Arab *'adat* had great relevance as long as Islam was confined to the Arab society. But once it spread out to far off areas, the need to incorporate other practices also became equally important. And now the changed consciousness about women's rights can also not be ignored.

There is yet another problem about the *hadith* literature which is, as pointed out above, an important ingredient of Shari'ah. The *ahadith* were generally reported by the Prophet's companions. In this respect even the most authentically reported a*hadith* present different kinds of problems. Firstly, most of the *ahadith* reported by the companions were not the exact words of the Prophet but the overall meaning of what he said. There are hardly few *ahadith* which can be said to be the exact words of the Prophet. Secondly, the *hadith* literature also incorporates the reports about what the companions saw the Prophet doing. Thus the Prophetic *Sunna* includes both what the Prophet said as well as reports about what he did in different situations.

Now among the Prophet's companions there were all kinds of people. There were companions who had sharp memory and good understanding and comprehension of the problems. There were companions who had very poor understanding of the complex issues and also there were companions who had poor memory. And there were companions who spent several years with the Prophet and there were companions who spent only a few hours with him, and even those who saw and heard him from a distance. All that these companions reported having heard from the Prophet became part of *hadith* corpus which then was used for formulating Shari'ah laws.

Not only that. There is yet another problem. The *ahadith* have been reported by people who heard it from the companions of the companions (tab'i tabi'in) and companions of the companions of the companions of the Prophet. Thus there is whole chain of narrators known as rijal (the narrating men or women). The collectors of a*hadith* did try to develop the science of *rijal* (i.e. *'ilm al-rijal*) criterion to judge the honesty and integrity of the narrators. But this criterion judged the honesty and integrity of the narrators rather than his or her understanding, comprehension or intelligence. Moreover, there were often missing links. And also the cases wherein much was not known about one or more of the narrators in the chain. Many narrators were of totally different cultural backgrounds - some narrators being Arabs and others non-Arabs not properly acquainted with the Arab affairs. Also, many narrators had their own biases for or against women (also about other matters) and these biases definitely affected their narrative or reports.

It was for this reason that the Prophet had strictly prohibited his followers from compiling his sayings. He knew very well that his sayings may not be reported faithfully to future generations for various reasons. Also, he was fully aware of the fact that the future generations will insist on strictly following what reaches them as the sayings of *Allah's* Messenger though they may be facing different circumstances. Even the first Caliph Hazrat Abu Bakr did not permit compilation of a*hadith* for similar reasons. Still people did compile these *ahadith* though much later. And by the time they were compiled spurious ones had mixed up with authentic ones.

Thus it will be seen that *hadith* literature, even if entirely authentic, presents several problems. Thus it cannot be considered as highly reliable source of Islamic legislation. But the Islamic juris corpus is as much based on the problematic *hadith* literature as on the holy Qur'an. Still the *'Ulama* project it as unquestionable divine and hence immutable. They refuse to admit any change even though sweeping changes are taking place in the social, cultural, economic and political circumstances. The doctrine of taqlid (mechanical imitation) is emphasised by the contemporary jurists in the world of Islam. They maintain that rethinking about the formulations of the great Imams is not permissible. In fact these formulations are treated as divine. Also, most of the *'Ulama* do not even permit taking more favourable provisions for women from other schools of law. They insist that any one school should be followed in its entirety. Some '*Ulama* of course permit such an approach. But they are fewer in numbers. Now more and more '*Ulama* are coming around to permitting this approach which has given some relief to women. The Ottoman rulers had adopted this approach in the 19th century itself. But still it is not widely accepted. Taqlid is the generally established rule.It is causing great deal of hardships to Muslim women everywhere.

The holy Prophet had anticipated the problems which will arise in future. He took care to leave some guidance in this respect. First, he encouraged what is known as *ijtihad* (i.e. exerting oneself to solve newly arising problems if no precise guidance was available in the Qur'an and Prophet's Sunnah). The *hadith* regarding Ma'adh bin Jabal is well known about this. When the Prophet appointed Ma'adh as governor of the Yemen, he asked him how will he govern. According to the Qur'an, Ma'adh replied. And if it is not in the Qur'an? the Prophet asked him. According to the Prophet's Sunna, replied Ma'adh. And if he does not find anything of the sort in the Sunnah also? the Prophet inquired. Then I will exert myself to solve the problem (*ana ajtahedo*). The Prophet patted his back in approval. Also, the Prophet is reported to have said that even if one makes mistake in doing ijtihad he/she will earn one merit and if one does not err he/she will earn two merits. The Prophet did this to encourage Muslims to solve problems which were likely to arise in future.

From this many modernists argue that one must resort to ijtihad to solve new problems and issues including women's issues. However, the orthodox '*Ulama* argue that the gates of ijtihad were closed long ago and also that now there are no qualified persons to do ijtihad. They feel the great Imams and some of their followers had the *requisite* qualification and none today has such impressive merits. Some '*Ulama* do feel the need for *ijtihad* but they too stop short of resorting to it for fear of consequences. Some who did faced the wrath of the fellow jurists and even ostracised. The debate is raging in the Islamic world for and against *ijtihad*. And when it comes to women's issues and rights, the resistance to change and rethink is much greater in the male-dominated Islamic world.

Muhammad Iqbal, a noted Urdu poet and thinker from India (d. 1938) was greatly in favour of *ijtihad*. He wrote in his Reconstruction of Religious Thought in Islam '"The ultimate spiritual basis of all life, as conceived by Islam, is eternal and reveals itself in variety and change. A society based on such a conception of Reality must reconcile, in its life, the categories of permanence and change. But eternal principles when they are understood to exclude all possibilities of change which, according to the Qur'an, is one of the greatest 'signs' of God, tend to immobilise what is essentially mobile in its nature." (pp.147-48).

Iqbal states in the above book very boldly, "The only alternative open to us, then, is to tear off from Islam the hard crust which has immobilised an essentially dynamic outlook on life, and to rediscover the original verities of freedom, equality, and solidarity with a view to rebuild our moral, social and political ideas out of their original simplicity and universality." (p. 156). Iqbal thus maintains that ijtihad is necessary to rebuild the law of Shari`ah in the light of modern thought and experience.

Ijtihad, I would like to emphasise here, is even more necessary today in respect of Shari'ah laws pertaining to women. It is highly regrettable that the Shari'ah law is almost inoperative in many other respects (like property and contract laws, criminal laws, financial transactions etc.) but when it comes to women's issues, the Shari'ah laws are sought to be strictly applied. In several Muslim majority and minority countries modern secular laws are applied in respect of all other things except laws pertaining to marriage, divorce, maintenance, inheritance etc. i.e. in the sphere of what is called personal laws. The greatest resistance, in the name of Shari'ah, is manifested by men when it comes to according better status to women. In this respect the Shari'ah becomes sacred and immutable and arouses great passions. The Islamic world, if it has to understand the dynamic spirit of Qur'an, and enact it in real life, will have to enact changes in the Shari'ah laws and accord women an equal status. In fact time has to come put the Qur'anic vision of sexual equality in practice.

As pointed out earlier there are verses in the Qur'an which have contextual significance. These verses formed the legal foundations of Islamic law in that age. But these were not the verses having impress of permanence and principles. There are certainly the verses which lay down norms and principles. Today, the Islamic legislation should be based on these verses. Before we examine these verses, we would like to set out certain values which are fundamental to the Islamic teachings. Any legislation which ignores these fundamental values could be anything but Islamic. It is necessary to understand that the classical jurists though did not ignore these fundamental values but the application of these values was constrained by the social ethos of the age. The Prophet's traditions also had to take these constraints into account.

The most fundamental values in Islam, as expounded by the Qur'an are justice, benevolence and compassion. The Qur'anic terminology for these values is *'adl, ihsan* and *rahmah*. The Qur'an talks of these values in imperative category. The Qur'anic verse 16:90 testifies to this: And surely *Allah* enjoins justice and benevolence (to others). Thus it will be seen that justice is very central to the Islamic value system - as central as love to the Christian ethics. No legislation in Islam which ignores this value can be valid.

It is this concern for justice which makes the Qur'an show deep concern for the weaker sections of society. Thus the verse 28:5 expresses this concern for them and says: "And We desire to bestow a favour upon those who were deemed weak in the land, and to make them the leaders, and to make them the heirs." The Qur'an desires to bestow the mantle of leadership of this earth upon the weak. The Islamic jurisprudence has to imbibe this spirit towards the weaker sections of society. And, women certainly belong to this category as far as the patriarchal society is concerned.

It is important to note that the values like justice and compassion cannot be applied independent of the age. In the medieval period the understanding of the concept of justice was very different from what it is today. Our era is a democratic era and justice in our era cannot be deemed to have been done if equality of all humans irrespective of sex, race and creed, is not ensured. Discrimination between one and other human being on any ground, including the sexual one, will be taken as injustice. But in medieval ages these discriminations were thought to be quite natural and non-violative of the concept of justice. Even slavery was thought to be natural and in keeping with the principles of justice. In fact if a slave ran away from the master it was thought to be an unjust act. Today, let alone slavery, even bonded labour or child labour is considered as grossly violative of justice. Thus the concept of justice greatly varies in a democratic era from that of feudal one. And yet justice as a value remains important in both the ages. The expression of the concept of justice in a particular era is not fundamental but justice per se is. However, in religious traditions, including in those of Islam, give more importance to the expression of justice in a particular age then to the notion of justice itself. It is because of this that the expression of justice in the *hadith* literature is more important than the notion of justice as fundamental value in the Qur'an. What was thought to be just during the classical period of Islam is thought to be just even today. And not only that the orthodox think the expression of the notion of justice today is violative of divine will. It is this attitude which impedes change in Islamic legislation so as to accord women equality with men.

However, one finds in the Qur'an full support for sexual equality in several verses. The Qur'an was certainly mindful of what was just in that era when it was revealed and what ought to be just in the transcendental sense. When the Prophet permitted a Muslim wife retaliation against her husband as a measure of justice, the Qur'an overruled him and permitted a measure of conditional male domination, though conditionality of justice was stipulated (see the verse 4:34). It would have been thought to be unjust if the Qur'an had permitted wife to retaliate against her husband and it would not have found acceptability in that society.

However, the Qur'an also did not intend to eternalise the then acceptable notion of justice. The dynamics of 'is' and 'ought' or interaction between history and eternity informs the whole spirit of Qur'an. Unfortunately, the orthodox miss this very spirit while reading the Qur'an form their own perspective. The verse 33:35 is much more fundamental in this respect as it clearly accords women equality with men in all respects. While 4:34 is informed by the spirit of that era, the verse 33:34 deals with the eternal dimension. The orthodox, however, do not wish to go beyond the divine injunction expressed in 4:34. They have frozen their minds in the classical age of Islam. What was temporal has become permanent for them and what is permanent is just brushed aside as of no consequence.

The Qur'an must be re-read and re-interpreted in today's context as the classical jurists read and interpreted it in their own context. No reformation is possible without such re-reading and re-interpreting the Qur'anic verses. The real intention of the Qur'an - that of sexual equality - comes through several verses. Those verses need to be re-emphasised. The verse 2:228 ("And women have rights similar to those against them in a just manner") is quite definitive in this respect. It hardly needs any comment. Maulana Muhammad Ali, a noted Pakistani commentator says commenting on the above verse, "The rights of women against their husbands are here stated to be similar to those which the husbands have against their wives. The statement must, no doubt, have caused a stir in a society which never recognised any rights for the woman. The change in this respect was really was a revolutionising one, for the Arabs hitherto regarded women as mere chattels. Women were given a position equal in all respects to that of men, for they were declared to have rights similar to those which were exercised against them. This declaration brought about a revolution not only in Arabia but in the whole world, for the equality of rights of women with those of men was never previously recognised by any nation or any reformer. The woman could no longer be discarded at the will of her 'lord', but she could either claim equality as a wife or demand a divorce." (Maulana Muhammad Ali, 1973, p. 97).

However, much of this spirit of justice and equality was lost when the Islamic doctors legislated under the influence of their own social ethos. The Qur'anic categorical imperatives were ignored, as pointed out before, in favour of those verses which were of the nature of concession to the age. There are many instances of this. The polygamy, for example. Firstly, it was a permissive measure in some circumstances (large number of war widows and orphans to be taken care of as many men perished fighting in the battle of *Uhud*) with great emphasis on justice to all the wives (their number not exceeding four). It was great advancement over the pre-Islamic practice of marrying unlimited number and without any obligation towards the wives.

Secondly, the verse on polygamy (4:3) is followed by the verse 4:1 which emphasises sexual equality in the words that ..."Lord Who created you from a single being (*min nafsin wahidatin*) and created its mate of the same (kind) and spread from these two many men and women..." and the verse 4:2 which talks of justice for orphans and widows. Then polygamy is permitted provided one marries with widows and orphans (and not any women) and there also justice with all wives is a must failing which one must marry only one. No one before had insisted on such conditionalities for plurality of wives. Thirdly, the verse 4:129 states that even if you desire you cannot do justice between wives and ends by saying that do not leave the one with total disinclination and incline towards the other leaving the first in suspense. If the verses 4:3 and 4:129 are read together polygamy is as good as not permissible. But the jurists, in order to avoid implications of reading the two verses together invented various explanations and took resort of *hadith* to keep possibility of polygamy open. And, much worse, in practising it, conditionality for justice was hardly enforced. In today's conditions polygamy should be done away with in order to implement the Qur'anic conditionality. Abolition of polygamy will serve the end of justice far better than its practice today. The arguments that men are more sexual or that in case there are more women than men, it will be better to permit polygamous marriages to avoid immoral relations etc. are all attempts at human rationalisation than divine intention. These arguments do not hold much water as there may be excess of women over men in one country and excess of men over women in another. And prostitution and immoral sex thrived even when men could marry any number of wives and also keep slave girls without limit.

Also, normatively speaking the Qur'an has conceded all rights to women which were available earlier only to men. She could exercise her right to divorce her husband as men could divorce her at will. The Prophet permitted a woman called Jamila to divorce her husband - against his will and without consulting him - just because she did not approve of his looks. While the verse 2:229 permits her to liberate herself from an unsatisfactory marriage by suitable compensation to husband (i.e. returning the dowry amount) the verse 4:35 gives her right to appoint an arbiter of her own to settle the marital dispute or agree to divorce. Also, the Qur'an requires of men to keep their wives in goodly manner and to leave them, if necessary, in a benevolent manner. And the verse 4:19 lays down that women could not be inherited or taken as wives against their will. men are also exhorted in this verse not to take a portion of what they have given to their wives and to treat them kindly. It was also emphasised in 9:71 that believing men and believing women are each others friends and they (both men and women) enjoin good and forbid evil. Thus both enjoy equal obligations and from this verse jurists like Abu Hanifa have concluded that a woman can become *Qadi* i.e. judge as it is her obligation also to enjoin good and forbid evil.

It is argued from the verse 4:11 that a daughter inherits half that of son and hence man is superior. Some modernists also argue on the basis of this verse that it is injustice to a daughter as she has been given half that of son and hence it is bias against female sex. It is simply not true. From one perspective one can say it was a cautious reform in favour of daughters. In pre-Islamic society daughters did not inherit at all and now they were given right to inherit half that of son. From another perspective it could be argued that it was not bias against daughter that they were given half that of son but daughters were duly compensated by mehr (dower amount at the time of marriage) whereas sons had to lose out by paying dower to their wives. And the wives do not have to spend anything by way of maintenance as it is enjoined upon the husbands to maintain their wives. Also, a woman inherited as wife and mother too. Moreover, she did not contribute to family wealth in those days by way of earning but now she does and her portion could be increased in view of the changed conditions. Thus the Qur'an has done no injustice to her in matters of inheritance also.

Another question is of *hijab* (veil). There is no injunction in the Qur'an that she veil her face. The verse 24:31 only lays down that women should not display their adornment and fineries publicly and that they should cover their breasts (tribal women in those days used to leave their breasts uncovered) and that they should not strike heir feet with anklets in public so as to draw attention to their adornments. In this verse both men and women have been asked to lower their gaze (4:30-31) and to restrain their sexual passions. As for what constitutes adornment and what should be displayed and what should be not, there are sharp differences of opinion. These differences are human and every commentator has his views. But *Tabari*, the noted classical commentator has summarised the views of many eminent jurists in his 'Jami' al-Bayan'. According to him adornment means (1) adornment of dress or the clothes that a woman wears; in other words, she is not required to cover the clothes she wears; (2) it means the adornment which the woman is not required to cover, such as collyrium, rings, bracelets and her face; (3) the exception (*illa ma zahara minha*) relates to a woman's clothing and her face.

These were opinions of the theologians of those days. Today, the sensibilities in this respect are very different and the scope of the exception can be made much wider subject to - and that is real intention behind it - to restrain sexual passion and protect ones chastity. To prevent extra-marital sex is the responsibility of both men and women and not of women alone, as per the Qur'an. Also, both should avoid wearing sexually stimulating dress. They should wear dignified dress. Covering of face by women is not required in the Qur'an at all. It was cultural practice of some post-Islamic societies. The Qur'an also does not require women to be confined to homes. On the contrary, they could earn and what they earned was theirs alone as per 4:32 (And for women is the benefit of what they earn). The cultural practices like confining women to home were sought to be legitimised later by inventing suitable *ahadith* or by far fetched interpretations of the Qur'an.

In conclusion, it should be said that if one goes by those verses of the Qur'an which belong to the normative category or which are of the nature of laying down principles and givers of value, men and women should enjoy equal rights in every respect. It would be necessary to re-read and re-interpret many verses which were used for centuries to subjugate women in Muslim societies. This subjugation was more cultural and patriarchal than Islamic or Qur'anic. The whole *corpus juris* of Islam relating to women needs to be seriously reviewed on the basis of Qur'an

A Fatwas can be Changed

Recently, a conference of Muslim Personal Law Board in India saw huge crowd of two lac Muslims from all over Maharashtra (a state in western India) and the chairman of the Board, Maulana Rabe Hasan Nadwi made a highly emotional speech and said that shari'ah is divine and no change in it can be made and even if whole Islamic world changes shari'ah, Indian Muslims will not allow any change in it and will keep the traditional shari'ah close to their chest.

How appropriate is this stance? Today many women are agitating for certain necessary changes like triple talaq and unregulated polygamy etc. which cause suffering to them. Some concerned people including myself have taken initiative to codify Muslim Personal Law so as to minimise its misuses and give relief to Muslim women. To what extent shari'ah law can be misused can be judged from the fact that a well-known Islamic University from Hyderabad (Deccan) allowed a man to marry two young girls simultaneously on the assumption that Islam allows polygamy.

All this is based on the books written and *fatwas* issued hundreds of years ago and our ulama do not want to deviate from these written texts. Whenever any question is asked they simply consult these texts and issue a *fatwa* and again like court judgements these fatwas become precedent for subsequent fatwas and these fatwas are treated as universally applicable. Lay Muslims do not know that these fatwas are merely opinion expressed by as mufti and is not binding.

Should *fatwas* issued by eminent ulama be treated as unchangeable? Or can they be changed with change of time and place? Generally shari'ah is thought to be divine and immutable and no human being can make any changes in it. In fact shari'ah laws have been developed by eminent imams like Abu Hanifa and others to meet the requirements of their time and place. Thus shari'ah can be described as sincere human approach to divine intention. It is well known that Imam Shafi'I when he shifted to Egypt, he changed his opinion of several *fiqhi* (jurisprudence) matters.

Recently, I saw a book by Allama Yusuf Qardawi, a well known *'alim* highly respected in the Arab world. It is on the subject matter of fatwas and necessity for changes in fatwas. It has been published by a respectable institution Islamic Fiqh Academy. Yusuf Qardawi has invoked the principle of ijtihad in Islam to justify changes in tawas (Arabic plural *fatawa*). The *Allama* even maintains that the shari'ah cannot be useful for the *ummah* unless ijtihad (he indicates several forms of ijtihad) is exercised from time to time.

Shari'ah, it is important to note, must remain dynamic and relevant to the time and place where it is applied. Fundamental principles and values on which shari'ah is based cannot be changed but the laws based on these principles and values should and must change from time to time to keep them relevant and useful. That is why in most of the Islamic countries traditional shari'ah laws have been changed or codified to make them as useful as they once were.

Qardawi has given ten grounds on which fatwas can be changed and all these grounds are highly relevant. First he gives four grounds on which fatawa should change i.e. change in time, change in place, change in conditions and change in what he calls 'urf (i.e. social practices or traditions). Qur'an also uses the term *ma'ruf*) in this sense. Then he gives six more grounds for desirability of change which are as under: (1) change in knowledge; (2) change in needs of people; (3) change in capabilities of people; (4) spread of calamity (when some acute problem becomes common); (5) change in collective political or economic condition and (6) change in opinion or in thought.

These ten grounds, in fact, capture all possible changes which can take place in a given society. This makes it amply clear that Islamic jurisprudence is by no means static or immutable as commonly thought of but it has enough space for change. It is altogether another matter if our ulama are rigid or incapable and try to hide behind divinity of shari'ah. In fact any law if it remains static cannot meet the requirements of the society.

Today, personal laws as developed during medieval ages need many changes. It is also well known that shari'ah law then had incorporated many Arab customs and traditions as *ma'ruf* and triple divorce was one among them. The Prophet (PBUH) had denounced it as Qur'an intended to empower women and give them equal status and no one practiced it during his time but it was later on reintroduced for certain reasons.

Today, women are highly aware of their rights and such practices are against principle of equality which is more fundamental than any Arab practice. Still it is practices in countries like India and even thought to be divine. Similarly polygamy is much misused and also thought to be man's privilege. It has to be regulated and should not be allowed to be used as per ones whim. No woman would accept it today as they did in the past. Medieval formulations in respect of personal laws were also influenced by patriarchal values and today patriarchal values are being challenged especially by women.

Polygamy is increasingly using its '*urf* i.e. social relevance and popularity. It should be allowed only in cases where it is very necessary. Similarly other personal laws could also be reviewed if needed. It will greatly benefit if our ulama keep these ten grounds in mind while giving their opinion in matters of *Shari'ah* laws.

2

Muslim Women and Change

Muslim Women between Tradition and Modernity

Recently in a poetic recital on T.V. in Saudi Arabia a Muslim poetess Hissas Hilal burst out against the strict control regime for women in her country. It was voice of protest and very bold protest at that, perhaps unthinkable in her regimented society. It was of course in verses of her poem. She said through veiled face about Islamic preachers, who sit in the position of power, but are frightening people with their *fatwas* and preying like a wolf on those seeking peace.

What is equally important is that she got loud cheers from the audience and won her a place in the competition's finals. It also brought her death threats. Posted on several militant web sites. The Saudi regime controlled by salafi ulama in religious matters; are adamant on retaining strict control over women in the name of Islamic traditions. Women are denied their rights and free choice according to their conscience.

This may not be the condition in all Islamic countries but traditional Muslim societies impose several restrictions and still are not ready to relax. the kind of *hijab* many Muslim women wear covering their faces and looking at the world only through two eye holes remains controversial among Muslim scholars, theologians and modern intellectuals. Question is what is to be done.

No one can deny the fast pace of change in the globalised world and it is becoming increasingly challenging to retain present controls exercised on women in traditional societies. This controversy has been going on ever since modernity asserted itself since nineteenth century. Many reforms took place in Muslim countries and women could win a degree of liberation.

However, later part of twentieth and beginning of twenty-first century saw re-emergence of traditional Islam, particularly *salafi* Islam. No society registers linear progress and progressive measures, in turn bring more challenges. Reasons, not to be discussed here are both economic and political, apart from social and cultural. This complex nature of tension between tradition and modernity is both challenge and opportunity.

What is important in this debate, which is often ignored in these debates, is that what we practice in the name of Islam is more cultural than religious or scriptural and also that we depend too much on tradition while defending or opposing the restrictions applied on women. A good example of this is a recent book published from Pakistan on "*Chehre ka parda wajib ya ghair wajib*" (Face Veil – Compulsory or Not) compiled by Khurshid Alam. It is a very scholarly debate between two learned scholar one defending and the other opposing face veil.

However, the book depends entirely on contradictory traditions of the Prophet (PBUH) and his companions cited by various medieval scholars. You find in abundance both kinds of traditions (*hadith*) insisting on face veil or thinking it unnecessary and both the scholars use these traditions to strengthen their position. This approach only reinforces traditional cultural Islam.

We should not ignore the fact that the most of the traditions (except those on moral, ethical or pertaining to *ibadat* (matters of worship) reflect Arab culture on one hand, and medieval west Asian or central Asian culture, on the other. The jurists have also maintained that Arab *Adat* (customs and traditions) could become part of Shari'ah law and many Shari'ah laws incorporate the Arab '*adat*.

In the book I am referring to, there is very little direct approach to the Qur'an or fresh reflections on the relevant Qur'anic verses. Let Muslim jurists and scholars realize that Arab '*adat* are far from divine and should not necessarily form the basic structure of the Shari'ah law. Today we must change this cultural base through direct reflections and fresh understanding of the Qur'anic verses relevant to women. This attempt would establish individual dignity and freedom of choice for women. Freedom of conscience is an important doctrine of the Qur'an and so is the individual dignity. Qur'an is far more in harmony with human dignity and freedom that the traditional medieval cultural practices.

This approach will. In no way, injure the divine nature of Shari'ah las and also would liberate it from its traditional cultural basis incorporating patriarchal values of Arab culture rather than the divine spirit of the Qur'an. This would liberate Muslim women and give them sense of dignity and freedom reducing tension between tradition and modernity. This opportunity should not be lost causing more agony to women and creating dilemma of choice for them. Most of the Muslim women want to follow their religion and also enjoy certain benefits of modernity. The Muslim scholars and jurists should end this agony.

Muslim Women and Change

Mostly people think Muslim women are oppressed and forced to wear veil and confined to the four walls of their houses. This is mainly because we read every day in Newspapers that Taliban force women into veil, burn down girls schools and always portray them wrapped completely in black cloth from head to foot. This image of Muslim women was further reinforced by the burqa controversy which erupted in France.

This image would be justified if all Muslim women followed the strict dress code propounded by Muslim theologians which was evolved in medieval ages and which they keep on justifying even today. But there is big difference in what is theologically projected and ground reality. It may not be wrong, if I venture to say, Muslim women have been defying theological code for more than a century now.

And now a century later, Muslim women have gone even further in their public achievements. It is true even today some Muslim theologians debate whether women are *naqisul aql* (defective reasoning power) or not but many Muslim women have superseded even Muslim men in several fields. In Saudi Arabia where women are not even permitted to drive cars, a woman became a licensed pilot and has been flying aircrafts.

Now we got news from Malyasia that Farah al-Habshi, an engineer by profession, has been appointed deputy of weapons and electrical officer in spanking new Malaysian warship *KD Perak.* Today she is donned in white and blue Royal Malaysian Navy uniform. What is interesting is that she also wears *hijab* to cover her head though not her face. She feels her *hijab* in no way comes in the way of performing her duties.

Maylaysia is an Islamic country and orthodox ulama exercise great deal of control over people's lives. Recently even the government of Malaysia chickened out when *Ulama* took stand that Christians in Malaysia cannot use the word *Allah* in their religious literature or in their newspaper. Muslim women face several problems in that country at the hands of conservative ulama in respect of family laws.

It is in the same country that a woman has been appointed naval officer on combat duty. Even in India women have not won the right to be on combat duty in navy or are not permitted to fly fighter planes or serve in combat arms. They are also not allowed seafaring in warships. Farah al-Habshi, on the other hand, recently participated in Milan naval exercise along with some other women.

Farah is also highly articulate and answered all the questions put to her by the journalists. And it is not only one example out of many. There are several other examples. Many Muslim women have excelled even in theological fields and quite independently of the traditional theologians. They have shown courage to challenge orthodox ulama. Here I can give example of Amina Wudud of theUSA who teaches Islamic Studies in Washington.

She believed women can lead mixed congregation in prayer and she led around 100 persons, men and women in prayer a few year ago and that too on Friday and delivered Friday *khutba* (sermon), quite unthinkable in traditional Muslim world. It raised storm of controversy and even Yusuf Qardawi, otherwise a moderate theologian from Qatar, wrote an article, opposing a woman leading mixed congregational prayer.

Some Kuwaiti women, elected to Kuwaiti Parliament after great deal of struggle, refused to wear *hijab* and fought for their right to go to parliament sessions without wearing one and fought their case up to Supreme Court of Kuwait and won. Many more examples can be cited of Muslim women daring authorities for their rights.

But media, which is interested in sensationalising issues, refuses to highlight Muslim women's achievements and continues to portray them as submissive to traditional authorities and meekly accepting their situation. This image of Muslim women has to change and reality, which is much more complex, has to be understood.

This is not to deny that in many countries Muslim women are facing difficult problems and their liberation is not a foregone conclusion. However, it is also true that many of them are fighting and refusing to submit meekly. What gives us hope is their continued struggle and defiance of traditional authorities.

It should also be mentioned here that many 'ualam and jurists also have realised that medieval shari'ah formulations about women cannot be enforced easily any more and some of them like Muhammad Abduh of Egypt, Maulavi Mumtaz Ali Khan of India and Maulana Umar Ahmed Usmani of Pakistan have expressed their serious reservations about traditional theological formulations on women. The determined struggle on the part of Muslim women will force many more theologians to revise their position and take Qur'an, and not medieval theology, more seriously on women issues.

The Muslim 'Ulama and Status of Women

The other day, I read a news item in Urdu daily from Mumbai Inquilab about the coming session of Muslim Personal Law Board. I was utterly shocked to read that Personal Law Board is worried that the Government of

India has passed a law against domestic violence whereas our '*Ulama* and *fuqaha*' (jurists) have always permitted beating of women. According to the law against domestic violence Muslim men have lost right to beat their wives.

Could there be any more shocking news about the status of mind of our '*Ulama*, if this news item is true? Can it be right to beat ones wife? Does Qur'an or Holy Prophet's *Sunna* allow this? Did the holy Prophet ever beat his wives? Can anyone quote any instance of this? Is there any verse in the Qur'an permitting wife beating? Yes, generally the '*Ulama* refer to one verse 4:34 which, according to them, permits wife beating. The translation of the verse is as under:

"Men are maintainers of women, with what *Allah* has made some of them to excel others and with what they spend out of their wealth. So the good women are obedient (to *Allah*), guarding the unseen as *Allah* has guarded. And (as to) those on whose part you fear ill-will admonish them, and leave them alone in the beds and chastise them. So if they obey you, seek not a way against them."

This is the only verse in the Qur'an which '*Ulama* hold against womenÆ. All other verses exhort men to fulfill their duties towards women and remind them of women's rights/ In fact entire discourse on women in Qur'an is right based and for men duty based. This above verse occurs in chapter 4, which is on women. There is no chapter on men in Qur'an. Qur'an emphasises equality of men and women (2:228). About 2:228, Maulana Azad says in his 'Tarjuman al-Qur'an' that this is revolutionary declaration of sexual equality 1300 years ago.

In the light of all this how can one think that Qur'an will allow women to be beaten? Now let us come to the word 'chastise them' which in Arabic is *wadribuhunna*. Now the word *daraba* in Arabic has several meanings. In Lane's dictionary one will find at least two full pages of meaning of this word *daraba* of which only one meaning is to chastise. Among other meanings is, according to Imam Raghib Asfahani, a distinguished scholar of Qur'anic terms, for he camel to go near she camel.

Thus if this meaning is taken then it would mean when she is persuaded go near her and not to chastise her. And this interpretation is much more congenial to the entire discourse on women in the Qur'an. It again and again exhorts men to be mindful of women's rights. Then how can it permit men to chastise them? And even when this meaning of chastisement is taken into consideration Tabari, highly respected exegete of the Qur'an refers to one *hadith* in which the Prophet only permitted very light strike with tooth brush or kerchief, and no more.

According to this *hadith* only symbolic light strike, so as not to injure, is allowed. But in the first place this meaning goes against the spirit of the Qur'an. All modern commentators have rejected this meaning. A Turkish scholar who has worked on the translation of the Qur'an for more than two decades maintains that *daraba* here means to strike out i.e. if a woman rebels against her husband then he should, in the last measure, remove her and divorce her as they cannot carry on together.

Another women scholar from Iran Laleh Bakhtiar who has translated the Qur'an from feminist point of view and has spent 40 years on this work also disagrees with translation of *daraba* as chastisement. She says, "After 40 years of studying and translating books related to the Qur'an, I realised that something was missing: an objective universal and inclusive translation of the Qur'an from its classical Arabic into contemporary English. Most of the 17 English translations I had seen included some interpretation of the verse making a direct comparison between the English and Arabic extremely difficult. Plus, many of the English translations continue to use Arabic words and names such as *Allah* for God, which can be confusing or even off-putting to new readers."

Two things she says about the method she followed is quite striking: she has looked at all different uses of the word in the text in context before determining the appropriate meaning in English. She used computer to create database of 40,000 nouns and verbs of the Qur'an 50,000 particles of speech. This method is most appropriate as then alone one can understand the significance of a word, both as verb and noun. The methodology of understanding the Qur'an which I have discovered is also collating all the verses of the Qur'an on one subject and then inferring most appropriate meaning.

Also, one should always remember no *'alim* (scholar) can avoid being influenced by his/her circumstances, both cultural and political, for understanding the scriptural text. There is no surprise, if the commentators of early Islam understood chastisement by the word *daraba* in their own cultural and political milieu.

Also, Prophet's Sunna plays an important role in evolving shari'ah laws. No one, even the most conservative *'alim* or jurist, has ever referred to the holy Prophet ever chastising any of his wife even when they made unreasonable demands on him. The Qur'an itself refers to an incident in which the Prophet's wives made demand for more worldly goods which the Prophet could not afford. Let alone chastising them, he did not even utter harsh words against them.

He simply withdrew into a room and did not speak to his wives for a month and then, as per the *Allah*'s instruction, explained to his wives that either they should opt for this worldly goods and separate from him or live with him and expect their reward from *Allah*. This incident has been referred to in the Qur'anic verses 33:28-29 and also in 66:1-3 and we find in 'Sahih Bukhari' reference to this incident that the Holy Prophet temporarily separated from his wives for a month and then reconciled to them.

This incident from Holy Prophet's life also clearly illustrates the real meaning of the verse 4:34 referred to above. That when wives rebel or try to become difficult, persuade them, then isolate them in bed and then reconcile with them and do not try to harass them or find way against them. Also the word *daraba* has been used in the Qur'an in number of ways and in different forms. For example in the verse 24:31, the word *daraba* has been used in gerund form for covering breasts with head coverings (*aurhani*). Here *daraba* does not mean beating or chastising.

Also, the occasion of revelation of the verse 4:34 as described by Tabari and Kasshaf, both highly respected commentators is that one woman approached Holy Prophet complaining that "my husband chastised me without any fault. What should I do?" The Holy Prophet thought for a moment and advised her to go and retaliate. This caused jubilation among women in Madina. But men were worried and rushed to the Prophet and said how will they control their families if their women retaliated against them? Then this verse was revealed saying men are maintainers of their families and if women rebel, persuade them, then isolate them in bed and then strike them away, if they are not persuaded, or according to Imam Raghib Asfahani, go near them after conciliation.

This verse often quoted by men for license to beat their wives but this meaning is not at all in keeping with the Qur'anic spirit. I would urge upon the '*Ulama* to revisit this verse in the entire Qur'anic context and reinterpret it. After revelation of the verse 4:34 women came to the Prophet and inquired if they have inferior status to that of men. The Prophet (PBUH) replied I will wait for *Allah*'s revelation. And then he received concerned revelation in verse 33:35, which reiterates that men and women are equal in every respect and that they will be equally rewarded for their spiritual merits.

Thus the verse 33:35 settles the matter conclusively. This is the last verse in respect of men and women. Also, while referring to relation between husband and wife (though the Qur'an does not use the word husband and wife, as the word husband denoted authority but only *zawj* and *zawja* i.e. one of the couple again denoting equality between the two) Qur'an says *Allah* has created love and compassion between them. It also says in the same verse that *Allah* has created your mate so that you find peace of mind in them.

If *Allah* has created love and compassion and source of peace in women how can it ever permit beating of wives? Thus one has to take all verses on the subject and read them together to find the real intention of the Qur'an. Chastisement was inferred by the medieval scholars under the influence of their patriarchal cultural milieu. One can discover new meanings as Qur'anic words are pregnant with many meanings, each meaning to be discovered in different circumstances but in keeping with the Qur'anic principles and values.

It will not only be unfortunate if Muslim Personal Law Board opposes domestic violence bill, it will also bring Islam to ridicule. And they will injure the real spirit of Qur'an and Sunnah. Islam greatly raised the status of women more than 1400 years ago and unfortunately our '*Ulama* (though not all) still understand the Qur'an in ways which denigrates position of women as during pre-Islamic days which Qur'an describes as *jahiliyyah* (period of ignorance) and Qur'an came to dispel *jahilliyah* and create enlightenment. Will our '*Ulama* choose ignorance over enlightenment?

Why Codification of Muslim Personal Law

Islamic Law or what is called Muslim Personal Law comes under attack not only by Hindutva forces but also is criticised by secular forces who stand for gender equality. The Hindutva forces attack it not for their love for gender justice but out of hostility for Islam. But same cannot be said for secular forces. They find existing Muslim Personal Law as gender biased in favour of man.

Most of us think that the Muslim personal law as applicable in India today is Shari'ah law. However, it is not so. Those Muslims who defend Muslim personal law as Shari'ah law do not understand the difference between Muslim personal law applicable today and Shari'ah law. In fact it was called Anglo-Mohammedan law before independence but was renamed as Muslim personal law after independence.

The British government, after it seized power from the Mughals, established its own courts, which also heard cases pertaining to Muslim marriage, divorce, inheritance etc. In most of these courts there were either British or non-Muslim judges who did not know Shari'ah law or if even Muslim judges heard these cases, most of them were trained in British laws.

What these judges did was to consult Hidayah, written by Mirghayani, a Hanafi scholar, and translated into English by Hamilton. Often they also consulted some Maulavi before delivering the judgment. Since the cases were heard in these British courts, the procedural law followed was English law and substantive law was based on *Hidayah*, it came to be known as Anglo-Mohammedan law.

The judgments in these cases delivered by higher courts became precedents for subsequent cases and thus whole corpus of law came into existence based on these judgments which came to be known as Anglo-Mohammedan law and renamed as Muslim personal law as calling it Anglo-Mohammedan law was now rather embarrassing. Thus to call it Shari'ah law would be a misnomer.

Unfortunately, what we Muslims or rather Muslim Personal Law Board is defending is not divine law but Anglo-Mohammedan law known by another name. It is unjust in many respects to women and we try to rationalize these injustices in the name of Islam. In fact Islamic law has to be based on Qur'an and *Sunnah* and then alone it could be called Shari'ah law and such law would not tend to be unjust.

In all Muslim countries too traditional laws have been amended to bring them closer to Qur'an and *sunnah* thus giving more rights to women as in the Qur'an. In Turkey too what came to be known as *Tanzeemat*, was based on different provisions favouring women taken from different schools of Sunni law like *Hanafi, Shafi'I, Maliki, Hanbali* etc. In India too, the Dissolution of Muslim Marriage of 1939 was based on Maliki School as in *Hanfi* law a woman has to wait for 90 years if her husband disappears without a trace.

If we codify the present Muslim personal law, many shortcomings in the present law can be removed thus making it much more gender? just than it is at present. In fact in its original spirit Islamic law in matters of marriage, divorce, inheritance etc. was most progressive and empowered women as no other law had done before. However, over period of time this original spirit was lost due to then prevailing social ethos and values. And customary laws acquired greater importance over Qur'anic and Prophet's (PBUH) pronouncements. Codification can remove these accretions over a period of time and restore original Qur'anic spirit.

We are doing this codification precisely for this reason. And our team is meeting noted ? *Ulama* and Muftis, Muslim lawyers and Muslim women activists to evaluate their views and problems encountered by them. Our team has recorded their interviews based on properly designed questionnaire prepared in consultation with some experts on Islamic law. It is important to know that we are interviewing *Ulama* of various schools i.e. *Hanafi*, *Shari'I, Ithna Ashari, Ahl-e-Hadis* etc. those who have presence in India.

These views will be very much kept in mind while actual codification is done. And it need not be reiterated that this codification will be based on Islamic framework and nothing outside it so that it is acceptable to all. It will not be based on anything outside Islamic laws. However, codification need not follow only one school of law as in some schools there are provisions more favourable to women, than other schools. Thus partly we may follow what was done in Turkey in framing *Tanzimat* laws.

It is interesting to note that so far our interviews are very encouraging and many *Ulama* from Deoband, Lucknow, Aligarh, Azamgarh and other places have fully supported our views about making present Muslim personal law gender-just by bringing it closer to Qur'anic spirit and spirit of Sunnah of the Prophet (PBUH). It was indeed very pleasant surprise to us. They also do not agree with Muslim personal board in maintaining status quo and causing problems to women.

Most of the *Ulama*, with some exceptions of course, agreed with us that polygamy cannot be permitted unregulated as Qur'an makes it strictly conditional, on ability of men to do equal justice to his wives as Qur'an clearly states in 4:3 and 4:129 that if justice is not done, one should marry only one. In fact 4:129 is very very emphatic on justice so much so that it says you cannot do justice even if you want and do not leave first wife suspended or neglected.

Thus in Qur'an priority is not for number but for justice. However, in Muslim personal law in India spirit of justice is totally lost and number has replaced it. Qur'an laid so much emphasis on justice 1400 years ago and today in 21st century when women are much more educated and aware of their rights, justice has receded into background.

It is interesting to note that some *Ulama* maintained that one need not even obtain consent of first wife as it is 'privilege' of men to marry up to four wives and they even denied that verse on polygamy was revealed after the Battle of Uhud in which more than ten per cent of men were killed and widows and orphans had to be taken care of.

Their ignorance was indeed very shocking as they maintained that polygamy is needed to take care of sexual need of man and if polygamy is not allowed prostitution will flourish. If one wife is undergoing menstruation or is pregnant or has delivered man must have other wives to fulfill his sexual need. This is not mentioned in Qur'an even indirectly and yet these few ulama justified polygamy on these un-Qur'anic grounds.

Some prominent *Ulama* from Deoband, Lucknow and Aligarh, to our pleasant surprise, favoured abolition of triple divorce and they were critical of Muslim Personal Law Board on its insistence to retain it. One of them pointed out that if triple divorce in one sitting is justified on grounds of 2nd Caliph Hazrat Umar permitting it, why don't they take into account that he later punished those who resorted to it.

These *Ulama* pointed out that divorce should be pronounced on three different occasions as described in the Qur'an so that reconciliation could be brought about in the meanwhile, if possible. Some even maintained that it should be only thrice in lifetime. All of them agreed that as per Qur'anic requirement prior to divorce arbitration should be attempted failing which divorce procedure may be started (4:35). This verse too emphasises reconciliation rather than divorce.

Thus these are two main issues in Muslim Personal Law, which are causing injustices to Muslim women. If polygamy and triple divorce are properly regulated Islamic personal law will not only come much closer to the Qur'anic spirit but would become much more progressive than what it is today.

Though incidence of polygamy is not very high among Muslims in India still some men do marry second wife (rarely four wives as in Hindutva propaganda) by either deserting first wife or refusing to divorce her when wife asks for *khula'*. Thus there is need to regulate polygamy by stipulating strict conditions as required by the Qur'an and no man should be free to take another wife according to his whims. Codification would attempt to lay down such conditions and make it justiciable as per law.

Also, triple divorce should be replaced by talaq al-*sunnah* or Qur'anic form of divorce both are quite fair to women. Even divorce where inevitable has to be fair to women and Qur'an repeatedly exhorts men to either retain her (in marriage) in goodness or leave her (i.e. divorce her) in kindness (2:229). She cannot be thrown out arbitrarily as it is usually done through triple and oral divorce. Law must prevail and proper procedure must be followed as laid down in Qur'an and *sunnah*. Triple divorce is not in keeping with either of the two,

Rethinking Muslim Personal Law as prevalent in India is certainly not to violate divine injunctions as often maintained by some people but to bring in much closer to divine injunctions i.e. to infuse in them really divine spirit. Well it may not always be possible to achieve complete unanimity but certainly we will attempt to create a broad consensus around codification so that Muslims women really enjoy equal status as they are entitled to according to Qur'anic injunctions and also in accordance to modern laws.

Can Veil be Enforced?

Can veil be enforced by throwing acid as announced by the Lashkar-e-Jabbar, a militant organisation in Kashmir? First of all one has to understand the nature of Qur'anic injuction on veil before we discuss what the Lashkar-e-Jabbar is doing. It is important to note that there is no concept of *hijab* (veil) in Qur'an for all believing women in the sense of covering one's face. What the Qur'an states should be seen in the light of the practices of women in the *jahiliyyah* i.e. pre-Islamic period.

In pre-Islamic period since the Arabs belonged to different tribes, the tribal women did not cover their breasts and also many of them would publicly display their sexual charms zeenah; wear anklets and would, in the market place beat their feet to attract attention of men. Since Islam was basically a civilising mission and gave greater dignity to women lifting their status from being mere chattles and sexual objects to dignified humans enjoying equal rights with men, it prescribed certain norms of behaviour and style of dressing. The Qur'anic prescriptions should be seen in that light in order to appreciate its main thrust.

The 24th chapter of the Qur'an deals with some of these issues. Before Islam, it must be noted, the sexual morality was quite lax. Man and women indulged in free sex in many cases. It was not considered social evil to indulge even in adultery. Thus when women embraced Islam the Prophet would take an oath from these women not to indulge in adultery. Thus to remove this laxity in sexual behaviour the Qur'an prescribed punishment for adultery in verse 24:2. There was no such punishment for adultery in the pre-Islamic Arabian society.

Also, to deal with the problem of displaying one's sexual charms (zeenah) publicly the Qur'an said that "And say to the believing women that they lower their gaze and restrain their sexual passions and do not display their adornment except what appears thereof." (24:31) Thus what the Qur'an is prohibiting is to display ones adornment publicly. And here too the Qur'an makes an important exception i.e. "except what appears thereof". Thus women are not asked to hide everything publicly. What should appear publicly, should appear.

Most of the '*Ulama* and Islamic jurists maintain that the phrase "except what appears thereof" means a woman can keep her face and hands open and that she can apply collyrium to her eyes and can wear ring in her fingers and bangle in her hands and display the same. Tabari, an important commentator of the Qur'an maintains this in his commentator on this verse.

Other '*Ulama* also concur with him on this issue and let us remember any interpretation of the Qur'an is mediated by sociological and cultural factors. Had those commentators lived in our times when social and cultural changes have taken place would have interpreted this verse even more liberally in favour of women. Thus even the medieval commentators have permitted women to keep their faces and hands open. Today women should have even greater measure of freedom. But even going by the medieval interpretation and conforming norms laid down by medieval jurists Muslim women should be allowed to move about publicly without veiling their faces.

In Iran, women do wear *hijab* but in keeping with the above verse of the Qur'an, are not compelled to hide their faces and hands. They wear an overall and cover their heads. The women in Iran enjoy considerable degree of freedom. They are far from confined at home. They are quite active publicly, are members of parliament and one of them is also vice president of the Iranian Islamic Republic.

The Qur'an, in another verse, also prescribes that women cover their breasts with the sheet of cloth which he wears (24:31) Thus it will be seen that when the Qur'an is asking women to cover their bosoms with their head-coverings how can it ask women to cover their faces? Covering bosoms is much more dignified for a woman and hence this is being prescribed by the Qur'an. Maulana Muhammad Ali of Lahore comments on this verse as follows: "Before Islam women used to appear in public with their breasts partly uncovered?and women were thus required to cover their breasts with a part of their head-covering as worn in the East conceals the arms, the neck and the bosom, as also the ornaments worn in the ears or on the neck or over the bosom.."

It should also be noted that the Qur'an permits to display her adornments before her husband, her parents, her other relatives with whom she cannot marry. However, more important to note is that this prescription by the Qur'an does not follow by any punishment for not following the Qur'anic prescription. Some even maintain that the nature of verses in this regard is recommendatory rather than mandatory.

How can then anyone enforce veil forcibly on women? The very nature of threat is un-Islamic and un-Qur'anic. If at all it is to be enforced it cannot be enforced by any organisation on the road; it can be enforced by the Islamic state. India is a secular state and in this country even state cannot interfere with one's personal freedom. In the Shari'ah legislation no punishment has been prescribed for not observing the code of dress prescribed or recommended by the Qur'an.

It is strange that such organisations do not speak out against men in any respect even if they violate the Qur'anic prescriptions about sexual morality. It is not that the Qur'an does not prescribe any code of conduct for men; it does. It requires both men and women to lower their gaze and restrain their sexual passions. Thus the Qur'an says in verse 24:30, "Say to the believing men that they lower their gaze and restrain their sexual passions. That is purer for them."

Thus men are first exhorted to observe sexual morality before women are exhorted. Yet every time these male-dominated and patriarchal organisations enforce sexual morality for women and keep silent about men. They never launch a campaign even if men continue to tease women on road and other public places or even molest or rape them. So much for their "Islamic morality".

In fact, such threats have been possible because of culture of violence having been perpetrated by the militants in Kashmir. Once violence is resorted to for solving problems it has terrible consequences. It results in killing of innocent people rather than solution of the problem. The concept of jihad also has been not only grossly misunderstood it has been grossly exploited by all sorts of unscrupulous elements. Women in Kashmir have greatly suffered in horrible ways due to violence being perpetrated by the *Jihadi* groups. It is the Kashmiri women who have payed the greatest price.

It is common knowledge that Kashmiri women have been raped by armed forces in retaliation to what the *jihadis* do. Several instances have been reported in the media. When the houses of Kashmiri people are searched for hiding militants the women are molested or even raped. The militants too hardly display exemplary sexual morality. They too do not hesitate in abducting women and either forcibly marry them or even rape them. Also, it is Kashmiri mothers who have lost their sons, or wives their husbands. Thus so called jihad by the militants, has done greatest disservice to women of Kashmir.

One should thus strongly condemn Dashkar-e-Jabbar for forcibly enforcing veil on Muslim women of Kashmir. Even Islam, let alone the secular government of India, does not give them any such right to enforce veil. Such threats have been condemned rightly by different sections of society in Kashmir. Even Hurriyat leaders have condemned it except of course Gilani who is known for his extremist views.

In a secular country like India even the government cannot prescribe any dress code. All citizens including women are free to follow their own choice in matters of dress. The threats in Kashmir has also emboldened some little known organisations in Mumbai and Hyderabad also to hold similar threats for Muslim women to observe veil. And not to be left behind the Hindutvawadis have also issued threats for the Hindu women not to wear jeans and mini-skirts. Where will be democracy if such threats are held out and women are forced to wear this or that dress.

One is free to observe veil or not to wear jeans but the freedom of choice should be exercised by women without any external coercion. The government should also see that no one, however militant, is allowed to take law in their own hands. Otherwise they will lose their legitimacy to govern and people will find it difficult to lead lives of their choice. There cannot be democracy without freedom and dignity.

The common citizens should also see to it that women are not openly coerced in this way. They will also have to resist attempts by such elements if they want to protect their own freedom. One shudders to think where this rot will stop if we surrender to such forces? All sorts of fanatics and religious fundamentalists will take law in their own hands and enforce anti-diluvian laws, which have nothing to do even with religion It is well-known fact of history that there was no system of veiling the face during the early period of Islam. It came from Romans and Persians i.e. Sassanids during the

Umayyad period. Many Islamic scholars have pointed this out. It is for the Muslim women also to know the Qur'anic provisions first hand rather than pitifully depending on the orthodox viewpoint in this regard.

Fatwas, Acceptability and their Relevance

Controversial *fatwas* are often issued and media strongly reacting to these *fatwas*. Some *fatwas* have been issued by well-known institutions like the Darul Ulum Deoband and some by individual Maulavis or Imams leading prayers in the mosques. Not only that the *fatwas* are controversial in themselves but also there is great deal of misunderstanding about the nature of these *fatwas*. We would like to throw light on all these aspects.

First, let us throw some light on the nature of *fatwas* and their significance for Muslims. It is important to note that there is no concept of priesthood in Islam, much less church like hierarchy. No authority, howsoever eminent, can claim sole right to pronounce any binding opinion for all Muslims. Thus no *fatwa* issued by any eminent authority is binding on any Muslim, even on one who asks for it.

There is wrong conception that once a *fatwa* is issued, all Muslims automatically follow it. It is far from truth. Even among Sunni Islam there are four surviving schools of jurisprudence (*shari'ah*), *Hanafi*, *Maliki*, *Shafi'i* and *Hanbali* and besides these there are other schools among Shi'ah Muslims like *Ja'fari, Ismaili* and *Zadiyah.* Even in every school there are differences of opinion on several matters.

Whenever any *fatwa* is issued it is issued according to the position in the particular school. Whatever *fatwas* are issued by Darul Uloom Deoband, they are issued according to the Hanafi school of Shari'ah. The founders of these schools had no arrogance about absolute truth about their own position. For example, Imam Abu Hanifa used to say if my two disciples differ from me, listen to them as they are two and I am one. Imam Ibn Hanbal, founder of Hanbali School refused to allow the Abbasid Caliph to enforce his *maslak* (i.e. Shari'ah law according to his formulations) throughout his regime. He maintained it would deprive people of their freedom to follow an opinion different from him. He also refused to become chief qadi in his establishment, as his maslak will reign supreme.

When these eminent imams founders of their respective schools never allowed their opinion to prevail on all thus depriving others of their freedom of opinion, how can lesser beings claim that their opinion is final and binding. Thus no *fatwa* should be taken as final and binding on all Muslims. In many respects opinions of different schools differ widely though principles (*usul*) do not differ. Each Imam derived different conclusions depending on which verse of the Qur'an or which *hadith* is being used by the *mufti* (one who issues the *fatwa*).

The *muftis* in India who issue *fatwas* follow mechanically their school of shari'ah. They simply consult their rule- book and pronounce the *fatwa*. For example the *fatwa* issued in case of Imrana was in keeping with the Hanafi school. If someone had asked this very question in Kerala where Shafi'i school prevails, the mufti would have issued *fatwa* just opposite to what Deoband issued. Because according to Imam Shafi'i what is permissible (i.e. marriage) cannot be cancelled by what is not (i.e. rape or adultery). Thus a Shafi'I mufti would have asked Imrana to continue in her marriage with her husband and her father-in-law would have been punished for committing rape.

Those who issue *fatwas* are not men of vision or great understanding of the issues involved. They do not investigate the merits of each case. They only consult the rule-book and pronounce their verdict, as pointed out above. Mostly those who ask the opinion of the *alims* (scholars) are poor and illiterate people from rural or semi-urban areas. Imrana and her relatives live in a village in U.P. The family is of labourers or rickshaw drivers. Her husband is a rickshaw driver.

A *fatwa* is to be located in its sociological moorings. A backward society consisting of illiterate and poor people have backward outlook. Their only asset is religion, which gives them some comfort in their otherwise life full of struggle and hard labour to eke out their livelihood. One cannot expect them to exercise their own intelligence in the matter. The *fatwas* should be criticised but keeping these factors in mind. Mere condemnation will not do. One should also understand why such *fatwas* are acceptable.

Those who criticise these *fatwas,* and rightly so come from educated middle classes living in comforts of urban environs. They have benefit of best of education and training. But poor and illiterate whose only asset is religion cling to the traditional religion. Any pronouncement from even the imam of a mosque is divine law for them. The same thing applies to the urban poor also who are far from intellectual and material benefits of modernity and post-modernity even though they live in urban areas.

Darul Ulum authorities of *Darul Ifta*' (department in charge of issuing *fatwas*) should also give a thought to re-organise their methodology of issuing *fatwas*. Darul Ulum Deoband, is one of the leading seminaries of the Islamic world. When they issue such poorly rated *fatwas*, it brings bad name to them. Whenever any question is put to them, they should not simply consult the rule- book and pronounce their opinion. They should thoroughly investigate the whole issue and apply their minds in the light of experiences of our own age.

The great imams like Abu Hanifa, Imam Hanbal and others when they pronounced any opinion they spent great deal of time considering every aspect of the issue. Of course they derived their conclusions from Qur'an and *hadith* but did not neglect the social situation. Now our *ulama* simply follow these great imams mechanically without giving any thought to the circumstances today. A mufti has great responsibility to discharge. He has to have social vision and thorough understanding of modern society. Allama Iqbal suggests in his Reconstruction of Religious Thought in Islam, that every generation of Muslims should re-think the issues and legislate according to their own needs.

The *fatwa* that a woman either should not participate in elections or if she does, should wear purdah is issued without applying the mind at all. They don't even realise that *hijab* is not an end in itself by means of preserving ones chastity and there are other means to do that. If a woman does not wear *hijab* does not mean she is morally corrupt or likely to become morally corrupt. Chastity does not depend so much on wearing or not wearing *hijab* but much more on her inner determination and moral training. In medieval society for reasons not to be discussed here, *hijab* was considered the only means of protecting her chastity. Women at that time were not publicly active and were not much educated. They were confined to household work and hardly participated in public life. Today, the circumstances have changed.

Today women are participating in public life. In Muslim counties like Pakistan and Bangla Desh they have achieved highest office of prime ministership. Now even Saudi Arabia has permitted a woman to become a pilot. Can she perform such functions observing *purdah*? The Qur'an itself lays, more emphasis on lowering the gaze (ghassul basar) and protecting ones private parts (i.e. chastity). Our ulama should learn to make distinctions between means and ends. For them often means themselves become ends. For example, for them purdah has become more important than chastity.

A mufti from Hyderabad issued a *fatwa* that a man can marry two wives simultaneously as the Qur'an permits man to marry four wives at a time. This *fatwa* was issued to enable a middle aged Arab to marry simultaneously marry two teenage girls. Such *fatwas* bring shame to Islam. The Qur'an had permitted to marry more than one wife to meet a crisis situation created after Battle of Uhud in which ten percent of man population was killed and large number of widows and orphans had to be taken care of. And this permission was also given, subject to rigorous conditions and warning Muslims that they cannot do justice to all wives even if they want to and they should not leave their first wife suspended in air.

Such *fatwas* as issued by a Hyderabad *mufti* do great injustice to the real spirit of Qur'an. They not only injure the spirit of Qur'an (which is monogamy in normal circumstances as per verse 4:129 of the Qur'an) but reduce it to a license to enjoy sexual pleasure with women. The Arabs come for this purpose and bribe their way through to marry young teenaged girls from poor families. The muftis should be ashamed to issue such *fatwas* thoughtlessly.

Our national media also preys upon such cases and instead of investigating thoroughly all the circumstances write more out of misunderstanding, if not hostility towards Islam and Muslims. Some papers even write out of downright hostility. Media should realise that such hype on *fatwas* creates tensions between communities and put entire Muslim community in the dock.

They do not even care to report that there are liberal and progressive Muslims who oppose such *fatwas* and that today an internal debate is raging among Muslims. Also, such things are not happening among Muslims only. Such things are happening along all sections of society. A woman is not treated with dignity due to her in all the communities India and all of us are in need of reorienting our attitude towards women and their rights. Sooner we realise better it is for our society and our country. Let us not point fingers at each other but treat the issue with seriousness it deserves.

Adultery and Qur'anic Punishment

Recently there was news about *rajm* i.e. stoning to death of some women and men in Iran for the offence of adultery. They were `buried up to the waist, and stoned to death. Before doing that they were given ritual *bath* (*ghusl*), wrapped in shroud and then buried up to the waist and stoned. This makes a shocking news and raises the question whether Qur'an permits such cruel punishment.

Before we take up discussion on the Qur'anic punishment we would like to discuss the very approach to crime and punishment in Islam. It must be remembered that the Qur'an is basically not a book on crime and punishment. It is a book of moral guidance and Qur'an dealt with all those issues which would make a human person a model human being in the eyes of *Allah*. The Qur'an should not be treated as a book of law, crime and punishment.

But since the Qur'an was revealed in a society where there was complete vacuum and there were no laws, legal or state institutions, no courts or judicial system, the believers sought Prophet's (PBUH) guidance in every question they were confronted with. In order to guide people the Qur'an came out with answers at different levels. At times it provided answers which were normative and went beyond immediate situation i.e. of eternal nature and at times it provided answers which applied to immediate situation by upholding or reforming the existing custom or tradition.

When it provided answer in terms of existing tradition it made it clear either in following or subsequent verse(s) that eternal answer was something else. Normally Qur'an takes very humane approach which does not violate human dignity but at times it also provided for exemplary punishment in view of the gravity of the crime. But the very word *hadd* (plural hudud) (had means limit) shows they were maximum punishments and cannot be given in every case. Only a judge or the *Qadi* will decide the gravity of the crime and decide whether maximum punishment is needed or not.

Our *muftis*, *qadis* and judges apply such punishments as a matter of course. The Qur'an also emphasises reformation of the person by using words like *tauba* (repentance) and that *Allah* is *Ghafur* (pardoner) and Rahim (compassionate). The Islamic authorities while giving punishment straight accord maximum punishment without taking into consideration these aspects of the Qur'anic approach. Normal approach should be to reform the person who commits offence or crime than to punish. Only when a person persists in committing offences, he/she should be accorded maximum punishment (*hudud* punishments). Qur'an's maximum emphasis is on reforming the offender through repentance and *Allah*'s compassion than to punish.

Also, severity or otherwise of the punishment also indicates severity of the crime in the society in which the punishment is prescribed. No punishment should be treated as permanent. However, our jurists and qadis, even if some punishment is mentioned in *hadith* about which there is controversy, will apply the punishment unthinkingly arguing it is Prophet's (PBUH) *sunnah.* This is in complete disregard of Qur'anic spirit and modern legal and judicial approach. On one hand we claim Islam is for all times to come and on the other we refuse to re-think practices not sanctioned by the Qur'an. And even if some punishment is prescribed by the Qur'an it has to be seen in the perspective of then prevalent conditions, and not to be blindly applied.

The Holy Prophet lived in a tribal society which had not even known or developed institution of marriage (except in Mecca) and hence sexual morality was lax among the Bedouins. Also, there were certain prevalent customs and Jewish prescriptions. At times the Prophet (PBUH), in the absence of Qur'anic injunctions accepted these prevalent customs or Jewish injunctions and when revelation came, it was abandoned. All this has to be kept in mind while accepting or rejecting any punishment mentioned in *hadith* literature.

It also has to be kept in mind that the shari'ah laws evolved over a long period of time and after considerable degree of controversies. In this respect we would also like to point out difference between *al-shar*' and *al-shari'ah.* *Al-shar*' is a divine command something emanating from *Allah* and al-*shari'ah* is systematic formulation of ordinances into a legal statement. Thus al-shari'ah came into existence through complex processes in a human society incorporating social needs and human opinion. It should not be treated immutable and unalterable. It is divine injunctions applied to a given social conditions. It should not be treated something eternal which cannot be re-thought.

Many issues which are part of one or the other schools of jurisprudence which we treat as divine and immutable were thoroughly debated by Islamic jurists and differing opinions were expressed and incorporated in different schools of law depending upon which *hadith* was accepted or rejected and how a particular verse of the Qur'an was interpreted. That is why all eminent jurists kept the door of *ijtihad* (in view of further social needs and changed circumstances) were kept open. But after a few centuries these lively debates and controversies atrophied and doors of *ijtihad* were shut. The shari'ah laws as evolved earlier by founding fathers came to be followed mechanically.

The punishment for adultery is one controversy among them and needs to be seriously and critically re-examined. Stoning to death for adultery is not at all a Qur'anic punishment. Qur'an prescribes 100 lashes for what it calls *zina. Zina* is Arabic word which means fornication, adultery as well as rape. In Arabic there are no different words as in English. This has become part of the problem. Imam Raghib defines *zina* as sleeping with a woman without legally marrying her.

And the Qur'an prescribes the punishment using the word *zaniyah* and *zani* i.e. women guilty of zina and man guilty of zina which can mean all three i.e. fornication, adultery or rape. Generally translators have translated the word *zaniyah* and *zani* as adulteress and adulterer. Thus Muhammad Asad translates verse (24:2) as "As For the adulteress and the adulterer - flog each of them with a hundred stripes, and let not compassion with them keep you from [carrying out] this law of God, if you [truly] believe in God and the Last Day: and let a group of the believers witness their chastisement." (Muhammad Asad, The Message of the Qur'an, Gibralter, 1980). Abdullah Yusuf Ali, on the other hand uses both the words adulteress and adulterer and fornicator. Thus he translates it as "The woman and the man guilty of adultery or fornication, flog each of them with a 100 stripes?"(Abdullah Yusuf Ali The Holy Qur'an (Hyderabad, n.d).

Thus Qur'an is obviously referring to both adultery and fornication and does not prescribe separate punishments for fornication and adultery. Had *Allah* intended harsher punishment for adultery, He could have clarified that for adultery punishment would be stoning to death and for fornication hundred stripes. What could have stopped *Allah* from saying so? There was no separate verse needed. It could have been specified in the same verse. And even if a separate verse was needed it could have been revealed leaving no ambiguity.

Also, the words of the verse "? and let not compassion with them keep you from [carrying out] this law of God" and also that "let a group of the believers witness their chastisement" clearly shows wrath of God for such act of illegal sex and thus flogging in itself is harshest punishment *Allah* prescribes and no harsher punishment should be instituted. *Allah* has expressed His wrath in this verse in very harsh words and so the punishment prescribed (of hundred stripes) is the harshest the Qur'an thinks of.

Now as for the prescribed punishment of *rajm* (stoning to death) in the corpus of shari'ah law today is based on highly controversial *hadith* of *hadrat* 'Umar that this verse of *rajm* was in the Qur'an and that we have recited it. This verse referred to here is called verse of *rajm* and one finds it mentioned in all major traditions as the missing verse. Thus we read in 'Ibn Ishaq' (pg. 684): "*Allah* sent Muhammad and sent down the scripture to him. Part of that He sent down was on stoning. Umar says, 'We read it, we were taught it, and we heeded it. The Apostle [Muhammad] stoned, and we stoned after him. I fear that in the time to come there will be no mention of stoning in *Allah*'s book, and thereby go astray in neglecting an ordinance *Allah* has sent down."

Thus according to Umar [ibn al-*Khattab*] the stoning verse was part of the Qur'an, the revelation which *Allah* sent down. But now it is missing. Thus adultery was not only a capital offence but demanded death by stoning.

Now the question is when Umar [ibn al-*Khattab*] is saying so assertively that the verse on stoning was there in the Qur'an and that we have read it and the Prophet (PBUH) stoned those to death who indulged in adultery, then why this verse was omitted? The Qur'an was finally compiled by Hadrat Uthman (which was certainly after the death of Umar), then why this verse was omitted? There is no conclusive answer to this, if we accept the above *hadith* as authentic and acceptable.

And if Uthman omitted the verse why did he do so? Specially after Hadrat Umar expressed fear that it might be omitted and people may forget it and thus not carry out *Allah*'s injunction? We do not find any satisfactory explanation for this. And whenever a verse was revealed it was committed to memory by some and was recorded by some. Even if written record was not found, someone who had committed it to memory (and there were many) could have pointed it out to Uthman and that verse could have been included in the Qur'an. It is highly unlikely that no one pointed out when final copy was being compiled that such an important verse has been left out from divine book about which Umar had expressed his fear that it might be left out. This seems to be highly unlikely scenario. While compiling, Uthman had consulted all *huffaz* (those who had committed Qur'anic verses to memory) and all written records.

Let us carefully see what Umar had said. According to *hadith* narrated by Ibn Abbas Umar said, "I am afraid that after a long time has passed, people may say, 'we do not find the verses of the *rajm* (stoning to death) in the Holy Book', and consequently they may go astray by leaving an obligation that *Allah* has revealed. I confirm that the penalty of *rajm* be inflicted on him who commits illegal sexual intercourse, if he is already married and the crime is proved by witnesses or pregnancy or confession." Sufyan added I have memorised this narration in this way." 'Umar added, "Surely *Allah*'s Apostle carried out the penalty of *rajm*, and so did we after him." (see Sahih al-Bukhari Vol. 8, Book 86, 'The Book of Al-Hudud', *hadith* no. 6829).

The words of above *hadith* clearly shows that it was very important verse and Umar feared that after a long time people may say we did not find this verse in the Book. Despite that why then was it left out as the final version of the Qur'an we have today, and about which there is no controversy among Muslims? Surely, Uthman too would have taken care to include all verses, much more the one on *rajm* which was so important. But he did not and this itself means, the *hadith* quoted above should be treated carefully and critically. It should certainly not be accepted uncritically as many tend to do. It is highly doubtful that the Holy Qur'an really intended to prescribe *rajm* for adultery.

We do not find any mention of *rajm* in Tabari's *tafsir* also. He simply explains meaning of jald, how hard one should hit and how many people (*ta'ifah*) should witness it. Had there been verse of *rajm* in the Qur'an he would have mentioned it while explaining the meaning of the verse 24:2.

Also, a careful examination of *hadith* literature shows that the Prophet (PBUH) used the words had, *ta'zir* and *'uqubah* interchangeably. Had is obligatory Qur'anic punishment while *ta'zir* and *'uqubah* are discretionary punishments depending on the circumstances of the crime and those who commit crime. Maulana Madudi also opined that hudud punishments can be applied only in Islamic society which is strictly based on Islamic principles and not in every society.

We also find a *hadith* narrated by Hadrat A'ishah that the verse on *rajm* was eaten away by a goat. Such an approach to Qur'an is dangerous and will open the Qur'anic text to various arguments and others will also claim that such and such verse was also in the Qur'an but was lost. We find in 'Sahih Muslim' (chapter CCCXI, p. 500, tradition 2286) that Abu Musa Ashari invited Qur'an readers of Basra and three hundred of them responded. It was said by one of them that we used to read a chapter in the Qur'an similar to *Bara'ah* in length and seriousness but I forgot it. I can remember from the chapter only the following words: 'Should a son of adam own two valleys full of wealth, he should see a third valley and nothing would fill Ibn Adam's abdomen but the soil. Now here it is maintained that whole chapter as long as chapter of *Bara'ah* is missing. We find many such a*hadith* in Sahih Muslim which refer to missing chapters and verses.

Umar is also reported to have said that Chapter 33 (Al-*Ahzab*) is incomplete. Al-Muttaqi Ali Ibn Husam-Din in his book 'Mukhtasar Kanz al-Ummal', printed on the margin of Imam Ahmad's Musnad, V2, P2 in his *hadith* about chapter 33, that said Ibn Mardawayh reported that Huthaifah said: Umar said to me: How many verses are contained in the Chapter *Al-Ahzab*? I said 72 or 73 verses. He said: it was almost as long as the chapter of the Cow (*al-Baqarah*), which contains 287 verses and in it there was the verse of stoning.

Thus we can see to what danger we are exposing the present text of the Qur'an on which there is complete unanimity by arguing that verse on *rajm* was revealed and then lost. We must resist temptation of such arguments, in order to justify *rajm* for adultery.

We also find one more narration from Imam Ahmad in which Umar said that if people would not say that Umar included in Qur'an what is not in it I would have written (this verse on *rajm*) in one corner of the Qur'an. This *hadith* is contradictory in itself. If the verse on stoning was there in Qur'an why Umar should fear accusation of including in it what is not there in it and if it was not there, where is the question of writing it down in one corner of the Qur'an. Those who accept such *hadith*s do not pay heed to contradictions in what is being said.

Some make another strange argument that verse of stoning in the Qur'an was revealed but its recitation was annulled but its implementation as punishment was retained. How strange is this argument. Why its recitation should be annulled. Any reason? The fact is that such verse never existed and *rajm* should not be justified by any means defying all rules of logic. The verse on punishment of *zina* is crystal clear in the Qur'an and only punishment prescribed is 100 lashes.

The Qur'an also prescribes half the punishment for married slave-girl. (4:25). How one can make stoning to death half in case of slave-girl? Only if punishment is 100 lashes one can make it half. The Qur'anic injunction about adultery by slave-girl is also so clear that no other explanation is possible. In fact, *Khwarij* uses this very argument to deny the punishment of stoning for adultery.

Also the argument that the Prophet (PBUH) gave this punishment is also not very tenable. It is far from proved that the Prophet gave this punishment (stoning to death) before revelation of this verse or after revelation of 24:2. If he gave punishment of stoning before revelation of 24:2 obviously he was guided by the prevailing custom in the society and especially its mention in Torah.

But it is difficult to maintain that he gave this punishment after revelation of the verse 24:2. Can the Prophet (PBUH) contradict injunction of the Qur'an? If so, what are other instances in which he did something which was in obvious contradiction to the Qur'anic injunction. This again has really serious implications, besides saying that the Prophet used to do what was not there in the Qur'an.

This is all the more problematic when we find in narration by Ahmad that during Umar's khilafah people used to say that there is no injunction in the Qur'an for *rajm* so how can we practise it? (the Arabic words of this *riwayah are inna unasan yaquluna ma al-rajm fi kitabillah wa innama fihi al-jald*).

Then again the following verse after 24:2 i.e. 24:3 "The adulterer cannot have sexual relations with any but an adulteress or an idolatress, and the adulteress, none can have sexual relations with her but an adulterer or an idolater; and it is forbidden to believers." How can an adulterer or adulteress have sexual relations with adulteress or adulterer, if they are stoned to death?

They can have such relations only if they are alive. This verse is also so clear that no other explanation is possible and any number of a*hadith* cannot justify any other explanation. What Qur'an intends is to make men and women give up zina whether it is fornication or adultery or rape. Qur'an wants to create a society where sexual relations would be for perpetuating human species, and not just for fulfilling ones lust.

Qur'an wishes to strengthen institution of family and, as pointed out at the outset, pre-Islamic Arabia did not have strong family institution. Also, tribal structure was breaking down and new society was coming into existence due to impact of socio-economic changes and on account of transition from tribal to commercial society. Family institution is highly necessary in such a society as new property relations were developing.

The Qur'an wanted to denounce sex outside marriage which weakens the institution of family and destroys its stability. But Qur'an was also ushering in a civilised society and its whole emphasis was on reforming human character rather than punishing in barbaric or harsh manner. Thus it prescribed punishment of 100 lashes in presence of a group of believers so that it brings him or her shame and creates strong barrier for repeating such action. In a way sentence is harsh enough within a civilised society but not barbaric so as to take away life in a cruel manner.

Once an adulterer is punished in presence of a group of believers, he will prefer thereafter to repent rather than repeat. Also, for any punishment we have to keep Qur'anic values in mind. Most fundamental Qur'anic values are justice (*'adl*), benevolence (*ihsan*), compassion (*rahmah*) and wisdom (*hikmah*). No punishment should go against these values. These are *Allah*'s names also in the Qur'an (*'Adil*, *Muhsin*, *Rahim* and *Hakim*).

Surely stoning to death goes against these fundamental values and kills an erring human being rather than giving him/her a chance to repent or reform. There is need for Muslim jurists (fuqaha') to rethink such punishments. It will make Islam humane which it is and which under influence of feudal values in medieval ages, undergone un-Qur'anic changes. Thus there is great need for bringing changes in Islamic fiqh in keeping with the Qur'anic values. Qur'an provides transcendent dimension to human life but Muslim jurists have imprisoned it in medieval values depriving Islam of its dynamic spirit.

Evolution of Shari'ah Law and its Potentiality for Change

Shari'ah law is considered quite central to Islam and one can hardly think of Islam without it. Its centrality to Islam is unquestionable. However, very few Muslims know that it evolved over a period of time and that much human effort have gone into its evolution. It is considered as wholly divine and hence immutable. This assumption comes in the way of any re-thinking on issues like rights of women, which is quite crucial today. It is therefore, very important to understand the nature of Shari'ah law and its evolution.

Arabia was by and large a Bedouine society except Mecca and Madina etc. which had sedantic population. Nomadic societies have no written laws and hence nomadic Arabs too, had no such laws. The settlements in Mecca and Madina came into existence out of nomadic populations settling around watering places but continued to follow their oral customary laws and traditions. They did not evolve any written laws unlike their Jewish and Christian neighbours who had revealed laws. The Arabs, in fact, had no tradition of learning and Arabic to them was more sacred to ears than to eyes. Even before Islam appeared on the scene there were no more than 16-17 people who knew how to read and write.

In fact the Arabs looked down upon scholarship as to them nomadic life was more precious and settled life was a sort of economic compulsion. They used to send their children to nomadic tribes for learning proper language. Thus they were nearly illiterate and were quite proud of their nomadic culture. Thus this pre-Islamic culture was referred to later as jahiliyyah i.e. one based on ignorance. The Qur'an brought to them, for the first time, the written culture and written laws. No wonder than that the first revelation of the Qur'an began with iqra' i.e. read. (see 96:1)

Thus the Qur'an became every thing to the Arabs, a storehouse of knowledge, knowledge (*'ilm*) they had never known. The Qur'an repeatedly stresses the word *'ilm*. *'Ilm* is a very comprehensive word in Arabic which embraces entire range of human knowledge. Thus the Qur'anic revelation was highly enriching experience. It gave them great wealth of knowledge and also laws to organise their society in keeping with just laws. The Arabs had very little in terms of knowledge (*'ilm*) and laws except some tribal customs and traditions which could not go too far. The Arabs were acquiring wealth as some of them were in international trade but they had no higher knowledge which could give them a place in the world.

It is important to note that the Arabs were surrounded by Roman and Sassanid Empires both of which were highly cultured and had highest achievements in terms of learning and scholarship. The Arabs, on the other, were at the bottom compared to their achievements. But once the Qur'an was revealed to them and they became masters of new knowledge this equation changed fast and Muslims raced far ahead and Baghdad evolved as a centre of knowledge and boasted of world's treasure of knowledge.

Thus the Qur'an was more than a miracle for the Arabs and all those who accepted it as the book of guidance. It was treasure house of science, philosophy, religion and law. However, often it provided guidelines and one had to extract from it what we can call *istinbat*. It has whetted the Arabs thirst for knowledge and as long as the Prophet (PBUH) was alive they went to him asking for guidance and the Prophet obliged them abundantly. Often many verses were revealed in response to questions from the believers.

The Qur'an, needless to say, became the major source of the Shari'ah law. As the Arabs wanted to base every thing now on the religion they embraces and which meant so much to them, they would ask flurry of questions so much so that at times the Prophet had to tell them not to ask too many questions lest all this become binding on them. Thus next to Qur'an Prophet's sayings and doings called (*sunnah*) became another source of Shari'ah law. However, the Prophet and hence his guidance was not available forever after his death. Other sources had to be found as new problems continued to arise particularly as Islam spread to other areas outside the Arabian peninsula.

Even within Arabian Penisla problems arose after the death of the Holy Prophet necessitating proper guidance. For example the Qur'an does not mention the punishment for drinking and this problem arose during the *Khilafat* of Hazrat Umar. Neither there was anything in the *sunnah* of the Prophet as everyone had stopped drinking completely after prohibition and the Prophet had no occasion to punish anyone. Thus analogical reasoning (qiyas) had to be used to prescribe punishment for drinking. Thus third source of Shari'ah law became qiyas i.e. analogy.

Then it was also necessary to develop a consensus among the learned of the *ummah* for acceptability and universality of the law so evolved and this was known as ijma' i.e. consensus. Thus *ijma* became the fourth source of Shari'ah law. The corpus of Shari'ah law developed over centuries using these four sources. However, it must be made clear here that this applies to Sunni Islam and the Shi'i Islam does not accept two later sources i.e. qiyas and *ijma*'as sources of Shari'ah law. For the Ithna 'Ashari Shi'ahs and Isma'ili Shi'ahs qiyas and ijma' are replaces by the sayings of the imams. For Shi'ahs imams are considered as *ma'sum* (i.e. infallible) and hence what they say about law becomes part of the law.

For Isma'ili Shi'ahs the final compilation of the Shari'ah laws took place during the time of the 14th imam Mo'iz and compilation was done by his Chief Da'i Sayyidna Qadi al-Nu'man and this compilation is known as 'Da'im al-Islam' and there is now no question of re-opening any issue. All these laws are based on the Qur'an, *sunnah* and sayings of Ali and imams from Hasan to Ja'far al-Sadiq and finally approved by Imam Mo'iz. The principle of ijtihad cannot be applied. Whatever is written in Da'a' im al- Islam is final.

However, it is not so, at least theoretically, as far as other sects of Islam are concerned. As we referred to above spread of Islam outside Arabian Peninsula gave rise to many new problems and these problems had to be satisfactorily tackled, especially after the death of the Prophet. The main guidance was available from the companions of the Prophet after his death.

These problems had to be solved within the frame-work of Islamic teachings but real problem arose when the Qur'an and *sunnah* were silent on the issue. Here before we proceed further it is necessary to point out that the Shari'ah can be sub-divided into matters pertaining to *'ibadat* and mu'amalat. According to us *'ibadat* (though there are differences among different sects in these matters too) should be re-opened for a discussion. 'Ibadat of course include prayers (*salat*), fasting (*saum*), haj, and zakat. These are fixed and immutable and cannot be affected by social changes. These are thus beyond scope of any discussion and are matter between human beings and *Allah*.

However, in what we call *mu'amalat*.i.e. matters between human beings and human beings, social changes can have an impact and the Shari'ah law can be reviewed in these matters and here it is useful to understand how social conditions have affected compilation of these laws. Among these laws too we can sub-divide these laws as those pertaining to crimes (jara'im) like theft, robbery, rape, adultery, murder etc. for which the Qur'an or Shari'ah law prescribes punishment and personal laws like marriage, divorce, maintenance, inheritance, custody of children etc.

In most of these matters pertaining to crime or personal matters the Shari'i-i.e. law giver has given clear guidance and detailed laws have been compiled. The basic theory, it is important to note, is that Shari'i-i.e. the law giver is *Allah* and all these laws are divine and hence immutable. But this is to be qualified as in common perception every bit of Shari'ah law is divine and hence immutable.

It is important to note that in Sunni Islam out of four sources two i.e. qiyas and ijma' are non-divine and part of human efforts to solve the new problems arising. There are four main schools in the Sunni Islam i.e. *Maliki*, *Hanbali*, *Shafi'I* and *Hanafi*. Of these *Maliki* and *Hanbali* are traditionalist while Hanafi is categorised as based on ra'i i.e. opinion. Imam Abu Hanifa lived in Kufa and Baghdad and had to face very complex situations. Baghdad was confluence of Arab and non-Arab civilisations and problems being thrown up were also far more complex and not easily found in first two sources i.e. the Qur'an and *sunnah*. Thus Abu Hanifa had to resort to his opinion.

Imam Malik and Imam Hanbal, on the other hand lived in *Hijaz* and were much closer to the Arab traditions and it was easier for them to find guidance within traditional sources especially within the frame-work of Prophetic *sunnah* itself. Thus they had no need for resorting to opinion or ra'i.

Thus according to Mahmasani "If we were to arrange the various schools in accordance with the degree of their recourse to opinion, the Hanafi school would be placed first and the Zahiri school last. The remaining Sunni schools would be placed in the following order: the *Shafi'I*, the *Maliki* and lastly the *Hanbali*. It is necessary to point out, however, that the above classification is but an approximation, for it is unlikely to find a particular situation in which we can justify a diametrically opposite listing. For example, we shall see in the Hanbali school's acceptance of one witness for purposes of evidence a less rigid stand than the Hanafi school." (Mehmasani Falsafat al-Tashri fi al-Islam, tr. By Farhat J. ZiadehI, Leiden E.J.Brill 1959, p.18)

After the death of the Prophet (PBUH) people use to consult prominent companions who had spread to different parts of conquered territories. These companions like Abdullah bin Abbas, Abdullah bin Umar, Abdullah bin Mas'ud and others. They were considered good at fiqh problems and their opinions had lot of weight. After them came another generation called *tabi'in* i.e. followers of the companions of the Prophet and then *taba' tabi'in* i.e. followers of the followers.

It was then that need was felt for systematising Shari'ah rules into different schools and the famous four schools came into existence i.e. Maliki, Hanbali, Shafi'i and Hanafi. These schools or madhaib spread in different parts of Islamic world. And it must be said that Imam Ja'far al-Sadiq played very important role as directly or indirectly all the four imams befitted from his *fiqhi* thinking.

During early period there were many re schools one of which was that of *Tabari* who was also a great commentator of the Qur'an. But these schools didn't survive and among Sunni Islam only these four schools survived. The Fiqh *Ja'fari* was followed by the *Ithna* 'Ashari Shi'ahs and the Isma'ilis also developed their own fiqh complied as Da'a'im al-Islam in two volumes.

Thus it will be seen that there are significant differences in these schools both in the category of *'ibadat* and mu'amalat. These differences were due to both ideological differences as well as those of socio-cultural conditions. The earlier period i.e. up to second century hijra was quite dynamic and productive. This was mainly the formative period for Islamic Shari'ah. This was also the period when Islam was spreading to other territories in Central Asia, South Asia and parts of Africa. These converted Muslims entered into Islam with their cultural and mental baggage.

It is important to note that any law has to have some social base. It cannot be created out of vacuum. Even divine pronouncements have a social base. That is why the Shari'ah law provides space for what is called *'aaḍat* i.e. customs and traditions which do not clash with divine objectives. Thus many Arab customs became part of the Shari'ah laws. Some customs were of course modified suitably so as to make them conform to the divine objectives and goal of justice.

Thus *nikah*, *mehr* and certain forms of divorce all existed before Islam appeared on the scene. These were suitably changed to make them acceptable with Islamic values. Earlier these were followed by the Arabs just because they happened to be the customs and traditions but the Islamic law giver made justice central to these practices.

In pre-Islamic period or period of *jahiliyyah nikah*, *mehr*, divorce, inheritance etc. were not based on the concept of justice whereas in Islam justice is quite central. These customs such as above were heavily loaded against women. Women had absolutely no say in matters of her nikah. Her father or grand father or brother could give her away to any man and take away the *mehr* himself. This was obviously very unjust to women.

The Qur'an, therefore, adopted nikah as a valid procedure for marriage but changed its nature and made it quite just for women. No nikah could be valid without woman's consent in presence of two witnesses and it was she who would fix the *mehr* amount and *mehr* would belong to her, not to her father as a wali or a marriage guardian. Thus it would be seen that Islamic marriage became very just to women.

It is important to note that in pre-Islamic Arabia women did not count for much in social and family life. Islam gave her a place of dignity and elevated her to status of equality with man (2:228). It was a great revolutionary step. As far as the Qur'an is concerned women as believers had in no way inferior status. This has been spelled out unambiguously in the verse 33:35. This verse leaves should not leave anyone in any doubt about equal status of women.

However, society was not ready for such revolutionary step. As pointed out above socio-cultural norms of a society overrides religious ideals and jurists succumb to social pressures in bringing women's status to given social levels. This is precisely what happened with the status of women in the Shari'ah formulations. For example, father hardly ever allowed her to make free choice for her marriage and exercised his authority to compel her to accept his choice and Shari'ah developed the doctrine of *kufw* i.e. of status. Also, even if she cried it was taken as her consent as she is thought to be crying for being separated from her parents. Such extrapolations eroded her free choice.

Thus we see cultural practices find their ways into juristic pronouncements. No Qur'anic pronouncement confines women to four walls of home. Women are seen as active social agents like all believers. She is charged with all Islamic duties including that of enforcing good and fighting evil (*amr bi'il ma'ruf wa nahiy 'an al-munkar*). This is most important duty a believer has to perform and a believing woman is also charged with this duty. No woman can perform this duty sitting at home. She as an active and sincere believer must perform this role with great sense of responsibility. It was for this reason that Imam Abu Hanifa was of the opinion that she can become a *qadi* as she is also charged with the function of enforcing good and fighting evil.

However, it was our cultural influence that she was required to sit at home and look after her husband and children. This is nowhere mentioned in the Qur'an as part of her duty. But it became part of juristic thinking and almost a sacred duty of a woman to look after her husband and children. One can easily see how cultural norms become part of so called 'Islamic behaviour' and part of Shari'ah law. In early Islamic society particularly during the Prophet's time and immediately thereafter she performed active public duties. Hazrat 'Umar had even appointed her as inspector of weights and measures.

There is another controversial issue of *hijab*. Our conservative jurists under the influence of their own socio-cultural practices interpreted the Qur'anic verses in such a manner as to restrict her freedom. In fact there is no mention of *hijab* in Qur'an for all Muslim women. It has been particularly mentioned for *azwaj-I-mutahharat* i.e. wives of the Prophet (33:53). The word *hijab* has not been used for other believing women at all.

The women in fact have been advised not to display their adornments publicly as during the period of ignorance the women would stand in public places dressed in their best and also wearing anklets and try to attract men's attention towards them and their adornments by striking their feet. This was not in keeping with the dignity of women. The Qur'an thus advised them not to display their adornment publicly except what should be displayed (24:31).

Basically it is an advice from *Allah* to protect her chastity and again exception has been made for what should remain open thereof and there is near unanimity among the fuqaha' that she can keep her face and hands up to elbows open. This opinion too, needless to say, culturally mediated. The then prevailing culture permitted face and hand to be kept open. The purpose is to protect her chastity, not to confine her within four walls. In fact in a given culture a dignified dress should suffice for her.

However, in the Shari'ah law great deal of restrictions were imposed on her and she was held responsible entirely for her chastity though the Qur'an lds holds men equally responsible for this. In the preceding verse i.e. in verse 24:30 it is said "Say to the believing men that they lower their gaze and restrain their sexual passions. This is purer for them." Thus primarily it is men's duty to restrain their sexual passion but in Shari'ah law all the restrictions have been imposed on women, not on men,

This is also because of cultural influences and not the Qur'anic pronouncements. The men has, equal, if not greater responsibility, to maintain sexual norms and chastity. Men also have to dress properly in this respect. To cover head or not to cover head is more cultural than Qur'anic requirement. We must learn to distinguish between cultural and what is Qur'anic. Our Shari'ah formulations in respect of female norms have been greatly influenced by our cultural norms.

Even practice of polygamy, as we have discussed separately in our article on the subject, was made more pervasive due to our cultural norms than due to the Qur'anic pronouncements. If we read the Qur'anic verses 4:3 and 4:129 together polygamy is hardly permissible. The Qur'an was the first divine Book to stipulate such harsh conditions for polygamy so as to make it almost impossible. Justice is so central to the Qur'anic pronouncements on polygamy that without fulfilling that condition it would never be permissible and there is great deal of debate whether material justice is enough for polygamy or equal love is also part of it. The verse 4:129 leaves us in no doubt that equal love is also part of it.

In this brief discussion on sources of influences on the jurists it becomes obvious that social dynamism ultimately leads to legal dynamism and the legal philosophy should not be based on outdated medieval concepts. Legal philosophy while based on Islamic and Qur'anic values should not become stagnant but should remain dynamic and *ijtihad* should be a continuous process. *Ijtihad*, of course, should reflect consensus of ummah and all leading minds of ummah should be involved. The Qur'anic values unfortunately were neglected in favour of our cultural norms and because of this slam began to stagnate. We must again make these Qur'anic values central to our jurisprudence and Islam would become the most progressive religion of the world.

Old Game of Personal Law Continues

It was huge gathering on the last day of Muslim Personal Law Board (MPLB) in Mumbai on 22nd April 2012. It was three day conference from 20-22 April and lot of efforts was made through announcements in the mosques, local processions and individual efforts to mobilize Muslims in support of MPLB and to prove its clout. As usual emotional speeches were made to warn government against interference in Muslim Personal law called *shari'at-e-mutahhira* (holy *shari'at*). It is interesting to note that this time the work 'holy' was added to what is usually called *shari'at* probably to emphasise its divine character,

Maulana Rabi' Hasan Nadwi, President of the MPLB made highly emotional speech and said that Muslims will lay down their lives if government interfered in the holy *shari'at* and that even if whole Islamic world makes changes in *shari'at* law Indian Muslims will not allow any change in it and will continue to embrace as it is without any change. Of course this emotional rhetoric greatly appeals to the masses who hardly know anything about the way *shari'at law* came into existence and for them the words of *Ulama* are like 'divine' words.

Today, shari'at law in India as it is practised unregulated is causing lot of suffering to Muslim women who are also part of Muslim *ummah*. Today the shari'at law is biased in favour of men as if women are not part of Muslim ummah. That is why almost all Muslim countries have made necessary changes to remove this male bias and make it more just towards women. The cent6raql principle of Islam is justice and it is divine will to do justice to all including women.

If the Maulana *sahib* considers shari'at law as evolved in 8th and 9th centuries more central than justice (the holy Qur'an says 'do justice, it is closest to piety') it is for him to decide. In fact shari'at is nothing but human approach to the divine injunctions and human approach is influenced by the circumstances and the context in which the law is developed. As human circum stances and context were involved there is nothing wrong in reformulating these laws and regulating them within the frame-work of Qur'an and *sunnah* (the holy Prophet's words and deeds) and that is precisely what Muslim countries have done. These Muslim countries also have great ulama and Islamic thinkers who care as much for Qur'an and *sunnah* as India's MPLB does.

Why talk of other Muslim countries the Fiqh Academy, New Delhi recently held an international conference in Mhow and decided in presence of ulama and eminent Islamic jurists that Muslim women are entitle to khula', if they insist on it, without permission from their husband. Also a few days ago a *fatwa* from Darul 'Ulum Deoband advised the person who asked whether he could take another wife while first wife he is married to, is alive as far as possible. Generally polygamy is considered in India as man's privilege. These changes are taking place and must take place in the changed circumstances.

A great '*Alim* (theologian and jurist) from Qatar Allama Yusuf Qardawi has published a book in which he says that *fatwas* can and must be changed with the change of place and circumstances and has give 10 different grounds in which these *fatwas* can be changed. He pleads that one should not simply consult books written in the past and issue *fatwa* but should deeply reflect on changes of place and circumstances before issuing any *fatwa*. Allama Qardawi is highly respected '*alim* of the Islamic world. Does Yusuf Qardawi not know that shari'at is divine? Shari'at is divine as much as it is based on Qur'an and *sunnah* but it is also human as much as it is also based on human inte3rpretations of these divine sources. And to that extent it must change, with the change in places and circumstances, as Allama Yusuf Qardawi insists.

Our Institute of Islamic Studies. Mumbai has also tried, in consultation with prominent ulama, Muslim lawyers, women activists belonging to *Bhartiya Muslim Mahila Andolan* and other women activists to codify the Muslim Personal Law strictly within the frame work of Qur'an and *sunnah* to make it more just for women who suffer mainly because of triple divorce and polygamy. A representative of Fiqh Academy also attended the consultation along with some teachers of Zakir Husain Institute of Islamic Studies, Jamia Millia Islamia and each and every provision of codified law was discussed thoroughly in the light of Qur'an and *sunnah* before it was incorporated.

I must point out here that the Shari'at law as it is today is much more empowering for women than any other religious law but it also must be accepted that it has male bias and to that extent it must be corrected in 21st century by excersising *ijtihad* (creative re-interpretation), a principle which the Prophet (PBUH) himself propounded while sending Ma'ad bin Jabal as governor of Yemen anticipating that he might encounter new situation there. Ijtihad makes enough space available for necessary changes in law with change of place and time. The Prophet (PNUH) give clear approval for such change to Ma'adh bin Jabal and patted his back when he said that I will exert my brain for appropriate changes in law to meet new situation. The principle of *ijtihad* is an appropriate tool to bring about necessary changes. However, the Indian '*Ulama*, for reasons best known to them, have failed to rise to the occasion and make shari'ah law more gender just.

The *Ulama*, if they care for the security of the community, could have raised the question of communal and targeted violence bill in such huge gathering which has been thrown into cold storage by the UPA Government. However, the MPLB failed to do that. This bill is much more relevant in the present circumstances than anything else.

3

Muslim Women : Yesterday, Today and Tomorrow

Purdah – Social and Qur'anic

I head read in a newspaper from Lucknow that a Muslim Lady, about 50 years Old, and chief of a Muslim women's welfare organisation, declared her candidature for forthcoming parliamentary election from Lucknow. She wanted to contest so that she could project women's problems in Parliament. It was also reported that as soon as he declared her candidature, she began to receive phone calls from some maulavis that women are supposed to be 'purdah nashin' (one who wears veil and sits at home) and are not supposed to contest election.

However, she did not pay heed and is determined to fight election. A few years ago a Muslim woman candidate, under 33 per cent reservation, filed her nomination for municipal election from Deoband which is seat of famous Islamic seminary Darul 'Uloom, a *fatwa* was issued that a woman cannot contest election as she is supposed to observe purdah. She too did not care and fought election but was told to wear veil while campaigning.

Now the question arises is observing purdah obligatory in the Qur'an? Or it is social custom which is strictly observed in certain families Qur'anic or merely a social custom. I also read many articles in Urdu press which glorifies purdah and maintains it is no obstruction in normal day today work but enhances women's capacity to work. Unfortunately we tend to accept anything in the name of Islam and begin to praise or justify it.

It is also to be noted that there are different types of purdah observed in different Islamic countries or communities. Women wear *abaya* in Saudi Arabia which covers woman's entire body from head to foot. In Iran women are required to wear *chador* which generally covers head. In Indian subcontinent some Muslim women wear an overall of black colour and cover entire face with two eyes popping out. Others wear overall but do not cover face.

Thus the kind of purdah we observe differs from country to country and from one community to another community. What is Qur'anic position? In Arabic veil is called *hijab* which means to cover, to hide or to stand in between. Qur'an does not use word *hijab* for women in general. Instead it exhorts women not to display their *zeenah* (adornments, charms) publicly (see 24:31).

This was to check rich and neo-rich women displaying their most charming dresses and embellishments publicly. However, they were permitted to do so before all those men and women who were their close relations whom they cannot marry. Qur'an nowhere requires women to cover their faces or much less, sit at home. In fact the verse 31 of chapter 24 begins by exhorting both men and women to lower their gaze when they meet each other. If women were required to wear veil, covering their face, where was the question of lowering their gaze.

Word *hijab* has been used in Qur'an only for wives of the Prophet (PBUH) that too this verse (33:53) exhorts men not to enter Prophet's (PBUH) house except when invited and not to linger on talking to his wives and if at all you have to ask for something, do so from behind *hijab*. This was because some men had the tendency to linger on after dining and indulge in talks with Prophet's (PBUH) wives.

What we make our women to observe in the name of *hijab* or call them *purdah nashin* is social custom from feudal ages when all sorts of restrictions were imposed on women and it was thought rightful position of women is at home, to serve their husbands and children. Even most orthodox Ulama agree that the verse 24:31 does not imply that women cover their faces. In fact there is consensus (*ijma'*) that women should cover their heads and other parts of body except face and two hands.

Since the crucial word in this verse is *zeenah*, not *hijab*, Ulama agree that women can not only keep their face open but also can apply collirium to their eyes and can wear rings in their fingers. Qur'an, has put no restrictions on women as we find in our societies. They are free to move out, exercise their rights and even earn their living. One does not find this culture of *purdahnashin* anywhere in the Qur'an. Women are supposed to be active agents like men. They even took part in battles during Prophet's (PBUH) time. In fact it was a woman who saved Prophet's life in battle of Uhud by taking sword's blow on herself. They also took part in public debates and Hazrat Umar even appointed a woman as market inspector.

Let us thus follow Qur'an and not social customs and tradition which reflect social values more than Qur'anic injunctions. Let us not paralyse half our population in the name of Islam. If women too become active agents our society will become much more dynamic and healthier.

Women and Inheritance

I am often asked both by Muslims and non-Muslims as to why a daughter gets half that of a son in her father's inheritance? Is it not injustice? All say men and women have equal rights in Islam and if she gets half that of her brother in inheritance, how can then we say man and woman are equal? Today, women feel that it is injustice with them and they should get equal portion in father's property.

Well, traditionally this objection has been with in various ways. First, there was no share in inheritance for daughters, Islam created it. Secondly, women were not earning and contributing to the family wealth and thirdly woman goes to her husband's place and gets share there in her husband's property. Also, her husband gives her *mehr* at the time of marriage and also is obliged to maintain her. So it is not injustice even if she gets half the share in father's property.

In the encyclopedic work *Ikhwanus Safa* there is a debate on this issue. The Master tells his disciples that Islam has given twice to weaker sections. The disciples ask are women among weaker sections? The Master says, yes. Then disciples ask then why women have been given half in father's property instead of twice? Master says you have not understood the Qur'anic logic of giving half to daughters. In fact Qur'an has given twice that of sons.

Bewildered disciples asked how half can be twice? The Master then explains: If a father leaves behind 1000 dirhams, his son will get 55 and daughter will get 250. When son will marry, will give away 250 dirham by way of *mehr* and will be left with only 250 dirham. And when daughter marries she will get 250 by way of *mehr* and will have 250+250 i.e. 500 dirham with her whereas her brother has been left with only 250 dirham after giving mehr. Thus who got twice? Son or daughter? Obviously the daughter.

But this explanation assumes certain situations which may not be true in practical life. First, daughter may not always get substantial *mehr*. At times she gets just nominal mehr. Secondly, these days both working class women and middle class women work and contribute to family wealth so she is entitled to a larger share. In those days women did not work (though in some cases they did).

Thirdly, in many cases women may not get married and not only that they would not get *mehr* but also after parent's death will have to maintain themselves. Then the above *Ikhwanus Safa* explanation will also not work. But various schools of law remain insistent that she cannot get more than half. But Qur'an certainly is not insensitive and leaves space for justice.

The Qur'anic verses on inheritance end with proviso that after paying of "a bequest you may have bequeathed or a debt" (4:11-12) The Qur'an has repeated this twice again also. Thus we see four times Qur'an lays stress on bequest or debt, if any on the part of deceased and then remaining will go to the inheritors as laid down by the Qur'an. Thus the person who leaves behind his property has every right to make will in favour of anyone he likes.

The jurists have argued that these verses were annulled after the verses on inheritance were revealed. Here we do not have space to argue that it is not so. Those who are interested in this discussion may see books of jurisprudence and differences between jurists on this question. One finds very interesting discussion on this in Maulana Umar Ahmad Usmani's book *Giqh al-Qur'an* 7th Volume (Karachi, 1986).

Thus the Qur'anic injunction for will stands and father has every right to will extra in favour of his daughter who cannot or does not want to marry so that she can carry on comfortably after her father's death. Or in some cases daughter may be physically challenged and may not get married and hence she cannot be looked after properly. Also, these days women from middle classes work and contribute to family wealth and hence they may be even given equal share in property.

Qur'an created share for her where it did not exist among Arabs in pre-Islamic period and Qur'an gave them equal rights in all spheres so it will be in keeping with the cannons of justice if more is given to them, especially by way of (*wasiyyah*) will by her father to safeguard her future.

Divorce in Qur'an and Shari'ah

Once, I read an article on divorce in Inquilab, an Urdu Daily from Mumbai written by a well known '*alim* and member of Muslim Personal Law Board Khalid Saifullah Rahmani. The title of the article was "*Ghusse ki haalat ka f'al m'utabar hota hai to talaq kyun m'utabar nahin hogi*" i.e. if generally anything done in anger is valid why not a divorce given in anger? If any lay person had written this article even then it would have been considered outrageous and when written by one who is considered an 'alim, it is much more so.

The Maulana argues that generally divorce is given in state of anger only and he argues if a husband is happy with his wife, will he gift her divorce? Divorce is given only when husband gets angry with his wife due to some act of hers. And then he says not only divorce but also several things are done in the state of anger. One would not like to comment on such arguments had it not involved fate of hundreds of Muslim women. One can only ring ones hands at such status of our prominent 'ulama. They take divorce so lightly and break up of family for them is only a matter of husband's anger with his wife.

Maulana Rahmani also maintains in this article that all *fuqaha'* have consensus that divorce takes place if given in state of anger because in this state as in this state man remains conscious of his act. Then the Maulana goes on to quote noted jurist Allama Abidayn Shami who has quoted Hafiz ibn Qayyim (very well known jurist and 'alim and disciple of Ibn Taymiyyah) and argues that anger has three stages: one that no change has occurred in his reasoning power due to anger and what he says, he should be understanding that and he should remain aware of its consequences and divorce pronounced in this state of anger will be valid. Second state is of extreme anger when man is unable to understand consequences of what he is doing and lacks in his will power. In this status divorce will not be valid since such a status of anger borders on madness and divorce given in a state of madness is not valid. Third state of anger is between the two states i.e. when man is partially aware of what he is saying and doing and partially not and divorce given in this state will also not be valid.

These are hardly acceptable arguments and at best these are rationalisation or justification of divorce given in a state of anger. One would like to ask Maulana and the jurists he quotes who will determine what state of anger one is when pronouncing divorce? Is there any objective criterion available to measure husband's anger at the time of pronouncing divorce? Has any instrument like thermometer available for measuring the degree of anger? And for these jurists even two witnesses for divorce are not necessary as prescribed by the Qur'an?

A divorce simply takes place if a husband pronounces divorce thrice in one breath and no witnesses are required. If witnesses are not required who will bear witness as to which state of anger divorce was pronounced? Will husband's own statement will be relied on? And if husband is determined to divorce his wife, how can his statement as to what state of anger he was in at the time of divorce can be acceptable. Who will decide what state of anger he was at the time of pronouncing divorce? Very strange rationalisation indeed for justifying divorce in a state of anger.

Also, these arguments are completely at variance with what Qur'an says about divorce. First, Qur'an requires, as pointed out earlier, two witnesses for divorce. Also, there is not even indirect evidence in Qur'an for giving divorce in a state of anger. See these two verses of Qur'an from Chapter 65 (Surah Al-*Talaq*) "O Prophet, when you divorce women, divorce them for their prescribed period, and calculate the period; and keep your duty to *Allah*, your Lord. Turn them not out of their houses - nor should they themselves go away - unless they commit an open indecency. And these are limits of *Allah*. And whoever goes beyond limits of *Allah*, he indeed wrongs his own soul.." (65:1)

And we find in second verse of this chapter (65), "So when they have reached their prescribed time, retain them with kindness or dismiss them with kindness, and call to witness two just ones from among you, and give upright; testimony for *Allah*. With that is admonished he who believes in *Allah* and the Latter Day. And whoever keeps his duty to *Allah*, He ordains a way out for him.

Let Maulana Rahmani note that Qur'an not only does not talk of divorcing in a state of anger but requires husband to divorce her (fariquhunna) with kindness. Also, she should not be thrown out of her marital home by the husband nor should she herself leave her marital home unless she comes with an indecent act (*bi fahishatin*). Also, Qur'an wherever talks of divorce, requires husbands to divorce them or separate them, with kindness. The verse 229 of Chapter 2 also talks of kindness while letting them go or separating them.

The verse is as under:" Divorce may be (pronounced) twice; then keep them in good fellowship (*bi m'arufin*) or let (them) go with kindness (*tasrihun bi ihsan*). Also so ensure full justice for women Qur'an requires arbitration before divorce (4:35). Thus there cannot be fairer method for divorce than the one prescribed by the Qur'an.

It is so unfortunate that Muslim jurists, under the influence of patriarchal ethos of their societies, they ignored all Qur'an injunctions and gave more credence to prevalent social practices and that too in the name of Islam. All this corpus of laws are referred to as Islamic laws of divine origin. In total contradiction to what Qur'an prescribes, the jurists, not only justified divorce given in a state of anger but also described states of anger.

What is more central to Islam - justice (*'adl*, *qist*) or state of proper consciousness in anger? Forget about anger, Qur'an does not approve of divorce in normal state of consciousness if proper method is not followed for giving divorce which ensures justice for wife. Any unjust act is *zulm* (oppression, wrong doing). According to the Qur'an women must be treated with fairness and justice and no act, committed in a state of anger (whatever the state of anger) can be a just act.

Maulana Rahmani's argument is very strange indeed that husband if not in a state of anger, will he divorce when he is happy with wife? Divorce, in fact should never be given in a state of anger at all. Whatever state of anger, intense, extreme or moderate, one does lose control of oneself and even if he is conscious of consequences of his act, is unable to think coolly and rationally. And Qur'an requires husband to remain kind even when divorcing her. Can anyone be kind while pronouncing divorce in a state of anger? Kindness and anger are two opposite states of mind.

Also, there are several instances in which husband pronounce divorce on getting angry on petty quarrels with wife. Can then such divorces be justified? Often husband repents after pronouncing divorce thrice in a state of anger but our jurists maintain his wife has been irrevocably divorced and he cannot take her back unless she marries some other man and he divorces her.

Husband and wife often quarrel and husband gets angry temporarily and is provoked to pronounce divorce. So such petty quarrels would become basis for divorce. This is not only legally wrong but also morally totally wrong. But such are our jurists and 'responsible' members of the MPLB. Can Muslim women then ever expect justice from them?

On one hand these jurists will argue that Islam greatly raised status of women and in pre-Islamic society women were treated as chattels and, on the other hand, to maintain manly authority, bring back those pre-Islamic practices in divine garb. Qur'an put the entire responsibility of treating women fairly and with kindness on men and our jurists gave total authority to men to throw their wives away whenever they liked.

There is not a single verse in Qur'an which exhorts women to treat their husbands with kindness while in their *nikah* (marital bond) whereas there are several verses requiring men to treat their wives with kindness. This was because women were in weaker position in that society and Islam has all the sympathy for weaker sections of society. In fact Islam laid greatest stress on giving justice to weaker sections of society including slaves, servants, orphan, widows and the poor.

As we have repeatedly pointed out Qur'an's sympathy is with *mustad'ifin* (those who have been weakened) (5:28) and our Ulama show all the sympathy with men who had all the power over women in that society (and still this continues even in most modern society) and juristically gives all the power over them. Let us remember justice is more central than opinion of any jurist howsoever eminent that jurist may be. Justice is Qur'an's central principle which cannot be sacrificed on the altar of any jurist's opinion.

If we have to project Islam as religion of justice and compassion for weaker sections of society we will have to revise our jurisprudence completely and prioritize justice over opinions of all past jurists of eminence. Eminence is not a principle it is only a social status whereas justice is a moral value central to Islam. Divorce is a very serious act and should be treated with utmost caution and responsibility. It breaks families and causes trauma to wife and children. According to a well-known *hadith,* Allah has permitted act of divorce with utmost reluctance. Thus neither Qur'an nor authentic *hadith* are problem for women, it is male authority which is.

Women's Rights in Saudi Arabia

The question of Muslim women's rights continue to occupy centre stage throughout the world. This question will assume greater importance in coming days also. The main reason for this is increasing education and awareness among Muslim women in all Muslim countries. Modernisation is also having its impact. Also more and more women are getting drawn into job market thus becoming independent of their fathers and husbands.

No country is exception to this process. Even in Saudi Arabia where women are under strict control, this process is on and they too are debating issue of their rights and are demanding more and more freedom.

Recently, there was a conference in Madina, in Saudi Arabia, the second holiest city of Islam wherein both men and women participated to debate women's rights. This was the third conference of its kind. Various issues including participation in work and representation in public institution came under discussion in this conference. But Saudi women were not satisfied even with such conference. They felt it is men who did most of the talking and women did not get opportunity and they were not properly represented.

The debate about women's rights and issues continue in the Saudi press as well as in the media in other Arab countries. Thus in an article in the leading English paper of Middle East, 'The Arab News' of 16 July 2004, Mody al-Khalaf writes, "For some time now, there has been a lot of talk, nationally and even internationally, about women's rights in Saudi Arabia. Westerners often make the assumption that we are totally deprived of all rights. Saudis, mostly conservatives terrified of any change, think that Saudi women enjoy all the rights they are entitled to by Islamic law. Both groups, of course, are wrong."

This article discusses the trauma of a Saudi divorced wife Mona and her struggle to lead dignified life and to give best possible education to her three children. It is really an inspiring story as to how Mona successfully struggled for her rights and for her children's rights. And that too in the Saudi Kingdom. This clearly shows that the Saudi women who are thought to be mere prisoners in the hands of men is not true. They too fight for their rights and dignified existence.

An interesting survey was conducted in the Saudi kingdom for the work participation of women. The study revealed that Saudi women can get involved in six major fields: worship, family duties, education, management in the private sector, and public sectors, and social services.

The study conducted by Khaled al-Baloush, deputy director of the Saudi Management Association in Jeddah and in which 2,550 Saudi women had been surveyed, said that 47 per cent (1,181 of the sample) opined that they are just as capable at work as men, sometimes even better, while 53 percent of the respondents said they could be more efficient for many reasons other than physical ability, which was the only aspect covered in the study.

In June 2004, a conference "Challenging Limitations: The Redefinition of Roles for Women in the GCC" was organised by the London Middle East Institute (LMEI) at SOAS with support from the Saudi Embassy in London, the Kuwait-British Friendship Society and Abdul Salam Al-Awadi, one of the keynote speakers Princess Lulwah al-Faisal, vice chairwoman and general supervisor of Dar Al-Hanan School and Effat College Board of Trustees, gave a comprehensive overview of the remarkable growth in female education in Saudi Arabia and said pioneers women, famous for their civic roles, are now standing to play an important consultative role.

She said that the basic challenges faced by Saudi women include the rapid rate of population growth of 3.1 percent a year, the mismatch between education and demands of job, and the social awareness of women's rights in Islam. Princess Lulwah noted that technology was an area that is particularly appropriate for Saudi women, and she expressed the hope that that will be adequately reflected in academic institutions.

The conference speakers included two dynamic Saudi women Dr Fawziah Bakr Al-Bakr, associate professor at the college of education, King Saudi University, and Dr Hayat Sindi who was the first female Saudi scientist to receive a doctorate in biotechnology from the University of Cambridge. Dr Sindi, in her paper, entitled "A Life Sentence" described the many obstacles she had to overcome in her passage from being a girl growing up in Makkah to obtain a masters degree from London University and a doctorate at Cambridge.

Dr Sindi who is a holder of many awards, stressed the importance of self-belief. Dr Al Bakr took the audience in a wide-raging tour of girls education and the role of women in the labour force in a paper full of information and statistics. She ended by presenting an eight-point plan to encourage women's role in business and economy and made number of recommendations.

All these developments among Saudi women are indicative of winds of change blowing in the Muslim world. It is no longer possible to deprive Muslim women of their Islamic and human rights. Even the Saudi society can no longer deal with women it used to deal in earlier times. Though the struggle ahead is by no means easy and smooth, yet signs of change are unmistakable. The patriarchal societies denied women their Qur'anic rights so far. The Qur'an unmistakably declared gender equality fourteen hundred years ago but Muslim men denied it to them even elementary rights until today.

There is a serious misconception about finality of the Shariah law in the Islamic world. The evolution of the Shari'ah law has been a process and it kept on evolving for centuries after the death of the Holy Prophet. The early doctors of law who founded various schools of Shari'ah like Imam Hanbal, Imam Malik, Imam Abu Hanifa and Imam Shafi'i, never thought that their opinions are final and binding on coming generations. Imam Malik did not allow the Abbasid Caliph to prescribe his magnum opus *Muwatta* to be prescribed for all Muslims. He maintained that he would not like it to be imposed on all Muslims. They can have their own opinion.

But later generations started following these doctors of law blindly and mechanically as if it was divine. Now ordinary Muslims following these doctors and the *ulama* belonging to these schools do consider opinions expressed by these doctors of law as final and consider it a sin to challenge the finality of their opinion. But all great Islamic thinkers have maintained that these opinions cannot be treated as final.

No one can doubt the scholarship and greatness of their learning. Still they were humans and product of their own time. The Qur'an, a divinely revealed text gives principles, values and guidelines. One has to develop detailed rules in the light of these principles, values and guidelines. Fundamental values are divine but instrumental values to implement them in given conditions, are not.

No law developed by learned men of one generation can be binding on people of subsequent generations. The Qur'anic verses were interpreted differently by different theologians of the same generation, then how can subsequent generations forfeit their rights to interpret Qur'anic verses according to their needs and requirements. May be throughout medieval ages no need was felt to reinterpret and develop Shari'ah law further after the learned men codified it as medieval society remained almost static for several centuries.

But since ninteenth century revolutionary changes in social and economic structure began to take place and new generations of Muslims began to feel great need for fresh thinking on issues of Shari'ah law. A great struggle began in almost all Muslim countries. The Napoleon's invasion on Egypt brought it under French influence and Egyptian society became the hub for intellectual debates on women's rights. Many books were written one of which 'Al-Mara't al-Muslimah' (The Muslim Woman) was most stimulating.

In India too, after the British rule was consolidated in nineteenth century, many Muslims scholars like Sir Syed Maulavi Mumtaz Ali Khan, Justice Amir Ali, Maulavi Chiragh Ali and others began to rethink on Shari'ah laws pertaining to women's rights. Sir Syed himself made insightful comments in his commentary of the Qur'an pertaining to verses on women and their rights.

Maulavi Mum'taz Ali Khan, a close colleague of Sir Syed Ahmed Khan wrote a book *Huququn Niswan* (Rights of Women) which boldly advocated equal rights for men and women at a time when women were not even allowed to come out of their houses and they were confined to *zanankhana* i.e. women's compartment. Even Sir Syed was disturbed by such a bold venture and advised the Maulavi not to publish it as it would cause great stir among Muslims and opposition to his mission of spreading modern education would assume greater fury. However, Mumtaz Ali Khan did not accept Sir Syed's advice and published the book.

Maulavi Chiragh Ali also advocated changes in the Muslim law so that women could get their Islamic rights which have been denied them for centuries. Thus modernity and modern changes directly impinged on the Muslim thinking and some scholars began to advocate changes in the traditional Shari'ah law. But so far only enlightened men were advocating rights of Muslim women. Women were still deprived of modern education and confined to their homes and *zanankhana* in their homes.

It was only in later part of twentieth century that Muslim women began to go to schools and colleges. Also, the educational institutions were dominated by men who often thought that woman's right place was in their homes and this was repeatedly injected into their minds. Naturally, the women also thought along these lines. But it was post-independence situation which began to bring fundamental change in the attitudes of Muslim women.

The Indian Constitution gave all citizens the right to vote including women and politicians had to cultivate women voters as well. Thus the democratic discourse in the country created greater awareness among all women, including Muslim women. Also, from seventies onwards more and more NGOs advocating women's rights came into existence and suffering Muslim women also formed their own NGOs. The NGO culture certainly helped women's cause.

In Muslim countries too, more and more women are getting educated and a new awareness is fast developing. Today, in Saudi Arabia there are more girl students than boy students, including at the university level. The oil revolution forced Arab governments to open more and more educational institutions. That is why the women in conservative kingdom like Saudi Arabia, are no longer content with their old situation and are demanding equality with men.

In Kuwait, women were not allowed to take part in the political process and could not vote. But many university-educated women were demanding right to vote during eighties. However, it was denied to them. When Kuwait was invaded by Iraq in 1990 and resistance movement began, the women participated in the resistance movement on condition that they would be enfranchised. The ruling dynasty of Kuwait promised that it would come through.

However, after Kuwait was liberated no such law was passed for a long time and only after great deal of agitation by educated Kuwaiti women, the ruling Sheikh issued an ordinance giving women right to vote but it was voted out in the parliament dominated by conservative men. However, the Kuwaiti women did not give up and now at last a bill is being introduced to empower Kuwaiti women to vote. One hopes, the bill will be passed. This again shows that educated women in Muslim countries are agitating for their rights and nothing will be gained without struggle.

Needless to say, there is long way to go. There are serious inequalities between the two sexes in Muslim societies. Though Malaysia is a highly developed Muslim country yet highly conservative views prevail as far as women's rights are concerned. The Sisters in Islam is an NGO in Malaysia which is struggling for women's rights. It is pressing Malaysian government for progressive legislation. They are aspiring, and rightly so, for equal rights. However, they have to face tough opposition from highly conservative *'ulama*. In certain states like Kelantaon the conservative Muslim party is in power and it has introduced *Hudud* laws (Islamic laws for adultery etc.) which are highly loaded against women.

In Indonesia too, after democratisation of political regime and end of Suharto dictatorship, a movement for rights of women has gathered momentum. In Indonesia the rate of literacy among women is quite high. There are several institutions catering to women's education, including Islamic universities and other Islamic institutions. These educated women are demanding better status. The books on rights of women are in great demand. Many women are working for Ph.D. on the rights of women.

In Pakistan and Bangladesh, women have succeeded in forcing authorities to bring about certain necessary changes like abolition of triple divorce and restricting polygamy. The then President Ayub Khan had promulgated an ordinance in 1961 known as Muslim Family Law Ordinance, which ushered in these measures. Bangladesh retained them after cessation from Pakistan in 1971 and despite Zia-ul-Haq's attempts to abolish the ordinance during 1980s when Islamisation of Pakistani state began, did not succeed. The women of Pakistan resisted abolition of the ordinance. It is thus in force even today.

However, the *Hudood* ordinance promulgated by Zia-ul-Haq is causing severe problems for Muslim women in Pakistan. There is some pressure on the Musharraf Government though there is fierce opposition to it from the *'ulama.*

In India, Muslim women are suffering because of lack of any reform in the Islamic law. Here the main obstacle is the minority status of Muslim community. Any move for change is strongly resisted both by the *'ulama* as well the political leadership saying it amounts to interfering in religious freedom of minorities. The article 25 of the Constitution, is quoted. This article allows all to profess, practise and propagate ones religion. The personal Law, it is maintained, is part of religion and cannot be interfered with. It is true that Shari'ah law is part of religion and government cannot interfere with it and this has stalled all reforms.

Even the Supreme Court judgement of 1985 in the famous Shah Bano case had to be reversed by the then Rajiv Gandhi Government under pressure from Muslims. It caused great setback for Muslim women's movement in India. The reversal of the Supreme Court judgement caused great resentment among non-Muslims and gave impetus to majority communalism. The secularists otherwise quite sympathetic to the Muslim cause, were also greatly upset.

The Shah Bano movement is an indicator of momentous difficulties in bringing about any change in favour of Muslim women. However, there is increasing pressure on the MPLB to effect certain essential changes like abolition of triple divorce. There are some liberal *'ulama* but they are greatly constrained by the conservative *'ulama* who are in majority.

The MPLB consists of Muslims of different sects, Sunnis, Shi'as, Bohras, Deobandis, Ahl-e-Hadis and so on. Different sects take different positions and it becomes more complicated to bring about any change e.g., , recently the MPLB announced that it was going to consider abolition of triple talaq in its Kanpur session in July 2004. The Barelvi *'ulama* from Mumbai belonging to Raza Academy immediately threatened to launch an agitation if the MPLB touched the issue of triple talaq. The MPLB had to retrace its step and had to announce that it had no intention to abolish triple talaq. The whole issue was thus again shelved.

There are two main obstacles for any change in the Muslim Personal Law in respect of women: (1) conservatism of some *ulama* and (2) political competition for leadership of Muslims. If one set of *ulama* give in to progressive change, their leadership is immediately threatened by conservative *ulama*. Thus under pressure from conservatives the comparatively liberal ones retract. This happened on 13 September 2004. The vice president of the MPLB Maulana Kalbe Sadiq announced in a press conference that the Board will promote family planning among Muslims in view of little higher rate of growth of Muslim population. He gave example of Iran where zero rate of growth has been achieved. If the Iranian Muslims can achieve zero rate of growth under the rule of '*ulama* why can't Indian Muslims slow down their growth under a secular set up.

However, the president of the MPLB Maulana Hasan Rabe' Nadwi immediately announced that this is not the stand of MPLB but only personal views of Maulana Kalbe Sadiq and he is entitled to his views. Thus any progressive reform suggested by one section of '*ulama* is resisted by another section and reforms are thus stalled. It is only increasing pressure from Muslim women which will create climate for change.

The conception among common Muslims that the Shari'ah law is divine and immutable has to change for any reform. Thus progressive Muslim intellectuals committed to women's rights have to educate the Muslim masses that the every succeeding generation of Muslims, has right to reinterpret Shari'ah law according to their needs. The Shari'ah law is not the body of static laws, but a corpus of dynamic laws creatively responding to changing times.

What was evolved by the Islamic jurists in earlier centuries was in response to the socio-political needs of the time. The Qur'an provided the ideal of equal rights of men and women but the society then could not cherish this ideal and the then doctors of law had to respond to their socio-political needs by watering down the Qur'anic ideal of equality of gender by invoking certain *ahadith* of the Holy Prophet or by resorting to the institutions *ijma*' and *qiyas* (consensus and analogical reasoning). Both *ijma*' and *qiyas* are human institutions and had to be developed to meet the needs of the time. These same institutions can be used for responding to the present needs.

This is the only way of keeping the Islamic law relevant and upholding the Qur'anic ideals of justice and gender equality. It is from this point of view that we have stated positions and views of various authorities in this book like Mohammad 'Abduh of Egypt, Sir Syed and Maulavi Mumtaz Ali Khan of India, Maulana Umar Ahmed Usmani of Pakistan and others to support the case for reform and change. My appeal to Muslims in general, and Muslim '*ulama* in particular, is to reflect dispassionately and try to implement the Qur'anic ideals and this is right time to do so.

Sharia, Fatwas and Women's Rights

Every now and then media reports *fatwas* issued by muftis in India, Saudi Arabia and other countries. One mufti in Saudi Arabia even suggested that if a Muslim woman has to keep a man for household work and interact with him though he is not *mehram* (from prohibited degree for marriage), she should suckle him from her breast to make him *mehram*. This *fatwa* was based on a *hadith* narrated by hazrat A'isha.

Darul Uloom Deoband, though does commendable work for peace and communal harmony, issues *fatwas* when it comes to women which reduce women as mere secondary to men or something subservient to them. Recently someone from Dubai jocularly typed on his computer talaq thrice he was told your wife has now been divorced and he cannot marry her until she marries someone else who divorces her and then only she can revert to her former husband who jocularly typed the dreaded word.

In Iran, a middle aged woman called Sakineh was punished to death by stoning as she was alleged to have committed adultery, though Qur'an no where mentions such a punishment and prescribes only 100 lashes for *zina* and in Arabic there is only one word be it rape, fornication or adultery. More recently, Darul Uloom Deoband issued a *fatwa* saying that her husband said word *talaq* thrice on mobile and even is she did not hear it triple divorce has taken place and she must marry someone else as a necessary condition.

These *fatwas* are issued just because some jurist or the other had so opined hundreds of years ago keeping in view the conditions then prevailing in society. On most of these issues there is no *ijma*' (consensus) and many of them are even based on controversial *hadith*. The opinion given by jurists hundreds of years ago were based not only on Qur'an o *hadith* but also on social structure and social ethos then prevailing.

Most of the Ulama or jurists, when asked for *fatwa* consult only those medieval sources and never bother to apply there own reasoning power. *Taqlid* (mechanical following) is considered as safest by all these jurists. However, even in those days many jurists had strongly condemned *taqlid.* Ibn Taymiyyah and Ibn Hazm both were great jurists and both have condemned thoughtless imitation.

Ibn Hazm was from Spain and used to give great importance to freedom of thought and independence of thinking in his juristic thinking. In this he was influenced by his teacher Abul Khayar. He was also of the opinion that one can be called '*Alim* as long as one engages in seeking knowledge. But one who thinks he knows enough is, in fact, jahil (ignorant). And seeking knowledge is seeking truth which is possible only through intellectual process. Our *Ulama* and jurists, as we know, have long since stopped thinking.

Qur'an is very fundamental source for Islamic jurisprudence but Ibn Hazm, very rightly puts Qur'anic verses in three categories: (1) those verses which need no other source to understand; (2) those verses which can be understood in the light of other verses of the Qur'an and (3) those verses which can be understood in the light of authentic *hadith* and authentic is one which has been narrated by most reliable and many narrators. Even if this method is followed Islamic jurisprudence, especially in respect of family laws, can be revolutionised.

Most of the jurists unfortunately rely, in matters of family laws, more on weak *hadith* than on Qur'an. Ibn Hazm, who apparently followed Zahiri School (but not by way of taqlid) strongly criticizes who do not think by themselves and simply resort to taqlid. And Ibn Hazm said all this in 14th century Spain. Our jurist live in the 21st century and yet resort to mechanical following of their respective schools.

In fact another Spanish jurist Al-Shatibi was also very creative in his thinking about shari'ah laws. He said that one must first understand the *maqasid* and *masalih* i.e. basic objectives and welfare of people for whom shari'ah laws are being framed. Our *muftis* and jurists do not at all keep these objectives and welfare of people in mind and simply consult standard books of their respective schools (of jurisprudence) and issue *fatwas*.

It is because of these *fatwas* that Islam is negatively projected in media and them we complain against media for its Islam bashing. A truly religious person should look at his/her own fault first before blaming others. As someone said we try to remove dust from mirror instead of from our own face. The mirror is going to show dust on our face in any case as long as it is on our face.

Today, it is highly necessary to dust off our own face and restore dignity of Islamic shari'ah by re-thinking several issues pertaining to personal laws restoring dignity and rights of women as given by Qur'an and taken away due to personal opinions of jurists in their own circumstances. Imitation should be thrown out of window and all eminent jurists from entire Islamic world should come together and compile corpus of laws giving equal rights to women in matters of marriage, divorce, inheritance, etc.

There is no doubt if we keep *maqasid al-shari'ah* (objectives) and *masalih al-shari'ah* (welfare of people) and resort to independent thinking and freedom of thought the Islamic laws would become not only highly just but a model to be followed by all. Ibn Hazm, for example, was of the opinion that if a man is economically weak and woman who wishes to be divorced well off, it is for divorced wife to maintain her former husband, something which modern law stipulates. We must go directly to Qur'an and accept only very authentic *hadith* and Muslim women will be more equal than in other laws.

Wearing Burqa will Now be a Crime?

Now a draft bill is under consideration of French Parliament imposing a fine of Euro 700 on any woman wearing *burqa* covering her whole body in any public place and her husband twice as much if he forces hear to wear *burqa*. This is for the first time that women would be penalised for wearing *burqa*. Earlier France had banned Muslim girls wearing *hijab* in schools. It argued that these religious symbols interfere with its commitment to secularism and its secular culture.

In fact nothing happens without political ideology being behind it. This measure is being championed by rightwing politicians who are exploiting anti-Islam feelings in France among a section of people under the cover of secularism. However the socialists are opposed to any ban on *burqa* though they are also not in favour of women wearing *burqa*. They feel women should be discouraged rather than banning *burqa*.

The socialist spokesman Benoit Hamon announced that wearing *burqa* is not desirable but is not favourable to legal ban which would amount to an inconsistent ad hoc ban. Mr. Hamon said on the RTL Raido "We are totally opposed to the *burqa*. The *burqa* is a prison for women and has no place in the French Republic", he said. "But an adhoc law would not have the anticipated effect".

The stand taken by socialists appears to be quite logical. One cannot stop women from wearing *burqa* through a legal ban. It is quite undemocratic to punish one for wearing certain type of dress. It is anti-democratic and anti-secular for a multi-cultural society. Let it be very clear that to cover entire body including the face is not necessarily an Islamic way.

The *ulama* hold different views on the subject. Majority of them hold that covering face and hands is not prescribed by Qur'an or *Sunnah*. Only very few theologians and jurists want women to be fully covered. To compel women to so cover their bodies and face is indeed against women's rights and dignity. And a woman should be a free agent to decide for herself what to wear within decent limits and cultural ethos.

However, this freedom also includes right of women to cover their face, if thy so desire and if they think it is requirement of their religion. When I was lecturing in Bukhara University among a class of women students all of whom were wearing skirts and their heads were uncovered, two women came fully covered including their faces. All other women demanded that these two *burqa* clad women should be thrown out.

I said imagine *burqa* clad women were in majority and two women had come wearing skirt and uncovered head and majority of *burqa* clad women had demanded those two women being thrown out, what would you feel. I, therefore, argued that let us not get violent because someone dresses unlike us. We should dialogue with them and persuade them, if we can, not to wear such dress fully covering themselves.

There could be a number of reasons why one prefers to wear certain kind of dress. May be there is coercion by parents or husband which is undesirable. Or may be one thinks it is a religious requirement and one tries to assert ones right. Or may be one is trying to fight cultural alienation. Certain dresses also become identity markers. Many Muslims who migrate from Asia and Africa experience cultural shock when they see French or other European women wearing scanty dresses, even wearing bikinis. Thus they feel all the more compelled to wear their traditional dress.

Also, in France and several other European countries migrants are marginalised and have feeling of alienation which pushes them into practising their own cultural norms. And then it is also to be remembered all Muslim women in France do not wear such dress covering themselves fully. In fact many Muslim women have integrated themselves into French society by taking to western dress.

Thus legal ban will only build up resistance among traditional Muslim women and they would try to defy the law resulting in social tensions. It would be far better to resort to persuasive ways to discourage traditional Muslim women not to wear all covering *burqa*. And persuasion alone will not work unless backed by other measures economic as well as social to fight alienation of religious and cultural minorities.

Thus one needs multi-pronged measures to contain this problem. Muslim *ulama* and intellectuals living in France also have to adopt creative ways to reinterpret Islamic traditional sources to suit new conditions. It is quite necessary to revisit traditional sources rooted in medieval feudal culture.

Religious Diversity and Tolerance in Islam

Diversity and tolerance are considered very basis of modernity as one of the modernity's fundamental principles is individual and community rights and also, as modernity implies democratic rule, tolerance and right to pursue any ideology or religion assumes great importance. The western countries consider themselves as role models for democracy and freedom. Bush, after 9/11 attack often used to say why [read Muslims] are jealous of our democracy and freedom?

Most of us believe in this myth that west stands for freedom of conscience, democracy and liberty. In theory it is quite correct. But is it is in practice? First of all let us one question did they ever consider non-whites, non-Europeans as equal and entitled to equality and liberty? The history tells us, no. The white superiority was always underlying assumption and the blacks (now known as African-American) were always discriminated against. Even Jews, until Second World War, did not enjoy equal rights. They were always discriminated against and forced to live in ghettoes, apart from what Nazis did with them.

Also, until Second World War when the western world was mono-religious and mono-cultural, its tolerance for non-western religions and cultures was never tested. It is only when economic migrations began from the erstwhile colonial countries that the west began to experience what they now call multi-culturalism and western society became multi-religious and multi-cultural.

It was then that strains appeared and we saw number of cases of prejudice and discrimination against non-white, non-western people migrating to the west. The most recent case is of Switzerland voting to ban minarets for Muslim mosques. In the poll held 57 per cent Swiss people voted against allowing minarets to Muslim mosques. In Switzerland close to four million people are Muslims.

It is heartening that the New York Times editorially condemned this proposed ban. It is worthwhile to quote excerpts from the editorial which was published on 30 November 2009, immediately after the referendum in Switzerland: "Disgraceful. That is the only way to describe the success of a right-wing initiative to ban the constitution of minarets in Switzerland, where 57 percent of voters cast ballots for a bigoted and mean-spirited measures."

Further the editorial says, "But the vote also carries a strong and urgent message for all Europe, and for all western nations where Islamic minorities have been growing in numbers; and visibility, and where fear and resentment of Muslim immigrants and their religion have become increasingly strident and widespread. The warning signs have been there: the irrational fierceness of official French resistance to the *shawls* and *burquas* worn by some Muslim women; the growing opposition in many European quarters to Turkish membership in the European Union."

The editorial is, indeed the voice of sanity in the growing intolerance in the western world towards Muslims in particular and, non-western cultures and religions, in general. We would again like to reiterate here that in principle the west does stand for equality, freedom of conscience and human rights which most of the Muslim countries have yet to learn. But, as we will show herein below that Islam also stands for tolerance and respect for other culture and faiths and believes diversity is creation of *Allah* but the test really comes in practice.

It is also true that terrorist attacks in some countries, and especially after the 9/11 has intensified hatred against Islam and Muslims but then in Switzerland, the Muslims have been peaceful and there have been no instances of such attacks and it appears quite irrational that people of Switzerland should display such intolerance towards their peaceful minority. However, the signs were in the air.

I had delivered a lecture on Islam and non-violence way back in 2004 in Zurich which was held in collaboration with the local church. When question of answer session began, the journalists present there said how Islam can ever be non-violent and peaceful. I said, I have based my speech on the Qur'anic text and anyone can verify what I have said but the journalists did not seem to be convinced. They kept on arguing until the church official intervened. What these journalists must have been writing about Islam is obvious. In modern society media plays a very important role.

This is further borne out by the TV debate between noted Swiss Muslim intellectual and my friend Tariq Ramadan and Oskar Freysinger on ban on minaret. It became evident from the debate that the real issue was not minaret, but Islam itself. Dr Patrick Haenni, a researcher at Religiouscope, who believes that religion, not politics, was the core of the initiator's discourse through a perspective full of misconceptions and stereotypes.

The ban on *burqa* in France by the government is another instance of this intolerance for non-western religions and cultures. This writer is no advocate of *burqa*s covering entire body and face from head to toe but the question is not one should wear *burqa* or not, more fundamental question is of individual right and choice? Whatever reason for wearing *burqa*, personal conviction, social or peer pressures or identity issue, does one have right to wear or not? Should one ban it outright?

Here, I would like to narrate an interesting experience. I was lecturing on secularism in the University of Bukhara and in the audience were mostly young women dressed in skirts as western women do. During the lecture two *burqa* clad women (wearing *burqa* from head to toe) entered and sat down. After my lecture was over some of those women stood up and agitatedly said sir, why should we not throw out these two women (wearing *burqa*)? I was shocked at the aggressive tone of these agitated women.

I enquired why do you want to throw them out? These women (all of them Muslim) said why are they wearing *burqa* and why do they cover themselves? I said I ask you one simple question suppose all these women were clad in *Burqa* and two of you had come wearing skirts and with modern haircut and if they had asked by not throw these two skirt-wearing women out, what would have been your response?

I said throwing out or banning a practice is not the solution but to dialogue with each other and to understand each other. They then appreciated my viewpoint and sat down quietly and we continued our discussion. Thus to accept the other, as the other is (not with prescriptions) is the essence of democracy. Prescription for the other violates the very spirit of others' rights and dignity which is the basis of modernity. Now it has been universally accepted that it is not only individual rights which are important but also group rights of minorities as well are equally important.

The west, whatever its principles and values, is yet to come to terms with non-western others. Also, it should not depend on the doctrine of reciprocation but group rights should be absolute. I remember in the U.K. there was debate in 1980s how Muslims treat Christian minorities in Muslim majority countries. Do they give them equal rights and freedom of religion? If not, why do they expect such rights in western countries?

This reciprocative approach contradicts the very spirit of democratic values and principles. These values and principles are absolute and no conditionalities could be prescribed. Of course there are complex reasons for the growing intolerance towards Muslim minorities in the western world. As everywhere the rightist forces thrive on hatred of the other and the ban on the minaret in Switzerland is also the result of rise of rightist politics. The Muslims in India too have experienced it when the BJP tried to come to power through hate politics of *Ramjanambhoomi.*

In France too, ban on *hijab* came under the regime of Sarkozy who is known rightist. Secondly, the rising number of immigrants also creates fear in the minds of original inhabitants of the country and, in order to press the issue, these numbers are highly exaggerated. Muslims, both by way of migration and birth, are the fastest growing minority in the Europe. Thirdly, most of the Muslim migrants are non-whites, many of them blacks from African countries and here both religious as well as racial prejudice combine and intensify hatred and intolerance.

In France, for example, most of the Muslim migrants are from former French colonies and hence happen to be black. Discrimination against them and their marginalisation totally alienates them and this alienation finds expression through complex ways through aggressive behaviour or overemphasis on their identities which in turn further intensifies their alienation.

And, if this is followed by an economic crisis as Europe is undergoing these days, majority fear against the migrant becomes even more aggressive born out of fear and the rising tide of rightist forces in such circumstances further aggravates it. Also, the US policies in the Middle East has resulted in intensifying extremism in a section of youth in the Muslim countries resulting in terrorist attacks such as the 9/11 which excites even more hatred against Muslims in the west.

What is the way out then? Where to stop this vicious circle of action and reaction? It is for sure that we cannot control all the factors. But it is also equally certain that we need a wise political leadership who is not after power but welfare of people. Democracy ideally speaking is for people's participation and for their well being. However, like other political systems, democracy too, has become means of grabbing power by certain groups and classes. Also, it tends to be majoritarian i.e. heavily tilted in favour of racial, religious or linguistic majority. There has been hardly any exception to it in the world.

Certain Muslim countries who swear by Qur'an as their constitution also flagrantly violate Qur'anic provisions. Qur'an gives certain ideals and values for governance, an idea of the desirable society. It says diversity is *Allah*'s creation and must be respected and celebrated. And this diversity includes linguistic, racial and religious and human beings, whatever religion, race or linguistic group they belong to, must be accorded equal dignity and which means all of them should enjoy equal rights.

However, you will not find any Muslim country swearing by Qur'an as the book of *Allah* implementing these ideals. You find discrimination on the basis of religion, even sects, language and ethnicity. You very much find discrimination for example in Saudi Arabia, against non-Arabs, against non-*Wahabi* Muslims and against other ethnic and racial groups. One finds discrimination in Iran against Sunni Muslims, against Arabs, against Bahais and against non-Persians.

In Pakistan, one finds discrimination against certain linguistic groups like Baluchis and Sindhis. It is dominated by the Punjabi majority. Not only that there is sectarian violence between Shi'ahs and Sunnis besides Christians and Hindus. It is the Punjabi majority which rules the roast. One has yet to see any Muslim country which does not violate injunctions of the Qur'an while swearing in by it as one has yet to see any western democracy not violating injunctions of their own constitutions enshrining ideals and values of modern democracy.

As long as the goal remains power, this is bound to happen. Another bane of the situation is current rise in the rightist forces which arouse emotions of people on the basis of religion, race and language. Again no country is an exception to it. Education system itself, which prepares children and students for future material of the society, is controlled by, in most, if not all cases, by rightist elements.

The Netherlands is also undergoing severe problem of anti-Muslim tirade. One politician made a film called *Fitna* and refused to take it back. Also, a Muslim fanatic murdered a film maker from the Netherlands who caste slur on Islam and this further led to anti-Islamic surge there. I met a professor of Islamic Studies from the Netherlands in Germany who spoke on Islam. The seminar was on progressive Islam.

I was stunned by his anti-Islamic outpouring. It was nothing short of hate-Islam speech. When we protested the organisers maintained that all views are allowed to be expressed from this forum. May be it was so. But what was worrying factor was that the person was teaching Islam in the Netherlands. If such Islam is taught in universities of a country what mindset would be generated? One shudders to think.

Media is no exception. While it must be made clear there are honourable exceptions and some newspapers and TV channels which are quite objective or tend to be so but then such papers and channels are, more often than not, popular. They are read or watched by serious viewers. Popular media tend to be prejudiced. Also, media is often owned by certain interests and it is not committed to the cause of objective reporting.

And media plays most crucial role in democracy. I would say if media plays responsible role rising above all interests modern democracies would be far more conflict-free than they are today. And in answering the question raised above media provides one of the crucial factors. Despite all the laws made by the state, media behaves the way it wants to as various state organs fail to implement the laws.

It is true we cannot have ideal democracy as the German philosopher rightly points out ideal is not real and real is not ideal, still one has to try to come as close to ideal as possible. Even such efforts are lacking in modern democracies. Invariably, it is powerful interests which determine the shape and direction of things and there is always tension between vested interests and the ideals and interests seem to win.

Of course if the conflict remains manageable it is one thing but disaster takes place when it goes beyond manageable proportions. The attack on the 9/11 and subsequent attack on Afghanistan and Iraq took this conflict between Islam and the west beyond all imaginable proportions as here too very powerful interests were involved. However, it would be wrong to consider it a self fulfillment of Huntigntonian prediction of 'clash of civilisation'. It was, instead, clash of political interests on both sides.

It is interesting to note that Huntington's book received such media attention in the west precisely because certain interests in the west wanted such book written to promote conflict. Of course things may not have gone as planned but to an extent those interests were served but at a great social cost. It greatly sharpened prejudices in the west against Islam. And this has been going on for quite some time now.

Since Muslims began to immigrate to the western countries in the post-colonial period the anti-Islam prejudices began to acquire sharper edge. The Rushdie's book 'The Satanic Verses' in the eighties and the support it received in the west was also part of this process. The enthusiastic support was not for the sake of freedom of opinion. There was a purpose behind it. The Islamic revolution had occurred in Iran which was anti-west in its thrust and made Iranian oil beyond western powers.

Thus the west adopted anti-Iran posture and when Khomeini, for his own political compulsions, issued *fatwa* against Salman Rushdie, the swords were drawn on both sides and west lent unqualified support to Rushdie in the name of freedom and Muslims stood by Khomeini's *fatwa*. It was neither freedom nor Islam but who will dominate Iran and its oil, west or people and rulers of Iran.

All these developments through 1980sculminated in 9/11 attacks and everything was complete for anti-Islamic prejudices in western countries and media. As far as Arab oil is concerned the clashes are likely to continue and will go through different phases. It reached its culmination during the Bush's unqualified support to rightist policies and outright adventure in the West Asia.

However, since it crossed critical limits in conflict management Obama took over the reigns of administration. But it would indeed be too much to expect that Obama would resolve the conflict. But yes, certainly he may succeed in managing the conflict a shade better and he appears to be sincerely trying. He is far from free agent as many think. His hands are tied by so many uncontrollable factors.

Al-Qaeda and Taliban issue is not here to disappear in few years. Afghan people are fiercely independence loving and even Muslim rulers like Moghuls failed to subdue them, much less totally aliens like Americans. American policy makers should study history of Afghan rebellion much more seriously than they have done. US jackboots cannot crush Afghans. Obama has to an extent realised this and though he is sending more forces but has also promised to withdraw by 2011.

Withdraws or not but certainly solution does not lay in trying to crush Afghans but to resolve it through dialogue and accommodation which again is not easy. The US is also not in Afghanistan for just to wipe out Al-Qaeda and Taliban but to control rich gas and mineral resources in Central Asia. It did not invaded Afghanistan for nothing. And as long as the US wants to control rich resources of Central Asia it cannot find accommodation with Afghan Taliban and as long as Taliban issue continues anti-Islam prejudices will remain strong as ever.

It is also absolutely necessary to solve Palestinian problem if one desires peace in West Asia. While Afghan Taliban are more concerned about peace in their region but Al-Qaeda is more focused on West Asia and to solve both the problems sans the US interests in both the regions is asking for let us say impossible. Should we despair then? Not really. But it is a challenge which few politicians can succeed in facing.

The Muslim countries too will have to seriously contemplate policy changes and have to make concerted efforts to project peaceful Islam on their part. They will have to fight powerful interests and confrontationists mindset on their part. The rulers in the West Asia have to go for modernisation, changes in their education system and promoting spirit of understanding and dialogue with the other.

King Abdullah of Saudi Arabia is wiser than his predecessors and following strategies to contain extremist elements in his own country. Like Obama his hands are tied too. In Pakistan military establishment is too powerful to be contained easily and for quite sometime to come civilian rule will not be able to ascertain its independence and Pakistan is very crucial for peace in Afghan-Pakistan region.

Well, while working for greater understanding let us understand these challenges too.

Women's Right and Personal Law

Like other women Muslim women, are also becoming increasingly conscious of their rights and are asserting themselves for realisation of their rights. Women in general and Muslim women in particular are suffering because of denial of their rights in this patriarchal society. Greater the degree of illiteracy, greater the lack of consciousness and hence greater their suffering. There being much greater illiteracy among Muslim women in India there is woeful lack of awareness among them about their own Islamic rights. Islam, as I have repeatedly pointed out, lays great emphasis on sexual equality and, accordingly, granted women equal rights in marriage, divorce, ownership of property etc. However, except for very brief period of early Islam, women could never enjoy equality of these rights. The '*Ulama*, with all their sincere commitment to Islam, were after all product of their time and interpreted the divine word from male perspective. They were also influenced by dominant male attitude of their times and took for granted in right earnest the prevalent male attitude towards women.

One of the prevailing assumptions in medieval ages was that women had deficient intelligence (*naqis al-'aql*) and hence should not be entrusted with responsible jobs. As late as mid-twenties of twentieth century Maulana Ashraf Thanavi, a great '*alim* in his own right also said that since women were deficient in intelligence they should not be entrusted with the responsibility of pronouncing divorce. Recently when Hosni Mubarak, President of Egypt, got a law passed in Egyptian Parliament empowering women to divorce their husbands, the '*Ulama* opposed it vehemently saying that women were emotional and hasty in decision making and if women were given right to divorce family life would be destabilised. The opposition from the '*Ulama* was so intense that Mubarak had to drop other measures in order to get the law giving women right to divorce passed.

Many rights which were accorded to women by the Qur'an were denied to them under such assumptions. It is important to note that the Qur'an by itself does not make any such pronouncements. It addresses all human beings - men or women - as u'lil *albab* (i.e. people of intelligence) and makes no discrimination between men and women on such counts. Though there is difference between men and women on certain functional matters there is no difference between them in matters of rights. Also, though the Qur'an nowhere says that a woman's duty is to look after her husband and children and do household work, the whole Islamic juristic literature is full of such assertions. Such assumptions come not from the Qur'an but from the prevailing social ethos.

The Muslim Personal Law in India is also based on many such assumptions. As pointed out above, Maulana Ashraf Thanavi himself thought that the women were deficient in intelligence, and from such assumptions all the problems of Muslim women flow. What is shocking is that despite evidence to the contrary the *'Ulama's* assumptions acquire divine status and are thought to be immutable. The Qur'an grants women right to divorce on giving fidyah (compensation) if she fears she cannot observe *Allah*'s limits, the *'Ulama* made it subject to husband's consent on the assumption that she would take hasty decisions and would destabilise family life.

The Muslim women today are demanding their Qur'anic rights. They want to liberate themselves from medieval interpretations of the Qur'an. However, the Muslim personal law board is resisting such demands from women. Some Muslim women, aware of their Islamic rights, drafted a standard *Nikahnama* and submitted it to the Board. Since marriage is a contract in Islam, standard contract conditions can be drawn up and signed at the time of marriage. A woman is entitled as much as a man to lay down certain conditions at the time of entering into marital contract. A woman thus can lay down a condition that her husband will not take second wife, or that he will delegate right to divorce to his wife (*talaq-e-tafwid*) etc. These conditions and similar other conditions, if incorporated into a standard *Nikahnama* as prepared by some Muslim women and men, could solve much of the problems being faced today by Muslim women without bringing any change in the personal law.

Such *Nikahnama* is well within the Islamic law and even the *'Ulama* of the stature of Maulana Ashraf Thanavi had drawn up such a standard *Nikahnama* way back in the thirties of the twentieth century. However, the members of the Muslim personal law board are sitting tight over the proposal. The *Nikahnama* submitted to the Board more than an year ago was sent to several 'Ulama for their approval before it was submitted to the Board and it received their approval. There is no condition in it which can be construed as un-Islamic. Even then the members of Personal Law Board are reluctant to approve it.

Recently there was news that the Board is going to consider the *Nikahnama* in its sitting in October in Bangalore. According to some sources, there are differences among the members of the Board regarding the draft *Nikahnama*. It is reported that the Board has scripted its own *Nikahnama* which is rather watered down version of the one submitted by the Muslim women from Bombay. A five member panel set up by the Board for this purpose has prepared this script. A spokesman of the Board has said that once this standard *Nikahnama* comes into force triple divorce on account of which many Muslim women are suffering today, will no more be possible. Abolition of triple divorce in one sitting will be a great relief for Muslim women. This form of divorce which all *'Ulama* agree is altered form of divorce and one which has been condemned by the Prophet (PBUH) is still valid in India though it has long been abolished in other Muslim countries.

It is reported that the *Nikahnama* being considered by the Board lays down special conditions for divorce, including the right of wife to claim *khula'* (divorce initiated by wife). The *Nikahnama* under consideration of the Board is also likely to restrict polygamy. Like triple divorce, polygamy is another serious problem for the Muslim women. The Qur'an has permitted it under exceptional conditions but these conditions are violated in practice. The Board should strictly regulate it as has been done in other countries including Pakistan.

With restriction of triple divorce and polygamy, Muslim women will not face much legal problems. Other laws of Islam are very fair to her and do not pose any problem. Triple divorce also is not universally practised by all Muslims. The Shi'ah Muslims do not recognise it and even among the Sunni Muslims Ahl-e-Hadith reject this concept. But the Shi'as and Ahl-e-Hadith are in minority and hence large number of Muslim women continue to suffer.

It will be a great change if the Muslim personal law board approves of the *Nikahnama*, which its own sub-committee has drafted. Its present chairman Maulana Mujahidul Qasmi is more liberal and is in favour of approving the new *Nikahnama*. He is also connected with the Fiqh Academy (the academy of the Islamic jurisprudence) which is actively engaged in taking up newly emerging problems and proposing changes. The Fiqh Academy has also prepared a volume on *Ishtirat fi al-Nikah* (The conditions in Marriage). This volume has examined in great details the conditions which can be stipulated by husband and wife at the time of marriage and has the approval of large number of 'Ulama in India from different schools of thought.

Thus it is a good news that the Muslim Personal Law Board has almost decided to finally approve the standard *Nikahnama* in its sitting at Banglaore on 29th October. If finally approved, it will be a first significant step in the direction of the reform of Muslim Personal Law in India. Most of the Muslim countries, with some exceptions, have already carried out reforms benefiting the women. In fact the secular India should have taken lead in this direction. However, the things seem to be moving although belatedly and these changes should be welcome by all those concerned with the plight of Muslim women.

Rights of Women in Muslim Societies

Muslim women's issues have acquired great deal of importance for several reasons. Muslim women are going for higher education all over the world and even among the poorer sections the rate of literacy is increasing. In fact, women's education which was a taboo a few decades ago is becoming acceptable. Education brings greater awareness among women and they, in turn, demand their rights. Also, there are many women NGOs working for the rights of women among the Muslims today which take up women's issues especially those pertaining to marriage, divorce, maintenance, custody of children etc. These tend to be crucial issues.

However, the Muslim clergy is highly reluctant to change and Islamic seminaries still provide training in Islamic jurisprudence developed during medieval ages when women's role in public life was extremely limited and they were supposed to be subservient to patriarchal authorities. The body of laws developed by the Islamic jurists is known as *Shari'ah* and the methods followed and intellectual efforts made is known as Islamic *fiqh* (jurisprudence).

It is a common belief among Muslims that Shari'ah laws are divine and hence immutable and for every Muslim it is obligatory to follow them. However, this is not a correct view. The body of Islamic laws developed over several centuries by eminent jurists is a result of human engagement with divine pronouncements in the Qur'an and *Sunnah* (Prophet's pronouncements and practices as reported by his companions and their followers).

Since the *Shari'ah* is a result of human endeavours to understand the divine, it is as much human as from *Allah* and cannot be made immutable. The modernist, liberal and reformist Muslims have been campaigning for change, with a view to removing gender inequalities and give women equal rights as Qur'an clearly stipulates. Thus one would see clear difference between what the Qur'an stipulates and what *Shari'ah* laws require.

This gap between Qur'anic pronouncements and *Shari'ah* requirements should not surprise us as the seventh century society and subsequent medieval values could hardly be expected to accept gender equality. It would be better to quickly survey the gender situation in seventh century Arabia:

The Arab society of the Prophet's time could be divided in two broad categories: urban i.e. sedentary and Bedouin i.e. nomadic. Culturally and socially both the societies were poles apart. Mecca, where the Prophet was born and grew up was highly urbanised region at the centre of which there was a highly respected religious sanctum sanctorum known as *ka'ba,* so named because of its cubical shape.

Mecca was also a centre of highly profitable commercial and financial operations and tribal chiefs, especially those belonging to the tribe of *Quraysh* (the Prophet also belonged to this tribe) had acquired great expertise in international trade and accumulated great deal of wealth.[1] Since women were not active economic agents, they had become quite subordinate to men. Further, as the Arab society was highly patriarchal, women had limited role to play in public life.

In Mecca women were treated as chattels having no rights whatsoever, except a few powerful women among whom was Khadija who was a rich trader and who, later married the Prophet.[2] But these were exceptions. Also, as we know, among tribals, there was no written law and only oral traditions were followed or there were time honoured customs. Accumulation of wealth made some individuals quite powerful and they began to violate even oral traditions and customary laws.

This made women, especially the widows and the orphans who had no protection, even more venerable. Women in Mecca enjoyed no property rights and strangely enough father's widows, except one's own mother, were inherited by the eldest son and he could even cohabit with them. Also, one could marry as many women as one liked.

A girl could be given away in marriage by her father or uncle or grandfather and the bride price pocketed by him. Child marriages were quite common and such marriages could not be revoked later. It became binding when the child became adult. Also, she had no right to divorce, while the husband could divorce her any time he liked just by pronouncing three words *talaq, talaq, talaq*.Once he pronounced these three words, he could not take her back even if he repented later, thus sealing her fate. And if at all he wanted to re-marry her she was required to marry another man who, after consummating marriage should divorce her. Then only she could marry her former husband and this procedure was called making her *hallalah* (permissible).

Also, there was a form of divorce called *zihar* i.e. a man would say to his wife 'you are like my mother'. He would utter these words, "Thou art (henceforth as unlawful) to me as my mother's back". The term mother in this case was a metonym for 'body'.[3] This divorce was considered irrevocable and what was worse, she could not remarry and had to live in her husband's custody for life.

Another form of persecution of wife was *al-'ila'* i.e. husband would take a vow not to go near his wife for a specified period which could extend from months to years and she would have to contend with her condition helplessly.

Above all, it was often considered a disgrace to have a daughter born. There was a practice, especially among the Bedouins, to bury a girl child alive. The Qur'an refers to this custom and strongly condemns it in verse 81:9. The Qur'an says, "And when the buried alive is asked for what sin she was killed." Muhammad Asad, noted modern commentator on Qur'an says that burying alive seems to have been fairly widespread in pre-Islamic Arabia, although perhaps not to the extent as has been commonly assumed. The motives were twofold: the fear that an increase in female offspring would result in economic burden, as well as the fear of humiliation frequently caused by girls being captured by a hostile tribe and subsequently preferring their captors to their parents and brothers.[4].

Bedouin Society

The condition of women in Bedouin society i.e. among nomads was somewhat different. Meccan society was, as pointed out before, highly commercialised and had developed the concept of property. Tribal bonds were being weakened, if not broken down and new practices were developing. But the nomadic society was quite static and strictly followed customs and traditions and also, in absence of concept of property, landed or otherwise, did not have strict family institution.

Women had thus little more freedom in sexual matters. According to Tabari, historian and commentator on the Qur'an, in Mecca, an urban complex, men could marry up to ten wives. In the Bedouin society, a woman also could enter into multiple marriages and she could divorce any husband she would not like to live with. The method of doing this was also interesting. The Bedouins lived in tents and the entry to the tent will have a particular direction. When she did not desire to live with a man she would change the direction of tent's entry when that man came to cohabit with her.[5]

But when a woman was captured in inter-tribal war, and such wars and raids were frequent among the Bedouins, the captor could cohabit with her without any formal marriage treating her simply as a slave. No ceremony of *nikah* was needed and her offspring would belong to the father. This custom prevailed both in the Bedouin as well as among the sedentary populations in Mecca or Medina.

Unfortunately, it remains a controversial issue till today in the Islamic jurisprudence, though now it is of only an academic interest whether such cohabitation with a slave girl or one captured in war is permissible. But this practice, we are told by historians, continued for long even after Islam raised the status of women as we will see, considerably.

Islam and Women

Now that we have seen the status of women in pre-Islamic Arab society which is referred to as period of *jahiliyyah* i.e. period of ignorance by Islamic historians, we would like to discuss how Islam brought about changes in her status. Is the status of women in Islam is low as often widely believed? Or her status in Muslim societies today is due to Islam or medieval cultural practices in Muslim countries?

Islam, if we derive its teachings primarily from Qur'an (as *hadith* literature is controversial) we will find a world of difference between Qur'anic teachings and Muslim practices. However, understandably Muslim practices, many of which are less than fair to women for variety of reasons, are thought to be Islamic practices. It is therefore necessary to distinguish between the two and also to understand reasons for such difference. We will throw light on this subsequently.

First, it is also necessary to understand that Qur'an was revealed to the Prophet (PBUH) in Arabian society during a period of 23 years in the early seventh century and hence there are many verses in the Qur'an which I call contextual. The Qur'an is a word of *Allah* and this belief is very basic to Muslims. However, the word of *Allah*, in order to be meaningful to the followers, cannot be devoid of socio-cultural context.

But that does not mean the entire text of the Qur'an is contextual. Certainly not. Its moral, ethical and value-oriented teachings are universal and normative. In fact much of the Qur'an contains what is universal and normative. There is controversy among the jurists and theologians as to which verses of Qur'an are contextual and which have been cancelled (known as *mansukh*). This is important for the debate on certain juristic and *Shari'ah* formulations including the ones on gender issues.

Another question is of understanding the treatment of an issue by the Qur'an. Generally many laymen as well as jurists pick and choose Qur'anic verses in order to prove their point or for juristic formulation. This is not correct. First, Qur'an has not been compiled strictly in order of revelation and secondly Qur'an treats one subject in different verses in different chapters. For example, women's issues have been treated in several different chapters like 2nd, 3rd, 4th, and 5th and so on.

Thus one has to study all the verses on a particular subject spread over several chapters and then bring them together to understand the real intent. As far as I know, no jurist has done that and hence differences among them persist. If we follow the above method of understanding the intent of Qur'an, many juristic formulations will have to be changed. Also, since certain Qur'anic verses are contextual, they must be read as such as core values are much more important than contextual injunctions.

There is one more factor which impacts on Islamic jurisprudence as it evolved in the past centuries, especially during the medieval period. The base for much of the *Shari'ah* formulations was provided by the seventh century urban Arab society and culture. Most of the early jurists came from there and were deeply immersed in their cultural traditions. All these became part of their juristic thinking.

The jurists themselves acknowledge this as Arab *adaat* (customary laws) being part of body of *Shari'ah* laws and in any reformist venture Arab *adaat* would not be binding on the reformer and this indeed would be a revolutionary step for Muslim women. Islam subsequently spread all over the world with radically different cultures and gender practices. Since the twentieth century Islam is spreading in Europe and North America which are basically western societies. Now even a term like Euro-Islam is emerging.

Unfortunately, for lack of proper knowledge and understanding most Muslims think even *adaat* part of *Shari'ah* is divine and binding. In fact many jurists agree that local *adaat* where Islamic *Shari'ah* is practised could be part of *Shari'ah*. But *adaat* or customary law of any region may not be gender-just. In that respect *Shari'ah* is more gender-just that any customary law.

In India, the *Khoja* and *Kutcchi* Memon communities of Gujarat were following the customary law, depriving their women of any share in inheritance. It was only after the *Shari'ah* Application Law of 1937 came into force that the women of these Muslim communities also got share in inheritance and property. It was for similar reasons that Qur'anic injunctions on gender justice got diluted as the Arabian society was not ready to give complete equality to women as required by the Qur'an and secondly they were psychologically conditioned to practise their own customary laws which subordinated women to male authority.

In fact it would not be difficult to demonstrate that Qur'anic formulations on women are all rights-based whereas men's are all duty-based.[6] But for reasons stated above, the Islamic jurists reversed this order by incorporating their own *adaat* and again made *Shari'ah* discourse duty-based for women and rights-based for men. What is needed today is to bring it in conformity with Qur'an by again reversing it and making the whole gender discourse rights-based for women and duty-based for men.

Now first we would like to deal with what changes Islam brought about in the status of women in the backdrop of pre-Islamic Arabian practices. Qur'an adopted a reformist approach in certain matters where sudden change could not have been acceptable and resorting to a radical approach in certain respects where change was much more urgent. Again those who want to bring about gender equality have to examine certain reformist and gradual approach in the light of core-values of Qur'an and make suitable changes.

For example, Qur'an did not abolish slavery right away as it would have caused more complex problems in the Arab society and would have thrown up great resistance from powerful vested interests. It, therefore, adopted a gradual approach and effected humanitarian reforms in the treatment of slaves. Qur'an encouraged liberation of slaves even for expiation for sins and even otherwise. Also, it required that slaves be treated with dignity and given the same food as the master ate, given the same clothes as master wore and be made to live in the same place where the master resided.

At the same time, it was made clear that all human beings have been created from the same parents i.e. adam and eve, and equality of all human beings and equal dignity is the norm.[7] Thus, according to this verse, slavery has to go if equality of all human beings is to be established in the society. Despite such radical approach we see slavery persisted in the Islamic world until it was abolished in the west, particularly in the USA.

Though Muslims claim Qur'an to be of divine origin, yet when it comes to their own culture, values, and interests, they violate its injunctions with impunity. If Muslims had followed true Qur'anic spirit and values they should have been the first to abolish slavery. Same could be said about gender discourse in Islamic countries today. Still Islamic world shirks responsibility of implementing gender- just laws and its *Ulama* and jurists continue to issue *fatwas* (legal opinions) which are violative of gender-justice and women's dignity.

Qur'an and Women

The Qur'an came out with a radical declaration that men and women are equal and women's rights are equal to their duties.[8] Maulana Abul Kalam Azad, a noted modern commentator on Qur'an, describes this verse as a revolutionary declaration of gender equality more than 1300 years ago.[9] Thus the basic principle in the Qur'an is of gender equality without any ambiguity whatsoever. But then, as pointed out above, in the context of the then Arab society there are some injunctions in Qur'an which, for those who talk of absolute equality, may find unacceptable in today's context.

But as pointed out already, Qur'an had to adopt a gradual reformist approach in certain respects while making the basic principles clear. The basic principle with regard to women is of gender equality. The *Shari'ah* laws must be updated in the light of this basic Qur'anic injunction. Until today, because of resistance on the part of *Ulama* and jurists, this basic principle continues to be in limbo.

One more problem which has to be encountered by reformists all over the world is that of *hadith* (Prophet's pronouncements). A major part of the body of *Shari'ah* law comprises *hadith* which is a highly controversial area. Because of *hadith* literature, several differences have arisen among Muslims on a variety of issues including the gender issue. Some Muslim historians tell us that the Prophet (PBUH) himself asked Muslims not to collect his *hadith* as it will give rise to differences among them. This is what precisely happened.

Ahadith (plural of *hadith*) were collected by several eminent personalities and their number reached to hundreds of thousands. Imam Bukhari, one of the greatest collectors of *ahadith* is reported to have collected more than six hundred thousand *ahadith.* As there were five others besides Imam Bukhari, we find six authentic collections of *ahadith* in Sunni Islam alone. The *Shiah* Muslims and *Isma'ili Shi'ah* Muslims and other sects have their own collections.

It was mainly because of these *ahadith* and interpretations of Qur'an in the light of such *ahadith,* that different schools of law arose and among theSunni Muslims of such several schools four survived i.e. *Hanafi, Maliki, Shafi'i* and *Hanbali* and among *Shi'ahs* three main schools are prevalent i.e. *Ithna 'Ashari, Isma'ili* and *Zaidi.* Thus, while Qur'an is one and its formulations divine and unambiguous, there are so many different legal schools differing from each other on several issues including issues pertaining to gender laws.

Most of the differences, as pointed out, are on account of two reasons; one understanding and interpretations of Qur'anic verses and two, the*ahadith* employed. Also, the jurists were located in different places and faced different socio-cultural issues, customs and traditions. Thus, local factors were no less important. For example, Imam Shafi'i was in Egypt where Coptic culture was prevalent and Imam Abu Hanifa was in Kufa which was confluence of Arab-Iranian culture.

Imam Malik and Imam Hanbal, on the other hand, were situated in the Arabian peninsula and were much closer, and hence influenced by, Arab *addat* i.e. customs and traditions. Besides the local influences, the methodology employed also influenced the formulations. When they faced a new problem and did not find any direct solution in Qur'an and *hadith,* they used what was called analogical reasoning (i.e. *qiyas*) and tried to obtain some kind of consensus on their formulation (*ijma'*).

Both *qiyas* and *ijma'* are human institutions and varied from one jurist to the other and also in the vast Islamic world (Islam had spread rapidly from Arabia to parts of Roman Empire to Central Asia to India to China to Turkey by the time these jurists codifying the *Shari'ah* laws). And it took almost three centuries in this great venture. We do not find the word *Shari'ah* for the body of Islamic laws almost for first three centuries of Islam. It was from the fourth century onwards that this word began to be used.

According to the noted Urdu poet Iqbal there were more than 100 legal schools of which only four survived in *Sunni* Islam.[10] If there were so many legal schools (called *madhahib*) one can understand the range of differences among Islamic jurists in formulations and the role of human endeavours in formulating the issues. There being no church or priestly hierarchy in Islam, every learned jurist was free to make his own efforts to understand these issues.

Since new issues kept arising which did not exist in Qur'an and classical *Sunnah* (as reported in its earliest time by the companions or wives of the Prophet) new *ahadith* were needed for legitimation and there began fabrication of *ahadith* and these *ahadith* directly contradicted Qur'anic teachings and even then they were accepted. It was because of such fabrication that many *muhaddithin* (i.e. experts of *hadith*) developed a separate discipline in the field of *hadith.*

The most important basis of this discipline was what came to be known as *'ilm al-rijal* (i.e. science of men reporting or narrating the *hadith*). The experts would examine the character and reputation of the narrator of *hadith* so as to know how reliable his or her narrations were and from whom he or she heard the *hadith* being narrated andalso to know whether the chain of narrators of a *hadith* being reported reaches right up to the Prophet or one of his companions.

Some experts also prescribed the criteria of *dirayat* (reason) as against mere *riwayat* (i.e. narration) i.e. to examine whether the *hadith* being narrated is in keeping with reason and moral standards or not. However, in *Sunni* Islam the narration and narrators became more central than reason and morality. In *Shi'ah* Islam reason (*dirayat*) retained its centrality but it was also more symbolic than substantial.

Thus it would be seen that in all schools of law in Islam *hadith* has played very important role in juristic formulations and over a period of time *hadith* did gain more importance for several reasons. The Qur'anic injunctions in respect of women were not acceptable in a basically patriarchal culture as they directly challenged men's authority and made women equal to men in every respect.

For this reason, even the very unambiguous formulations of the Qur'an were subjected to strange interpretations with the help of a*hadith* which contradicted Qur'anic formulations. These a*hadith* represented their cultural ethos rather than Qur'anic injunctions. Also, where Qur'an did not put any restrictions on women these *ahadith* were employed to put severe restrictions on them.[11]

Thus, Qur'an and *hadith* became two worlds apart and *hadith* was invoked more and more to subjugate women and to curtail their rights. For example one does not find mention in the Qur'an that a single woman cannot venture out of house without being accompanied by a male relative whom she cannot marry (*mahram*). On the basis of a *hadith* the jurists almost elevated it to the status of an obligatory practice for women. Even today in Saudi Arabia a single woman is not allowed to go out alone and by implication she cannot even drive a car herself. There could be some justification if such restriction is placed as a precaution if a woman has had no outside experience and if there are frequent cases of molestation or sexual assault. But certainly it cannot be elevated to the status of a legally binding practice.

Another example is that of veil (or *purdah* or *burqa*), which is so much in the news these days. Qur'an does not prescribe veil (*hijab*) for women. In fact the word *hijab* does not occur in Qur'an for veiling the face of an ordinary Muslim woman. It was meant for the wives of the Prophet and this verse for wives of the Prophet was revealed because some *Bedouin* Arabs, being nomads and not acquainted with cultural norms, sat long after a marriage dinner and talked freely with Prophet's wives, which Prophet did not like. Hence this verse was revealed that you must leave after the dinner and if you talk with wives of the Prophet, talk from behind *hijab* (i.e. curtain). Even here, the proper context is a reference to a curtain and not to face veil.

For other women, the word *hijab* or *burqa* does not occur in Qur'an at all. The verses which are often quoted in support of veiling women with the help of *hadith* have nothing to do with that practice. One verse pertains to display of adornments (*zeenah*) publicly and the other of eve-teasing in early morning when Muslim women went out for relieving themselves, there being no toilets at home.

As far as display of adornments is concerned, it is more of advisory in nature than obligatory. It begins with advising men to lower their gaze while meeting women and women also to lower their gaze while meeting men. Then it further goes on to say:

"And say to the believing women that they lower their gaze and restrain their sexual passions and do not display their adornment except that appears thereof. And let them let them wear their head coverings over their bosoms."[12]

There are two crucial elements prescribed for women in this verse. Firstly, not to display their adornments *except what appears thereof* and secondly that they should also cover their bosom with the *khimar* (known as *dupatta* in India, which is used either as headgear or for hanging on shoulders). While asking women not to display their adornments, a cultural space has been allowed by using words '*what appears thereof*'. What exactly these words mean has been keenly debated and various *ahadith* used for the purpose.

There is near consensus among early jurists that women can keep their face exposed and are permitted to apply corium to their eyes and wear rings in their fingers. However, Qur'an does not categorically prescribe any such restrictions. This opinion is also based on cultural practices of the societies of those days when except in certain cases, women were not active agents in the public arena. More fundamental to Qur'anic prescription is to lower the gaze and restrain sexual passion rather than hiding one's face behind *hijab*.

In fact *hijab* or face veil was later imitated during the Umayyad period when Islamic Caliphate was transformed into monarchy after conquests of parts of the Byzantine Empire and the Sassanid Empire of Persia as the wives of nobles of these courts observed face veil and even worst kind of restrictions due to large harams. Such imitation also strengthens men's hold over women. And in legitimising such practice, resort was taken to *ahadith* whose authenticity can be questioned.

The second verse of the Qur'an often used to justify face veil is about pulling one's *jilbab* (a kind of long and loose-fitting gown worn generally by Arab women) over their face (what is called *ghunghat* in north India). It is purely a contextual verse. When Muslim women went out to relieve themselves, some eve-teasers would tease them and when caught would say we thought they were slave girls as some slave girls were used by their masters for immoral acts (Islam strictly prohibited this).

The Qur'anic verse says, "O Prophet, tell thy wives and thy daughters and the women of believers to let down upon them their over-garments. This is more proper so that they may be known, and not be given trouble (or teased)."[13]

This verse cannot be of universal application and cannot set the norm for all Muslim women for all times to come. It was only about pulling the over garment on one's face to distinguish themselves from slave girls. No slavery exists now and no such practice is necessary. One cannot impose certain contextual practices of early Arabian society over women today. And yet some *Ulama* use such verses in Qur'an for justifying the face veil.

Here it would be interesting to throw some light on *burqa* ban controversy in Europe. Belgium has already banned it and French Parliament has also voted for it and may soon become a law. The argument in support of the prohibition is that it is meant to protect France's secular culture and to liberate Muslim women from oppression. Both arguments are flawed. Today Europe is multi-cultural and all cultures are to be respected. It is no more mono-cultural and such arguments are no more valid.

Secondly, it would be against one's individual rights to impose what one should wear. No restriction, however plausible from certain point of view, can be imposed on the free citizens of a country. Such imposition itself is an oppressive act. It would amount to replacing one kind of oppression by another. Thirdly, it is difficult to assume that all women wear face veil because of patriarchal oppression. Some might wear the veil due to their own conviction and free choice.

Thirdly, unless a woman complains that she is being coerced into wearing such veil it would be unjustified to punish her. Otherwise she will suffer doubly. When the family forces her to wear veil and if she refuses, she will suffer the wrath of the family and if she does, she will suffer the wrath of the state and made to either pay fine or go to jail. If it is estimated that in France no more than 400 to 2000 women wear face veil out of a Muslim population of four to five million. In Belgium no more than 30 or 30% women wear face veil and yet it has been banned. Thus reasons must be sought elsewhere rather than pretentious claim that such prohibition is meant to liberate women or to protect French culture.

Wife-beating and Qur'an

Again, there is a verse in the Qur'an (verse no. 34, chapter 4)in the chapter on Women. Today this verse has assumed great importance in women's rights debates. The orthodox argue that the said verse gives men authority over women and even the right to beat, if they rebel. The modernists are challenging its meaning and debating what exactly certain key words in the verse mean. Do they mean literally what the orthodox jurists claim? Or they mean something else. There are even some websites on this debate.

Before we discuss this verse, we would like to give its text the way it is translated even by some moderate Muslims like Muhammad Asad who otherwise adopt quite fresh approach on many issues. He renders it as under:

"Men shall take full care of women with the bounties which God has bestowed more abundantly on the former, and with what they may spend out of their possessions. And the righteous women are truly devout ones, who guard the intimacy which God has (ordained to be guarded). And as for those women whose ill-will you have reason to fear, admonish them (first); then leave them alone in bed; then beat them; and thereupon they pay you heed, do not seek to harm them. Behold, God is indeed most high, great."[14]

Now the key words in this verse are *qawwam, qanita, hafizat li al-ghayb and daraba,*of which *daraba* (usually translated as beat) is most controversial. Some orthodox translators render the word *qawwam* as authority implying men have authority over women. *Qawwam* does not have any such shade of meaning even remotely and yet, in a feudal, patriarchal culture such rendition became acceptable.

It simply means one who maintains or takes care of financial and other needs of women and since women in general were not active economic agents in those days, Qur'an made it obligatory on men to maintain them and take care of them as they earned and *Allah* bestowed His bounties on them. But Mohammad Asad's rendering of *ba'dahum 'ala ba'din* as "on the former (men) than latter (women)" is not correct.

Such a rendering would mean men will always earn and women will always be passive agents. It simply means "some over the others" and 'some' over others' are inclusive of both genders and leaves the possibility of women becoming active economic agents in future and they have become active agents today. Maulana Azad is nearer the truth when he argues that *qawwam* is a functional word and if women earn and maintain their family they also qualify as *qawwam*.[15] Today many women will qualify as *qawwam*.

Before we discuss this verse any further we would like to throw some light on the context in which it was revealed. The context of the verse will throw greater light on its contents. A woman, according to noted Qur'anic commentator Kasshaf, came to the Prophet and complained that she was slapped by her husband without any fault on her part. What should she do? The Prophet told her to go and retaliate (*izhabi was iqtasi*). Tabari, another noted commentator also endorses this story.

The women were jubilant and men worried. How will the men, who maintain women and spend their means over them, control them, if the Prophet has allowed them to retaliate? They also came to the Prophet (PBUH) and complained and then the Prophet said it was my personal opinion and I will wait for revelation from *Allah*. And this verse was revealed. That is why it begins with reference to men earning and looking after women.

Thus it will be seen that this verse is purely contextual and does not set any permanent norm of behaviour. Further let us take the term *qnaitat* which is translated by some as obedience to husband. This word is used only for obedience to *Allah* and Muhammad Asad has rightly rendered it as devout. As for *hafizat li al-ghayb* Asad has rendered it as 'guarding the intimate' thereby implying chastity. *Ghayb* actually means 'unseen'.

Modernist Turkish translator Edip Yuksel and his colleagues translate it as "they honour guarding the privacy".[16] The other key word is *nushuz* which Muhammad Asad translates as ill will and many others as rebellion or disobedience to husband or disloyalty in marriage. Edip Yuksel says:

"This phrase emphasizes the importance of loyalty in marital life, and helps us to make better sense of what follows." In the verse 4:128 the same word *nushuz* is used for husband and means misbehaviour. Thus for Edip rendering *nushuz* as disloyalty, in variety of forms is clearly appropriate for both 4:34 and 4:128.[17]

The most controversial word of course is *idribuhunna* usually rendered as 'beat them'. The modernists and reformists of course are rejecting this translation as the verb *daraba* has variety of meanings. It is equivalent to 'strike' in English. In Qur'an it is used in multiple meanings like to travel, to give example, to strike, to beat, to cover, to regret, to take away, to ignore etc.

Thus *idribuhunna* can be and should be rendered as 'separate' them i.e. if they indulge in disloyalty in marital matters separate them and the same thing will apply to husbands also, if they too indulge in disloyalty according to 4:128. Thus beating a wife is out of question and apart from this, the general approach of Qur'an and its advice to men as to how they should treat their wives also makes it clear that beating them is not correct translation.

For example Qur'an says: "And of His signs is this that He created mates for you from yourselves that you might find quiet of mind in them, and He put between you love and compassion." (30:21) and "that believing men and women are one another's friends and they enforce what is good and prevent what is evil" (9:71) and then even at the time of divorce men are obliged not to mistreat and leave them with kindness (2:229). How can the same Qur'an allow men to beat them? As explained above one must collate all verses together to know the final intention of Qur'an and should not decide the meaning just by reading one verse on the subject.

It is also important to note that Qur'an, except at three places, does not use the word husband or wife as usually husband implies authority over wife in a patriarchal culture. It either uses common noun like men and women or more often, and this is quite important to note, the word *zawj* i.e. couple, which indicates complete equality. It is a unique feature of the Qur'an that it treats men and women on such parity though it was revealed in a highly patriarchal society. It is unfortunate that Muslims preferred to revert to their old ways rather than abide by divine instructions.

Is Woman a Half Witness

Muslim jurists' patriarchal values are reflected in interpreting various verses of the Qur'an totally ignoring its real spirit and Qur'an's repeated assertion that men and women are equal. Qur'an went an extra mile to assert gender equality knowing fully well how men will try to bring in inequality in gender relations as their minds have been conditioned over centuries.

It asserted in 33:35 "Surely Muslim men who submit and Muslim women who submit, and the believing men and believing women, and the truthful men and truthful women, and the patient men and patient women, and the humble men and humble women" and the charitable men and charitable women "and the fasting men and fasting women, and men who guard their chastity and the women who guard, and men who remember *Allah* much and women who remember – *Allah* has prepared for them forgiveness and mighty reward."

In what other way could gender equality be asserted than in these words? And yet we see all over Muslim world that women are treated unequally in every respect. What do we ascribe it to? To Qur'an or to male prejudices? It is a bitter fact that gender equality does not prevail even in the west despite all their gender-just laws. It is a matter of attitude, not of laws. When the western society is passing through post-industrial era and yet gender inequalities prevail, what could one say about the Afro-Asian societies where feudal values are predominant and hence gender equality remains only a dream. And Qur'an desired to bring about gender equality more than 1400 years ago. The reversal of Qur'anic teachings should not surprise us.

Another legal myth established by Islamic jurists was that a woman is a half witness compared to man as the Qur'an requires two female witnesses in place of one man in financial transactions. First let us quote the relevant Qur'anic verse:

> "O you, who believe, when you contract a debt for a fixed time, write it down. And let a scribe write it down between you with fairness; nor the scribe should refuse to write as *Allah* has taught him, so let him write. And let him who owes the debt dictate and he should observe his duty to ALLAH, HIS Lord, and not diminish anything from it. But if he who owes the debt is unsound in understanding or weak, or (if) he is not able to dictate himself, let his guardian dictate with fairness. And call to witness from among your men two witnesses; but if there are not two men, then one man and two women from among those whom you choose to be witnesses, so that if one of the two errs, one may remind the other....(2.282)

This elaborate verse on writing down a debt transaction itself may surprise some people as to why was it necessary in the Qur'an. The reason was though the Arabs had taken to international trade, very few of them were literate and hardly ever indulged in written transactions. Most of their dealings were oral and often resulted in disputes; hence the emphasis on writing. This would minimize disputes. Let us be clear that the whole verse is recommendatory in tenor and not obligatory.

And if two witnesses signed what was written it becomes more credible and trustworthy and hence the recommendation for signature of two witnesses. Why did Qur'an require two women in place of one man? Was it because she was half witness as many commentators and jurists assumed? Qur'an does not say so at all. It clearly says 'if one of the two errs, the one may remind the other.'

The verse above, as pointed out before too, must be read with other verses on women to understand Qur'anic approach. Qur'an makes it clear that men and women are equal in abilities, capacities and intellectual gifts and we find in 3:1934 men and women will be equally rewarded and we find in 24-6-9 that in matters of witness also they are equal. Thus if we read all these verses in totality it is not difficult to conclude that here in matters of financial transaction in those days, women, not being very experienced, could err and hence if one errs, the other could remind her.

There are other explanations offered by some liberal and progressive commentators. Maulavi Mumtaz Ali Khan[18] for example, maintains that the requirement of two women is a sort of privilege, rather than disability. If one woman is menstruating or has delivered or suckling her child, the other may go and bear witness. Such privilege has not been given to man. And it is also not true that all jurists have considered woman as half witness.

Ibn Qayuyim, a prominent disciple of Ibn Taymiyyah, maintains that a single woman, if she be reliable, can be acceptable as a witness. He says:

> "When the woman be perfect in retaining in memory what she observes, is wise and also religious-minded the object is served by her evidence alone....On many occasions the evidence of one woman alone is considered sufficient. The better proposition, therefore, would be that a matter be decided on the evidence of two women and; the oath of the right holder plaintiff (which means it should not be necessary to produce a male witness along with them). This is what is stated by Imam Malik and it is one of the views attributed to Imam Ahmad...."[19]

Thus it will be seen that even Ibn Taymiyyah and his disciple Ibn Qayyim who are considered quite orthodox in their approach do not maintain that the Qur'anic verse makes woman a half witness. Everything depends on her understanding, honesty, capacity, intellectual ability and experience and even one woman's witness will suffice. Today women specialize in finance and deal in complex operations of high international finance. How can one then maintain that she would not be able to bear proper witness and would need the other to remind her? The verse was purely contextual and should not be used to deride women today. Ibn Taymiyyah and Ibn Qayyim were in 14th century and maintained even one woman is sufficient as witness then how can in 21st century when women are far more educated and experienced, cannot handle financial transactions by themselves?

Should Woman Inherit Half that of her Brother?

This is another aspect of woman's right which is often held against her by men. It is true that Qur'an allocates her half the portion of that of her brother in her father's property. But this verse too has to be treated as contextual rather than normative. As I referred to above Qur'an goes gradually for reform and then gives norm for normative change. Women in pre-Islamic society had no right to inherit father's property.

A woman came to the Prophet and complained that her husband died and she had only a daughter and that her husband's brother had seized all the property of her husband arguing that Arabs do not give share to their daughters in inheritance. It was on this occasion that the verse on inheritance was revealed and Qur'an created inheritance right for daughters half that of her brothers. What was important was that she got the right to inherit where it did not exist. Secondly, we must bear in mind that she was not, in those days, an active economic agent and had very limited public space.

Thus Qur'an tried to compensate her in other ways. First, she was given right to demand *mehr* from her husband to be and unlike pre-Islamic period, she was entitled to keep the *mehr* amount or property whatever she demanded, and not her father, as in pre-Islamic days. No marriage was valid without *mehr* being paid to her and Qur'an said she could demand even a heap of gold.

Thus *mehr* tended to be a very substantial amount and the amount of *mehr* increased so much that the second Caliph tried to put a ceiling. It was objected to by a woman called Fatima and she recited the Qur'anic verse about *mehr* and argued, "O Umar, when *Allah* has allowed us to demand heap of gold who are you to put a ceiling over it? Umar immediately withdrew his proposal.

Secondly, Qur'an makes it obligatory for the husband to maintain his wife even if she has means to maintain herself and has substantial property or income. And interestingly, the *Ulama* defined maintenance, during Aurangzeb's time (included in *Fatawa Alamgiri*) as serving her cooked food (it is not her obligation to cook food), stitched clothes, independent house to live in and if the husband cannot afford independent house, an independent room with separate access (if she does not want to live with her it laws) and other necessities to maintain her health and beauty.

Thus the concept of maintenance is quite comprehensive in Islamic *Shari'ah* and if the husband does not pay her maintenance, the *Shari'ah* entitles her to take loan in her husband's name and the husband will have to pay off the loan. She is even entitled to take amount due from his pocket without his permission, in case he is avoiding paying maintenance to her. If seen in totality, with all these obligations, a son ends up having less, though his share is double, than a daughter, who gains from these benefits even though her share is half that of her brother.

The question arises what if she does not, or cannot, get married? The Qur'anic verses on inheritance clearly say that male and female relatives are entitled to inheritance from what is left after paying what a father has willed away and a father has every right to will a part of his property to an unmarried daughter or daughter with certain disabilities. No one can take away this right to will from him during his life time. But the only condition is that the will should be made during his life time and he should not die intestate.

Also, Qur'an has given her half the share but does not say anywhere that if conditions change, she cannot be entitled to more or even equal share, especially if she is an active economic agent and adds to the family wealth like the sons. Either she can keep separate account of her wealth and income, and if she merges it with family wealth, she can be entitled to full share like her brothers who too add to family wealth.

Though the traditional jurists do not agree with such proposition, if one goes by the Qur'an and its creative interpretation, it is a distinct possibility. Qur'an gives full property rights to women on par with men and makes it clear that what she earns is hers and neither her father nor her husband can claim what she has earned herself. Thus if she contributes to family wealth through her own efforts, her share in inheritance should also go up on par with brothers.

Marriage and Divorce

Marriage in Islam, as is well known, is a contract, not a sacrament unlike in Christianity and Hinduism and a woman has same rights in marriage contract as man. She can stipulate conditions; and if those conditions are violated it would amount to breach of contract and the marriage could be invalidated. But it is also important to note that in order to emphasize seriousness of marriage Qur'an calls it *mithaqan ghaliza*[20] (i.e. a strong covenant).

Thus it is both a civil contract but with an element of spiritual companionship since it is a strong covenant and should not be broken on petty considerations. Nevertheless, primarily it is contract of civil nature and without consent from both the parties it cannot be solemnised. Thus a father has no right to give consent to a girl's marriage without her specific approval. Also, her consent should be obtained in the presence of two most reliable witnesses and both witnesses should testify before the *Qazi* and she should specify conditions including the *mehr* amount.

Among the conditions she can also specify that her husband will not take another wife at all or without her consent and if he does, she is entitled to go for dissolution of her marriage on the ground that her husband has violated the marriage conditions. Many prominent women used to stipulate this condition in their marriage contract in the early history of Islam. Among those, according to some *Sunni* historians, was the Prophet's grandniece Sakina, daughter of his grandson Imam Husain, the martyr of Karbala, though according to the *Shi'ah* historians she had died in prison in Syria in her childhood. But besides Sakina, there were many learned women who would stipulate such condition. We find these instances quoted in early Islamic history.

Her consent for marriage was so fundamental that when father of a woman went to the Prophet (PBUH) and requested him to persuade her daughter to marry such and such person, the Prophet called her and asked her to marry such and such person. She asked: Are saying this as a Prophet of *Allah* or like any other man? If you are saying this as a Prophet it is my duty to obey you but if not I refuse to agree to marry the person chosen by the father and the Prophet let her go.

As in a patriarchal feudal society, there was institution of child marriage and ifa father gives away his daughter to someone, she is given right to accept or reject the marriage when she becomes an adult as without her consent marriage will not be valid and acceptance or rejection will have to be conveyed to the Qazi concerned. This right in *Shari'ah* language is called *khiyar al-bulugh* i.e. option of puberty. She has every right to exercise this option and cannot be coerced into accepting father's commitment in her childhood.

In pre-Islamic times women could be inherited. This was strictly prohibited by Qur'an. Thus Qur'an says, "O you who believe, it is not lawful for you to take women as heritage against their will. Nor should you straiten them by taking part of what you have given them unless they are guilty of manifest indecency. And treat them kindly...".[21]

This verse is referring to two pre-Islamic practices: one, when the father dies, his elder son could inherit his father's wives except his own mother. Qur'an prohibited this in this verse; second, Arabs would trouble their wives they did not like so that they would be forced to obtain divorce and take the dower amount back. This was highly unfair to women and hence Qur'an prohibited this too, unless they indulged in indecent acts like extra-marital relationship or some similar acts. This verse also exhorts men to treat their wives with kindness.

The next verse (4:20) also exhorts men that "if you wish to have [one] wife in the place of another and you have given one of them a heap of gold (*qintaran)*, take nothing from it. Would you take it by slandering [her] and [doing her] manifest wrong? Here too, two things have been emphasised: one, do not make false accusation in order to divorce the wife and two, do not take away dower from her even if you have given a heap of gold i.e. the dower could be as high as the wife demands.

In pre-Islamic times a marriage guardian was required and was known as *wali.* No *nikah* could be performed without the agency of *wali.* But Qur'an does not refer to this institution of *wali* which clearly means that an adult woman could enter marriage contract herself without the agency of her father or in the absence of father, grandfather, uncle or brother. But again it was too radical a step for Arabs to accept.

The jurists retained the institution of *wali* in the case of *bakirah* i.e. a virgin who was marrying for the first time but allowed a *thayyib* i.e. a widow or a divorcee to marry without *wali.* The argument is that a virgin is not experienced and hence requires her father or nearest male relative to act as marriage guardian but a widow or a divorcee is experienced enough to dispense with marriage guardian. But marriage guardian or no marriage guardian, her consent is necessary.

Qur'an has instituted further reforms in the institution of marriage and details of these reforms are given in the verse 4:23. In pre-Islamic days there was no sanctity of blood relations in marriage; one could marry half-mothers or half-sisters or father's sisters or mother's sisters etc. The following verse prohibits such marriages. It says:

> "Forbidden for you are your mothers, your daughters, your sisters, your father's sisters, your mother's sisters, the daughters of your brothers, and daughters of your sister's your foster mothers who suckled you, your sisters from suckling, the mothers of your wives, and your step daughters residing in your homes from your wives which you have already consummated the marriage with; if you have not consummated the marriage then there is no sin upon you; and the wives of your sons that are from your seed, and that you join between two sisters except what has already been done. God is forgiving, Compassionate." (4:23)

This is a very thorough reform of the pre-Islamic institution of marriage which, among others, restores dignity of women. It was indeed humiliating that one could marry one's father's wives or step mothers or children from other wives of their fathers. Even marriage with a girl whom one's mother has suckled was forbidden. But Qur'an allowed marriage with one's cousin's i.e. children of one's maternal or paternal uncle or aunt.

Qur'an also did not approve of triple divorce in one sitting as was the case in pre-Islamic days. And such divorce was considered irrevocable and the divorced woman was required to marry another man who had to consummate the marriage and then divorce her so that she could become *hallalah* i.e. permissible for her former husband. It was even more humiliating for her to so marry another man in order to become permissible for the former husband for no fault of hers.

Qur'an brought about reform in this form of divorce and required divorces to be spaced at one month's interval and to pronounce one divorce at a time after checking that she was not in a state of menstruation. And he could take back his wife before one month was over and, if not, he could pronounce divorce a second time and wait for another month until she was in a state of purity. He could either take her back or finally pronounce third divorce which would be irrevocable.

The Prophet also denounced the practice of *hallalah* and forbade it. After pronouncing third divorce she could marry another person of her choice and if at all, for some legitimate reason, he divorced her (not for making *hallalah*) then she was also free to marry her former husband. These instructions are specified in the verse 2:229. It says:

> "The divorce is allowed twice. So either remain together equitably, or part ways with kindness. It is not lawful for you to take back anything you have given the women unless you fear that they will not uphold God's limits, then there is no sin for what is given back."
>
> "So if he divorces her again, then she will not be lawful from him until she has married another husband. If the other husband divorces her, then they are not blamed for coming back together if they think they will uphold God's limits;" (2:230)

The Prophet (PBUH) strongly denounced combining three divorces in one sitting instead of spacing them over three months. There was great wisdom in spacing them over three months in that if a divorce was pronounced in a state of anger or in haste, there was whole month available for friends to intervene or arrange for arbitration and bring about reconciliation and again one more month was available if divorce was pronounced second time also. And by making it obligatory to pronounce divorce only after menstrual period was over, there was wisdom that man, after his anger was over, could cohabit with her if she is in a state of purity and thus take her back.

Thus in the matter of divorce also abuses were removed and women's status improved considerably. However, after the Prophet, when Islam spread to parts of the world far and wide and non-Arab societies and cultures became part of the Islamic world, women's status came for a shocking set back. Women in feudal societies like Persia and Byzantine Empire had very low status and people who converted to Islam from these areas entered Islam with their own cultural capital, heritage, customs and traditions.

Thus women, to begin with, in these areas relapsed to low status as they were found in during pre-Islamic days. What was worse, many Islamic jurists (*fuqaha*) who interpreted Qur'anic verses or used *ahadith* came from non-Arab background and their formulations resulted in lowering the status of women. Not only that, the capital of the Caliphate shifted from Medina to Syria (Damascus) which was part of Byzantine Empire during the Umayyad period. And when the Abbasid captured power it shifted from Damascus to Baghdad, a former part of Persian Empire.

Thus all eminent *Ulama* and jurists also flocked to these capitals and also due to access to higher Islamic education in capital cities new jurists and *Ulama* from among non-Arabs came into existence with a thoroughly feudal outlook. Women's rights received setback in this feudal environment. The Arabs themselves were not ready to accept revolutionary change in women's status and give them equal status. They too had suppressed women for centuries.

As in Sunni Islam *qiyas* and *ijma'* (i.e. analogical reasoning and consensus) played important role, both Arab and non-Arab jurists and *Ulama* developed consensus on the lower status of women. As Qur'an was not easy to tackle in this respect, another floodgate was opened i.e. that of *hadith*. Qur'an could not be tampered with but *ahadith* could be fabricated with some efforts and then Qur'anic verses interpreted in the light of these *ahadith*. This proved to be very useful tool for the jurists with patriarchal outlook.

For example, there is no mention of child marriage in the Qur'an as marriage is civil contract but in all these cultures child marriage was prevalent. Thus *ahadith* was fabricated that Prophet (PBUH) married Aisha when she was seven years old and marriage was consummated when she was nine. Modern researches clearly show that this *hadith* is far from genuine and appeared almost 300 years after the Prophet's death. But since marriage was a civil contract the jurists also had to concede right of option for puberty (*khiyar al-bulugh*) i.e. she could accept or reject marriage on becoming adult.

We have already discussed the verse 4:34 which has been mainly interpreted with the help of *ahadith* and even beating of women justified which was not in keeping with the status Qur'an gives to women. Her conjugal rights also suffered a setback in the light of such *ahadith* and entire Qur'an discourse on women which was right-based was reversed, as pointed out above and became duty-based.

The triple divorce in one sitting which the Prophet had so strongly denounced was also restored and in many cases it became the main form of divorce, though the Prophet had clearly indicated that the best form of divorce (*talaq-i-ahsan*) was to pronounce one divorce and to leave her with kindness after a month after giving her dues (*mata'*) and maintenance during the *iddah* period.

Though the Prophet also had denounced in no uncertain terms the practice of *hallalah,* ittoo came back into practice and sometimes even the *Qazi* would offer his services to make a woman *hallalah* i.e. marry her for a day, consummate the marriage and get her a divorce so that her former husband could marry her again. Also, the patriarchal philosophy that a woman is supposed to be obedient to her father, then to her husband and look after them and serve them became widely accepted philosophy.

In one of the tracts written in Persia (*Perfumed Garden*) in 3rd century, *hijra* it was said that an ideal Muslim wife will always be at the service of her husband and would not step out of the house without his permission even if her father was seriously ill or on his deathbed. And that she would smile to keep her husband happy even if she is in serious trouble.

Then from India, Maulana Ashraf Thanavi, a great *Alim* and jurist from India wrote a book in Urdu called *Bihishti Zaiwar* (i.e. *Jewellery of Paradise*) which deals with Islamic behaviour of women and is given as part of dowry to every Muslim woman in North and Central India so that she behaves as an ideal wife and mother and daughter. The Maulana's views, to say the least, are thoroughly soaked in feudal culture and yet these views are considered Islamic.

Ashraf Thanavi is even against women acquiring literacy, much less acquiring learning. He feels that if women are made literate they would write love letters and would be corrupted. What a reason to keep women illiterate! It is very close to the Persian tract *The Perfumed Garden* referred to above. It is its almost Indian version and several generations of Muslim women in North India grew up reading this book. It is a best example of how Qur'anic teachings were distorted by Muslims in their own cultural milieu and yet all these practices were considered as Islamic.

Women's Status in Contemporary Muslim World

The Muslim world today is facing two major problems viz., gender justice and terrorism. The problem of terrorism is limited to certain areas but that of gender justice has become almost universal in the Islamic world. Saudi society happens to be most restrictive of women's freedom and empowerment, followed by some other Muslim countries though one must concede that changes are taking place and situation is not entirely static.

It would be interesting to discuss why Islamic world tends to be so behind in giving equal status to women despite Qur'anic teachings to the contrary. Generally even scholars and academics ascribe it to Islam and its teachings, as these academics are not well versed in Qur'an and Islamic studies. They happen to be either social scientists, activists and observers or develop stereotypes and prejudices generally prevalent in the society and judge things from these stereotypes.

In fact, the causes of Muslim women's backwardness are socio-cultural and political. First, we would like to throw some light on socio-cultural aspects which are most importantand which account for major hindrance towards change. We will then discuss political causes also.

In fact the Muslim world, especially the Middle East is located very strategically for the western colonial interests. The colonising countries of the west, especially France and England, supported monarchs and dictators in the Middle East and sustained feudal culture and encouraged feudal elite along with religious elite. These feudal lords too, in turn, supported conservative *Ulama* to prevent any progressive social change.

Egypt was the only exception where there was some intellectual ferment thanks to some western educated elite like Ahmad Amin and also a progressive religious cleric like Muhammad Abduh (1849-1905) who spent a few years in France during his exile from Egypt by the British. Muhammad Abduh later devoted himself to the cause of education in Egypt and rose to become Chancellor of Al-Azhar University and also the Chief Mufti of Egypt. He was committed to women's rights and tried to persuade his people for progressive reform and women's education and did make some dent. However, on the whole society was too enmeshed in traditional socio-cultural institutions to accept change on wider scale.

The condition of other Muslim countries was worse and even poverty-ridden with high rates of illiteracy. Before discovery of oil, Middle East was immersed in poverty and illiteracy and colonialism remained a great hindrance in bringing about any socio-economic changes. Later on Iraq, where Baathist (socialist) revolution took place, underwent some revolutionary changes and Baathists were committed to empowering women. Hence till the advent of Saddam Husain's regime women enjoyed gender equalityin Iraq. However, now after US invasion situation has become much more complex with increasing influence of Shi'ah clerics.

In Iran, the Shah regime, however politically repressive and reactionary, was in favour of gender equality and women, especially from the upper classes, took to westernisation and Shah even abolished *hijab*. However, such fiats do not bring about real change in the society until there is thorough change in socio-economic structures from below. The rural areas in Iran continued to be quite conservative and under strong influence of feudal lords or conservative clergy in alliance with feudal land-holders.

In India where Muslims are a large minority happen to be poorest and most illiterate even slipping below *Dalits* in poverty and illiteracy. Most of them are converts from artisan classes and castes and even today a bulk of the Muslims belong to these socio-economic categories. The feudal elite migrated to Pakistan after partition but the poorer masses chose to remain in India.

Political Factor

Since western powers formed alliances with authoritarian regimes in the Islamic world, democratic revolution was prevented. When Iran experienced revolutionary change and oil industry was nationalised in 1952 under Prime Minister Fatimi, the CIA staged a coup with the help of Ayatullahs and other clerics and brought back Shah again. Thus it was CIA, for the oil interests that authoritarian Shah regime was restored.

In Saudi Arabia too monarchy is surviving with the help of America which has established its military base there along with other Gulf countries like Kuwait, Qatar etc. where Sheikhs rule with US support and suppress all democratic freedoms. Egypt too is ruled by highly suppressive regime of Hosni Mubarak who has support of not only US but also of Israel and human rights is considered a dirty word and human rights activists put in jail accusing them of receiving foreign funding.

Because of authoritative regimes in the Muslim world, clergy gets greater political importance as they can be relied upon to provide religious legitimacy to such regimes and the clergy, in order to strengthen its religious influence, oppose any change and insist on strict application of *Shari'ah* laws. The best example is of Pakistan where Zia-ul-Haq, after establishing his military dictatorship announced 'Islamisation of Pakistan' and enforced strict *Shari'ah* laws with the help of mullahs.

Afghanistan is another country which is in a gender mess because of politics than anything else. The Taliban apply tribal laws which are worse than even *Shari'ah* laws and suppress women's rights and burn their schools and colleges. They want women to be confined strictly to home and bear children and serve the family.

Though Malaysia is economically and educationally much better off compared to other countries, it lacks genuine democracy which is manipulated by the Malay leadership from above and seek alliance with religious leadership and bows before its dictates. The Malays who form the majority (about 60 per cent) are comparatively more backward and some states ruled by princes cling to traditional laws and Islamic laws and thus Malay women too enjoy limited rights. The clergy vehemently opposes any change.

Thus we see politics plays very important role, especially politics where politicians seek legitimation through alliance with clergy who extract their own price. But there are more enlightened rulers too who have brought changes to empower women like in Morocco, Tunisia, Jordan and to some extent in Kuwait where women extracted some basic rights as they had joined struggle against Iraq when it was invaded by Saddam Husain's forces.

Even in Saudi, as female students far outnumber male students in universities, some changes are taking place and women are raising their voices and even debating with the conservative clergy for their rights. Though progress is extremely slow and tardy, nevertheless it is taking place. Women can't even drive cars in that country.

Codification of Personal Law

Many secularists and rationalists reject religion-based laws known as personal laws (*ahwal al-shakhsiyah*) altogether and want them to be replaced by secular laws. However, as far as Muslims are concerned it would remain a pipe dream for a long time to come. Their socio-cultural conditions are not suitable at all for such drastic change. What is the way out?

The way out is codification of *Shari'ah* laws. Even the traditional *Shari'ah* laws are based on concept of justice. Justice in the Qur'an is so fundamental that even a most conservative interpretation of the Qur'an could not ignore it. What codification has to do is to apply it more rigorously and in the spirit of Qur'an. Also, though many *ahadith* are anti-women, there are quite a few which are in keeping with the Qur'anic spirit. Our Centre is attempting to codify these *Shari'ah* laws so as to create gender equality within the Qur'anic frame-work

The codification applies to laws pertaining to marriage, divorce, inheritance, custody of children in case of divorce, maintenance during persistence of marriage and after divorce. These are most important areas of personal law.

Marriage

Marriage **is, as already pointed out above, a civil contract in Islam.** What is important therefore, is to enforce it rigorously making it a legal requirement. The *Qazi* or one who performs *nikah* must obtain specific consent of the bride herself in person in the presence of two reliable witnesses. The consent should specify the *mehr* amount (in currency, gold or silver or property with all details of the property) and whatever other conditions she wants to stipulate like not taking any other wife or delegated right to divorce (*talaq-i-tafwiz*) if he violates any of these conditions. All the details shall be entered in the *nikah* form and signed by bride and bridegroom, two witnesses and the *qazi* himself.

Mehr

If there is any deferred payment is involved it should be properly specified along with the time-frame within which it shall be paid and also how much will be paid immediately. Also, it is proposed that minimum *mehr* amount to be three months' earning of the bride groom and maximum could be without any limit, of course depending on the capacity of the bridegroom. *Mehr* also could be in terms of gold or silver or shares or fixed deposits. *Mehr* in terms of gold or silver is preferable as inflation erodes the value of currency. It could also be in terms of property.

Polygamy

Polygamy should not be normally permissible, as even in the Qur'an it is allowed in certain exceptional circumstances, especially to help widows and orphans and subject to condition of rigorous justice (see 4:3 and 4:129). Either the bride can stipulate that the man cannot take any other wife at all during the persistence of the marriage with her or if she agrees for a co-wife, it should be subject to conditions such as capacity to maintain two wives with equal amount of maintenance and spending equal time and paying equal attention to both.

Also, there should be reasons listed for taking another wife like (a) it is medically proved that the first wife is unable to give birth to a child and she allows her husband to take another wife for child; (b) doctors certify that the first wife is suffering from terminal disease or some such disease that make cohabitation impossible. But even then, the first wife's consent should be obtained and the *Qazi* will satisfy himself that the husband will be able to maintain both the wives justly as specified above. Polygamy should not be treated as husband's right as is clear from the Qur'anic verses also.

Divorce

Most of the Muslims in India (*Sunni Hanfis* and *Shafi'is* in south) practise triple divorce in one sitting which becomes absolute and even if he later repents he cannot take her back unless she marries someone else. This form of divorce should be banned and only *talaq-i-ahsan* i.e. one divorce should be pronounced and when one month is over either he should take her back or let her go by making divorce effective and two witnesses should be present when divorce takes place. No other form of divorce should be admissible.

He will pay the remaining part of the *mehr* (*mehr muwajjal*), if any, along with other dues or jewellery or dowry items etc. and what the Qur'an calls *mata'* (a onetime consolidated amount which should be substantial so as to help her in need or in distress) along with three month's maintenance for the *iddah* period. Divorce should be in writing and with signatures of two witnesses and the *Qazi.* Oral divorce should not be admissible.

Before a divorce is finally pronounced, the *Qazi* should appoint two arbitrators (*hakamain*) as per Qur'anic requirement who will try to bring about reconciliation and if such attempt fails, the husband should pronounce divorce once for the period of *iddah* (three months) and after *iddah* is over the divorce will take place. Written divorce should be made compulsory.

Khula' and Dissolution of Marriage

A woman should be able to go for *khula'* by approaching a *Qazi* if she is unwilling to live with her husband. If she asks for *khula'* there should be no need for husband's consent as the Prophet (PBUH) granted *khula'* to Jamilah without consulting her husband as she insisted on it. In case of *khula'* she will return the *mehr* amount or property which she had received from her husband but if the husband waives it off, it will be better for him. If he is not ready to waive it off she must return the dower.

Dissolution of Marriage

A Muslim woman should also have an option of dissolution of her marriage as per the Muslim Marriage Dissolution Act of 1939. All the grounds for dissolution have been specified in the Act and need not be repeated here. This Act also has given her substantial relief and is to her great advantage.

Inheritance

As pointed out above, a woman's share in inheritance will be half that of her brother and we have explained the reasons. Often she does not get even half, either because she does not know about it at all or the brothers take her signature on papers on some pretext or the other. Or, even if she knows she does not want to quarrel with them as she thinks that if is divorced she may have to knock on their door again.

What is needed is to make a woman aware of her rights and if triple divorce is banned and if divorce is no longer unilateral as it is today, she may not have to knock on brothers' doors and she may feel more empowered economically too. Secondly, one of the reasons as to why she gets only half that of her brothers was that she was a passive economic agent and did not contribute to the family wealth and income.

Now a Muslim woman often works and is quite active as an economic agent and helps increase family income and wealth. She should either get full share in inheritance like her brother or her contribution be recorded separately and given her at the time of marriage. Also, now there is trend, and Iran has taken a lead in this respect, to take into count her domestic chores, treating it as work converting it into wages. Had she not performed these chores, the husband or father would have had to employ a servant. In Iran, even at the time of divorce, she is compensated for her domestic chores depending on the number of years she remained a wife. It is quite an important step for her empowerment.

And if for some reason a woman remains unwed, it should be made obligatory for her father to make provision for one-third of his wealth to be willed in her favour so that she is compensated for the maintenance she otherwise would have received as a wife or home maker. Such a provision should also be made up to one-third if a son predeceases his father. It has already been done in most of the Muslim countries.

Conclusion

It would thus be seen that there is enough scope within Islamic *Shari'ah* to bring about changes so as to ensure gender justice, justice being a very important ingredient in *Shari'ah* laws. Since the changes proposed are all within Qur'anic framework and in no way contradict *Shari'ah* law but only tries to remove certain injustices that have crept in due, not principles or fundamentals but to cultural and customary practices.

In fact, as already pointed out, if Muslims had carried out Qur'anic injunctions without adding their cultural practices the Islamic world would have been a great pioneer in ushering gender equality in the world. However, feudalism destroyed, in practice, the revolutionary spirit of Qur'an.

Shari'ah, Women and Traditional Society

There was a disturbing news of a Muslim woman Mukhtaran Mai in Pakistani part of Punjab having been raped by men of her village by the order of Panchayat. Another woman called Imrana from Bijnor district of U.P. in India was raped by her own father-in law and the village Pachayat at the instance of a local mullah asked her to marry her own father-in-law and treat her husband as her 'son'. These are absolutely shocking rulings in the name of Shari'ah.

Similarly few persons raped Mukhtaran Mai in Pakistan as a result of Panchyat's decision as her brother had done something wrong. These persons were released by the Punjab High Court though later on an appeal filed by Mukhtaran Mai Supreme Court of Pakistan again ordered these alleged rapists to be rearrested. What is shocking is that the government of an Islamic Re-public of Pakistan black listed her so as to disallow her to travel abroad and on public hue and cry removed her name from the black list but took away her passport. Again under pressure from human rights activists passport was returned to her.

In Mukhtaran Mai's case whole state machinery was ranged against a helpless woman to deny her justice. All this raises important question: what is the place of women in Muslim societies? The Muslim men never tire of repeating that Islam gave women rights and human dignity they deserve and also keep her wrapped up in veil to protect her chastity and on the other, readily condone such disgraceful treatment in the society. In almost all Muslim countries (I would hesitate to call them 'Islamic' countries as usually they are referred to) women is treated as secondary to men or even worse. The Taliban even denied her right to education and closed down all schools meant for girls and disallowed them to work and earn their livings even when there was no man member in the house.

The Saudis do not allow women to drive cars and deny them right to vote even in Municipal elections. In Kuwait women won right to vote recently after a long drawn struggle. In Pakistan women are more often punished for rape and men go scot free as she cannot produce required four witnesses. Also, we find in Sindh what is known as 'karo kari according to which she is killed if she is found talking to a stranger of the other sex. In Bangla Desh the village mullahs do not allow women even to pillion ride with her husband or some male relative. They issue *fatwas* if women work with some NGOs for their living.

They dub all activities outside home as 'un-Islamic' and issues *fatwas*. Mukhraran Mai was raped at the instance of village panchayat simply because her brother was guilty. Such punishment cannot be given in Islam even if she was guilty of some serious crime, much less for what her brother did. Yet not only the government remained silent spectator but even took steps against her.

The question is whether the Muslim *'ulama* consider all this as Islamic (which no one even with elementary knowledge of Islam would uphold as Islamic) or connive at these horrific acts against women because they are men. In India too all Hanafi and Shafi'i *'ulama* consider triple divorce as bid'ah (i.e. sinful) and yet while holding such divorce valid according to their school of law never ever launched campaign against it and never tried to educate Muslim men that they should avoid this form of divorce as it is sinful and they should resort to other forms of divorce like talaq-i-sunnah or talaq-i-hasan or ahsan which were approved by the Qur'an or the Prophet's sunnah. Whenever the case of triple divorce came to them they would decree that his divorced wife has now become haram (prohibited) to him.

We can conclude from all this happening in Muslim countries that to our *'ulama* are more committed to patriarchy and patriarchal values than to Islam. In North West Frontier province where Muttahida Majlis-e-Amal, an Islamic Front, has won elections and formed the government, maximum number of such cases take place and yet these *'ulama* who agitated for enforcing shari'ah rule in this province keep silent when such atrocities are committed against women. Even most conservative shari'ah law would not approve of shooting down a woman if she is found to have relations with any stranger and yet *'ulama* keep quiet at such incidents and do not try to educate men against such atrocities.

Thus the commitment to Islam is skin deep when it comes to women's rights. The shari'ah itself is a result of patriarchal interpretation of the Holy Qur'an and even patriarchally loaded shari'ah also is ignored when it comes to persecuting women and depriving them of their rights. There is nothing in the Qur'an which prohibits women from dealing with men other than those who are prohibited to her for marriage and yet in several Muslim societies she is not allowed to deal with them in any manner in the name of Islam.

Thus all of us Muslims need to seriously reflect upon condition of women in Muslim societies. The Qur'an gave her all the rights which modern societies have given her in the beginning of twentieth century and yet she never enjoyed these rights except for a short period when the Prophet (PBUH) was alive and until the Caliphate lasted for 30 years. With the Umayyad period she began to loose her rights until she was completely subjugated and became confined to four walls of her house and this began to be considered as her highest virtue.

It is now that women are getting educated and becoming aware of their Islamic rights and challenging medieval interpretations laded with patriarchal values and agitating for their rights. In Saudi Arabia too women are challenging their conventional status and asking for more rights and Saudi Government is grudgingly responding to women's demands. In Saudi Arabia women graduates from universities constitute about 50 per cent and hence their enhanced awareness.

In western countries, now Muslim women have taken yet another step - leading the mixed congregational prayer and delivering Friday sermon. After Amina Wadood now another Muslim woman from New York Pamela Taylor led mixed congregational prayer in Canada on 1 st July 2005 well, it may be too radical for men in Asian ad African countries but it is undoubtedly an irreversible trend. What is considered 'unIslamic' at one stage by our *ulama* becomes perfectly Islamic after a few decades, or even after a few years, in some cases.

Now a large number of Muslims live in non-Muslim countries and face new dilemmas every day and for which there are no answers in conventional shari'ah books or they conflict with law of the land or modern social ethos. This also necessitates a serious reflection on the state of affairs of Muslim law by committed scholars to Islam. The traditional *ulama* are by and large unfit for the job. Only those who have in depth knowledge of the Qur'an, *hadith* and early Islamic history and process of evolution of shari'ah law can do justice to Muslim women's question in modern times.

The blanket assumption that shari'ah is divine and hence unchangeable has to be contested. This is the popular view in the Muslim world. At the cost of repetition I would like to assert that such a view is misplaced. Shari'ah law is a result of man interpretation of divine injunctions and it took several centuries to evolve. The law makers faced new problems and new situations and provided for it through analogical reasoning (*qiyas*) and consensus (*ijma*') among '*ulama* for those problems for which they did not find any answers in divine sources. This is the reason why there are differences in various schools of law (madhahib) like Hanafi, Shafi'I, Maliki, Hanbali, Ja'fari, Isma'ili, Zaidi, Zahiri and so on. There were even more schools which did not survive.

This became possible for two main reasons: absence of the concept of priesthood in Islam and the Qur'anic doctrine of freedom of conscience (2: The early jurists were very well aware of this and hence developed different schools using different interpretations of the divine sources or using different a*hadith* (reports of Prophet's sayings). Some used one *hadith* whole others rejected it in favour of the other. Or some used one Qur'anic injunction and some *hadith* giving its interpretation while others used different interpretation using some other *hadith*.

In some matters, one Imam was more liberal while in other matter the other imam took more favourable view for women. That is why many modernists and even traditional *'ulama* suggest that one can borrow from another school if ones own school creates problem for a woman. This is what could have been done in case of Imrana affair also. As the Hanafi school maintains that even in case rape by her father or father- in-law a woman cannot retain her marital tie with her husband one could have taken help of Shafi'i school which takes different view.

Again the problem is with our traditional mullahs that they find nothing unnatural in taking such positions which conflict with modern societal values and enhanced awareness of women. The village panchayat consulted a local maulavi who with his half backed knowledge of shari'ah law even decreed that *Imrana* should marry the rapist father-in-law and treat her own husband as her 'son'. This was beyond belief and utterly shocking that any such *fatwa* can be issued. But then our rural areas are far behind in special matters. Here one should not take religious but sociological view of the matter. This is what happens in backward social milieu.

Everyone will agree that to issue any injunction in the name of shari'ah is a highly responsible job. The mullahs in rural areas have half backed knowledge and give their opinion more on the basis of their bias then on the basis of proper knowledge. In fact the Mullah consulted based his opinion on the Qur'anic verse 24:3 which says, "The adulterer cannot have sexual relations with any but an adulteress or an idolatress and the adulteress, none can have sexual relations with her but an adulterer or an idolater: and it is forbidden to believers."

Since in the Imrana case father-in-law had intercourse or adultery with her it was decreed by the maulavi that she now live with her father-in- law and treat her husband as her son an opinion which was totally wrong and immoral. According to the Qur'anic verse both should be guilty of adultery and here Imrana is not guilty of adultery but victim of rape. This verse cannot apply to her at all. Moreover this verse is of the general nature and does not deal with daughter-in-law, father-in-law situation. One will have to think twice before applying it in such a situation.

Now question arises about the *fatwa*' issued by Darul 'Uloom Deoband which is entirely of different category. One cannot say that this *fatwa* was issued by someone having no knowledge or half baked knowledge. According to this *fatwa* she should separate from her husband. After adultery by her father-in-law she can no more live with her husband as he happens to be his son and according to the Qur'an prohibiting marriage with the wife of the father. The Qur'anic verse says "And marry not women whom your father married, except what has already passed. This surely is indecent and hateful; and it is an evil way." (4:22)

This verse obviously refers to the *jahiliyyah* (pre-Islamic) practice of marrying father's wives other than ones own mother. It was indeed a hateful practice. It appears it was on this basis that Darul Ulum Deoband issued this *fatwa*h. This is also based on Imam Abu Hanifa's ruling that when a woman has sex after marriage with her husband she becomes mother of all his children and so can't marry his son, even though that son may be from previous marriage.

The Darul Ulum *fatwah* may have taken both - above Qur'anic verse as well as Imam Abu Hanifa's ruling into account and issued the edict. But a *fatwa*h in favour or against any person could be issued not only on general rulings but after through investigation of the case concerned. In *Imrana's* case it was rape, not marriage or sex with consent. How such ruling can apply to her case?

Only thing that can be said in favour of Deoband is that *fatwah* was issued without any knowledge of a specific case. One, however, does not know whether with the knowledge of the specific case same *fatwa*h would have been issued or not. It is only a matter of conjecture. It is also to be noted that Imam Shafi'i differs from Imam Abu Hanifa in his ruling on similar case. According to Imam Shafi'I what is haram and impure i.e. rape cannot annul what is halal (legitimate) and pure i.e. relationship. This marriage which is legitimate relationship cannot be annulled by an act of rape.

Thus in no case *Imrana's* marriage with her husband can be dissolved just because she was raped by her father-in-law. Even if *fatwah* is issued according to Hanafi ruling, in view of gravity of the case (a woman is married with five children) and as far as possible such a long established perfectly legitimate relationship should not be dissolved specially when it is case of rape on unwilling woman.

Now the personal law board's inquiry that no such rape has taken place and it is likely to be false allegation due to property dispute between son and father, is an altogether different matter. It should be left for the courts to decide, no such hurried conclusion should be drawn on wither side.

We are more concerned with the *fatwa* rather than allegations and counter-allegations from both sides. Let us assume the rape took place and then only we can discuss the merit of the *fatwa*. My point is that in modern times one has to bear in mind the rights of women. One cannot simply quote a ruling given more than thousand years ago to decide a case in twenty first century. For justice to be done one has to keep concrete circumstances into mind.

All women issues unfortunately get politicised and becomes a game in minority-majority politics. Majority communal leaders rush in to demand uniform civil code in any case related to minority women, be it Shah Bano case or Imrana case, the minority community leaders also rush with equal haste to accuse majority community of being anti-Muslim and showing false sympathy for Muslim women. The male leadership of both the communities do not care whether justice is being done to the woman victim or not.

Women thus invariably become victim of male politics, particularly so in South Asia. It is therefore highly desirable that one should rise above such considerations and consider women as dignified as men and accord them full dignity honour and rights. It is unfortunate that Qur'an gave women equal status but in all Muslim societies, as pointed out above, they were denied their rightful place and their rights were taken away in the name of Islam.

Men want to retain their dominant position in any case. During Shah Bano movement referring to the verse 2:241 it was maintained by some *'ulama* that even one time provision was obligatory only on pious Muslims referring to the word muttaqin and not on all Muslims. This shows strong bias against women of their own community. Thus it is men who give enough opportunity to anti-Islamic forces to ridicule treatment of 'Islam' towards women. In fact it is men to blame for such interpretations of the Holy Qur'an.

Many verses in the Qur'an were revealed when believers men or women came to the Prophet (PBUH) asking certain questions and revelation brought answers in that particular context. The whole asbab *al-nuzul* (occasions of revelation) literature is there on the subject and many shar'i positions were based on such revelations. But now keeping these asbab *al-nuzul* in mind we have to reinterpreted these Qur'anic verses.

We have to go by Qur'anic values rather than certain verses relating to concrete historical conditions then prevailing. The most central value in the Qur'an is justice, followed by ihsan and *rahmah* (compassion) and hikmah (wisdom). These values will override all juristic decisions or rulings of the great *imams*. Taking contemporary conditions into account one must apply these values.

If this method is followed then in the Imrana case no such *fatwa* should have been issued compelling her to dissolve her marriage. As in the case of Shah Bano (Shah Bano was compelled to disown the Supreme Court judgement in her favour and declare that she would stick to shar'ah rather than accept Supreme Court ruling) *Imrana* was also compelled to say she would follow shari'ah ruling and be prepared to dissolve her marriage.

It is vitally necessary to train our *'ulama* in modern social sciences and muftis in modern principles of jurisprudence so that they can be more careful in issuing ruling rather than simply repeating what this or that Imam said. One should also thoroughly understand how the great imams applied the principles usul *al-fiqh* in their own circumstances and on what basis they applied those principles to their own circumstances and how modern jurisprudence evolved and how certain fundamental values were applied to modern conditions. This comparative study will immensely benefit our 'ulama, particularly those who deal with shar'i rulings.

But even the higher madrasas of learning only repeat what was evolved during early period of Islam. And this despite the fact that Holy Prophet specifically permitted ijtihad (intellectual efforts to re-apply Islamic principles to new conditions). Even the great *imams* like Abu Hanifa and Shafi'i faced new situations and challenges and they exerted themselves to apply Qur'anic provisions to these new situations and looked for a*hadith* to find answers and when they could not, they used analogical reasoning to find answers.

The whole process needs to be imitated today rather than their rulings, to find answers to modern problems. One will have to clearly identify what is fundamental and what is incidental to the situation and then decide on the ruling. In Indian subcontinent and specially in India there is urgent need to codify Islamic law as it exists today. Unfortunately our personal law board is not even ready to codify whereas during the British period *'ulama* like Maulana Ashraf Thanvi codified the Islamic law pertaining to dissolution of marriage which gave so much relief to Muslim women at that time. The MPLB should work on codification of Muslim personal law and that itself will give great relief to Muslim women.

Now Muslim women are becoming more aware due to spread of modern education and they are challenging all the decisions of Muslim personal law board and they have challenged the present *fatwa* too. It is a healthy sign and one hopes now women will not accept male domination in the name of Islam and will work for realisation of truly Qur'anic status of equality with men. We have to replace earlier juristic rulings with modern laws based more on Qur'an than on earlier opinions.

France Needs Pluralism

The utterances of French President Sarkozy that *burqa* will be banned in France and that wearing veil was not religion but torture and punishment for women, have caused great stir among Muslims and lot is being written in the media on this subject. As it was expected most Muslims, men and women had come out in support of wearing veil and was defending it in various ways theological as well as non-theological. Earlier French Government had banned wearing veil or scarf over head by Muslim girls in schools. The Sikhs also suffered as their children were banned from wearing turban in schools. At that time also there was strong reaction from various sections. Sikhs were also greatly agitated and Sikhs from various European countries and even from North America demonstrated on the streets of Paris but nothing came out of it. There are two things involved here one, the question of democratic rights and two, theological arguments. As far as democratic rights are concerned all Muslims as well as non-Muslims, should thoroughly debate this issue and as far as theological arguments are concerned the Muslim theologians as well as Muslim intellectuals should equally thoroughly debate it and see whether covering of whole body from head to toe including the face is divine ordained or is cultural and patriarchal practice being justified in the name of religion.

First, let us examine the issue in the light of democratic rights. One perspective in this regard is that it is democratic right of an individual what to wear and what not to wear. A government cannot dictate citizens in matters of what to wear and what to eat. The French Government, if at all it bans *burqa* (still the issue is under discussion and a parliamentary committee is examining whether to ban or not to ban), it will go against democratic norms and practices.

In this regard I would like to point out that countries like France are yet to come to terms with pluralism and multi-culturalism. Europe, throughout centuries has been mono-cultural and mono-religious (Catholics and Protestants are offshoots of Christianity and both are embedded in western culture) and it was migration from Afro-Asian countries, mainly former colonies to Europe after Second World War when de-colonisation began, European countries experienced pluralism and multiculturalism. The argument by French President that wearing Burqa, a religious apparel cannot be permitted in 'secular' France is based on this mono-cultural practice of secularism. France too, is multi-cultural today as many African Christians and Muslims from its former French colonies have come to France but unlike U.K. France has really not come to terms with multi-culturalism. French culture really reigns supreme. It is intolerant of other cultural practices though tolerance is great democratic value. It is surprising how intolerant French Government is towards other cultures and religions.

A truly democratic nation would respect other cultural and religious practices and would not treat its own citizens as aliens and ban their practices. If some Muslim women decide to wear *burqa* covering their bodies from head to toe, it is their decision even if it tortures them. Indian Court has also approved of right of Jain monks to go on fast unto death as their religious practice though it involves extreme torture to the body. After all they are torturing themselves, not others and particularly because it is their religious belief. Thus French government will be better advised if it becomes more tolerant of other cultures and other religious practices.

Now coming to Islamic theological argument it is not correct to believe that Qur'an prescribes covering of women's body from head to toe and also the face. What Qur'an advises is not to display their adornments publicly and the word used in verse 24:31 is zeenah (adornment), not veil (*hijab*). And the words of the verse are also advisory, not obligatory. It is better if they do not display their adornment (zeenah) publicly but they can do so privately in their own homes and before their own people, like parents, parents in-law, uncles, other women and children.

There is no mention of *hijab* in the sense of covering face in Qur'an at all. All Muslim jurists and theologians agree that according to verse 4:31 women can keep their face open and apply collyrium to their eyes and can also keep their hands open and wear rings in their fingers. However, they insist on covering their heads and hence in Iran women are officially required to cover their heads with what they call chador but can keep their face open. This verse also asks women to cover their breasts.

This clearly shows that in pre-Islamic Arab society women were keeping their breasts at least partly, if not wholly, open as many women in western societies do today. Also, there is debate between theologians whether this verse refers to external adornment or beauty of the body itself, which would necessitate covering of whole body from head to toe so as to hide the beauty of the body.

The other view is that it refers to only external adoration, not the beauty of the body and this view is supported by what is said in the end of the verse i.e. "Let them not strike their feet so that the adornment that they hide may be known." Many Arab women used to wear anklets and strike their feet to attract attention to their adornment which the Qur'an advises them not to do.

This verse 24:31 makes an exception for covering and says, "..do not display their adornment except what appears thereof ". Throwing light on this exception Tabari, one of the noted early commentator on the Qur'an says what she may not cover under this exception (1) adornment of dress or the clothes that a woman wears i.e. she need not cover the clothes she wears; (2) also she is not required to cover adornment like collyrium, rings, bracelets and her face. In support of his view Tabari also says while praying a woman does not cover her face and her hands up to her elbow while she covers rest of her body.

There is also a *hadith* the Prophet (PBUH) told Asma, his wife ?Aisha's sister, when she appeared wearing thin clothes, "O Asma, when woman attains her puberty it is not proper that any part of her body should be seen except this, and he pointed to his face and hands." (Sunan Abu Daud 31:30). This *hadith* settles it conclusively that face and hands up to elbow need not be covered. However, the *burqa* which covers woman from head to toe including face is widely spread in Islamic world. What is its origin? It is certainly more cultural than religious. One eminent scholar and judge Amir

Ali who wrote extensively on Islam and Islamic history maintains that it originated much after the Prophet i.e. around 7th century *hijra* (13th century A.D.) that is after sack of Baghdad. It was unknown during the early period of Islam.

However, another eminent Islamic historian Maulana Shibli who was also Justice Ameer Ali's contemporary challenged this position and wrote, in his article on Purdah that it existed in pre-Islamic Arab society and Islam simply accepted it. Whatever the position one thing is absolutely clear that Qur'an does not recommend covering of whole body from head to toe, nor it requires covering of face. And whether *Shibli* is right or Justice Ameer Ali, it became part of Islamic culture. Today many Muslim women wear it out of social or family compulsion and many wear it voluntarily as a mark of Islamic tradition. There are other reasons too. For many purdah is mark of Muslim identity but then it is also justified as protective of woman's dignity. These women say they feel quite safe and have nothing to fear and no one can molest or rape them. They are taken as serious and no nonsense women. May be to some extent but women can be much more safer if proper social environment is there and enforcement of law and order is stricter.

Many women wear *burqa* as a matter of tradition and some under family compulsion. These women also say it is not in any way hindrance for their work. Well, may be it is rationalisation of a tradition. Also, sometimes what appears to be out of choice may not really be so. Choice is also dictated by the environment we live in. In consumer society too we feel are choosing out of free will but it is more often our choice is dictated by high pressure advertisement of products.

Cultural traditions also exert silent pressure and what appears to be 'choice' is really not free choice. Whatever the case *burqa* or *hijab* for Muslim women in their own cultural environment is not really burden or chain as it appears to those totally alien to this tradition. Westerners are shocked because their cultural traditions are radically different. The contemporary western culture revels in exposing larger part of woman's body than hiding it. Western tradition is just the opposite. In my opinion neither woman's body should be exposed nor completely covered. They should be neither treated as object of man's lust nor something to be hidden or imprisoned. She should dress to maintain her dignity and individuality as a free agent that is what is most desirable and that is what her status is in Qur'an. Her sexuality should neither be feared nor used as lust but celebrated as a divine gift.

References

1. See, Asghar Ali Engineer (1975), *The Origin and Development of Islam* (Orient Longman, Delhi).
2. *Ibid.*
3. Muhammad Asad (1980), *The Message of the Qur'an* (Dar al-Andalus, Gibraltar), comments on verse 33:4, pp. 639. f.n.3.
4. Muhammad Asad, *Ibid* pp. 933, f.n.4.
5. See, Asghar Ali Engineer (1980), *The Rights of Women in Islam*, Chapter on "Status of Women during Jahiliyah" (Sterling Publishers, Delhi).
6. See Asghar Ali Engineer, *Islam and Modern Age,* January 2007.
7. see Qur'an 17:70.
8. See Qur'an 2:228.
9. See Maulana Azad (1996), *Tarjuman al-Qur'an* (Vol. 2), Commentary on verse 2:228.
10. See, Sir Muhammad Iqbal (n.d), *Reconstruction of Islamic Thought in Islam* (Lahore).
11. See, Asghar Ali Engineer, *Qur'an, Hadith and Women*, Volume X, No. 5 February 4, 2008 (Asian Human Rights Commission—Religious Groups for Human Rights).
12. See Qur'an 24:31.
13. See Qur'an 33:59.
14. Muhammad Asad, *The Message of the Qur'an, op.cit.,* pp. 109-110.
15. Maulana Abul Kalam Azad, *Tarjuman al-Qur'an* (Sahitya Academy, Delhi, 1980), commentary on verse 4:34.
16. See EdipYuksel *et al. Qur'an: A Reformist Translation* (Bainbow Press, USA, (2007) under 4:34.
17. *Ibid* 4:34.
18. Maulavi Mumtaz Ali Khaqn, *Huquq al-Niswan* (Centre for Study of Society and Secularism, Mumbai).
19. Ibn Qayyim *Islam al-Muewaqqa'* (Lahore, n.d.), Vol. I, pp. 71-77.
20. Qur'an 4:21.
21. *Ibid* 4:19.

4

Period of Reconciliation

Shari'ah Law and New World Order

These days Swat Valley pact with Pakistani Taliban and enforcement of Shari'ah law is very much in news. The Pakistani Government has agreed to allow the Swat authorities to enforce Shari'ah law in Swat Valley and nearby Malakand. Everyone knows how the Shari'ah law is understood by Taliban. Earlier they had burnt more than 400 girls schools saying it is not permissible for girl to go to school. Today the media has reported that now they have agreed to restart schools provided girls wear *hijab*.

Which Shari'ah position is correct according to them? If the girls could have gone to schools with hijab why did then they burnt it down earlier? Has their Shari'ah law changed? It is anyway quite strange that anyone could try to stop girls from getting education in the name of Shari'ah law. Islam is the first religion which made it obligatory for male and female both to acquire education.

According to a well known *hadith* acquiring *'ilm* (knowledge) is obligatory (*faridat*) on all men and women. Also the Qur'an uses the word *'ilm* and its derivatives hundreds of times but has not said anywhere that women cannot obtain education. The first *wahi* begins with the word *iqra'* (i.e. recite) and many women accepted Islam much before their men folk did and recited the Holy Book regularly.

Women used to go to the Prophet regularly with their problems and even insisted that the Messenger of *Allah* fix one day especially for them and they used to flock to the Messenger of *Allah* asking him several questions. In many cases they used to be more eager to know than the men. Several women are counted among the *sahabiyat* (i.e. female companions of the Prophet.

Whenever the Qur'an uses the word *'alim* or *'ulama'* it includes both men and women and never for men only. Other religions may or may not have put curbs on women and prevented from acquiring knowledge but not Islam. And if Taliban burnt schools earlier in sheer anger to protest against Government of Pakistan would it then not imply that they politicize Shari'ah? Shari'ah is the law of Islam and cannot be allowed to be politicized.

And it is wrong to think that Islamic law is static and only the medieval '*ulama* had right or knowledge to determine the law and no changes can be made in it in keeping with the new problems and challenges appearing in the world. It is a mistaken belief that Shari'ah law takes static view of the world. No student of Islam can deny that *ijtihad* (which implies utmost intellectual efforts to understand new emerging problems and challenges) is integral part of Islamic law. Iqbal, the noted philosopher-poet calls it the dynamic principle of Islam.

Shari'ah is based on certain core values of Qur'an which can never be ignored in any formulation of law. Justice ('*adl*) is one of them and most fundamental value and is among Allah's names (*Allah* is 'Adil). No law can ever violate this fundamental value and it is for this reason that even in two verses on polygamy (4:3 and 4:129) justice is most important condition and Qur'an clearly says if you fear justice cannot be done then marry only one.

Let us remember law is an instrument of justice and not end in it self. However our traditional '*ulama* unfortunately consider Shari'ah law as an end itself. Justice is the end. A law may appear just in given circumstances but may not remain just with passage of time. Also, new problems and challenges may appear for which rethinking may become necessary. In no civilisation law remains static. Even prominent jurists differed from each other living in different cultural context.

For Taliban who are basically tribals first and then Muslim, law has got stuck in the past. It does not change as their society does not change. Hence they are incapable of understanding dynamics of the changing world. Even it is not Allah's Will to keep the world He created static. We find in Surah Al-Rahaman verse 29 "..Every day He manifests Himself in yet another (wonederous) way."

Thus *Allah* Himself manifests every day in new ways and His law too cannot remain static. The Shari'ah Law also has to change (only values and norms will remain constant). Pakistan has modernized but tribal areas have lagged behind and remained ferociously patriarchal and hence Taliban want to suppress women's rights and apply same medieval patriarchal values, not Qur'anic values which are equally fair to both genders.

Gender is after all not biological but a social construct and hence if society remains static the idea of gender all remains static and frozen. It is thus for government of Pakistan to do justice to all its citizens and make people of Swat and Malakand also partners in progress and not allow Taliban or any agency to enforce medieval understanding of Islamic laws.

Attack on Taslima Nasreen - Love of Islam or Love of Power?

It was shocking that three MLAs of Ittahidul Muslimin in Hyderabad gatecrashed into the book release function of Traslima Nasreen book *'Lajja'* translated into Telugu and tried to beat up Taslima and shouted slogans using unbecoming words, even using abusing language. And all this in the name of Islam as if it stands for such hooliganism.

The party leadership instead of condemning such wayward behaviour, approved of it and patted them on back. They were even given hero's welcome. One MLA even said that if Taslima comes to Hyderabad again, she will be beheaded. If elected representatives take law into their own hands, there cannot be greater tragedy. If they had done it without invoking Islam, it would have been a different story, though equally condemnable.

Was this for love of Islam? No way. It was love of power, pure and simple. The party leadership thought it was good opportunity to strengthen and widen its electoral base. Human behaviour, especially political behaviour is extremely complex. Politicians, while acting in self-interest, invoke high ideals in order to cover up their utterly selfish motives.

One Imam even declared from Calcutta that he would pay Rs. 50,000 if anyone blackens Taslima's face. An *imam* is supposed to be very respectable and responsible person who leads people in namaz (prayer) but also leads them in social and political matters. An *Imam*'s behaviour should be highly restrained and responsible. I totally disagree with Taslima's views and think she is completely ignorant about Qur'anic teachings but that does not give anyone right to violently attack her or incite people to attack her.

Apart from the fact that such hooliganism is morally reprehensible, it is unwise from the viewpoint of those who are opposed to Taslima's attacks on Islam. This gives her much more publicity that she deserves. Now this attack that took place in Hyderabad will give her worldwide publicity on one hand, and would make her celebrity in the eyes of those who are already hostile to Islam. Now reams and reams of papers will be blackened in her praise.

She would also be now much more hostile to Islam than ever before. She would really hate Islam because of hooliganism of some members of Ittihadul Muslimin. If we really love Islam then we should try to win her heart and soul through love and compassion. And that is what the Prophet of Islam did. It is a well known story that a Jewish woman who hated the

Prophet (PBUH) used to throw garbage on him whenever he passed from below her house. Once when she did not throw garbage on him, he inquired why she did not and was told she is sick. He immediately went to inquire about her health. She was so moved that immediately accepted Islam then and there.

What a contrast! Those who claim to love Prophet and Islam are attacking a woman and making her hate Islam more than before. This is madness, not wise behaviour and must be condemned as strongly as possible. These MLAs and crowd accompanied them have brought utter shame to Islam and Muslims. It is heartening that many religious leaders of Muslims and intellectuals have condemned it. Maulana Mustaqim of *Jamiat ul-ulama-i-Hind*, Shiah leader Maulana Ather Abbas Rizvi and several others have strongly condemned attack on Taslima Nasreen.

The book which was being released in Hyderabad had nothing to do with Islam. It was Telugu translation of her book on persecution of Hindu minority in Bangladesh. After demolition of Babri Masjid like hooligans of Hindutva attacked Muslims all over India and engineered communal violence in number of cities and killed Muslims, the hooligans of Jamat-e-Islami of Bangladesh attacked Hindus and demolished their temples and set fire to their houses. In Lajja (shame) she has condemned all this. Do we Muslims not heave sigh of relief when some fair-minded Hindus stand by Muslims when Hindu communal forces attack us? Should we not stand by fair-minded Muslims of Bangladesh if they stand by Hindu minority?

It is true Taslima has written provocative articles on Islam. We must counter it by arguing on the basis of Qur'an rather than attacking her physically, and in very dignified language befitting a true Muslim. No one can cite a single verse of Qur'an or any *hadith* to support violence against others, even enemies, as long as they are peaceful. On the other hand we can cite several verses from the Qur'an, to support dignified behaviour.

The Qur'an says, "Call to the way of thy Lord with wisdom and goodly exhortation, and argue with them in the best manner" (16:125). Again what a contrast? the hooligans of Ittihadul Muslimin beat up a woman and other journalists and others present there. Also, *Allah* says in the Qur'an "..do not be aggressors, *Allah* does not love aggressors." (2:190). And even if a Muslim renounces Islam and becomes unbeliever, no one has right to punish him except Allah.

"Those who believe", says Qur'an, "then disbelieve", again believe and again disbelieve, then increase in disbelief, *Allah* is not referring to any punishment for those who repeatedly believe and disbelieve and increase in disbelief, let alone human beings punishing them of their own. Even if Taslima has ceased to believe and has increased in her disbelief, no one has any right among human beings to punish her. It is matter of her conscience. All one can do is to dialogue with her in dignified way and then leave it to her conscience.

II

Democracies in socially backward countries like India face an acute dilemma. The entire functioning of democracy depends on rights of people and freedom of conscience and right to believe or disbelieve. Both individual and collective rights are sacred in democracy. However, politicians greedy for votes of illiterate masses, and even educated middle class people, try to incite religious feelings and get their votes. Most of the politicians find this easy way to legislative assemblies or Parliament. They emerge as champions of this or that religion and grab their votes.

This is what the Sangh Parivar did by launching an aggressive movement for *Ramjanambhoomi* and demolished Babri Masjid and took pride in that act of lawlessness and destruction. The *Sangh* leaders launched not only aggressive campaign but Sangh leaders like Uma Bharti and Sadhvi Rithambara used abusive language against Muslims and the government did nothing. They allowed hate campaign to go on.

If the authorities had taken stiff action against Uma Bharti and Rithambara, it would have sent a strong signal to all others that they cannot get away with such aggressive campaigns against all norms of democracy. Democracy cannot succeed without following rule of law. If Uma Bharti and Rithambara had been punished, MLAs of *Ittihadul Muslimin* would not have dared to indulge in this hooliganism.

However, as the Swedish scholar who wrote Asian Drama observed India's is the soft government and refuses to act until all damage is done. Taslima Nasreen's attackers also got away with symbolic arrest and were released on bail immediately thereafter. It speaks volumes about our indifferent approach and also fear of votes.

So many communal riots take place because no guilty is ever punished. All of them know this and have nothing to care for consequences. And riots keep on taking place. In Mumbai riots more than 800 persons were killed, many of them most brutally, and yet state is extremely reluctant to act lest Shiv Sena may not approve of it. Can this ever be the reason for not acting at all for a democratic government?

This is indeed a bad omen for Indian democracy. The people involved in such public crimes must be severely punished to send strong message that hooliganism will not be tolerated in any case. Rule of law must be applied under any circumstances. Politicians should not be allowed to incite people publicly to indulge in mayhem and murder. This is repeatedly happening in our democracy.

It is a heartening sign that many religious personalities among Muslims and secular intellectuals among them have come out strongly condemning the attack on Taslima Nasreen. Still many columnists, even waiting for a day started demanding where are those Muslims and secularists who immediately condemn *Hindutvawadis* but keep quiet when some Muslim fanatics indulge in such extremist action. Many such columnists will come out with many such articles and further aggravate feelings in majority community.

We are not a mature democracy and should come out against any act of hooliganism and violence whosoever perpetrates it, Hindus, Muslims, Sikhs or Christians. We must promote zero tolerance towards any act of violence. It should be our litmus test. If we want to enjoy fruits of secular democracy we must shed all forms of partisan feelings. Politicisation of religion in our democracy has already done enough damage. How much more damage we want to inflict?

Is any one listening?

Fatwa that Stirred Muslims

Recently Darul Ulum, Deoband issued a fatwa saying that if a woman works in any government or public office with other men, the income will be haram (prohibited) for her family. This *fatwa* was published prominently in *Times of India,* a leading newspaper. This stirred a hornets' nest and a large number of Muslim women and men, including some *ulama* opposed the *fatwa* and Darul Ulum had to say it never issued such *fatwa* and that it had only responded to a question about women working in public offices.

There are two things involved here. One is that Muslims no longer unquestioningly accept whatever our *ulama* say in such matters, particularly relating to women and their rights. Even some *ulama* questioned the legitimacy of this fatwa. Secondly, and this is disturbing aspect, our *ulama* are totally text-oriented, not problem-oriented. Whatever text was produced by our predecessors under very different conditions has become sacred for them and must be adhered to irrespective of drastic changes in the society.

Most of the *ulama* who defended the fatwa argue that women can work in what they keep on calling *shar'i hudud* (limits of shari'ah). Secondly, question why apply these *shar'i hudud* only to women? And thirdly who will define these limits? For these *ulama* any mixing of men and women is an act of *fitna* (mischief). For them a woman's character and integrity has no meaning or significance at all. If she raises veil from her face in a mixed gathering, she is transformed into a *fitna.*

There are several instances in the Holy Prophet's life when men and women came together and Hazrat A'isha even led the battle of Jamal (Camel) and there were hundreds of *sahaba* (companions) were around and no one told her not to venture out of home to take part in the battle. Shifa bint-e-Abdullah, a leading lady, was appointed by Hazrat Umar as market inspector and no one protested. What was she doing as a market inspector? Dealing with women alone?

The *Qur'an,* which is the primary source of shari'ah, does not refer to hijab (veil) for ordinary women at all. On the other hand, it advises women not to display her *zeenah* (adornments) publicly (24:31) but refrains from defining what constitutes *zeenah* or adornment. It has been defined by various commentators depending on their cultural environment. Qur'an does not even say whether they should cover their heads, let alone faces. It says, on the other hand "except what appears thereof" leaving space for interpretation. There is near agreement among commentators that face and two hands should remain open. However, it advises women to cover their breasts.

This above verse is preceded by advice to both men and women that let believing men that they lower their gaze and restrain their sexual passions (protect their sexual organs) and let believing women lower their gaze and protect their sexual organs. (24:30) In fact this is most important part of these two verses. The verse 30 is often ignored in which men is equally responsible for lowering his gaze and restraining his sexual passion.

Instead entire responsibility is put on women that they should cover themselves including their faces lest they should become source of *fitna* (mischief). Qur'an has put this responsibility on both men and women to restrain themselves. It is unfortunate that when it comes to women, we totally ignore even what can be called *maqasid al-shari'ah* (i.e. intentions of shari'ah) and only woman is held responsible for her behaviour.

Throughout the *Qur'an* men and women have been described as equally responsible for their deeds (*a'mal*) and will be given equal reward or punishment for whatever they do. If one needs any clarity on this let him carefully study the verse 33:35, besides several other verses in the Qur'an. If men and women are equally responsible for all their deeds both men and women will be equally responsible for their sexual conduct also and men would be equally source of fitna, not women alone as in our fiqh today.

In fact what our *ulama* call shar'i hudud were fixed by men who considered women as secondary to men and unequal in status due to cultural attitude towards women in the medieval era. The whole *fiqh* has to be thoroughly revised in keeping with the true spirit of Qur'an. Also, one needs to develop proper methodology and frame-work to understand Qur'anic intentions in totality, not in pieces, as our commentators have been doing.

Sticking to medievally understood shar'i *hudud* and culturally defined one, instead of religiously defined, will not serve the purpose any more to avoid such *fatwas* in future.

Role of Women in Karbala

These days we find lot of restrictions on women. In many cases they cannot even venture out of homes and are required to restrict themselves to household chores. Very few Muslim women have public role, much less participating in tumultuous events of life. And all this was being done in the name of Islam. However, if we caste a glance on early history of Islam we find women taking part of various events along with men. The Prophet (PBUH) had from Khadija four daughters and brought them up as model women participating in Islamic revolution.

Islam was not only a spiritual but also a social revolution. It empowered women and gave them equal rights which was just unthinkable in those days. Women could play at best a secondary role in any civilisation, in any part of the world. However, Islam upheld their human dignity and assigned them equal rile in all worldly affairs along with men. Many women like Umm-e-Ammara even took part in various battles which the Prophet (PBUH) had to fight. In the Battle of Uhud *Umm-e-Ammarah* took the attack of sword on her arm and saved the life of the Prophet (PBUH).

Hazrat Fatimah, as all Muslims agree, was one of the five bodies (*Panjatan*) whom Muslims highly revere and she who was brought up by the Prophet (PBUH) himself in the highest values of Islam, gave birth to Imam Hasan, Imam Husain along with Hazrat Zainab who played pivotal role in the aftermath of the Battle of Karbala. Hazrat Banu, many Muslims believe, was daughter of Kisra, the King of Iran who was defeated by Muslims and Hazrat Ali married her to his son Husain.

Hazrat Banu also faced the tragic events of Karbala very bravely and sacrificed her two sons Ali Akbar and Ali Asghar with dignity in the way of Allah. It is important to note that when Imam Husain was leaving Mecca for Kufa (Iraq) in response to the letters he had received from many important citizens of Kufa to lead them in a fight against Yazid who had usurped Khilafat in violation of the condition laid down by Imam Hasan while abdicating in favour of *Mu'awiyah*, he (Imam Husain) was advised by many of his well wishers not to take his family members with him to Kufa and go there alone as people of Kufa may betray him and side with the rulers.

However, despite the risks, Imam Husain turned down the advice and took all family members including women with him. He knew, better than his advisors, that these women which included his wife, sister and daughters, would play very important role. Even if he has to fight against Yazid's forces in or near Kufa. The people of Kufa and those very people who had invited him to lead them in fight against Yazid and his counter-revolution betrayed him.

Yazid stood for all that which was against Islam. Not only his life-style was against that of the Prophet (PBUH) and his companions but he also tried to destroy the institute of *khilafah* and *Imamat* and introduced reactionary institution of monarchy which was totally against the revolutionary political system introduced by Islam Husain knew, before he left for Kufah, what was in store and he deliberately took women along with him to show to the world that women can also play very important role in saving the Islamic revolution.

And these women did play a role which was no less significant than that of male companions of the Imam. And Imam was right, particularly his sister Hazrat Zainab book the lead. After the martyrdom of the Imam and his colleagues Imam Zainul Abidin, all women and children were arrested and taken to Damascus on bare camel back via Kufa. Syeda Zainab, a brave and bold woman addressed Muslims everywhere exposing Yazid and his evil actions and un-Islamic acts and his counter-revolutionary designs.

Syeda Zainab and the Imam's entire family was kept in prison in Damascus and when they were brought to Yazid's court, Zainab, eloquently spoke in front of all Yazid's courtiers and thoroughly exposed him. She never shied away in exposing him so much so that he had to release her and Imam's entire family and sent them back to Madina ensuring their security.

Syeda Zainab's role was exemplary and it very well showed how bold were Muslim women and how they played the important role in consolidating Islamic revolution. Today despite so much progress and spread of education still Muslim women are suppressed and in some countries like Saudi Arabia even their voice is considered *'awrah* (not be publicly heard) and here Zainab and other women from Imam's family were the main speakers.

Hazrat Zainab was eldest among those women and was leading entire family including Imam Zainul Abidin who was then quite sick and unable to play an active role and it was Hazrat Zainab who had to lead role and she proved be first among equals. Today, women have to learn much from her leadership. Her public role and oratorical skills have much to learn from.

It is wrong to think, as many Muslim men do that women belong to weaker section and cannot achieve much. Hazrat Zainab's public role is very inspiring for Muslim women today and should be an example for those who feel they are fit only for domestic chores.

Life after Triple *Talaq*

The Muslim Personal Law Board (MPLB) has taken a bold decision to review practice of triple talaq at one go. The Board undoubtedly deserves congratulations from all those who are committed to women's rights and had been campaigning for this essential reform. Hundreds of Muslim women have suffered because of the pre-Islamic practice which, came back into *Hanafi* and *Shafi'I* Islamic law for the reasons not to be gone into here.

It is unfortunate that the Sunni Barelvi *ulama* have threatened to launch an agitation if the MPLB approves of abolition of triple divorce. They maintain that though it is *bid'ah* (sinful form of divorce), nevertheless once pronounced thrice, it is valid. They have stated nothing new. It was because of this view by the *Hanafis* that triple divorce was practiced so long in India though it was abolished in most of the Muslim countries. The Barelvi threat should not deter the members of MPLB from abolition of triple *talaq* though the Board would like to evolve a consensus on the matter. It would be better if the MPLB persuades the Barelvis to agree.

It would be better if such consensus is worked out as Barelvis are in majority and if they do not agree to the abolition of triple *talaq* by the Board may not be very effective. An overwhelming majority of Muslims in India follow the Barelvi school. It is also important to note that unless it takes the form of legislation it may not be effective if triple divorce is challenged in the court of law.

Suppose despite the MPLB abolishing it if someone pronounces triple divorce it will remain valid in the court of law unless it is abolished by law. Thus what the MPLB has to do is to prepare a draft and give it to the government to enact it. Such a precedent already exists and the Dissolution of Muslim Marriage Act was drafted by the *ulama* led by Maulana Ashraf Thanvi and others. It was enacted in 1939.

But if such an exercise is undertaken by the MPLB, it has to be quite comprehensive. There is great need for codification of Muslim Personal Law today. It should be done as early as possible. What is known as Muslim personal law today, it is interesting to note was known as either as Anglo-Mohammedan Law during the British period or simply as Mohammedan Law and was enacted by the British. But after Independence the terminology changed and the Anglo-Mohammedan Law, in order to wipe out its colonial stamp, came to be re-named as Muslim Personal Law. However, its contents did not change.

Thus mere change in its terminology was a political act, not a harbinger of social change as in other Muslim countries. To decolonise its name is not enough, one must docolonise its content wise as well. During the colonial period women were not supposed to play an active role in socio-political matters, at least among Muslims though there were exceptions like Bi Amma (Mother of Ali brothers) and many other women who played important role in freedom struggle.

But now 56 years after the Independence much water has flown down the Ganges and Muslim women are also in the forefront of many social movements. They are far more conscious today than they were during the colonial period. It is after great deal of efforts that the MPLB has agreed to abolish triple divorce. Very important as this measure is, it is not enough. There is a crying need for a comprehensive legislation to be drafted under the guidance of the MPLB by the *ulama* and Muslim intellectuals and lawyers.

As I have often pointed out, Islamic law is so progressive that it can become basis for a uniform civil code. However, conservative Muslim society dragged the Qur'anic pronouncements to its own level and introduced, through human reasoning many measures, which curbed women's rights. Despite reforms in other Muslim countries women have not got full measure of equality, which the *ulama* theoretically concede. Iniquitous measures vary from country to country.

In Saudi Arabia, for example, women are not allowed to drive and they are jailed if they drive. In Kuwait until recently women were not allowed to vote and had to wage struggle for years before this right was conceded recently. There is a debate raging in Saudi Arabia as to why women cannot drive while they can drive in other countries. Obviously issues like driving and voting were not in existence in early Islamic period. It is the *ulama* in Saudi Arabia and Kuwait who, using their own reasoning prohibited them form during. And now women are waging a struggle in these countries against these restructuring and *ulama* are opposing it saying it is 'sin' for women to drive or vote.

In many other Islamic countries like Indonesia, Malaysia, Pakistan and Iran women drive and vote without any religious constraint. Qur'an is the only unanimous divine source for Muslims and it remains most progressive in respect of women's rights. Ideally it grants equality between man and woman and should be the main source of legislation about women's rights.

The past interpretations of the Qur'an were constrained by socio-economic conditions and should not be binding on the present and future generations of Muslims. All great Islamic thinkers have repeatedly made this point and have accepted the central role of *ijtihad* (creative interpretation). It is only our social conservatism, not lack of theological sanction, which prevents our *ulama* from exercising it.

The attacks on Muslim identity by the Sangh *Parivar* also have been one of the reasons for resistance to any change. These attacks may continue and demand for the Uniform Civil Code persist and find legitimacy if there is no initiative for change. Its attacks may even continue after such initiative. Our initiative for change is not motivated or restrained by these attacks. It should be based on the merit for change. Muslim women should not suffer and get justice.

My plea with the MPLB and concerned Muslim intellectuals is to initiate measures for drafting a comprehensive law duly codified which will embody the Qur'anic spirit. Triple divorce and unregulated polygamy has often been the cause of attacks on an otherwise quite progressive Islamic personal law. Polygamy may not be abolished completely but strictly regulated as directed by the Qur'an. In fact both the verses on polygamy i.e. 4:3 and 4:129 should be read together to understand the real Qur'anic intent. Even the first verse i.e. 4:3 requires rigorous justice to all wives and ends by warning that 'if you cannot do equal justice then marry only one'.

The second verse 4:129 makes it clear that equal justice is humanly impossible and does not leave the first wife in suspension. With such warnings polygamy should not be practised unregulated. All other Muslim countries except Saudi Arabia and Kuwait have introduced strict measures to regulate it. Thus a draft law should introduce such regulatory measures and specify circumstances in which one could take second wife as has been done in Pakistan. Those circumstances could be when the first wife is terminally ill, or medically proved to be infertile or barren and that too with the permission of the first wife and the court of law.

Today, though by no means polygamy is widely prevalent among Muslims (it is much more among tribals, dealits and upper caste Hindus), still one finds cases of desertion of first wife and marrying another without giving justice to the first wife. This should not happen and this is strictly prohibited by the Qur'an. The Qur'an permitted polygamy to help women in distress like widows and orphans, not to do injustice to them. It is the duty of the *ulama* to educate Muslims in this respect.

Thus there is a crying need for a new draft law which the MPLB can draft with the help of Muslim lawyers and intellectuals incorporating all these changes and ask the government to enact it. If it is properly drafted I am sure, it will become a model law for others to follow as in Islamic law women enjoy all the rights which modern laws have given to women like widow remarriage, compulsory arbitration before divorce, inheritance, right to property, right to earn and so on. And all these rights are unconditional and a wife also has a right to lay down conditions at the time of marriage.

As such a law may take time since it is not easy to develop a consensus due to sectarian differences. The board in the meanwhile should launch an awareness campaign against misuse of polygamy. It should also see that the amount of *mahr* paid is substantially high (part of which can be deferred) to discourage easy resort to *talaq*. The Qur'an itself encourages high amount of *mahr*. And *mahr* is woman's own untrammelled right. In case of divorce it can provide her with a measure of economic security. It is regrettable that in some Muslim communities *mahr* is only nominal and as low as Rs. 41 or Rs. 51.

In all these matters MPLB can play an important role as it has come to be acknowledged an authoritative body and in a sense representative too. Though it is understandable that it cannot rush into things, it can certainly cautiously proceed further leading the way. If the women suffer after all half the umma suffers and Qur'an does not admit injustice in any case.

Personal Law in India

Muslim Personal Law Board is in the news. In 2005 it was into four and was Muslim women themselves formed two personal law boards of their own. This is big news for media and many Muslims were worried about unity of Muslim Ummah in India. The Personal Law Board itself was maintaining that it was not split but that new boards have come into existence and no member of the existing Board had resigned and formed new board.

Some members of the existing Board have even alleged that 'some vested interests (mainly political) are behind formation of these boards. Such stand is at best unfair accusation or at worst insulting to those who have formed these boards. It is not only Shiahs who have formed a separate board but also the Barelvis who are *Sunni* by sect. Also this is not the best way of sorting out grievances. Instead of hurling accusations the wise leaders should try to sort out differences or solve grievances.

As for unity of Ummah it has remained mere rhetoric for centuries. Despite one God, one Messenger and one Book Muslims have remained divided along sectarian lines for last 1400 years. All our Muhaddithun (i.e. those who narrate Prophet's sayings) have narrated a *hadith* from the Prophet (PBUH) that my ummah will be divided in 72 sects and that only one sect will be naji (i.e. on the right path). Of course the Qur'anic ideal is of one ummah but there is a condition attached: the ummah will remain united if it remains best of the people (khayrah ummatin). This qualification could not be fulfilled except perhaps by the first generation Muslims and once they ceased to be best of the people they were divided in several sects. Thus we find description of these sects in Baghdadi's book Al-Farq bayn al-Firaq (Difference between Sects).

Also, it is well known that even in *Sunni Islam* there are four different schools. Thus differences between Muslims have been there historically and we have lived with these differences. If one Personal Law Board has ceased to represent all Indian Muslims there should not be so much breast beating. Either our '*Ulama* should show wisdom and bring about reconciliation in the best of spirits or if reconciliation is not possible we should learn to live with these differences.

The claim of Muslim Personal Law Board that it was sole representative of all Muslims in India does not bear any scrutiny. It did come into existence in 1972 in response to one Hamid Dalwai's repeated attacks on Shari'ah law and campaign for uniform civil code. The Government of India had never announced any intention of enacting uniform civil code. Let alone enacting it, it had not even indirectly hinted at such a possibility. Also, Hamid Dalwai had no backing from Muslims. He was backed by communal forces and even today these forces consider uniform civil code as their agenda.

All secular forces today have disowned uniform civil code as communal forces have adopted it. Even women's organisations no longer demand UCC as communal forces are demanding it. Thus today there is no threat of Shari'ah law being in any danger. But unfortunately if it is in danger it is from conservative '*Ulama* of the MPLB. They have robbed the Shari'ah law of its dynamism and are perpetrating old formulations arrived at centuries ago. We would like to throw more light on this aspect.

However, first we would like to assert that the MPLB does not represent opinion of all Muslims from day one. Let alone any voting it was not constituted even by any broad consensus among opinion makers among Muslims. Few '*Ulama* and Muslim advocates and others got together and decided to constitute the board and later gave representation to other Muslims sect-wise. No opinion of prominent Muslims was sought about its representative character.

It is true that among Muslims in India there is no unanimity about application of Shari'ah law. Not only there are sectarian differences but also polarisation among them on the lines of progressives and conservatives. It is not easy to push through any decision unanimously among 150 million Muslims and differences are bound to arise. Thus MPLB should not claim in the first place that it is representative of cross section of Muslims in India. And the way it has functioned it has represented at best only ultra-conservative sections of Muslims.

Real protector of any thing is one, which also ensures its healthy growth. One cannot claim to be real protector of something when it begins to stagnate and cause injustices. MPLB has seriously failed in really protecting Sharia'h law by ensuring its healthy growth. It missed great opportunities repeatedly. It always showed its conservative face. The Shah Bano judgement is the best example. It was great opportunity for the Board members to give healthy lead to Indian Muslims by properly interpreting the Qur'anic verse 2:241 which says make provision for the divorcees in goodly manner.

However, the MPLB gave in to ambitious Muslim political leaders who were exploiting the Supreme Court Judgement for their own political ambitions without regard to interests of Muslims in general and Muslim women in particular. It should be remembered that the Qur'anic laws are very progressive and equitable and give women equal status with that of men. It was the first religion in the world which kept interests of divorcees also in view and required men to make provision for his divorced wife since she is usually in helpless situation when divorced. The Qur'an did not mention any period for such provision and left it to the requirements of time. It was opinion of the early jurists that provision be made at least for three months of iddah (waiting before she could remarry after divorce). This opinion could not have been binding as the Qur'anic injunction is.

However, the *'Ulama* in MPLB simply protected the opinion of early Muslim jurists rather than true spirit of Qur'anic injunction i.e. to protect the interests of divorcee and do justice to her. All non-Muslims in general and many Muslim women in particular thought that Islam is unjust to women's rights. The reality is quite contrary to this. Islam has shown greatest concern for women and their rights. The Qur'anic pronouncements in respect of women are far ahead of time.

If today Muslim women have formed their own board it is because of gross failure of the MPLB to meet their demands, which are quite just and within Islamic frame-work. The triple divorce has been causing serious problems to Muslim women. It has nothing Islamic about it. The *'Ulama* themselves maintain that it is sinful form of divorce (talaq al-bid'ah) and one fails to understand why sinful practice should be perpetrated in the name of Shari'ah. The Holy Prophet did not approve of it and Hazrat 'Umar enforced it in certain circumstances and those circumstances do not obtain at all. Is Prophet's (PBUH) opinion more sacred than that of Hazrat 'Umar? And those circumstances also do not obtain under which it was temporarily enforced. It is mere orthodoxy and refusal to change and nothing else. All Muslim countries also have abolished this unjust form of divorce. But our *'Ulama* refuse to take notice of these developments.

A standard *nikahnama* was prepared after long deliberations by several Muslim groups and given to MPLB to approve of it. But the Board sat tight on it and dithered time and again and postponed its implementation. And even when it announced its approval it was its watered down version, which hardly benefits Muslim women. Should it then surprise them if Muslim women, tired of Board's inaction in the matter announced formation of their own Board. However, what is sad is that Muslim women have formed two boards. They should come together and form one board together and include women having proper knowledge of Qur'an and Shari'ah and with ability to creatively interpret the Qur'anic and Shari'ah injunctions to bring about reform and change and to make Shari'ah law more just for women in today's circumstances.

In Islam women have every right not only to recite the Qur'an but also to interpret it. Ijtihad (creative interpretation) is every Muslim's religious right given proper knowledge and understanding of the text and causes of its revelation. As scholars of Islam know every verse in the Qur'an was revealed in response to some questions in the minds of believers or in response to some major events why then Muslims should not understand the Qur'anic verses in response to their own situation?

All major modern thinkers of Islam have maintained that ijtihad represents the dynamic principle of Islam and that every generation of Muslims have right to re-think Shari'ah issues in the light of their own experience and wisdom of their own time. However, since power is wielded in Muslim societies by conservatives such thinkers were either persecuted or totally ignored. Even great thinkers like Muhammad Abduh of Egypt met with the same fate.

It is high time for the Indian '*Ulama*, particularly those associated with the MPLB to shed bit of their conservatism and ensure healthy growth of Shari'ah law in secular India. In fact, given proper spirit and commitment, Islamic law can become model for UCC. Qur'anic law is most modern in its approach to women's rights. Its very spirit was killed by social conservatism and stagnation. Even Sir Syed and Iqbal, though proponent of change, did not assert themselves in view of social conservatism of Indian '*Ulama*. Sir Syed requested Maulavi Mumtaz Ali Khan not to publish his Huquq al-Niswan (Rights of Women) in view of such conservatism. But the Maulavi did and it is a model book even today. The Maulavi was great scholar of Islam in his own right.

If the MPLB does not learn any lesson from these developments, it will have itself to be blamed. Instead of blaming vested interests it should seriously reflect on its own policies and help infuse dynamic spirit in the Shari'ah law. Least it can do is to codify Muslim personal law with the help of progressive lawyers. They should take initiative which Maulana Ashraf Thanvi took in codifying certain aspects of Muslim law in 1939 and got Dissolution of Muslim Marriage Act.

Women Delivering Sermons

Amina Wadud, an Islamic scholar of repute from US led the mixed congregational prayer on 18th March 2005 in New York and also delivered khutba' (i.e. sermon). It was a historic step as it was a unique development in history of Islam. Not that it was first time but it happened after centuries. Amina Wadud invoked principle of spiritual equality of men and women in Islam. She led some 130 women and men in prayer. Subsequently another woman led Jum'ah prayer and delivered a sermon in Canada too. Asra Nomani, a former Wall Street journalist also led prayer in University of Brandeis, near Boston in the USA. In fact Asra was main motivator behind the movement for a woman leading the mixed gender prayer.

It greatly disturbed conservative Muslims who denounced it as against Islam. Fatwas were also issued against it. Some extremist Muslims in USA even threatened to throw bomb and hence the venue had to be changed. Libyan leader Gaddafi in condemnation of a woman leading mixed gender prayer went to the extent of saying that women led prayer 'creates millions of Bin Ladens' according to Daily News (March 24, 2005). There was time when Gaddafi was fervent advocate of gender equality and used to say that gender inequality in the Muslim world is a western colonial conspiracy to immobilise half the Muslim population. That time Gaddafi was more of a rebel and now perhaps he is finding back his mainstream roots in Islamic world. He has also given up his militant image and has come closer to USA.

In Egypt the Great Mufti (*Mufti-e-A'zam*) Ali Goma also denounced a woman leading the mixed congregational prayer. He said it is not permitted in Islam. He said no woman can lead mixed congregational prayer, much less a jum'ah prayer and she cannot deliver khutbah. He said that majority of imams and muftis agree that a woman cannot lead mixed congregational prayer. However, all '*ulama* agree that she can lead only women in prayer.

It is important to examine this claim from the Qur'anic viewpoint. Is there any authoritative argument (nass) against a woman leading mixed gender prayer in Qur'an? Certainly not. All agree that there is no such denial in Qur'an. Though the Qur'an does not refer to the issue directly, there are verses in Qur'an, which can support a woman leading such mixed congregational prayers. We will throw more light on this little later.

Prophet's *hadith* also allows a woman to lead congregational prayer. The Holy Prophet had asked Umm Waraqah bint Abdallah to lead prayer in her dar, which included men. She was well versed in Qur'an compared to others, including men, and hence the Prophet (PBUH) asked her to lead the congregational prayer. Now generally dar (house) is interpreted as her family and according to this interpretation she was asked to lead her family members in prayer including her husband. But it is also stated in *hadith* that the Prophet (PBUH) appointed a mu'addhin (caller to the prayer) who was a man. This means it was not her family but most probably her locality. Here dar should not mean household or family but locality as dar al-Islam would not mean family of Islam but a locality, even a country of Islam.

This *hadith* relating to Umm Waraqah has been narrated by Abu Dawood, also by Ibn Khuzaimah, who rates it as 'sound' (i.e. authentic). Umm Waraqah was also one of the few who handed down the Qur'an before it was compiled in written form. It was because of this *hadith* that jurists like Al-Mozin, Abu Thawr, and Al-Tabari held the opinion that a woman can lead prayers of mixed congregation. Ibn Taymiyyah, another noted jurist, was of the opinion that a woman can lead Tarawih prayers of mixed congregation.

Though there is unanimity among ulama' and jurists that *hadith* relating to Umm Waraqah is authentic but then there is debate whether permission by the Prophet was specific to Umm Waraqah or it implies permission for all women to lead mixed congregational prayers. However, there is noting to indicate that it was specific to Umm Waraqah. Since she was an 'alimah who was well versed in Qur'an and elements of *salah* (prayer) so she was asked to lead prayer in her locality. It was certainly her ability and sincerity, not her tribe or standing in the society which earned her that distinction.

It is well-known principle of jurisprudence that of the two one who is greater 'alim would lead prayer and of the two one who is physically more sound would perform function of imamah and of the two, one who is from the same locality would lead the prayer. Extending this to sex, the *'ulama* concluded that since woman is physically weaker than man so man is superior and hence must lead the prayer. However, on this basis all *'ulama* and jurists agreed that woman can lead other women in prayer.

But a woman can be greater 'alimah than a man and it was on this principle that the Prophet (PBUH) allowed her to lead mixed congregational prayer. It was 1400 years ago and now in 21st century there is such opposition to a woman leading the prayer. It is really strange. Stranger reasons are being given to oppose a woman leading mixed congregational prayer.

A leading Arab 'alim Sheikh Yusuf al-Qardawi says in his fatwa that "Throughout Muslim history it has never been heard of a woman leading the Friday Prayer or delivering the Friday sermon, even during the era when a woman Shagarat Ad-Durr, was ruling the Muslims in Egypt during the Mamluk period. It is established that leadership in prayer in Islam is to be for men."

With due respect to the Sheikh I must say first of all Muslim men, particularly *'ulama* have decided that a woman cannot be ruler or head of the state. How then Qardawi is approvingly quoting that during a woman's rule in Egypt no woman led congregational prayer. Qardawi, like other traditional 'ulama, I am sure, considers woman's rule as illegitimate. And if he does not, then he should not object to a woman leading mixed congregational prayer.

Secondly, his argument that it is well established that "leadership in prayer in Islam is to be for men."The question is who has established that? The Qur'an? No. The holy Prophet's Sunnah? No. And every one agrees that Islamic Shariah is based on Qur'an and Sunnah. It is not for anyone to establish Islamic rules. This assertion on the part of Yusuf al-Qardawi is not right and certainly not based on Islamic sources.

Sheikh Qardawi, in order to justify traditional practice that man alone can lead congregational prayer comes out with very strange logic, even obsession with sex. He argues "Prayer in Islam is an act that involves different movements of the body ? Moreover, it requires concentration of the mind, humility, and complete submission of the heart to Almighty Allah. Hence, it does not befit a woman, whose structure of physique naturally arouses instincts in men, to lead men in prayer and stand in front of them, for this may divert the men's attention from concentrating in the prayer and the spiritual atmosphere required."

I really wonder on the Sheikh's logic. On one hand he says prayer is an act of concentration and submission to *Allah* and humility to Him and on the other he argues that woman's sexuality will interfere with this concentration. Of what use is a Muslim's concentration if he gets sexually excited even in the sacred and spiritual act of prayer and submission to Allah. Better he des not pray. *Allah* says in the Qur'an that "Surely prayer keeps (one) away from indecency and evil." (29:45) and our *Ulama* are arguing that a woman through her posture in prayer will excite a man's sexual desire. Whom should we listen to? To *Ulama* or to *Allah* who says prayer is antidote for all indecency and evil?

Qardawi further argues "Hence, it is to avoid the stirring instincts of men that the Shari'ah dictates that only men can call for Prayer and lead people in the Prayer and that women's rows in Prayer be behind the men." This may be Sheikh's view; it is certainly not the Qur'an's and Sunnah's view. Qardawi thinks the Prophet did not know what he knows about the men's sexuality and permitted Umm Waraqah to lead prayer. And he also thinks that only men's sexual feelings can be stirred, not women's when they pray behind men.

The problem is not with sexuality but with men's ego that he does not want to pray behind a woman. Men have total control on all social and religious institutions and in no case wants to give up this control. Islam came as a liberator for whole humanity, much more for women who were totally subjugated. The Prophet of Islam (PBUH) was personally great supporter of women's cause. Apart from revelation he did what he could for women and their liberation. He wanted women to be equal to men both in material and spiritual sense. The Qur'anic verses as well as the Prophet's conduct are clear proof for that. Not only that he wanted women to pray inside the mosque but also wanted them to lead men in prayer. When some men obstructed women from entering into mosque to pray he said do not prevent Allah's servants (amatullah) from praying inside Allah's house. Men do not allow women to enter into mosque in several countries even today, particularly in South Asian countries like India, Pakistan and Bangladesh.

Who do they follow? Their own version of Islam or *Qur'anic* and Prophetic Islam? The Qur'an stands for complete equality in human dignity, freedom, duties and rights as far as women are concerned. The *Qur'an* puts in four words when it says wa lahunna mithlul ladhi 'alayhinna (i.e. and women have rights similar to those against them in a just manner. 2:228).

These four words are of great significance. These words ushered in revolution in gender relations in a period of darkness in the world. These words gave women what the world could give them in early twentieth century. The Prophet (PBUH) naturally brought these words into practice in their true spirit. The world until then had believed animals and women have no soul. The Qur'an, on the other hand, not only preached men and women have been created from what it calls nafsin wahidin (from one soul) but also accorded them full human dignity.

The Qur'an made another revolutionary statement wa laqad karramna bani Adam (And surely We have honoured children of adam. 17:70). Children of Adam being collective noun all are included including men and women, black and white, Arab and non-Arab. Thus to the Qur'an all human beings have equal dignity and no gender discrimination is allowed as no colour, racial or linguistic discrimination is permitted.

But when Islam spread to other parts of the world where all forms of discriminations, including gender discrimination, were practiced this revolutionary message of Islam was lost and all prejudices sexual, racial and linguistic began to be practiced. The Muslims who embraced Islam with their pre-Islamic prejudices could not appreciate the Islamic spirit and there was no person of the Prophet's (PBUH) spirit among them or status of immediate companions of the Prophet to infuse true spirit of Islam among them.

Women enjoyed very low status in all cultures and races and this low status continued despite acceptance of Islam among those people who embrace Islam decades or even centuries after the death of the Prophet (PBUH) and his companions. The new generation of '*ulama* from Persian, Roman and Turkish stock too engaged themselves in formalistic juristic issues without fighting their deeply embedded cultural prejudices against women. And to serve these deeply embedded gender discriminatory opinions new *ahadith* (sayings of the Prophet) came into existence and qiyas and ijma' (analogical reasoning and consensus) being purely human institutions too were influenced by these cultural prejudices.

Thus all sorts of discriminations began to be practiced against women. The early dynamism of women was severely restricted and she was confined to home. The Prophet (PBUH) had even allowed them to participate in the war, Umar, the 2nd caliph had appointed a woman as inspector of markets and now she, wrapped in black cloth could not move out without a *mahrim* (i.e. with a man closely related to her whom she could not marry).

Now all this was thought to be strictly Islamic and the '*ulama* and jurists issued fatwa after fatwa (legal opinion) making this low status of women as

Islamic. She then became mere appendage of her father or husband after marriage. Her salvation lay only in submission to authority and pleasure of her husband. She could not even step out without his specific consent. She lost her individual dignity. A *hadith* circulated wherein the Prophet (PBUH) was made to say that if it were permissible to prostrate before anyone except *Allah* I would have required wife to prostrate before her husband.

Thus one can see how later generations of Muslims immersed in their cultural values and completely alien to the Qur'anic spirit, degraded woman's status. No wonder if she was not permitted to lead congregational prayers as she was thought to be inferior to man. Yusuf Qardawi's argument that no woman in the history of Islam had led congregational prayer is based on this kind of logic, not on the Qur'anic spirit.

During the Prophet's time the women did not accept their degradation and fought for their Qur'anic rights. Once when an argument ensued about their status they went to the Prophet (PBUH) and inquired whether they are inferior to men. The Prophet waited for divine injunction and *Allah* responded: "Surely the men who submit and the women who submit, and the believing men and the believing women, and the obeying men and obeying women, and the truthful men and the truthful women, and the patient men and the patient women, and the humble men and the humble women, and the charitable men and the charitable women, and the fasting men and the fasting women, and the men who guard their chastity and the women who guard their chastity, and the men who remember *Allah* much and the women who remember ? *Allah* has prepared for them forgiveness and the mighty reward." (33:35)

If one reads this divinely revealed verse can he still argue that women are in any way inferior to men? If one still does then all one can say is that he is either not appreciative of Qur'anic teachings or that he is deeply immersed in his male-dominated values. To him Qur'anic message is not as important as is own values in which he has been brought up. The real tragedy is that one is born in a Muslim family and formally accepts Islam as religion without being deeply affected by the Qur'anic spirit. Or Islamic message reaches him through not only his cultural filter but also through the conservative *'ulama* themselves quite alien to real Qur'anic spirit.

After deeply studying the import of the verse 33:35 can one still seriously argue that women cannot lead mixed congregational prayers? That is why all those who are opposing women leading mixed congregational prayer are simultaneously admitting that there is nothing in the Qur'anic and *hadith* against women leading prayer. But since they are immersed in male values rather than Qur'anic values, they maintain women cannot lead congregational prayer and invent strange arguments like sexual excitement by looking at the back of a woman. What is much more surprising is that such arguments are advanced by the *'alim* of the status of Sheikh Yusuf al-Qardawi.

They do not realise that such arguments are external to the Qur'anic spirit. The Qur'an does not even remotely suggest that men are sexually more excitable than women and so women should be wrapped in cloth from head to toe to spare men the sin of rape or adultery. The Qur'an treats both man and woman equal even in this regard and proposes same punishment for both for such offences.

Even in case of polygamy men use such arguments. It is often argued that polygamy saves men from resorting to illegitimate relationship with other women. The Qur'an does not refer to any such argument. On the other hand the Qur'an reluctantly permits polygamy to take care of orphans and widows (4:3) and warns that "if you fear you cannot do justice then (marry) one". "Not only this in yet another verse 4:129 it says". And you cannot do justice between wives, even though you wish (it), but be not disinclined (from one) with total inclination, so that you leave her in suspense. And if you are reconciled and keep your duty, surely *Allah* is ever Forgiving, Merciful."

The message of this verse is very clear and if one reads both the verses i.e. 4:3 and 4:129 together it becomes quite clear that he can take more than one wife only in some exceptional cases but otherwise one should take one wife. Yet the *'ulama* throughout history made it almost a privilege for men to marry up to four wives and justice never remained an issue. On the other hand such arguments totally external to the Qur'anic spirit that one need to marry more than one wife to avoid life of sin were usually made.

Now women are much more educated and conscious of their rights and time has come to put in practice the real Qur'anic spirit and understand the Qur'anic teachings in right perspective and small steps like Amina Wadud and others leading mixed congregational prayers should be taken. The Islamic world urgently needs certain reforms and for that internal debate will be very helpful.

All these steps has stirred feelings and from the heated debate will come the much- needed light for healthy change. The vast gap between Islamic spirit and Muslim practices need to be bridged through dialogue and discussion. There is constant attack from non-Muslims about gross injustices perpetrated by Islam against women. Non-Muslims are not aware of Qur'anic teachings and hence they blame Islam for these injustices. Those Muslims who understand the Qur'anic teachings must come forward and initiate discussions both with Muslims and non-Muslims.

Muslim women also need to be properly educated in the Qur'anic teachings and we urgently need women theologians to spread awareness among them. Thus both Muslim men and women committed to human dignity and gender justice will have to seize initiative to bring about much needed changes in Muslim society. Thus we should welcome the initiative taken by sisters like Amina Wadud and others and spread this message.

A believer (m'umin) must be totally committed to justice, benevolence, compassion and wisdom as these are oft repeated Qur'anic values and any injustice to women cannot be acceptable to a believer. Throughout medieval ages Muslims lost the true message of Qur'anic values and now in the age of human dignity and human rights Qur'anic message of gender justice needs to be revived.

If we do not bring the real Qur'anic spirit even in today's circumstances we will miss the bus forever. *Allah* will never forgive us for this indifference to His Message. We have always sidelined reformers like Muhammad Abduh of Egypt who stood for gender justice and true Qur'anic spirit. We need not one but many Abduhs.

Women on the Move

There is widespread perception that Muslim women are among the most backward, illiterate and oppressed in the world. In media they are always shown clad in *burqa* or wrapped in hijab (veil). They are also perceived to be confined to the four walls of their homes totally cut off from outside world. While partly it is true but reality is much more complex and also not static. Generally we tend to oversimplify and assume reality to be static. In a fast changing world reality cannot taken to be static. We should always pay attention to changing and emerging reality.

What happens in the Muslim world is usually blamed on Islam. The underlying assumption is that Muslim behaviour is always determined by religious belief and since Muslim women are backward and do not enjoy rights like other women it is because of Islamic teachings. This impression is further reinforced by the pronouncements of some orthodox *'ulama* that want to see Muslim women wrapped in hijab.

It has to be borne in mind that firstly all Muslims do not behave according to what theologians or *'ulama* say or even according to the teachings of Islam; secondly, social customs, traditions and social milieu exert their own pressure. It is difficult to ignore all this. Thirdly, there are multiple interpretations of Qur'an. Fourthly, modern world-view also plays an important role in determining one's point of view as well as behaviour.

The question of Muslim women, their social status and rights cannot be understood without keeping these things in mind. First of all it must be kept in mind that Qur'an makes clear pronouncement in favour of equal rights for both sexes (2:228). However, this vision of Islam for sexual equality could not find practical implementation for number of reasons. Those who embraced Islam, however sincere they might have been, were product of a fiercely male-dominated society. The Qura'nic pronouncement on the other hand, was an ideal which required very different cultural milieu. From sociological viewpoint it was not immediately implementable.

The scriptural understanding is always mediated through culture. The Arab culture was patriarchal and had set its own understanding of women's position. Thus the Qur'anic pronouncement of sexual equality was understood and implemented through mediation of Arab culture. What is worse Islam spread through deeply feudal societies like those of Iran, parts of Roman empire and India. The '*ulama* certainly could not transcend cultural norms of these societies. Thus shari'ah formulations came into existence mainly in Iraq, Egypt and of course Madina. Iarq and Egypt were confluence of ancient cultures with age-old traditions of their own. These milieux greatly influenced the Muslim theologians in their understanding of Qur'anic pronouncement of sexual equality.

To meet the demands of their societies they selectively used Qur'anic verses and certain sayings of the Holy Prophet (PBUH) to formulate shari'ah approach to women problem, their status and rights. This became medieval religious heritage, which no one could question. However, under pressure from modern social norms these Qur'anic pronouncements are being rediscovered by modernists and a debate is raging in the Muslim world today about rights of women in Islam.

Meanwhile the Muslim women are on the move in various Muslim countries. In every Muslim country and countries with considerable Muslim population like India education is spreading fast among Muslim women. This certainly brings increased awareness among women themselves and they press for their rights both Islamic as well as secular. There are both types of movements among Muslim women in Islamic world. In some Muslim countries Muslim women theologians have emerged with thorough knowledge of the Qur'an, Islamic theology and shari'ah. There are women theologians like Fatima Mirsani from Morocco, Amina Wadood and Riffat Hassam from the USA and several others. Also there are women's organisations like 'Sisters in Islam' from Malaysia.

These Muslim women theologians and organisations are questioning the traditional interpretations of the Qur'an in respect of women's rights and developing new feminine oriented theology ensuring equal rights for men and women. 'Sisters-in-Islam' from Malaysia is challenging the orthodox '*ulama* from Malaysia. They are even trying to get the concept of 'marital rape' accepted as a valid law.

As pointed out above reality is not static in Muslim women's world. The women in as orthodox society as that of Kuwait are demanding right to vote which is being denied to them by the Kuwait ruling elite. It is hoped they will win this right sooner than later. In Pakistan the women agitated in early fifties itself against the Pakistani Prime Minister when he married his secretary and took her as second wife. The agitation continued until Ayub Khan who had captured power in 1958 brought Muslim Family Ordinance in 1961, which put certain restrictions on polygamy and oral divorce. This ordinance could not be undone even during Zia-ul-Haq's period when the orthodox '*ulama* were closest to state power in Pakistan.

The Pakistani society, despite its ups and downs as far as project of 'Islamisation' is concerned, is on the move in changing women's social status. Recently seven Pakistani woman diplomats have been appointed ambassadors. An official of Pakistani foreign ministry said that it is for the first time so many women have been appointed ambassadors in important world capitals. They are all career diplomats and have been posted to European capitals. One woman Asma Aneesa, who was ambassador to one of the Central Asian countries, has been appointed on directing staff of National Defence College. No mean achievement.

Bangladesh, though otherwise quite poor and backward, is not far behind. There recently twenty female officers have completed two year gruelling military training and passed out from Bangladesh Military Academy (BMA). This training was for the post of second lieutenant and their passing out ceremony was attended by Bangladesh Prime Minister Khaleda Zia.

The Saudi society too is by no means as static as we think of. The Saudi women too are facing complex choices. There is no doubt compared to other Muslim countries they are subjected to stricter traditions. But there is no reason to assume that they are passive and inert to modern changes in the society. The Saudi society as a whole is conceived as governed by purely traditional Islam and totally shut out to modern world. The Saudi society is undergoing pangs of modern change and this is causing social convulsions and these social convulsions occasionally assume violent forms. This is subject of another article and cannot be discussed here.

We will discuss here only other issues related to women in Saudi Arabia. The women in Saudi Arabia are taking modern education. The princess called Umm Abdul Aziz, for example, said (see www.amanjordan.org) "We have our own traditions, but they do not prevent women seeking education." Though there are obviously separate educational institutions for women and there is no co-education in Saudi Arabia. They strictly follow the tradition of sexual segregation.

The News Letter of Pakistani women's organisation 'Shirkatgah' of April 2003 says about changes among Saudi women, "Trying to balance the challenges of modernity with the demands of traditional past has meant that change is cautious and slow, but women insist that change is afoot." Mona Megalli says in her article "Saudi women face complex choices" in the above news letter, "Saudi women now outstrip men as graduates and other specialised colleges, making up 58 per cent of a total of nearly 32000 students in 2000." The female students listen to male instructors through closed circuit video an audio system.

There are many restrictions Saudi women have to grapple with. Women are not taught engineering and law, for example. They have to compete in touch job market in Saudi society. Similarly though women own 40 percent of private wealth and thousands of businesses from retail to heavy industry, they face frustrating legal and cultural restraints and they have to rely on male agents to deal with government offices.

It is also encouraging news from Jordan that it has amended law to give women equal rights. This was announced by Queen Rania. She made this announcement on the opening day of Arab first ladies dedicated to improving the conditions of women in the male dominated Arab world.

In Iran, women have to wear chador but *chador* has not been a constraint for them as far as work is concerned. Iran has very active women's movement in whole of Islamic world. They are active in practically every field of work and are present in large numbers in Iranian parliament too. In Indonesia too women have entered in educational field in a big way. There are large number of women in Islamic universities too and there is strong movement developing for women's rights.

Thus one must realise that reality is multi-layered and complex. Muslim women too are undergoing through throes of change the world over. The orthodox *'ulama* can hardly restrain this forward march. More and more Muslim women are either challenging medieval theological formulations or simply ignoring them. They are trying to carving out their own niche in this male dominated world.

Orthodxy and Change

The women's question is acquiring ever greater importance throughout the world. The women suffer discrimination whichever community or country they belong to. Women in western countries also suffer discrimination in the male dominated society though there may be difference of degree. Women in Islamic countries are perceived to be suffering more compared to other countries. What is happening in Afghanistan at the hands of Taliban has reinforced this perception. The Taliban are treating women in most primitive way. It is hardly Islamic. Yet they do it in the name of Islam.

The orthodox *'ulama* treat the question of women in Islam with hypersensitivity. They are opposed to any kind of change in general but on women's question, in particular. They imitate quite mechanically all the provisions in this respect formulated by the '*ulama* more than thirteen hundred years ago. Any re-thinking on the issue is no less than a sin. Also, the question of women has become an important question of Islamic identity vis-vis the west as far as the Islamic countries are concerned and also of Muslim minorities vis-vis the majority communities in countries like India. Thus any change in Muslim personal law is opposed vigorously as threatening Muslim identity and an unwarranted interference in Islam. One of the agenda of Islamic revolution in Iran was to reassert Islamic identity vis-vis the west and it found expression in enforcing chador (a head-gear) for women.

The Islamic revival throughout Islamic world is compelling women to take to veil. In many cases Muslim women are doing so voluntarily. In Iran too many women who had taken to miniskirts during the Shah's period, discarded them and began to wear chador of their volition to escape the charge that they were opposing the Shah at the instigation of the Soviet Union. Similarly in countries like Egypt the women, particularly the university students have taken to veil to assert their Islamic identity. In fact in the period of MTV when the western pop culture is being disseminated with all vengeance such a reaction appears to be quite normal. In the west women bares as much as she can whereas in the east she hides as much as she can. It is thus more of reaction rather than coercion. Women in Islamic countries assert 'modesty' to fight the western 'vulgarity'. These are two different cultures poles apart. Thus veil should not be seen as mere subjugation of women. The Iranian women are quite assertive of their rights despite wearing chador. They are recruited in all government offices, are members of parliament, hold political offices like Masumeh who is vice president of Iran. Not only this the Iranian women are fighting for equal status today and women's movement in Iran is quite strong, as strong as in any other non-Muslim country. Thus veil is cultural expression of modesty rather than any oppressive measure.

In modern era education is spreading fast in all countries including Muslim countries. Muslim women in almost all countries are going to universities in ever larger numbers. These educated women become far more aware of their rights than illiterate women. Thus there is hardly any country with sizeable Muslim population where women are not asserting themselves. Even in a conservative Sheikhdom like Kuwait women are demanding right to vote and right to hold political offices. There is large number of women in the universities in Kuwait. The women spearheading the women's rights in Kuwait is a dean of faculty of arts in the Kuwait University. In Pakistan and Bangladesh women have held highest offices of Prime Minister and hold offices in various governmental as well as non-governmental organisations.

However, that does not mean there are no serious problems. It is struggle all the way for women: struggle against orthodoxy, struggle against certain oppressive cultural norms which do not permit women to enter certain fields, struggle against dowry and bride burning and struggle against honour killing. As women assert their rights and struggle to find a place of honour in the society the society over which there is domination by men reacts more sharply and tries to put more restriction over them. This struggle will go on for a long time to come. What is shocking is that women are being denied even their well-defined Islamic rights.

It is important to note that Islam is the first religion in the world which recognised woman as legal entity and gave her all rights which man enjoyed. Thus Islam gave women right to enter into marital contract on her own condition. Her father or any male member of the family cannot give her away in marriage to any person of his choice. Her consent to marriage in presence of two witnesses is very necessary for finalisation of marriage. She could stipulate certain conditions which must be fulfilled for validity of the marriage. Any violation of the stipulated condition could lead to dissolution of marriage. What is most revolutionary is that she can insist on what is known as *talaq-i-tafwid* i.e. delegated right to divorce. According to this provision in the marriage contract she can insist on delegated right to divorce her husband on his behalf if he violates any condition of the marriage contract. It would be seen that even most modern law has no such provision for benefit of women.

Divorce is a recognised institution in Islam though it is not encouraged. Both man as well as woman have right to divorce. The Qur'an has made a very fair provision for divorce. It stipulates arbitration. Thus the Qur'an says, "And if you fear breach between the two (i.e. husband and wife), appoint an arbiter from his her people each. If they both desire agreement, *Allah* will effect harmony between them." (4:35) The very concept of arbitration is quite modern and this was stipulated 1400 years ago by the holy book of Islam. However, it is highly regrettable that such fair provision of the Qur'an is ignored by Muslims and they resort to triple divorce in one sitting which was part of pre-Islamic customary law.

Unfortunately, at least in India, triple divorce has become the most prevalent form of divorce among the *Sunni Hanafi* and *Shafi'i* Muslims. In fact, triple divorce is un-Qur'anic and is rejected even by Hanbalis and *Ahl-e-Hadith* among the *Sunni* Muslims and all Shi'ah sects. Triple divorce being unjust to women was not practised during the Prophet's (PBUH) time and also during the time of the ist Caliph Hazrat Abu Bakr and for two and half years during the reign of 2nd Caliph Hazrat 'Umar. It was during the later part of his reign that triple divorce in one sitting was enforced again on account of its misuse by some Arabs. Triple divorce has never been a part of Islamic teachings. It was, in fact, part of the Arab customary law. Even according to Shah Waliyullah, a great Islamic thinker with social vision of 18th century India it is unfair to apply the Arab customary law to non-Arab people. Many Shari'ah provisions include some aspects of the Arab customary law prevailing in the pre-Islamic times. Abolition of triple divorce on which there is no unanimity among Muslims will give great relief to Muslim women. Many men misuse it either to harass their wives or divorce them most arbitrarily leaving them in lurch. Hundreds of women are suffering today because of its validity. Fortunately, it has been abolished in Pakistan and Bangladesh.

Islam has also given right to Muslim women to divorce which is known as *Khula'*. Though this word has not been used in the Qur'an, a woman, according to it, can buy her freedom from her husband by giving fidyah i.e. compensation. And this right is absolute. Thus the Qur'an says, "Then if you fear that they cannot keep within the limits of *Allah*, there is no blame on them for what she gives up to become free thereby." (2:229). Commenting on this verse Maulana Muhammad Ali says, "These words give the wife the right to claim a divorce. It is one of the distinguishing characteristics of Islam that it gives the wife the right to claim a divorce, if she is willing to forgo the whole or part of her dowry." (Holy Qur'an, Lahore, 1973, p. 98). The Holy Prophet enforced this right in the case of Jamilah who wanted to free herself from her husband though she found no fault in his behaviour towards her except that she did not like him. According to Sahih Bukhari the Prophet (PBUH) allowed her *khula'* by returning the orchards which her husband had given her by way of mahr. But unfortunately the orthodox *'ulama* deprive her of this right also by insisting on consent of her husband. This approach is not in keeping with the sunnah of the Prophet (PBUH). Her right to *khula'* should be absolute particularly when they fear they cannot keep within the limits of *Allah* i.e. they cannot fulfil the marital obligations.

There is also a form of divorce what is called *mubarat*. It is in this form of divorce that mutual consent of both husband and wife is required. Unfortunately the *'ulama* have equated *khula'* with mubarat which is not correct. The Muslim personal law as it operates in India also does not allow woman right to *khula'* without her husband's consent and naturally husbands, more often than not, exploit this for harassing her and also for extracting much higher compensation than justified.

There is another provision in the Qur'an which is often exploited by men in the most un-Qur'anic way i.e. the provision for polygyny. A man has been permitted to take upto four wives. But this is far from being a general provision for man. It is permitted only in exceptional situation and subject to stringent conditions. Many *'ulama* feel that since this verse was revealed after the battle of *Uhud* in which ten per cent of male Muslim population was wiped out leaving many orphans and widows, provision up to four wives was made only to help these widows and orphans. Thus the relevant verse is as follows: "And if you fear you cannot do justice to orphans, marry such women as seem good to you, two, or three, or four; but if you fear that you will not do justice, then (marry) only one or that which your right hands possess. This is more proper that you may not do injustice." (4:3)

Thus it will be seen that there is so much emphasis on justice. Qur'an has exercised enough caution in this respect. Again in 4:129 Qur'an makes men aware of difficulty in exercising justice between spouses. It says: "And you cannot do justice between wives, even though you wish (it), but be not disinclined (from one) with total disinclination, so that you leave her in suspense. And if you are reconciled and keep your duty, surely *Allah* is ever forgiving, Merciful." Thus Qur'an makes it clear that equal justice is not possible and one should not leave the first wife in suspense by marrying the other. The early *'ulama* also discussed what is meant by justice and generally they emphasised equity in maintenance of all four wives. But some felt it included equal love for all wives and since it is not possible as rightly emphasised in 4:129, the intention of the Qur'an is to promote monogamy. Also, the verses on polygamy should be read along with other verses of the Qur'an on husband-wife relationship to understand the real spirit of the Qur'anic approach to this question.

In 21:30 *Allah* says, "He put between you, love and compassion." Thus the relationship between husband and wife is basically of love and compassion. Then how just relationship can exclude love between the two. Also Qur'an says that "They are a garment for you and you are garment for them. Thus if the verses on polygamy are read in conjunction with these two verses it becomes very clear that equal love and dignity in husband-wife relationship is a must. Libas (garment) stands for human dignity. And since equal love with all wives is not possible and human dignity cannot be upheld without love and compassion multiple marriages are not encouraged by the Qur'an. Thus polygyny is an exception and not a rule.

The women's question needs to be tackled with new sensitivity and freshness of approach. It is not true to say that what the medieval theologians thought on this question is immutable and divine. After all the *'ulama* are human beings, howsoever learned they may be and what is more important to emphasise is that they were product of their own time. What they thought on women's question reflected ethos of their period. The real vision of the Qur'an unflods itself with passage of time. The Qur'an really envisions equality of sexes and there is enough in the Qur'anic verses to draw this conclusion. Thus the verses 2:228 and 33:35 declare sexual equality in no uncertain terms. Yet in medieval ages these verses were by and large neglected or understood with differently. The time has come to unfold the real message of the Qur'an in this respect. Islam has treated women with great sense of dignity. True Muslims, therefore, should not allow an impression being created that Islam treats women unjustly.

It is not the intention of Islam to confine women to home and entrust her alone with the responsibility of minding household work and bringing up children. There is no where stated either in the Qur'an or any of the *hadith* that household work is her sole responsibility. It is, at best, a shared responsibility. In *Fatawa*' 'Alamgiri compiled during the reign of Aurangzeb Alamgir, the Moghul emperor we see that maintenance has been defined by the '*ulama* to include cooked food, sewn clothes and a separate house to live in. Thus a husband has to serve her with cooked food and cannot insist that his wife cook the food and serve him; on the contrary it is his duty to serve cooked food to his wife as part of maintenance. Minding children should also be a shared responsibility between the two. No faqih i.e. Islamic jurist can insist that man should not share household responsibility with his wife and that it is wife's function alone. Even the concept of *qawwam* in 4:34 has undergone great change. The earlier commentators and theologians thought it means either 'ruler' or 'controller of household affairs' or 'caretaker of the family' while wife is his subordinate. The modern scholars maintain that this verse does not entitle man to dominate woman but indicates his function of earning and maintaining family. It is only a functional concept and does not show any inherent superiority over women. Even a scholar like Maulana Azad maintains this and says that in those days it was man who earned (the word *qawwam* is an exaggerated form of qama which means to stand and since one who earns stands too much is called *qawwam*) and spent on his wife and chidren and looked after them he has been described as *qawwam* by the Qur'an. Maulana, therefore, argues that if wife earns and shares the expenses incurred on the family she will also be called qawwam as she also performs the same function as her husband does. There may also be cases in which wife earns and husband does not. In that case she will be *qawwam* and husband will not be. And there are many families today in which wife is the sole bread earner.

Thus whichever angle we look the woman's problem from, she is not the looser or unequal from the Qur'anic stand point. We should not impose our own thinking and explanations on the Qur'an. It is too much to think that what we feel is the real intention of the Qur'an. Thus for example, many people justify polygyny by saying that since woman gives birth to child and man cannot go near her for several months or she goes through the menstrual periods man needs to have more than one wife. It is purely un-Qur'anic approach and an explanation never intended by the Qur'an. Such explanations reflect sexual obsession. In fact the verse 24:33 says "Let those who do not find the wherewithal for marriage keep themselves chaste, until *Allah* gives them means out of His grace.."

Thus *Allah* requires that man remain chaste until he finds means to marry even one wife. Sexual obsession is obviously discouraged. Secondly, such explanations reduce a woman to be a mere sexual object, not a companion to be loved and respected as the Qur'an requires. *Allah* has created *mawaddah* and *rahmah* (love and compassion) between the two and not mere sexual instinct. Sexual instinct is more for propagation of species than mere pleasure. Even most orthodox '*ulama* would agree on this point. However most of the Muslims take another wife more for sexual reasons than otherwise. This defeats the very purpose of treating women with love dignity and as companion. One must thoroughly revise the whole outlook on polygamy. Today women are much more educated and much more aware and hence would consider it undignified to live with a co-wife and share her husband's attention and love with her.

As we hinted above the question of Islamic identity vis-vis the west is being treated in terms of women's rights in Islamic world. Why only women should bear the entire brunt of the question of Islamic identity. Her clothes, her hijab, her role in the society is seen as part of Islamic identity whereas man does not have to face any such restriction. He can continue to wear western dress and adopt new ways of life in the modern society without in any way violating the Islamic norms. Wearing western dress is even seen as more dignified as far as men are concerned. But if woman takes to different dress Islamic norm is violated. The Qur'anic verses with such interpretations as to restrict her role are invoked. All will agree that thrust of the Qur'ani'c argument is that women dress modestly. She should not expose her sexual charms. This is also in a particular context prevailing in Arabia. The Arab women used to stand in public places and attract men's attention by displaying their charms, wearing anklets and thumping their feet to attract men's attention. Also, she would bare her body as much as she could. It is these vulgarities the Qur'an wanted to stop. It is also important to note that Qur'an never took away her right to zeenah i.e. to adorn herself. She is allowed to display her charms before her husband and those close relatives with whom she cannot marry (*mahram*).

Thus the Qur'anic verse 4:31 gives the description of those before whom she can display her charms and adornment. This verse begins with the words which are quite significant "And say to the believing women that they lower their gaze and restrain their sexual passions and do not display their adornment except what appears thereof". The words "except what appears thereof" are quite significant. This clearly implies that certain parts of her body can remain open. There is almost a consensus among orthodox '*ulama* also that the face and hands can remain open and that she can apply collyrium to her eyes (which is part of adornment and wear rings in her fingers and bangles and these parts can remain open. We also find in *hadith*

(Abu Daud 31:30) according to which the Prophet himself is reported to have told Asma', his wife 'A'isha's sister, when she appeared before him in thin clothes, through which parts of her body could be seen: "O Asma', when woman attains her puberty it is not proper that any part of her body should be seen except this, and he pointed to his face and hands." This settles conclusively that Islam never enjoined the veil por covering of the face.

The preceding verse 24:30 also makes it clear what is real intention in observing modesty. It says, "Say to the believing men that they lower their gaze and restrain their sexual passions. That is purer for them. Surely *Allah* is Aware of what they do." Thus it will be seen hat it is not only the duty of woman to restrain herself from displaying her sexual charms but also of man to lower his gaze and restrain his sexual passions. In fact both men and women have to observe a moral code. It is also to be noted that the concept of modesty is culturally conditioned. There cannot be a universally valid concept. What is considered modest in one culture may not be necessarily so in other culture. Western way of dressing for women (except ultra-modern and fashion oriented which is promoted by the profit motives of the cosmetic industry) has its own dignity and modesty. All western women do not dress in ultra-modern and exotically fashionable way. Such way of dressing is not only vulgar but is based on exploitation of women.

What early commentators have prescribed for women to wear is based on their own culturally conditioned notions. The Arabs had their own notions of what is *zeenah* (adornment), what is sexually charming and exciting and what constitutes modesty and modest way of dressing. Thus what is binding on us is that women should refrain from displaying their sexual charms publicly and restrain her sexual passions and not wearing what Arab women wore and not to go by their concept of what constitutes modesty. We must distinguish between what is fundamental in the Qur'an and what is instrumental to achieve it in the society. What is fundamental alone is binding on the believers, not hat is instrumental in a particular society to achieve what is fundamental. While observing chastity and restraining sexual passions is a fundamental requirement and binding on all believers wearing hijab or a particular type of dress prescribed by earlier commentators of the Qur'an is not binding. One must make distinction between the two. Hijab, if it means hiding or covering the face is certainly not what is prescribed by the Qur'an. It is a totally wrong notion that the Qur'an prescribes hijab.

It is also a culturally conditioned notion that women should not venture out except in prescribed fields. It is neither proved from the Qur'an nor from the sunnah (Prophet's sayings and doings). The women during the Holy prophet's time used to take part in all fields including the battle field, and not only for tending the wounded. Their role was much mre than that of nurses. The case of Umm 'Umarah is well known among them. In the battle of 'Uhud it was she who protected the Prophet from being harmed by the kuffar (unbelievers of Mecca who were trying to kill him. '*Umarah* took sword in her hand and attacked those who tried to come near the Prophet and pierced sword into his body. She was, therefore, popularly known as '*woman of Uhud*'. The Prophet (PBUH) also had great regard for her and always used to inquire after her health. We also have to instance of Ghazalah, a Kharijite woman who was known for her bravery and who challenged Yusuf bin Hajjaj in the battle, an Umayyad governor who was feared even by all Arabs. He was a great tyrant.

Thus we see that women took active part in combat situations and proved their might. Why should then women be restricted from taking part in military or police service, if they want? Hazrat 'Umar had appointed a woman the chief inspector of markets in his time. In Aghani we read stories of highly skilled poets, musicians and lovers of art. They were greatly respected. Some of these women were women of highest achievements in the diverse fields in life. Zubeda, the wife of Abbasid Caliph Harun al-Rashid was a highly skilled administrator. She was often consulted before major policy decisions were taken. It is she who built a network of canal system which immensely benefited the people. Thus it will be seen in those days there were no restrictions on her which are being imposed today. It is again culturally mediated restrictions rather than prescriptions by the Qur'an or *hadith*.

Feudal culture put severe restrictions on women and confined her role to household affairs only. She was made to observe strict purdah. All that is changing but still there is lot of resistance to change. Cultural prejudices are not easy to fight. Thus it is feudal cultural sensitivities which are restricting her role. Muslim women should fight these restrictions and try to excel in any field of their choice. The Muslim community cannot progress if their women remain confined to the house. Early marriage is also culturally determined rather than religious requirement. Child or pre-puberty marriages should be ruled out. Islam, while permitting child marriage due to cultural reasons, had given her what is known as khiyar al-bulugh (option of puberty) i.e. she could annul the marriage on achieving puberty, if she did not approve of the same. Thus child marriage is discouraged by Islam.

Empowerment of Muslim women is not possible until she overcomes all such restrictions imposed on her by the feudal society. She must acquire modern skills and excel in all these fields. What Islam has given her by way of rights is being given to her now by modern society. She should overthrow her restrictive role and fight for her Islamic rights and this struggle for Islamic rights will empower her.

Muslim Women and Modern Society

The question of women's rights in general and those of Muslim women's in particular have remained at top of agenda in developing countries. Muslim women continue to face many problems in not only Muslim-majority countries but also in democratic secular countries like India and even in western countries where Muslim personal law cannot be practised. Their Islamic rights are also denied to them in the name of shari'ah law which is supposedly divine.

One reason for this is ignorance of Islam in general, and Qur'anic pronouncements in respect of women, in particular. There are two extremes among Muslim women: one, who accept Shari'ah pronouncements in respect of women totally and uncritically being totally unaware of circumstances in which the Muslim jurists made those pronouncements. Most of these women are either illiterate or educated in traditional Islamic sciences. Second category is of those women who are totally indifferent to religion and consider religion an impediment in realising women's rights. They even reject religion aggressively like Taslima Nasrin.

Both these extremes do not help as far as average Muslim women are concerned who, ignorant or otherwise, take their religion seriously and also are struggling against traditional shari'ah pronouncements about women. These women are in overwhelming number and one has to help them realise their rights in the Muslim society. This can be done only through the medium of Islam and by re-examining the Shari'ah pronouncements in the light of Qur'an and its normative verses.

There is enough in the Qur'an favouring rights of women but these Qur'anic pronouncements have so far been ignored or interpreted in ways loaded against women. It is, therefore, necessary to critically examine the Shariah pronouncements in respect of women in the light of Qur'an as understood by modern Muslim women in a democratic set up. We should bear in mind that cultural mediation affects our understanding of scripture.

Thus two things are important in this respect: reading the Qur'an from women's perspective and secondly from democratic cultural perspective since medieval cultural perspective has seriously affected our understanding of the Qur'an. It is heartening that some Muslim women are making serious attempt in this direction. Some of them are organising seminars and discussions and re-reading the Qur'an from women's perspective and are invoking the doctrine of *Ijtihad* which is dynamic principle of Islam. *Ijtihad* has been sanctioned by no less a person than the Prophet (PBUH) himself. Thus *Ijtihad* is integral part of Islam and has played a very important role in the entire history of Islam. The corpus of Shari'ah laws would not exist but for *Ijtihad*. It is unfortunate that after 11th century A.D. the *'ulama* began to frown upon *Ijtihad* for various reasons.

I have before me a compilation called For Ourselves- Women Reading the Qur'an. This is an important compilation by Women Living Under Muslim Laws. This is a serious attempt by believing Muslim women from various Muslim and non-Muslim countries to re-read the Qur'an and re-interpret it. It is also important to note that there are different translators of the Qur'an and translation, howsoever honest and liberal, does tend to be interpretation and translator's ideological dispensation sneaks in. For example, a presenter in the seminar points out, "Among translators there is a range from ultra-conservative to ultra-liberal, and Abdullah Yusuf Ali is a liberal translator." There are translators whose translations almost indicate as if women are secondary to men. The word *qawwam* in the verse 4:34 has been translated in number of ways as ruler, as manager, as protector, supporter, in charge etc. you find 30 different translations.

In this key verse men have been described as *qawwamun* by the Qur'an and conservative translators translate as "men are rulers over women" and prove the superiority of men over women. However, liberal translators do not accept this translation and translate it as 'in-charge', or 'protectors' or 'managers' and so on. But even this carries a sense of superiority and others have translated it as those who run around to earn and nothing more. This reduces the degree of superiority and also they add that being qawwam is a function, not any biological superiority or inferiority and a woman can also be *qawwam*, if she earns and many women earn today in modern society and hence she also becomes *qawwam*.

Thus the Qur'anic text per se cannot be decisive but how it is understood by the jurist or theologian, is equally important and as pointed out before, cultural mediation, plays an important role. The Qur'anic text cannot be understood in the same way today as it was understood centuries ago in feudal cultural ethos. Thus one great impediment in bringing about change even today is absence of democratic ethos in Muslim world. The women still continue to play subordinate role in these countries as in authoritarian societies the jurists and theologians too tend to be authoritarian and totally lack democratic perspective.

Thus a great struggle is going on in the Muslim countries for rights of women. More and more women are getting educated and becoming aware of their rights, Islamic or otherwise, and demanding changes in law. Something will definitely emerge from this great churning. Women scholars like Fatima Merssini from Morocco, having both Islamic and modern secular education have also shown the way. She has pointed out in her work The Veil and The Male Elite how to understand Qur'an'and *Hadith* literature. She has critically examined the Hadith literature which is one of the main sources of Shari'ah formulations.

It is of course, not easy to challenge traditional sources of Islamic jurisprudence. It would require not only great Islamic scholarship but also sustained efforts in that direction. After all we have inherited a rich corpus of laws which have been integral part of Islamic practices for centuries. They carry weight of great learned *'ulama* behind them. It is so difficult to disregard this juristic heritage.

But one need not despair. Much greater changes have taken place in the world in last two centuries. Until yesterday it was unthinkable that a Muslim woman can step out of four walls of her house and be active earning member of the family. But today it is an accepted practice even in countries like Saudi Arabia though with lot of restrictions. In other Muslim countries she can move freely, go out and earn and also hold important public positions. When Benazir Bhutto took over as Prime Minister of Pakistan many conservative *'ulama* objected quoting a *hadith* that if a woman becomes head of the state it would be a disaster for the country. Fatima Merssini effectively demolishes authenticity of this *hadith* in her scholarly work and the Muslim world also ultimately accepted women premiers in Pakistan and Bangladesh. In Bangladesh two women have been alternating as Prime Minister for last several years.

Despite the fact that there have been women prime ministers in Bangladesh and Pakistan it does not mean that women in these two countries are not suffering. Quite to the contrary, the Pakistani and Bangladeshi societies are very complex in structure and Muslim women are suffering a great deal. In North West Frontier Province tribal customs and traditions are going very strong and honour killings are quite common. Women enjoy very inferior status in tribal areas. In Sindh too, there are practices like karo kari (local Sindhi term for honour killing) and marriage with the Qur'an. The later practice is meant to prevent women from marrying outside family and thus keep the land within the family itself since a Muslim woman can inherit land also as per Islamic law of inheritance.

The mechanical interpretation of hudud laws (punishments for crimes like murder, theft and rape or adultery etc.) in respect of adultery and rape normally goes against women especially when she becomes pregnant or she goes to lodge complaint against man who raped her. This is taken as self-confession of illegitimate sexual intercourse and is arrested and jailed or even sentenced to death by stoning as it was the case of Amina Lawal in Nigeria.

The hudud laws also need to be properly interpreted in the light of the Qur'anic pronouncements and translators like Maulana Muhammad Ali, Abdullah Yusuf Ali, Muhammad Asad and others have tried to do that. Stoning to death is certainly not a Qur'anic punishment as there is no such verse in the Qur'an but is based on *hadith* literature and it is necessary to critically examine the entire *hadith* literature. Even Imam Bukhari whose collection of *hadith* is considered most authentic had rejected thousands of *ahadith* while collecting them. Some of the *ahadith* that he accepted as authentic also are problematic and should be re-examined; in the light of the Qur'an.

We have to re-codify the Shari'ah laws pertaining to women on the basis of the liberal, modern interpretation of the Qur'an and some *ahadith* which are in conformity with the Qura'nic spirit. Such an approach, it is hoped, will be an instrument of struggle for women's' rights for believing Muslim women. This requires a great deal of research in authentic Islamic sources. This would need great Islamic scholarship on the part of Muslim women activists in various countries, especially Pakistan, Malaysia and Indonesia and some Arab countries like Egypt, Jordan etc. They may have to face opposition from conservative '*Ulama* but there is no other way.

I think, this is the only way in the given situation. Rejecting religion altogether is not the way out nor total submission to what exists. A new way will have to be carved out by women themselves.

Qur'an, Hadith and Women

What is position of women in Qur'an and *hadith*? It is very interesting to compare what is stated in qur'an about women and what do we find on women in *hadith* literature? And here I am not referring to *ahadith* from an other source but from what is known as Sihah Sitta (i.e. six most authentic sources of *hadith*). I wish our *Ulama* reflect on the contrast between how Qur'an treats women and how *ahadith* treat them. Much of woes of Muslim women will be over if we follow Qur'an rather than these *ahadith*.

Women lost in *ahadith* what they had gained through Qur'an. Today if world thinks Islam treats women in very unfair way it is because we follow *hadiths* rather than Qur'an as far as women are concerned. In pre-Islamic period women had lowest of low social status and Qur'an lifted them far above and our '*Ulama* never tire of saying this. But within few decades of the revelation of the Qur'an women came down to their pre-Islamic status in a fiercely male dominated society. And this was accomplished through *ahadith* as a legitimizing factor.

Those who narrated these *ahadith* never thought for a moment how they contradict Qur'an as these *ahadith* served the social purpose very well. Qur'an provided ideals and values but society could not rise to that level and instead dragged Islam to its own level and *ahadith* served that interest best.

When Islam was confined to Arabian peninsula it was different but when it spread to far off places, parts of Roman empire, Sasanid empire (Iran), Central Asia etc. these regions were very different in their culture, religious values and social ethos and it was quite natural for Islam to adapt to what these societies needed. Even Shari'ah, all jurists (fuqaha') agree incorporated much of Arab *'adati* (customary law).

It was not easy to avoid these cultural values and customary practices found in non-Arab societies when people of these regions embraced Islam. Position of women in these regions was no different from what it was in pre-Islamic Arabia and when one embraces a religion which originated outside that region he/she does not automatically caste away his/her own cultural values and social ethos.

Also, it is a well-known fact that Islam spread far and wide much quicker than Shari'ah laws were compiled in different schools. In fact various Shari'ah schools (*madahibi*) came into existence in different regions where Islam had spread. Even before the Arabs could grasp full significance of Islam and adjust their lives to new values and ideals, it had already spread to various parts of the world, right up to China. In fact Islam spread to these regions with lightening speed.

It is also interesting to note that various companions of the Prophet (PBUH) also had spread to these parts of the world and these companions in many cases married local women and adopted cultural values of the region and being companions of the Prophet (PBUH) they were also source of Islamic knowledge and those converted to Islam would flock to them for guidance and hence number of *ahadith* were narrated by these companions relying on their memory and understanding. Thus along with authenticity of *ahadith* sociology of *ahadith* also becomes equally important.

While Qur'an was compiled during Prophet's (PBUH) life time and when some deviations from standard recitation was noticed (on account mainly of tribal dialects) Hazrat Uthman had wisdom to compile standard copy and destroy all others and thus Qur'an was saved from differences in the text. All other copies of the Qur'an were prepared from this copy.

Ahadith, on the other hand, were compiled two to three centuries after the death of the Holy Prophet and underwent much changes due to passage of time. Though there was chain of narrators and despite honesty and integrity of narrators, there was every possibility of change in text with different narrators with even differences in their understanding and cultural background. Unfortunately for *ahadith* honesty and integrity of narrators became the only criterion rather than its conformity with the Qur'anic approach, values and ideals.

Also, there were those who did not hesitate to produce a *hadith* to legitimize some action or requirement of someone powerful and influential. Thus while there never arose any differences about the Qur'anic text, there have been all sorts of differences about authenticity or otherwise of *ahadith*. In fact much problems could have been avoided if *ahadith* in such large numbers and in different compatios had not been accepted. For these very reasons the Prophet (PBUH) had discouraged from compiling these *ahadith*. But *ahadith* became socio-cultural and socio-religious needs in vastly different circumstances.

These needs were such that a doctrine was evolved that even if a *hadith* stands in contradiction of the Qur'an *hadith* will prevail. Many Shari'ah injunctions were developed on this basis. Then various questions arose whether *hadith* is *da'if* (weak), narrated by only one or by several narrators or its different variations or whether its narrators (*ravi*) were *da'if* (weak) and so on. The whole *hadith* literature is full of these controversies. Also different sects relied on different *ahadith* to legitimize their positions. In short many controversies originated due to excessive reliance on *ahadith*.

Much more so *ahadith* were used to lower women's status as Qur'anic ideals and values in respect of women could not be accepted by societies which treated women as subordinate to men. Men in any case wanted to retain his superiority. He thought he was ruler over women and many Qur'anic verses were explained under the ethos of men's superiority. Most of the Qur'anic verses on women are not explained in the light of other Qur'anic verses (only reliable methodology to understand real intent of the Qur'an) but in the light of *ahadith* which degrade women.

I would like in this article to compare *ahadith* about women with Qur'anic verses and show how mutually contradictory these Qur'anic verses and *ahadith* are. Qur'an talks of equal dignity of men and women and even story of Adam and *Hawwa* is narrated in a way which does not blame *Hawwa* at all for eating the fruit of a tree which Adam was prohibited to go near to. Qur'an talks of creation of men and women from one nafs and *hadith* says *Hawwa* was created from rib of adam. Qur'an says it is Adam who disobeyed his Lord and acted ignorantly Thus Qur'an says "And Adam disobeyed his Lord, and was disappointed" (20:121)

Also, the entire discourse in Qur'an on women is rights based but in Shari'ah, thanks to *hadith* literature, entire discourse is duty based for women and right based for men, something which one found during period of jahiliyyah. It was too hard for men to accept equal dignity for men and women in the feudal society within which Shari'ah rules were compiled.

Qur'an gives equal rights and equal dignity to both men and women but *hadith* literature is full of *ahadith* contradicting this Qur'anic approach. For example in Bukhari we find a *hadith* which stands in contradiction to the Qur'anic verse 33:35. The *hadith* is narrated thus:

"The Prophet (PBUH) urged the women to be generous with their gifts, for when he had glimpsed into the flames of Hell, he had noted the vast majority of people being tormented there were women. The women were outraged, and one of them instantly stood up and demanded to know why that was so. 'Because,' he replied, 'you women grumble so much, and show ingratitude to your husbands! Even if the poor fellows spent all their lives doing things for you, you have only to be upset at the least of thing and you will say, 'I have never received any good from you!', At that the women began vigorously to pull off their rings, and throw them into Bilal's Cloak. (Bukhari 1.28, Abu Dawud 439).

See the content and tenor of this *hadith.* It is full of anti women attitude and women are supposed to be, in this *hadith*, ungrateful to their husbands. As against this see the Qur'anic verse 33:35 which says, "Surely the men who submit and women who submit, and the believing men and the believing women, and the obeying men and the obeying women, and the truthful men and truthful women, and the patient men and patient women, and the humble men and humble women, and the charitable men and the charitable women, and fasting men and fasting women, and the men who guard their chastity and the women who guard, and the men who remember *Allah* and women who remember ? *Allah* has prepared for them forgiveness and mighty reward."

See how in this verse Qur'an treats men and women equally and talks of equal degree of forgiveness and equal reward. In the above *hadith*, on the other hand, more women than men are consigned to flames of Hell because they are ungrateful to their husbands. Qur'an no where requires women to be obedient to their husbands. It is husband who is exhorted to be kind to their wives (see 2:229) "keep them in good fellowship (*bi ma'ruf*) and let them go with kindness (*bi ihsanin*).

Also men and women are described each others garment (*libas*) (2:187). According to Qur'an men and women are each others zawj (one of the couple) thus indicating equal dignity and love and respect, not obedience or subordination. The Prophet (PBUH) never treated any of his wife as subordinate. He not only treated them with dignity, he often consulted them in various matters and even followed their advice. In fact Umm Salma's advice to sacrifice animal at Hudaybiya proved very beneficial.

Woman Half a Witness?

Let us examine one more *hadith* which apparently appears to be in conformity with Qur'anic provision but indeed it is not. We find it in Muslim. The *hadith* is narrated as under:

Prophet is reported to have said, 'I have seen none lacking in common sense and failing in religion but (at the same time) robbing the wisdom of the wise, besides you.' Upon this a woman remarked: 'What is wrong with or common sense and with religion? 'He observed: 'You lack of common sense (in) that the evidence of two women is equal to that of one man, that is the proof of your lack of common sense. And you spend some nights (and days) in which you do not offer prayer and in the month of Ramadan 9during the menstrual days) you do not observe fast; that is your failing in religion.' (Muslim 31)

This *hadith* has several flaws. Qur'an nowhere states that she is half witness, much less because of lack of common sense. And messenger of *Allah* will not say such things which degrade women whom he consulted in difficult times as pointed out above. Qur'an simply says that when you take loan, write it down and let two male witnesses be summoned as witnesses and if two men are not available let one man and two women bear witness so that if one forgets, other can remind. (2:282)

This verse no where says she lacks in common sense. She may have lacked in experience as in those days women did not indulge in financial transaction. Lack of experience cannot be equated with lack of common sense. Also, if women cannot offer prayers or fast during menstruation, how can it be construed as 'failing in religion'? It is state of disability, not lack of belief or commitment. Belief or religion has something to do with ones heart and soul, not physical condition. Our Prophet (PBU) had high respect for women and for his wives. It is unthinkable that he would say such degrading things for women. He loved Khadija, Fatima and Ayesha so much. All these women were highly intelligent and great upholders of Islam. In fact they were more firm in their belief of Islam than many men. Entire Muslim world holds these women in high respect. In fact Islam gave such high status to women and guaranteed their rights when all over the world women had no rights at all. In fact it was this general demeaning attitude towards women which is reflected in these *ahadith.*

Women Rulers Bring Bad Luck to those Over Whom they Rule

We find another *hadith* in Bukhari which is often quoted against women becoming rulers of countries or nations. In fact Bukhari has reported three traditions connected with this episode, two of which were in the chapter on "Letter of the Prophet to Chosroe and Caesar". Abu Bakr's *hadith* is No. 4425. The preceding *hadith*, No. 4424, was reported from Ibn Abbas who said that "the Prophet of *Allah* sent Abdullah Ibn Huzaifa with his letter to Chosroe. When Chosroe read it he tore it. I believe said Bin Musayyab said: Then the Prophet prayed to *Allah* that he tear them up completely." The third *hadith* is No. 6639 reported by Bukhari in the chapter on "how the oath of Prophet was" and it goes: "When Ceaser dies there will be no Ceaser after him. When Chosroe dies there will be no Chosroe after him."

Bukhari (4425) reports from Abu Bakr the following *hadith*: "*Allah* provided me with considerable benefit during the battle of the Camel with one word (or one statement). When news reached the Prophet (S.A.W.) that the Persians had appointed Chosroe's daughter as their ruler, he said: "A nation which placed its affairs in the hands of a woman shall never prosper!"

Now it is well known that Abu Bakr narrated this *hadith* after battle of Camel in which Hadrat Ayesha participated and the battle was aimed against Hadrat Ali. This *hadith* surfaces only with the narration of Abu Bakr who was aspiring for governorship of one of the provinces and wanted to please Hadrat Ali. Abu Bakr obviously had a purpose in narrating such a *hadith.*

It is quite contradictory to Qur'an in as much as Qur'an upholds leadership of Queen of Sheba (Bilquis) who over-rules the advice of her male advisors and makes peace with prophet Salman (Soloman). See verses 32 to 35 of Chapter 27. When Bilquis asks for opinion of all her male advisors whether we should fight or make peace with Sulaiman, they advise her to fight and not to surrender. But she over rules them and decides to make peace arguing "Surely kings when they enter a town, ruin it and make the noblest of its people to be low; and thus they do."

Thus we see that Qur'an upholds wisdom of a woman in not fighting and making peace with stronger ruler and saves the nation from ruin. But the *hadith* quoted above says just the opposite that if a woman becomes ruler it would prove ruinous for the nation. The *hadith* thus suggests that Prophet contradicts Allah's revelation which is not thinkable. The only conclusion in either the narrator had his own motive in narrating the *hadith* or could not at all understand what the Prophet said. I leave conclusion to the readers.

We find even more shocking *ahadith* ascribed to the Prophet regarding women. One such *hadith* found in Sahih Bukhari and narrated by Sahl ibn Sa'd which says "Evil omen was mentioned before the Prophet (PBUH). The Prophet (PBUH) said, "if there is evil omen in anything, it is in the house, the woman and the horse."

This *hadith* equates woman with house and horse. There cannot be any comparison between the three. Also both house and horse are extremely useful for human beings which facilitate his/her living and traveling. House is from basic necessity for human beings and horse was needed in those for travel and were valued highly. They were used in wars as well as their movement was quite swift. Such thoughts are product of very low kind of mind unfortunately ascribed to a mind *Allah* had graced with highest kinds of thought. He had chosen him to be His Prophet, His messenger. One cannot think he would say such things.

There is one interesting *hadith* found in Bukhari and narrated by Ayesha. The *hadith* is like this: the things which annul the prayers were mentioned before me (Ayesha). They said, "prayer is annulled by a dog, a donkey and a woman (if they pass in front of the praying people)".

Ayesha said, "You have made us (i.e. women) dogs. I saw the Prophet PBUH) praying while I used to lie in my bed between him and the Qiblah. Whenever I was in need of something, I would slip away, for I disliked to face him."

We can see how some narrators equated women with dogs and donkeys and Ayesha challenged them. It shows how men held women in low esteem and ascribed their despicable thoughts to the Prophet (PBU). Always there may not be women like Ayesha to challenge such low thoughts and *hadith* may be believed uncritically.

Similarly we find another *hadith* in Sahih Bukhari narrated by Osamah which is again totally contradictory to the Qur'an. The *hadith* says "And I advise you to take care of the women, for they are created from a rib and the most crooked potion of the rib is its upper part. If you try to straighten it, it will break, and if you leave it, it will remain crooked, so I urge you to take care of the women."

Very degrading to women, like similar such *ahadith.* It completely contradicts the Qur'an where there is no mention at all of *Hawwa's* creation from the rib of Adam. This *hadith* also has been created to prove inferiority of women. In all the verses on women in Qur'an there is not a single verse which degrades women like this or proves her inferiority to men in any way.

This was prevailing social attitudes of men towards women which made them create such *ahadith* so that they could rule over them and women could not use Qur'an to claim equality with men. Qur'an was revealed to the prophet so that he could give equal dignity and status to women but society was not prepared for this in any case and sought to lower the status of women by producing such *ahadith* as they could not temper with the Qur'an they used another weapon to bring down status of women.

It is unfortunate that still our *Ulama* are not prepared to critically evaluate these anti-women *ahadith.* On the contrary they keep on quoting them to keep status of women lower in the society and under the thumb of women. It is precisely for this reason that non-Muslims think very adversely about Islam and how Islam has 'suppressed' dignity and status of women.

Time has come for Muslim women to evaluate these *ahadith* critically and refute the fatwas *Ulama* issued on the basis of such *ahadith.* We need great scholars of Islam among the women who could take independent position. Where are such women?

Women in the Light of *Hadith*

Muslim Women are often deprived of their rights in the name of *hadith.* When it is pointed out that it is not keeping with the spirit of Qur'an they point out some *hadith* and say *hadith* is authentic and *hadith* will prevail even if it is not strictly in keeping with the Qur'anic pronouncement. But such people are equally selective in matters of *hadith.* They quote *hadith,* which serves their purpose and helps in maintaining man's authority over woman. Here we would like to throw light on those *ahadith* which are closer to the spirit of the Qur'an and which empower women. Such *ahadith* are often suppressed or at least not highlighted except by those who believe in justice to women.

Before we take up these *ahadith* we would like to throw some light on nature and treatment of *ahadith.* First most important thing in regards to *ahadith* is that unlike Qur'an there is no unanimity about *hadith* among Muslims. It is highly controversial area and it is not without grounds. No criteria had to be laid down for Qur'anic text as the Prophet (PBUH) used to recite vahi as soon as received and some of his companions used to either memorise it or write it down on palm leaf or camel bone or its skin. So never any controversy arose.

It is not so in respect of *ahadith.* A*hadith* were compiled more than 150 years after the death of the Holy Prophet. Prophet himself never encouraged collecting of *ahadith.* He was aware of controversies it will give rise to. Similarly Hazrat Abu Bakr and Umar also discouraged collection of *ahadith.* So not much attention was paid to *ahadith* until the period of four caliphs.

It was after them that all kinds of political controversies started and Muslims were divided into different groups and subsequently into sects. The Umayyads captured power and to the shock of Muslim Ummah Yazid was nominated as his successor by Amir Mu'awiyah. The *Umayyads* were conscious of their non-acceptance by Muslims and also the fact that Yazid had brutally killed Imam Husain and his colleagues. So the Umayyads had to somehow win legitimacy and *ahadith* began to be fabricated. This was one reason why so many *ahadith* came into existence, which were far from being authentic.

Second reason why large number of *ahadith* came to be fabricated was that Islam spread to vast non-Arab areas with their distinct cultures and traditions. They had to mould Islamic teachings in their own customary mould. Also many Sahabah (companions of the Prophet) were not available to travel to those areas and spread proper teachings of Islam. This was particularly so in respect of women. Each culture has its own traditions of treating women. It was difficult for those cultures to accept what Qur'an had taught them with respect to women. These were feudal cultures where women were greatly subjugated and patriarchal authority was supreme.

And to give legitimacy to their own customs and traditions over and above *ahadith* were needed and thus large number of *ahadith* came into existence. When large number of *ahadith* came to be fabricated many Jurists and *Ulama* were alarmed and had to develop science of *hadith* to separate authentic from fabricated. This was not easy with passage of time but nevertheless an attempt had to be made.

One of the ways developed was to examine the chain of narrators as to what was the reputation enjoyed by narrators. Were they quite honest and truthful? However, this became most important criteria rather than text of the *hadith* itself whether it was in keeping with the reason or in keeping with the Qur'anic teachings or not. Thus *riwayat* (what is narrated) became more important than dirayat (i.e. reason). Also, if a *hadith* was narrated by a single narrator it could not be as acceptable as the one narrated by several narrators. Most of the *ahadith* were judged on these criteria.

Those jurists who lived in Mecca and Madina like Imam Hanbal or Imam Malik used only those *ahadith* which were considered authentic there and thus used very few *ahadith*. Imam Abu Hanifa also was very careful in this respect but since he lived in Kufa which was confluence of more than one culture (non-Arabs outnumbering the Arabs) he had to face several other problems which were not faced by Madinese and Meccan jurists.

What is corpus of Shari'ah law which survived had come into existence in largely non-Arab areas and did caste its shadow on the corpus of Shari'ah law and such *ahadith* about which there was no unanimity were used in its formulation. These sociological aspects cannot be ignored while determining status of women Thus one has to be very careful while pronouncing our judgment about Shari'ah laws as regards to women.

With these introductory remarks we would like to deal with those *ahadith* which are more favorable to women than others which reduce women to man's subjugation and then it is justified in the name of *hadith*. Qur'an has not only given equal dignity but also has recognized woman as an independent entity in her own right, not mere appendage to her parents or husband. However, it is not so with Shari'ah law. She is treated as subject to father's or husband's authority.

Let us begin with creation of adam and *hawwa*. Qur'an no where says that *Hawwa* was created from the rib of adam and yet we find this in *hadith* literature and that too in Sahih Bukhari. Now it is true this *hadith* is accepted by Muslims almost unanimously and yet this cannot be the reason for accepting it uncritically. The Qur'an while talking of creation of man and woman says in 4:1 "O people, keep your duty to your Sustainer, Who created you from a single being (nafs) and created its mate of the same (kind), and spread from these two many men and women."

According to this verse both man and woman were created from one being and there is no question of one being superior to the other. But this was not acceptable to a culture which was patriarchal and wanted man to be invested with authority over woman. Hence a *hadith* was needed to sanctify man's authority over woman and this *hadith* said *Hawwa* was created from rib of Adam. This belief was more popular among Christians (though it is not stated in Bible also) and was borrowed from there.

In order to make woman subject to male authority it must begin with her origin itself. If it is accepted as revealed in Qur'an that both man and woman were created from the same being and from the same kind how could one justify superiority of man over woman. Also, unlike Bible *Hawwa* was not to be blamed for Adam's mistake and it was Adam himself who was to be blamed for defying Allah's fiat.

Thus the Qur'an clearly says "And certainly We gave a commandment to Adam before, but he forgot; and we found in him no resolve (20:115) then again Qur'an says, "And adam disobeyed his sustainer, and was disappointed" (20-121). In both these verses Qur'an blames Adam alone and *Hawwa* is no where in picture. Thus it is not *Hawwa* who, as in popular stories, induced Adam to eat the forbidden fruit. It is again very important verse as to how Qur'an treats woman.

Thus according to Qur'an woman is neither posed again man nor is she his competitor but in Qur'anic philosophy both man and woman complete each other and they are mutual companions, nothing less, nothing more. And according to one *hadith* the Messenger of *Allah* said both man and woman are equal in status. Yet our *hadith* literature is full of *ahadith* according to which woman is not equal partner but depends on the will of her husband. She has to be obedient to husband and not to do anything not approved by him.

Again according to *hadith* literature woman is temptress, often misleads man and seduces him and makes him deviate from right path. This is utterly un-Islamic and un-Qur'anic view of woman. And according to some *ahadith* she will be severely punished if she disobeys her husband and goes out of her home without his permission. She should not go to see even her sick father or mother, if husband has not given her permission.

And in Qur'an even if suckling is to be discontinued for a child it should be done with mutual (husband and wife's) consent. Thus Qur'an says (65:6), "But if both desire weaning by mutual consent and counsel, there is no blame on them." Thus even for weaning mutual consent and counsel is necessary and so woman should be equal partner in all such decision and not only husband.

Many marry off their daughters without her consent or even without consulting her. And it is surprising that even Imam Shafi'I, *Maliki* or even *Hanbali* (followers of Imam Hanbal) take such position which is found to be quite weak. Imam Taymiyyah and his disciple Ibn Qayyimj did not agree with them and refuted this position. Daughter's consent is a must for her marriage.

According to one *hadith* the Holy Prophet is reported to have said that if woman becomes head of a state that country will face disaster. A Moroccan sociologist Fatima Merrinisi has shown after meticulous research that this *hadith* appears thirty years after the death of Prophet (PBUH) and its narrator is one Abu Bakr who narrated this *hadith* after the battle of Jamal in which Hazrat A'isha fought against 'Ali. We do not find its narration by others. It is also important to note that Abu Bakr was aspiring for a post in Hazrat Ali's administration. The Prophet had highest regard for women and he can hardly be expected to have said such thing. Also, in a revelation to the Prophet Bilquis (Queen of Shiba) overrules opinion of her court nobles to fight against Soloman rather than make peace with him. Thus Bilquis showed more wisdom than her male nobles.

One thing is to be noted here that our apriori attitudes are of reflected in the use of *hadith* or Qur'anic text. If we are for subordination of women to patriarchal authority we either search for such *ahadith* ? weak or strong- or Qur'anic text by and interpret it the way we want and if we are in favour of women's dignity and equal status we search for *hadith* or Qur'anic text to suit our attitude.

Then what is the way out? How to determine what is really intended? We have to adopt proper criterion as well as methodology for that. In order to do so first we have to carefully examine the core value system of Islam and then to take other factors social, economic, political and contextual. These factors are contingent, not integral to the core value of Islam.

Now core value of Islam is gender equality and human dignity (2:228, 17:70). Thus if other factors do not seriously impinge on the situation gender equality and woman's dignity will prevail and laws made will have to reflect these two core values of Islam. Now when jurists of classical Islamic period 1st to 3rd centuries of Islam were compiling Shari'ah laws there were certain contingent factors they had to take into account which resulted in gender inequality. But since these Shari'ah laws were based on these contingent factors and not on core values, they cannot have status of permanence. If those contingent factors are no more valid, the laws may have to be changed in keeping with the core values of Islam.

First, when classical jurist were formulating laws the very social ethos were such as to subject woman to male authority.

Secondly, there was no concept of rights of women as an individual entity and this certainly influenced Islamic jurists while making laws. However, since Qur'an had clearly pronounced their rights they could not completely ignore rights but did find ways to make woman subordinate through arguments like she is biologically different and as a mother she has duties towards her children and so on or by using weak *ahadith* or used the Qur'anic text through their own interpretation.

Thirdly women in those days were economically totally dependent on man and hence could hardly assert their independence and also were brought up on those lines interiorizing their subjugation to man. So the jurists found no resistance from women to their formulations who took them quite natural as well as divine. Though there were few women who were learned and knew both *hadith* and Qur'an but they were far and few in between. Moreover such women also had to take prevailing social conditions into account.

Now take *hadith* like a mehram man (man relative who is prohibited to her by way of marriage) must accompany her when she goes out. She cannot go alone. In those days social conditions were such that there was no security available outside home and she was considered weak unable to defend herself from sexual attacks or molestation and hence a man must accompany her to protect her. Even today in many places women are generally unsafe and are often sexually attacked and raped and hence as a precautionary measure someone may accompany her.

But this cannot be elevated to a level of principle and stipulate that she cannot go out of her home without accompanied by a man which is what our jurists do and consider it a divine injunction. In principle a woman should be free to go out alone, if she deems it fit and social environment is secure.

Also, our muftis and jurists insist that she cannot earn her living and it is husband who will earn and look after his wife and children. This also has been elevated to the level of principle and many men do not allow their spouses to work. It is true it is Qur'anic injunction that husband will maintain his wife and children but Qur'an also permits woman to earn and whatever she earns will be hers and husband cannot take it away except by her consent (4:32).

Sometimes extremely weak and fabricated *hadith* is quoted to reduce her status and deprive her of her just rights unequivocally described in Qur'an or *hadith*. For example she is not allowed to enter mosque for prayer. There is absolutely nothing in Qur'an or in authentic *hadith* to prevent her from entering the mosque. Yet it is rigorously enforced in South Asia though not in South East Asian countries. In the Prophet's (PBUH) time women used to go to mosques even early morning and 'Isha (late evening) prayers. We find in Sahih Muslim that the Prophet (PBUH) said 'do not prevent Allah's female servants from entering the mosque'.

Another two *ahadith* often quoted to reduce woman's status are that women are deficient (naqis) in intellectual capacity and faith (iman) and that Prophet (PBUH) said that if it were permissible for human being to perform sajdah (prostration) before other human being I would have asked women to prostrate before her husband. Both these *ahadith*, Yusuf Qardawi, a well known *'alim* from Egypt (now living in Qatar), are baseless. But they are often quoted to degrade woman.

Similarly Yusuf Qardawi points out the *hadith* that the Prophet of Islam asked his daughter what is best for a woman and Fatima Zahra replied she should not see any man and no mans should see her. The Prophet kissed her and said you are my daughter. Qardawi says this *hadith* is baseless and is not even worth the ink it is written with.

The Qur'an, on the other hand says that when Moses met two daughter of prophet Shuaib and he gave water to their sheep they talked to him and he talked to them and then "One of them said: O my father, employ him; surely the best of those that thou can employ is the strong, the faithful one. (28:26)

This verse shows two things: one, women can talk to men who are strangers and that women's counsel can be sound. This is further reinforced by the story of Queen Shiba which we have already quoted earlier. Similarly it is well known that in Hudaibiyah when companions of the Prophet (PBUH) refused to sacrifice animals as the Prophet had agreed to humiliating terms for peace with non-believers of Mecca, he sought advice of his wife Umm Salma and her advice proved to be very useful. Despite all these some people maintain that do not consult your womenfolk and if you do, do opposite of what they say. It is great insult to her intelligence and her dignity.

Similarly one saying is ascribed to Hazrat Ali that woman is total evil and whatever she does is evil. How can Ali whose wife was Fatima, Prophet's daughter whom the Prophet (PBUH) loved intensely can say this? All this is reflection of what was thought of women in earlier medieval societies and how men treated women. The Qur'anic and Prophet's teachings about women were totally disregarded in view of prevailing social ethos.

It is true that it is very difficult to change social conditions through mere exhortations. It takes not only sincere efforts and commitment but also objective socio-economic conditions. The Islamic teachings could not be implemented and women continued to be treated with contempt and degradation for following reasons:

1. When the Prophet and his companions departed from the scene there

was none left with strong commitment to Islamic ideals to supervise Islamic values and ideals.

2. Islam spread to areas far and wide with culture in which women had much lower positions and they accepted Islam more for convenience than conviction and were immersed in their own cultural values and social ethos. Hardly anyone except some *Ulama* knew Qur'an and *hadith* and they too were surrounded by cultural traditions alien to Qur'anic teachings and hardly could do anything to change it.
3. The prevalent socio-economic conditions were also not at all favourable to raise woman's status. Mere religious teachings could, as pointed out above, hardly have brought about the necessary change.
4. Islam conquered parts of Byzantine Empire on one hand and Sassanid Empire on the other hand and both were feudal empire. Thus Islam entered a feudal society and got itself feudalized and women were further subjugated in Muslim society with feudal cultures.
5. Islam could not emerge from feudal societies until modern times and in modern times too basically no capitalist or industrial revolution could take place in entire Islamic world.
6. Those who migrate to western countries today also do so from these semi-feudal countries with their own traditions which remain part of their cultural baggage when they go there and attract severe criticism. Since the Muslims living in western societies are hardly acquainted with Qur'anic status of women, they consider such harsh criticism as 'attack on Islam' and is hardly able to respond creatively to such attacks.

We, therefore have to go back to Qur'an for restoring woman's rights and promote gender equality and reject all those *ahadith* which are weak and fabricated and develop proper criteria to develop new legislative parameters.

Uniform Civil Code or Legal Pluralism

Recently the Supreme court while disposing of a case on Indian Succession Act, 1925 filed by a Catholic priest voiced its distress that the government has failed to enact Common Civil Code to end discrimination among various religious communities in the areas of marriage, succession and property, and said that such a code would help in removing the contradictions based on religious ideologies.

The Supreme Court also declared as unconstitutional Section 118 of the Indian Succession Act, 1925 which applied to Christians alone and not to any other communities and imposed restrictions on the community from bequeathing property for religious and charitable purposes by will.

It is not for the first time that the apex court has voiced its opinion for enactment of such a code. In other cases too it did so particularly while delivering judgement on the Shah Bano case which had perturbed the Muslims. However, in other cases the Supreme Court judges did not hold unanimous view for enactment of common civil code. Earlier Justice Shah had held that any imposition of such a common code would be against the provision of the Article 25 which guarantees? freedom of conscience and free profession, practice and propagation of religion.

The Muslims have also always maintained that imposition of common code will violate the spirit of Article 25. The Muslim personal law is part of the Shari'ah law and the Shari'ah law is integral part of Islam. According to them the two cannot be separated. How can then the Constitution allow freedom of religion and impose, at the same time, a law, which is contrary to ones religion?

There is some truth in the argument but not the whole truth. We will come to this little later. First it must be pointed out that imposition of common civil code is rather an elitist view, not a popular one. In fact only those who stand for gender equality irrespective of religious provision to the contrary, would accept such a code. But a vast majority of people from all religious communities, including the vast majority of Hindus, would reject it.

Even the members and supporters of the BJP would show hardly any enthusiasm for it. In fact the Hindu law is much more iniquitous for women than the Muslim law. Even after the reforms in the traditional Hindu law, and enactment of the Hindu Code Bill, which was vehemently opposed by the conservative Hindus and, therefor, had to be watered down, it is more iniquitous than the Shari'ah law. A Muslim woman can divide the ancestral property as her right to inheritance in immovable property is unconditional whereas there are problems in partitioning the ancestral property for a Hindu woman.

The BJP has unfortunately made common civil code a Hindutva agenda thus imparting it a Hindu communal colour. The BJP has adopted it as its agenda not because it loves gender equality but only because it is opposed by minorities, particularly Muslims. It was for this reason that all women's organisations dropped the demand for common code, as it became the Hindutva agenda. In a highly communally charged atmosphere no minority community would welcome such a measure.

Today with a deepening of democratic processes each caste and community is becoming more conscious of its identity and today our polity is mainly based on these identities. The politicians have been fighting elections mainly on the basis of caste and communities and thus have aggravated feeling of identities. In Rajasthan when Rupkanwar committed sati the Rajputs defended it as a matter of their identity. The Rajput youth stood with swords to defend the memorial created there.

Thus it is very difficult in such political atmosphere to think of enacting common civil code. The caste practices among Hindus are far more important than any law of the country. Each caste has its own customs and traditions, which supersede all laws of the country. In several parts of U.P. if any boy of lower caste marries girl of upper caste they are publicly beheaded. Such cases have often taken place between *Jats* and *Jatavs* of U.P.

The diversity of laws among Hindus is so bewildering in different regions and castes that to create a uniform law among them itself would be a great challenge. In Tamil Nadu and some other parts of south the most preferred form of marriage is between niece and maternal uncle while in U.P. marriages even within seven gotras are unthinkable. How can one reconcile such diverse practices within one uniform law?

The reality in India is much more complex than western societies, which have been totally secularised. The process of secularisation in India though not negligible is yet far more slow and tortuous. In many cases traditions and traditional practices are assuming greater importance than ever before. In many ways it seems we are regressing rather than progressing. And no law, however ideal, can become acceptable if it alienates people and ignores social realities. A law has to be socially rooted, in order to be acceptable. Thus sociological view is as necessary as legal view.

Democracy in a country like India with its pluralist tradition lasting over thousands of years cannot succeed without respecting pluralist ethos. It is interesting to note that the west has discovered pluralism recently? after Second World War and hence calls it post-modernist phenomenon. But India has known it even during medieval ages. We lived more in peace and harmony as we respected pluralism, different religions and different traditions.

The modernisation brought new problems and we began to imitate the west without understanding our own social realities. These problems are getting intractable as our society is not changing, especially when it comes to mass of people, as fast as upper class economic elite. This is much more so as far as Muslim masses are concerned. There is much greater degree of power and illiteracy among them compared to other communities. There is very weak middle class among them to advocate modernisation and change. It is precisely for this reason that priestly class which itself comes from poor strata has much greater hold over the community.

And yes we have to find solution to the problem of gender discrimination in the given laws in all communities. How to go about it? Common civil code is no solution. The solution can be found in legal pluralism. If we accept this way of looking things it will be easier to remove gender discrimination. But legal pluralism does not mean we retain traditional or religious laws as they are. We must make suitable changes and enact reforms to remove gender discrimination embedded in these laws.

As far as Muslim personal law is concerned there are two main problems oral or triple divorce and legality of polygamy. The Muslim personal law board must bring about these desired changes within Islamic framework. Triple divorce is not a Qur'anic injunction. And the Prophet has also strongly disapproved of this form of divorce. The Qur'an has, in fact, prescribed most modern way of divorce through arbitration (4:35). It is highly unfortunate that Muslims in India ignore such a clear Qur'anic injunction and practice form of divorce disapproved by the Holy Prophet. Moreover *Hanbali*, Maliki, *Ahl-e-Hadith* and Shi'ah Muslims do not accept the validity of triple divorce. Thus it should be abolished and replaced with the Qur'anic form of divorce or by Talaq-i-sunnah which are very fair to women. Triple divorce in one sitting is not practised in most of the Islamic countries. Even Pakistan and Bangladesh have changed their laws in this respect.

Similarly as far as polygamy is concerned the Qur'an has given permission for it in particular circumstances and most reluctantly and if the two verses on polygamy i.e. 4:3 and 4:129 are read together it becomes impossible to practice polygamy. It is wrong to think that the Qur'an has permitted polygamy without any conditions. Its conditions are most rigorous and very difficult to fulfil and hence even in earlier Islamic period the Mu'tazila believed that it is as good as banned.

The Muslim women hardly suffer other disabilities i.e. widow re-marriage, property rights, inheritance etc. and are much better off than other women. Thus Muslim Personal Law Board should take the Qur'anic spirit into consideration in reforming the personal laws and remove such disabilities as mentioned above. The personal law thus will not come under legal scrutiny again and again and would also uphold the real Islamic spirit. Many illustrious Islamic scholars of nineteenth century and early twentieth century like Maulavi Imtiaz Ali Khan, Maulvi Chiragh Ali and a legal luminary like Justice Amir Ali had advocated these changes within Islamic frame-work.

Thus legal pluralism will be much more in keeping with the democratic spirit than a common civil code and all right thinking people should work for these necessary reforms to do away with gender discrimination of traditional laws. Moreover no one has framed any common civil code so far, not even the BJP which has been advocating it for political rather than reasons of gender justice. Very few men are prepared for gender equality in our society. Even if a common civil code is to be enacted one should frame one and publicise it for discussion by all concerned rather than simply talking of enforcing one. A social consensus will be highly necessary. Let us not simply politicise the issue.

Women and Understanding of Qur'an

Until recently it was monopoly of man to understand and interpret scripture and make laws according to their own understanding and man's understanding was very much colored by patriarchal culture. Now it has been well-established fact that patriarchy has played very important role in understanding of scriptures. What was considered as 'divine' was also as much male-oriented. It appeared as if God spoke through man only and women were, at best secondary in divine scheme of things.

Also, man was subject and women object of divine knowledge. Man legislated through divine ordinances and women were required to follow the laws. They could not even understand, let alone intervene, nor could they mediate in any situation. And they served God only through man. Father and then husband had to be obeyed almost as God had to be obeyed. In Islamic tradition this is well represented through a *hadith* which says Prophet (PBUH) said that had sajda (prostration) been allowed for human being I would have ordered women to perform sajda before their husbands.

Thus a woman was required to follow and obey man either as father or husband or even as elder brother. The right to be marriage wali (marriage guardian) was invested in elder or younger brother if father or grandfather or uncle did not exist. Thus in *shari'ah* marriage could not be solemnized without a man guardian. Woman was always like to err and hence needed male guidance.

Patriarchy was so strong an influence that even Qur'an, whose primary project appears to accord equal status to women, failed to achieve this objective in society. We have shown elsewhere (Islam and Modern Age, January 2007) that in Qur'an entire discourse on women is right based and for men duty based and yet Muslim society completely reversed this and again entire discourse on women became duty based and that of men right based. That was the power of patriarchy. Though the Prophet (PBUH) even in his farewell address remembered women and exhorted his followers to treat women kindly.

He said in his farewell address regarding women as reported by Ibn Ishaq, "O people! It is true that you have certain rights with regard to your women but they also have rights over you. (emphasis supplied). Remember that you have taken them as your wives only under Allah's trust and with His permission. If they abide by your right then to them belongs the right to be fed and clothed in kindness. Do treat your women well and be kind to them for they are your partners and committed helpers. And it is your right that they do not make friends with anyone of whom you do not approve, as well as never to be unchaste." (emphasis supplied)

The words in italics show that they were by any standard revolutionary when they were uttered (more than 14 hundred years ago). The Prophet (PBUH) was extremely supportive of women's rights, their equality with men and their dignity as human being. What was the urgency for the Prophet (PBUH) to exhort men for women's rights in the farewell address? Because he knew women are ill-treated by men in the society and even Qur'anic exhortation is ignored and hence he reinforced Qur'anic exhortation for women's rights through his farewell address. He mentions about women's likely unchaste behaviour for historical reasons. In Arabia before Islam it was not very uncommon to have extra-marital relations. Marital bonds were not strong among many tribes, especially outside Mecca and Islam laid great stress on chastity of women and strongly condemned extra marital relations and hence Prophet also emphasized that. It was in no way derogatory to women.

Now in contemporary world situation with regard to women is fast changing. Women are now not only well educated but also are becoming increasingly independent economically. They are not satisfied with traditional interpretation of Qur'an. Not only the Muslim women but also women from other faith traditions want to revisit their respective scriptures and reinterpret them from their perspective. All universities have also started women studies departments.

There are those women who are secular and reject role of religion in their lives but there are also women (majority of whom) want to abide by injunctions of their faith but are not at all satisfied by conventional understanding of their scriptures. This is much more so as far as Muslim women are concerned. They are convinced of truth and divinity of Qur'an and want to understand it from their viewpoint.

But important question is whether they need to be expert of Arabic language for understanding Qur'an? Some '*Ulama* would insist yes, anyone who wants to interpret Qur'an must have mastery over Arabic language. Not only that they also must have thorough knowledge of *hadith* literature. They should also know, according to them, good knowledge of how those words used by the Qur'an, were used in jahiliyyah (pre-Islamic) period. These are, according to the '*Ulama*, essential condition for understanding of the Qur'an.

The tribe of '*Ulama* know very well that generally Muslims do not fulfill these conditions and hence they would not dare understand Qur'an by themselves and will ever depend on them and Qur'anic understanding will remain their monopoly for ever. It was for this reason that '*Ulama* condemned anyone who translated Qur'an in any non-Arabic language.

Even great authority on Qur'an like Shah Waliyullah in 18th century was reprimanded and punished for translating Qur'an in Persian. But one must note that this is not Qur'anic position. Qur'an itself says it has been reveled in simple language so that people can understand it easily. Let us not forget that Qur'an was addressed to mostly illiterate people of Arab. It is well known fact that Arabs were never proud of learning but of knowledge of their lineage. They rather under-rated high degree of learning. In Islamic history even learning of Islam, theology, philosophy, philology etc. was enriched by non-Arabs. Arabs hardly ever, took keen interest in higher learning. It is for this reason Qur'an maintained that it has been revealed so that it could be understood easily (yessarnal Qur'an) so that even an illiterate Arab can understand it. This was when Islam was confined to Arabia. But new problems arose when Islam spread fast among non-Arab peoples.

One reason why non-Arabs took such keen interest in acquiring higher learning in Islamic fiqh, theology and philosophy was because it was only in this area that they could excel Arabs, not in the field of Arabness. After all in early history of Islam Arabs were the ruling class and despite repeated exhortation against it in Qur'an and *hadith*, Arabs remained very proud of their ethnicity and they continued to look down upon non-Arabs as inferior.

The non-Arbas did not want to depend on Arabs for understanding of Qur'an and they began to especialize in the knowledge and philology of Arabic language and thus it became highly specialized field of learning. Today non-Arab Muslims far exceed Arab Muslims and for them understanding Qur'an remains very serious enterprise. Of late Qur'an began to be translated into various languages and now is available in all the world languages.

It also needs to be noted here that there is no concept of priesthood in Islam, much less any church authorized to interpret Qur'an and issue binding injunctions. And women were never debarred from understanding and interpreting Qur'an. In fact throughout history of Islam there have been prominent Qur'anic authorities as well as authorities on *hadith* among women. In fact according to recent research at Islamic Centre at Oxford University, there were more than 38,000 muhaddithin (narrators of *hadith*) among Muslim women and their biographies have been published in eight volumes.

Thus women always took keen interest and developed appreciable learning in Qur'anic studies. But these women mostly accepted well-known male authorities as their model of learning and rarely developed an independent and autonomous understanding of Qur'an from women's perspective. Their excellence in learning was derived, more often than not, on male authorities.

But all those women who want to draw inspiration from Qur'an are not expert in Arabic language and specially in classical Arabic. Even many Arab women whose mother tongue is Arabic, speak dialects and are not well versed in classical Qur'anic Arabic. What should they do? If they go to already well-established authorities, they are all traditional authorities and do not admit of any new understanding of the Qur'anic text.

What should these non-Arab women or those Arab women not well versed in Classical Qur'anic Arabic do? Should their understanding remain subjugated to traditional understanding? In that case not only that they will not be able to achieve their liberation from male-orientation of Qur'anic interpretation, but also would not be inspired by Qur'anic injunctions which they aspire to.

The only alternative is that they should understand Qur'an in translation in their mother tongue and try to make sense of Qur'an from feminist perspective in their own language. understanding of the Qur'an reading it in their own language. One can be a good Qur'anic scholar by studying Qur'an in her/his own language, provided his study of Qur'an is thorough. I know people who do not know a word of Arabic and are yet able to quote appropriate verses of Qur'an on subjects of their interest.

Now the question is (1) of authenticity of translation and (2) viewpoint of translator. Both are important questions. As for authenticity of translation is concerned, there are some very authentic translations are available, especially in English and also in other languages. However, second question that of viewpoint is more crucial when it comes to feminist perspective.

It is not easy to find translations, which have been done in inclusive manner and with feminist perspective. Most of the translations have been done from male viewpoint and that is considered quite natural also. It is only after mid-twentieth century that some women scholars began to study and write on Qur'an from their own perspective. Some among them have been Riffat Hassan, Amina Wadud from America, Ziba Mir-Hosseini from the U.K., Asghar Ali Engineer from India and others.

They have written extensively on Qur'an and women's rights but none of them have translated Qur'an from feminist point of view. This has been done now by Laleh Bakhtiar of Iranian origin living in USA. Her translation is inclusive. (of both the sexes) and has translated verses pertaining to women in a very gender sensitive manner. Her translation of verse 4:34, for example, is quite interesting.

She translates it as under:

Men are supporters (qawwam) of wives because God has given some of them an advantage over others *(faddalna b'adahum 'ala ba'din)* and because they spend of their wealth. So ones (f)* who are in accord with morality are the ones (f) who are morally obligated, the ones (f) who guard the unseen of what God has kept safe. But those (f) whose resistance (nushuz) you fear, then admonish them (f), and abandon them (f) in their sleeping place then go away (from them (wadribuhunna) (f) then go away from them (f); and if they (f) obey you, surely look not for any way against them (f)."

Here there are few key words like *qawwam*, *nushuz* and *wadribuhunna*. Those who translate from male point of view translate qawwam as manager and some have even translated it as authority during earlier periods. Laleh Bakhtiar translates it very differently as 'supporters'. This translation is sensitive to female sensibilities. Actually it is also in keeping with meaning of the word qawwam which also means to maintain, to support financially.

Another crucial word is *nushuz* which generally means to rise against, to rebel. If we go by Prophet's farewell address after his last hajj (as reported by Ibn Ishaq) *nushuz* can also resisting husbands authority.

Thus if wife refuses to abide by husband's wishes or resists his wishes then he should persuade her and if not persuaded isolate her in sleeping place and even then if she persists in her resistance 'go away from her' i.e. leave her. Generally the word wadribuhunna has been translated as 'chastise her' which is offensive to modern female sensibilities.

Of course some people point out that actually *nushuz* means sexual misconduct quoting Prophet's (PBUH) last sermon and then maintain that chastisement is for sexual misconduct and hence justified as often husbands' would kill their spouse for such behaviour in Asian and African countries. But the Prophet (PBUH) is only advising chastisement (without injury) which is far more humane and sensitive to woman's feelings.

One Turkish scholar has rendered wadribuhunna as 'strike away' them i.e. divorce them if they persist in their nushuz (resistance, rebellion or misconduct). One more argument against chastisement is verse (2: 229) where it is said "keep them (wives) in good fellowship". If one has to keep them in good fellowship where is the question of beating them or chastising. And keeping wives in good fellowship recurs in the Qur'an number of times.

Of course one argument in favour of 'chastisement' could be the historical view of Qur'anic text. In seventh century Arabia one could, the argument goes, hardly expect otherwise. In those days wife beating was socially quite acceptable and Qur'an prescribed it only in extreme case of sexual misconduct (provided we mean by nushuz as sexual misconduct) and that too with advice not to injure them. More kindness to women could not be expected in seventh century Arabia.

But the counter argument could be when Qur'an accorded equal status to women (see 2:228 and 4:32) in seventh century which was equally unthinkable in 7th century Arabia, it could also prohibit wife beating which is quite undignified behaviour towards her. Well there could be arguments and counter arguments and much will depend on ones viewpoint whether it is feminist or not.

And today there are women experts who study Qur'an from feminist point of view and translate Qur'an in that perspective. Thus for those women who translate Qur'an into other languages expert knowledge of Arabic is highly necessary. But every woman who wants to know what Qur'an has to say about their rights, need not be expert in Arabic language. They can certainly select a translation which is more sensitive to their needs.

But there can be no two opinions about studying Qur'an on the part of those women who want to know their Qur'anic rights, whether they study Qur'an in Arabic language or in any other language.

Even those women whose mother tongue is Arabic, face a severe problem as far as '*Ulama* are concerned. They maintain, as against Qur'an, that it is not easy to understand Qur'an even if one knows Arabic and they need to study tafsir (commentary and explanation) of Qur'anic text in order to understand it. But Qur'an itself maintains, as pointed out above that it has been made easy to understand as it has been revealed for common people and for their guidance. Also, there are two types of verses in Qur'an what are called muhkamat and mutashabihat i.e. those verses which are quite clear and understandable and those which are ambiguous and capable of more than one meaning. Only those who aim at mischief refer to *mutashabihat*.

All verses pertaining to women fall in the category of *muhkamat* and hence can be understood directly with no intervention by '*ulama*. Moreover '*ulama* themselves differ widely from each other in understanding those verses. Even there are unending controversies about which *hadith* should be used to understand a verse and which *hadith* is not relevant.

In view of these controversies why a common person with knowledge of Arabic should not try to understand the divine intention by studying Qur'an. Also, the benefit would be new perspectives could be developed in understanding the Qur'an in today's context and in today's milieu. Did '*ulama* not tried to understand Qur'an in the light of their own experiences and in their own cultural milieu in early Islamic period? Is that understanding binding on us forever?

So far Qur'an was understood and commented upon only by men as women were not so highly educated in those days due to number of restrictions imposed on them during medieval ages. By then women had lost all rights and privileges accorded them by Qur'an and Prophet (PBUH). They are now retrieving that situation and more and more women are going for higher studies, women studies and divine sciences.

These women today are in much better position to understand Qur'anic text and from their own sensitivities. The real merit of divine text like the Qur'an is that it can be understood and interpreted in multiple ways and one can choose best possible ways. And women too have every right to understand these verses in best possible ways as they can keeping their sensibilities in mind.

Qur'an was revealed to create a new society, society based on values like justice, compassion, truth and love, not simply on tradition. However, social traditions asserted again and values were subordinated to traditions. Qur'an itself was sought to be understood in the light of traditions rather than values. Values like justice, love and compassion went in favour of weaker sections of society and women certainly belonged to that weaker section.

Hence if Qur'anic values were given priority over tradition, women would have enjoyed best possible status in the society. Since men, so far in authority, did not permit women to enjoy Qur'anic status, today time has come when women can choose to bring these Qur'anic values to fore and assert these values in their understanding of the Qur'an. It is their right and no one can take this right away from them.

Violence against Women and Religion

Religion is believed to be divine. It is divine in more than one sense. Firstly it is divine in the sense that its teachings are motivated by purest of intentions; secondly it is divine as its teachings are transcendent as religion exhort us to transcend what is to, what it should be in society as well as in our personal conduct. But soon after birth of religion it gets mixed up with customs and traditions already existing in society on one hand, and, on the other, powerful interests, often very negation of its teachings, begin to control it.

Thus what reaches us is far from religion in its divine form but a mixture of several things. Its divine teachings diluted or even negated and we begin to perpetrate certain dogmas in all their rigidity resulting in several problems and resisting all changes. We even forget that what is divine cannot be against reason and human progress both material and spiritual.

Rigid dogmas and doctrines are not product of religion, as we often believe, but of human mind which itself is product, not of divine teachings but of existing social ethos. Also, theologians and priests acquire, for followers of religion, status of demi-gods. An ordinary follower entirely depends on these scribes and priests for their understanding of religion. Also, psychologically speaking, most human beings feel highly secure by following some leader or authority. To think or act by oneself is quite onerous and avoided by ordinary human beings.

However, true religiosity consists in knowing, thinking and taking responsibility for ones own actions. Taqlid (mechanically following) is not a religious act as responsibility for what one does is not on oneself but on the leader whom one follows. Thus leaders acquire vested interest in their followers and anyone who effuses to follow becomes an heretic and is denounced, even ostracized.

I have said these prefatory words so that we understand real import of religion as against prevailing practices in the name of religion. Unless we discover the real spirit of original teachings we would continue to follow something far away from religion. It cannot be expected of any existing religious establishment to represent true spirit of religion. No establishment can ever represent true sprit of religion. They negate each other. Any establishment represents some form of interests and religion negates all forms of interests. It is an individual spiritual quest.

Today in all established religions we find women having secondary position. Religious leadership itself has become a male prerogative. Today all established religions represent patriarchal values and hence women cannot enjoy same rights and dignity as men. And this secondary position of women is sanctified through theological doctrines. Now no religion in its divine form can assign secondary position, much less vilify women. All human beings are creation of the Supreme Being. If at all women must have higher position as she partakes of creation through giving birth to human beings. If creation is a divine act, women too perform this divine act.

However, established religions, strayed from divinity, lost this divine dimension and patriarchy overtook divinity and women became subordinate to men and, at best became instrument of production rather than partaking of divine act. Conceiving and giving birth became her weakness rather than divine strength and even means of subjugation. And subjugation, in its extreme form, was enforced trough violence.

And since subjugation was theologized, so was violence against her. Thus violence against her came to be theologically justified in different religious traditions. Here we will discuss violence against her from Islamic theological point of view. When the Government of India passed the domestic violence Act, an Urdu paper from Mumbai *Inquilab* reported a statement of General Secretary of Muslim Personal Law Board that Government is depriving us of our Islamic right to 'beat our wives'.

It was a shocking statement as there cannot be divine right to beat ones wife. What is the source of this statement? It is a Qur'anic verse 4:34. Now according to all traditional commentators like Tabari, Zamakhshari, Ibn Kathir and others this verse of 4th chapter was revealed when a woman complained to the Prophet (PBUH) that her husband slapped her unjustly so what should she do? The Prophet (PBUH) who always gave priority to justice over anything else and also always accorded equal dignity to women, asked the woman to go and retaliate.

This created a crisis in the patriarchal society of Arabs and men surrounded the Prophet and said if our women have right to retaliate how will we control our families? It was natural concern in a patriarchal society. The Prophet had to tackle this crisis, according to this story and hence he waited for divine intervention to tackle it as it was of grave proportion. The revelation came in the form of 4:34.

This story also shows that many verses were revealed in response to certain social situation and hence importance of that verse could be understood only in that context. In other words such verses cannot be absolutized, as our jurists and theologians tend to do. This verse today is being debated between modernists and traditionalists and being differently interpreted.

First, let us take traditionalist point of view in understanding this verse. The verse has been translated as under by Maulana Muhammad Ali whom I can describe as semi-modernist i.e. neither completely traditionalist nor completely modernist: "Men are the maintainers of women, with what *Allah* have made some of them to excel others and with what they spend out of their wealth. So the good women are obedient, guarding the unseen as *Allah* has guarded. And (as to) those on whose part you fear desertion, admonish them, and leave them alone in the beds and chastise them. So if they obey you, seek not a way against them. Surely *Allah* is ever Exalted, Great."

I have underlined some words in this translation which are crucial in determining position of women in this divinely revealed book. We have already seen the context in which this verse was revealed. And to a great extent its meaning would also relate to this context. Traditional theologians and jurists read into it clear statement of subordination of women to men. The above translation, as I have said, is by semi-modernist theologian.

If we take traditional translation, it would be even more problematic from feminist viewpoint. The first underlined word in this translation is qawwam which the Maulana has translated as 'maintainer' but traditionalist translate it as 'ruler' or 'authority' and so translated it would mean 'men are authority over women'. However, root meaning of the word is maintainer and protector. So the Maulana is much closer to the root meaning than traditionalists. Maulana Abul Kalam Azad's translation in Urdu also supports this meaning.

The other underlined words are ba'duhum 'ala ba'din. Muhammad Ali has translated it as "some of them to excel others". However, Muhammad Asad, in his The Message of the Qur'an displays greater bias towards men when he translates these words as "God has bestowed more abundantly on the former (i.e. men) than on the latter (i.e. women). But again Maulana Muhammad Ali is much nearer to root meaning of ba'dahum 'ala ba'din than Muhammad Asad.

Next the words 'good women are obedient' are interpreted as 'obedient' to men. The Arabic word in the Qur'an is qanitatun which can only mean obedient to Allah, not to men. And to be fair to the Maulana, in the footnote to this word he has explained "Obedient here signifies obedient to Allah." Muhammad Asad has translated it as 'devout' which is closer to the root meaning of qanitat.

Another controversial interpretation is of the word what Maulana translates as desertion and Muhammad Asad as 'ill-will'. In Qur'an the Arabic word for this is *nushuz*. The root meaning of this word is to rise, to protrude. Thus its more acceptable translation would be to rise up against husband. It can be interpreted as desertion or also, as one Maulana Shoaib points out sexual misconduct. For this meaning of the word, he refers to Prophet's (PBUH) use of this word in this sense in his address after last Hajj known as Hajjat al-wada'.

The Qur'an, in this verse tells men that in case of *nushuz* (desertion, rising up or sexual misconduct) first they should admonish them failing which they should be isolated in bed and even then if they continue their nushuz then chastise (or beat) them. Now the Arabic word for chastisement used in the Qur'an is *wadribuhunna.*

The traditionalists argue that Qur'an clearly permits men to beat women (or their wives) though the Qur'an does not use the word wife but general word women. And that is why General Secretary of Muslim Personal Law Board gave a statement that this Act against Domestic Violence has deprived us Muslims of our God-given right to beat our wives. However, this translation (i.e. to beat them) is highly controversial and Muslim feminists and modernists are challenging it.

Then how Muslim feminists and modernists understand this word? Before we discuss this it would be better to point out that first major commentator of the Qur'an Tabari points out to few traditions (*ahadith*) of the Prophet which say that beating should be mere symbolic i.e. very light so as not to injure them. Tabari mentions the *hadith* that when asked how much can we beat? He was brushing his teeth with a brush; he lightly struck the brush on his body and said this much, no more. According to similar *hadith* also referred to by Tabari Prophet had a kerchief in his hand and he struck with kerchief and said this much and no more.

It is for this reason most of the translators write in the bracket while translating *wadribuhunna* 'so as not to injure them'. In other words do not thrash them. But then if they are to be struck so lightly like with the brush or handkerchief, what is the use? Beating is supposed to be a physical punishment and punishment for rebelling or sexual deviancy (if at all nushuz means that as Maulana Shoaib believes) cannot be as light as that. It should be such as to physically hurt.

Thus one should rethink the meaning of *wadribuhunna* here. It seems the Prophet's traditions referred to by Tabari may be later inventions. The word daraba translated as to 'beat' has no one meaning in Arabic language. It has several meanings. The meaning chosen should jell with the overall Qur'anic approach to women and not conflict with it. If word '*daraba*' is translated as beating, it certainly conflicts with the overall Qur'anic approach towards women.

If one carefully studies Qur'anic verses about women it becomes clear that Qur'an gives equal status both to men and women and equal dignity to both as human beings. Qur'an does no where distinguish between men and women except in matter of function. Qur'an even refrains from using word 'husband' and 'wife'. It often uses the word zawj i.e. couple which is much more equitable expression of marital relationship than husband and wife. Husband and wife indicate dominating and dominated relation.

Also, entire discourse in Qur'an about women is 'right-based' i.e. talks of their rights only and entire discourse about men is 'duty-based' i.e. talks of their duties only and repeatedly exhorts them how to behave with their wives. This was because in pre-Islamic Arab society women enjoyed no rights and were expected to discharge their duties towards their husbands. The Qur'an disapproved of this unequal relationship and enhanced her status by insisting on their rights and not on duties.

But patriarchal Arab society was not ready to accept such total transformation and with lapse of time again reversed the relationship and went back to original situation and hence Shari'ah discourse is full of discourse about her duties towards husband rather than rights though in view of clear Qur'anic verses jurists could not ignore her rights.

Also, Qur'anic verses talk of qualitatively different relationship between man and women. For example we find in verse 30:21 "And of His signs are this, that He created mates for you from your own kind that so that you might find quiet of mind in them and He put between you love and compassion. Surely there are signs in this for a people who reflect."

In this verse we find true Qur'anic approach towards husband-wife relationship which is neither of domination and dominated but of love and compassion towards each other. It is not only of sexual pleasure and procreation either. Men can find peace of mind in them (li taskunu). Thus there is no question of Qur'an allowing men to beat their wives even in the event of differences between them.

Also, the Prophet (PBUH) never ever beat his wives. Who knew Qur'an better than the Prophet? If the Qur'an allowed beating of wife Prophet would have surely known this and in the event of differences with his wives he could have used physical force, even symbolically as *hadith* ascribed to him shows. But we do not find any such event in his life. Prophet (PBUH) treated his wives most respectfully and with dignity. He knew Qur'an does not permit wife-beating under any circumstances.

The Qur'an refers to his differences with his wives when they demanded more material benefit from him which he could not afford. He did not even quarrel with them on the issue and only withdrew himself and sat in a room alone. When Umar whose daughter Hafsa had married Prophet, came to know about this, he came to meet him (and Prophet met him rather reluctantly) and Umar advised the Prophet to beat his daughter Hafsa as she had defied him. One finds reference to this in the Qur'anic verses 33:28-29.

Umar was known for beating his wife since his pre-Islamic days but the Prophet (PBUH) refused to accept his unsolicited advice. The tension between the Prophet and his wives was soon resolved and normal relationship resumed. Yet in another verse men and women have been described as each others friends. Thus Qur'an says, "And the believers, men and women, are friends one of another. (9:71)

Thus we should try to understand one verse of the Qur'an with another verse or verses of the Qur'an rather than with the help of *hadith*. Qur'an's authenticity can never be doubted though many *ahadith* (plural of *hadith*) are of controversial nature. Also, Qur'an gives norms and values and has transcendental dimension. *Ahadith*, on the other hand, are often product of patriarchal society and hence are to be treated with extreme caution.

Unfortunately all the commentators on Qur'an rely more on these *ahadith* than on the holistic approach to Qur'an as pointed out above. Even in formulation of Shari'ah laws, more reliance has been put on *hadith* than even Qur'an when several problems arose after the demise of the Prophet (PBUH). Most of the Arabs who embraced Islam were not in fact qualitatively transformed and social ethos and cultural values could not be easily caste away.

Thus patriarchy asserted itself again and again and even jurists could not completely disregard patriarchal values. Also, a theory was developed that the Shari'ah could incorporate the aadaat i.e. customs and traditions of the Arab society in which Islam was borne. This opened the door for much pre-Islamic practices to be incorporated into Shari'ah laws. In this process often Qur'anic values were compromised.

Thus the word wadribuhunna also came to be understood under prevalent cultural and social ethos of pre-Islamic society. In fact Meccan society was more patriarchal than Medinese society which had matriarchal traces and hence treated women with more dignity. But many of the prominent companions of the Prophet originally belonged to Mecca who had migrated to Madina either along with or after the Prophet. They wielded great influence in reporting *ahadith* and interpretation of the Qur'anic verses.

A careful exegetical literature would show that no scripture can be understood apart from existing social cultural practices. In other words understanding of scripture is culturally mediated. Thus no commentary on Qur'an can be an exemption. Though Qur'an is divine, its understanding is surely human and not binding. Human understanding can change in changed circumstances.

A modernist or a contemporary commentator may differ from earlier interpretations. Many modern scholars of Islam maintain that Qur'anic values can be much better appreciated and understood in today's circumstances when there is much greater awareness about women's rights and dignity. And surely Qur'an's transcendental approach can find much greater acceptability today.

Thus *wadribuhunna* should not be understood as chastisement but its other meanings must be explored to understand Qur'an's transcendental dimension. Even in medieval ages some Qur'anic scholar's like Imam Raghib Asfahani pointed out in his dictionary of Qur'an *mufradat* al-Qur'an that daraba 'ala in Arabic meant male camel going near female camel.

If this meaning is accepted and there is no reason why it should not be expected as it comes from a great lexicographer of Arabic language, the meaning of the expression radically changes. It would instead mean go near them if they are persuaded after isolation in bed and they give up their nushuz through persuasion. Many other modern commentators have also adopted other meanings of the term daraba.

Thus an American Iranian commentator Laleh Bakhtiar who has created a comprehensive data-base on Qur'an translates it as under: "But those whose resistance (nushuz) you fear then admonish them and abandon them in their sleeping place then go away from them (*wadribuhunna*) and if they obey you, surely look not for any way against them; truly Gid is Lofty, Great." (4:34) Laleh Bakhtiar 'The Sublime Qur'an').

Thus the medieval understanding of the Qur'an in such matters i.e. in women issues must make way for more modern and contemporary approach so as to give women their due which have been denied them for centuries and should no longer be denied today. The old approach cannot be sustained for long as women today are getting more educated and are active members of human workforce.

I hope, Muslim intellectuals and supporters of women's rights within Qur'anic framework would go for *ijtihad* (intellectual exertion for fresh approach) as it is long overdue.

5

Future Beckons All

Islam and Gender Equality

The question of sexual equality is very important parameter of modernity along with democracy and human rights. Whatever be the status of women in the Qur'an, status of women in Muslim societies is far from satisfactory. Be it in India, Pakistan, Bangla Desh or any other Muslim country in West or South East Asia like Malaysia and Indonesia. In all these countries the problem of women's status has acquired critical proportions. Many women's organisations have sprung up in these countries and are struggling for their rights. The problem is acquiring more and more serious proportions as modern education is spreading among middle class women.

Earlier, the orthodox in the community were strongly opposed to education for women. Even today in rural areas and smaller towns education for girl child is frowned upon. Nevertheless in bigger towns and among growing middle classes it is no more possible to stop women from acquiring education and hence proportion of educated women is increasing and with increased percentage of education among women awareness for their rights is also increasing. They increasingly demand equal status with men. Some women tend to become indifferent to religion and even consider religion as serious obstacle in their right to equality.

The orthodox among Muslims too, on their part, show stiff resistance to any change and want to maintain status quo. They of course quote from the Qur'an and *hadith* and also from opinions expressed by the Islamic jurists, to prove their case. This further strengthens impression among these women that Islam is not going to help them and they begin to reject it.

However, there are also women who are determined to use religion in their favour and for fighting their battle against the male understanding of the divine scripture. They believe in women reading and understanding the Qur'an. Thus there are various women's organisations doing this exercise and re-interpreting the Qur'an. It is a better sign and I believe, a more healthy sign. Women have as much right to understand and interpret the Qur'an from their perspective. Even most orthodox among the Muslims would agree that women have also right to interpret the Qur'an.

Sexual Equality and the Qur'an

The important question is whether the Qur'an accords equality to women or gives women an inferior position. According to conservative view, women have an inferior position and the *'ulama* quote the Qur'anic verses in their support as well as *ahadith* and opinion of the *fuqaha'* (Islamic jurists) in their favour. But this also raises an important question, which we must deal with.

Would sexual inequality prevalent in the past in the Muslim societies be binding on the modern generations too? Or to ask the same question in reverse i.e. can we be justified in projecting our modern values in the past? Should we expect that past generations follow our norms of sexual equality? Obviously, this would be an unfair position and so it would be equally unfair to expect that we blindly imitate the past generations and their opinion leaders. We have to evolve our own norms and values. But many of us do not accept changes in norms and values and consider it against Divine Will.

One also has to throw some light on the question of legal philosophy in Islam. The Islamic law is considered of divine origin and hence immutable. The time is not supposed to have any influence and external changes either have to be rejected or so moulded as to be acceptable to the immutable divine law. However, there have been an alternate point of view too inherited from past. Imam Shatibi of 14th Century Spain whose theory of Islamic law takes into account what he calls maqasid al-*Shari'ah* (i.e. purposes of Shari'ah) and masalih of umma (i.e. good of the community).

According to this alternate view it is *maqasid* (purposes) for which law has been framed, matters that law per se and keeping in view the maqasid changes can be affected to achieve these purposes and the good or welfare of the community should always be kept in view. One cannot sacrifice the purpose or the welfare of the community for the sake of law. Thus this alternate theory is more dynamic and change-oriented. But it was a minority view in the Islamic world.

But today there is more acceptability to this viewpoint. In fact Shari'ah was never meant to be static as it is assumed by many of us today. Shari'ah law was most dynamic and reflected needs of the time. The different jurists living in different places and in different circumstances adopted different views and they differed from each other on many issues. The eighteenth Century Islamic thinker from Indian subcontinent Shah Waliyullah also argues in his magnum opus Hujjat Allah al-Balighah that the Shari'ah is devised in keeping with the nature of the people and needs of the time. He devotes entire chapter of his book to develop this argument. He even gives an example of how ahkam (legal injunctions) change with circumstances.

The example given by him is quite interesting and pertains to law of inheritance. When the Prophet (PBUH) migrated from Mecca to Madina, his blood relations were left behind and so he established what is called *muwakhat* (mutual brotherhood) and the Qur'anic verse about inheritance was revealed. However, when those left behind in Mecca came back and joined their families and Islam flourished the verse, making inheritance a right of close blood relatives was revealed, cancelling the earlier one. Thus with the change of circumstances the hukm (religious injunction) also changed.

Thus Shah Waliyullah had this insight that Shar'i ahkam reflect social situations as far as mu'amalat (inter-personal and social) issues are concerned. The great Imams after whom Shari'ah schools are known are also categorised according to their social role. Thus Imam Malik was conservative and has been called as imam al-muhafizin (imam of those who wanted to preserve as much as he could). Imam Abu Hanifa, on the other hand, was more liberal and open and has been referred to as imam *al-mujaddidin* (the leader of modernists) and Imam Shafi'i was moderate and has been called imam al-wast wa i'tidal (i.e. leader of moderates). Imam Hanbal who was much more rigid has been described as imam al-mutashaddidin (i.e. leader of those who take extreme positions). In Saudi Arabia it is Imam Hanbal who is followed generally. This categorisation also shows that there were significant differences among the Islamic jurists and some among them were open and liberal and some quite rigid and unyielding. Changing social situations did influence thinking of eminent jurists like Imam Abu Hanifa and Imam Shafi'i.

The situation today has changed greatly and re-thinking on many issues like man-woman relations is highly necessary. Even the Qur'an, as pointed out by Shah Waliyullah and other Islamic *'ulama*, did respond to social situations and some verses revealed earlier were cancelled later with the changing situations. The debate about nasikh (verse which cancelled) and mansukh (verse which was cancelled) rages even today. It is important chapter of the Qur'anic *'ulum* (i.e. Qur'anic sciences).

Thus on man-woman relations also we find different verses which are selectively quoted by anti-equality and pro-equality of sexes. These verses were revealed in response to different situations and hence differing stances in these verses. Some verses make certain contextual concessions in favour of man and some lay down norms for long time to come. The Qur'an, it is important to note, does not confine to given situation or status quo (though has to make certain concessions to it) but basically wants to transcend the given situation. The most important characteristic of the Qur'an is its transcendence and anti status quo spirit.

Before the Qur'anic revelation woman's situation was far from satisfactory. She was not only unequal but subordinate to man in every respect though between Mecca and Madina there were significant differences also. Meccan society was highly patriarchal in ethos and Madinese society was perhaps matriarchal in distant past and its traces survived until rise of Islam.

Without this social background we cannot appreciate the changes Qur'an effected in Arab women's life at the time. However, the Arab men were not easily reconciled to these significant changes in women's status. We will throw some light on the kinds of debates, which took place on man-woman question at the time. Islamic revolution had brought lot of awareness among women of the time as modern democratic society has brought so much awareness among Muslim women today.

There are two significant verses in the Qur'an which reflect debate on men-women relationship in Madanese Islam. In Meccan verses we do not find these debates, as Muslims were too weak to think of these issues there. It was only in Madina that when Muslims began to acquire dominant position that these gender issues came to the fore. Women were far more aware of their rights after becoming Muslims and they posed questions to the Prophet (PBUH) about their status in response to which these verses were revealed.

Of these verses the two significant verses are 4:34 and 33:35. Both these verses make statements on men-women relations, which appear to be quite different. The modern scholars are keenly debating these verses. While 4:34 is often quoted by the orthodox to prove their point, there is controversy about 33:35 about its real status on sexual equality. Again the orthodox '*ulama* maintain that it is all about spiritual equality. Is it? It needs some discussion.

First, the verse 4:34 which is frequently quoted for Qur'anic position on sexual equality. The verse is translated as under by Maulana Mohammad Ali of Lahore: "Men are maintainers of women, with what Allah has made some of them to excel others and with what they spend out of their wealth. So the good women are obedient, guarding the unseen as Allah has guarded. And (as to) those on whose part you fear desertion, admonish them, and leave them alone in the beds and chastise them. So if they obey you, seek not a way against them..."

The same verse is translated by Muhammad Asad as follows: "Men shall take full care of women with the bounties which God has bestowed more abundantly on the former than on the latter, and with what they may spend out of their possessions. And the righteous women are the truly devout ones, who guard the intimacy which God has (ordained to be) guarded. And for those women whose ill will you have reason to fear, admonish them (first); then leave them alone in bed; and then beat them; and if thereupon they pay you heed, do not seek to harm them.."

However, Ahmed Ali in his 'Al-Quran' differs from both Maulana Mohammaed Ali and Muhammad Asad in translating the word 'wa'dribuhunna. Mulana Mohammad Ali and Muhammad Asad translate it as 'admonish then' and 'beat them' respectively. But Ahmed Ali translates it as 'go to bed with them' and cites Raghb's Mufridat fi Gharib al-Qu'an, Lisan al-Arab, and Zamakhshari. 'Daraba 'ala', according to Raghib is said for he camel mounting over she camel and thus Ahmed Ali translates it as 'going to bed' rather than beating the wife.

Thus we see there are significant differences in translation of this controversial verse. There are few key words in this verse '*qawwam*', 'qanitat', 'nushuz' and '*wa'dribuhunna*'. The understanding of the verse very much depends on understanding these words properly. 'Qawwam' traditionally has been translated as 'ruler', 'authority over women' etc. However, modernists and women rights activists are challenging this meaning. Maulana Mohammad Ali translates it as 'maintainer', Mohammad Asad as 'to take full care of' and Ahmed Ali as 'guardians'.

Thus '*qawwam*' should not mean ruler or an authority but one who takes care of or maintains wife or acts as guardian. It is thus not a statement of superiority of man over woman but an economic function. And it should also be noted that woman can also perform this function (and she does in our times) and hence she can also be 'qawwam' as per the Qur'an. Thus this verse cannot be understood properly unless we properly understand these key words.

Another key word is '*qanitat*' which is generally translated as 'obedient' and implying thereby 'obedient to ones husband. But that is also problematic. '*Qanitat*' means 'devoted to' or 'obedient to God' and not to husband. Then another important word is 'nushuz' which literally means 'rebellion' which has been rendered as 'ill will' by Muhammad Asad and Maulana Mohammad Ali as 'desertion' by wife and Ahmed Ali as being 'averse' towards husband. However, 'nushuz' as such applies to both husband as well as wife. The modern legal term for it is 'mental cruelty' and with respect to husband it also means 'ill-treatment' of wife in physical sense and we find mention of ill treatment of wife by husband (nushuz) in verse 4:128. Thus it clearly shows nushuz is applied to both husband as well as wife. And another key word '*wa'dribuhunna*' has already been explained. The word daraba has several meanings in Arabic language and here, as pointed out by Raghib himself could mean sexual intercourse with wife rather than beating or chastising the wife. Thus Ahmed Ali comes much closer to the meaning of the verse.

It is important to note that the Prophet (PBUH) has also strongly disapproved of beating ones wife. We find a *hadith* in authentic collections, which is as follows: "Could any of you beat your wife as he would a slave, and then lie with her in the evening?" And according to *hadith* in Abu Da'ud, Nasa'I, Ibn Majah, Ahmad bin Hanbal and others "Never beat God's handmaidens" i.e. he forbade to beat any woman.

In fact the above verse under discussion was revealed in response to a situation which has been described by Zamakhshari in his Kasshaf. This verse shows that there was practice of wife beating specially among the Arabs of Meccan origin. According to Zamakhshari Habiba bint Zaid complained to the Messenger of Allah that her husband Sa'd bin Rabi' slapped her. The Prophet told her to 'retaliate'. But this caused serious problem among men as they would not accept retaliation from their wives and hence they complained to the prophet and then this verse (4:34) was revealed.

However, it caused stir among women of Madina. They were disturbed and approached the Prophet and wanted to know their real status vis-a-vis men and then the verse 33:35 was revealed. The verse is quite important one as regards women's status and is translated by Maulana Muhammad Ali as under: "Surely the men who submit and women who submit, and the believing men and the believing women, and the obeying men and the obeying women, and the truthful men and the truthful women, and the patient men and the patient women, and the humble men and the humble women, and the charitable men and the charitable women, and the fasting men and the fasting women, and the men who guard their chastity and the women who guard, and the men who remember Allah and women who remember - Allah has prepared for them forgiveness and mighty reward."

This verse is an important statement of equality of men and women. It mentions ten times men and women being equal in all respects and their reward will also be equal. It is not merely in spiritual terms as some would like to believe as the verse mentions being truthful, guarding ones chastity and being humble and patient too. Thus men are no superiors to women in any respect, spiritual or material. This statement is being made when even Greek philosophers were discussing whether women have soul or not. The Qur'an, on the other hand declares that men and women both will be forgiven and would be given great reward in equal measure. There are other verses in the Qur'an which declare equality of men and women. The verse, 2:228 for example, is one among them. This verse says, "in accordance with justice, the rights of the wives (with regard to their husbands) are equal to (the husbands') rights with regard to them, although men have precedence over them."

Maulana Abul Kalam Azad, commenting on this verse says that the Qur'an through these four words (lahunna mithlul ladhi 'alayhinna) has made revolutionary declaration of equality of men and women. According to him these four words have given women all that was their right but they had never got them. These four words lifted women from the dust of deprivation and humility and made her sit on the throne of dignity and equality.

He also explains the words "and the men are a degree above women" by saying that they were earning and feeding them (the verse 4:35) and the Maulana, it is interesting to note also clarifies that men do not get any distinction by birth over women. If women earn and run the family women would also have this distinction of being a degree above men. Thus the statement of Qur'an "men are a degree above (women) is functional and not biological, in any way."

The meaning of the scripture reveals itself differently in different cultures and social conditions. Our jurists and the *'ulama* could not have understood the meaning in their social and economic environment which we can understand today. Thus the interpretation of the Qur'an should not be static leading to freezing of Qur'an's meaning in one particular age. While we should not fault the interpretations of eminent jurists and *'ulama* of earlier periods, we should not surrender our own right to understand and interpret the Qur'an under our own circumstances.

Thus our struggle is against the status quoist approach to the Qur'an and it is our duty to develop a new hermeneutics of the Qur'an which takes into account the economic and social needs and functions of our own times. Women are playing very vital role in our society and have even become economic leaders and managers. Thus the old hermeneutics cannot take us very far today.

When women were so aware of their rights in the time of the Prophet and were active on religious and social fronts, how can they remain passive today and accept the role assigned them by the orthodox *'ulama* who refuse to take into account the new socio-economic dynamics? It has always been a human endeavour to understand divine intentions as sincerely as they can. If our forefathers did it we can also do it today with same sincerity but different understanding mediated by our socio-economic needs.

Islam and Female Circumcision

These days a controversy is raging about female circumcision in India among a section of Muslims (Bohras). A woman belonging to the community has sent a petition to issue a firman banning the practice and is also preparing a petition to be filed in the Supreme Court to issue a ban order. Many newspapers and magazines are carrying articles on the issue condemning the practice and many have approach3ed me for interview whether it has Islamic sanction.

Needless to say, it is highly controversial subject and there is no unanimity among Muslims on this question. It is not found among all Muslims but among Bohras in India and among Shafi'is in Egypt, Sudan and Ethopia besides other African countries. Among Indonesian Muslims too, it is reported to be prevalent as they too are Shafi'is. But Shafi'is in India who are found in Western Maharashtra (Kokan area), in Kerala and Tamilnadu it is not prevalent. Thus all Shafi'is also do not practice it.

Whatever it is it has African connection. It appears this originated in Africa and spread in other parts of the world. It is important to note that Imam Shafi'I lived and compiled his fiqh mostly in Egypt and as for Bohras are concerned Cairo (Egypt) was the seat of power of Fatimid Imams and *Ismaili* book of jurisprudence *Da'aim al-Islam* was written by Sayyidna Qadi al-Nu'man In Cairo during the time of 14th Imam Mu'iz. Thus among Bohras also the African connection is obvious.

As to the Question whether it has any Islamic sanction the answer falls in rather grey area. One cannot say categorically either way. Qur'an does not talk of either male or female circumcision and that is why even male circumcision is referred to sunnah or Sunnat-e-Ibrahimi or Sunnat-e Mohammadi. But ib case of men it has almost considered obligatory and all Muslim sects are unanimous about it. Before Islam it was practiced by Jews and that is why it is also referred to as Sunnat-e-Ibrahimi too and according to some traditions Prophet (PBUH) adopted it from there.

While male circumcision is celebrated publicly and people are invited to public dinner female circumcision is done secretly (by those who practice it) and except family members no one cones to know about it. The *hadith* (tradition) cited is also considered weak by many Muslims. Thus we find in Abu Dawood (Book 41, no. 5251) that Umm Atiyyah al-Ansariyyah narrated that a woman used to perform (female) circumcision in Madina. The Prophet (PBUH) told her do not cut severely as that is better for a woman and more desirable for husband.

Similarly we find in Muslim too in Book 3 no. 684 Abu Musa reported. There cropped up a difference of opinion between a group of Muhajirs...He (Abu Musa the narrator) said I got up (and went) to A'isha and sought her permission and it was granted.... I said: what makes a bath obligatory for a person? You have come across one well informed! The Messenger of Allah (PBUH) said : when anyone sits amidst four parts and the circumcised parts touch each other a bath becomes obligatory.

We find similar *hadith* narrated by Abu Musa al-Ash'ari in Malik's *Muwatta* too. This *hadith* also refers to A'isha as the source. Similarly in

Malik's Muwatta Book 2 Number 2.19,77 it is said Yahya related to me from Malik from Naf'I that Abdullah ibn Umar "Ehern circumcised part passes the circumcised part *ghusl* (bath) is obligatory."

Similarly we find in the Shafi'I source book *Reliance of the Trqaveller* (*Umdat al-Salik*) written by Ahmad ibn Naqib al-Misri that female circumcision is obligatory. This book has been certified by al-Azhar University This book says "Circumcision is obligatory (both for men and women. For men it consists of removing the prepuce and for women removing the of the clitoris (*bazr* in Arabic). Hanbalis hold that circumcision of women is not obligatory but *sunna.*

Thus it will be seen that there is no unanimity among Muslims about female circumcision and it is found prevalent as pointed out mostly among African Muslims as among many African tribes. Whereas in case of men circumcision does not reduce sexual pleasure but is considered necessary from hygienic point of view, in case of female circumcision it reduces sexual pleasure and no hygenic function as in case of men. While men circumcision is universal among all Muslims, female circumcision, at least in practice, is confined to a few Muslim sects primarily those of African origin.

Since female circumcision interferes with woman's sexual pleasure, almost replacing old Roman chastity belt, it has become a human rights issue today. Female circumcision came into vogue to restrict her sexuality today women are demanding its abolition. It should also be noted that Islam does not, in nay way seeks to restrict either male or female sexuality but only restricts illegitimate sex outside marital bond and gives right to woman to seek divorce from impotent husband if he had hidden this from her at the time of marriage.

This Islam fully respects woman's right to sexual pleasure as it is essential for perpetuating human progeny. It is society which, in the name of morality does so but being patriarchal in structure, does not put any restriction on male sexuality. Actually both sexes should be permitted natural sexual pleasure as it is absolutely necessary for healthy human growth but also for perpetuation of human species. Justice demands that both sexes be treated equally.

Polygamy in Islam

Polygamy has been a very controversial issue in Islam. The Orthodox '*Ulama* maintain that it is part of Islamic Shari'ah and hence men can take up to four wives, if they want to, without any reasonable cause even. The modernists and champions of women's rights, on the other hand argue that the polygamy is only permissible in certain conditions with the strict proviso for equal justice with all the wives. According to the modernists, man just cannot take more than one wife simply because he likes some other woman or gets enamoured of her beauty. They also argue that the Qur'anic norm is monogamy but polygamy is permissible in certain exceptionable circumstances with strictly enforceable condition for justice.

The orthodox '*Ulama* justify polygamy on the grounds which have not been stated in the Qur'an. They argue that men's sexual needs are greater than those of women; secondly they argue that women go through periods or give birth to children and it is not possible to have sexual intercourse with them during these periods and hence man needs more than one wife. They also argue that if a woman is terminally ill it is better to marry another woman rather than divorce her and make her psychological wreck. Also, if she is barren and cannot give birth to another child, it is better to take second wife without divorcing her and add to her woes. She already suffers from lack of children.

Of course, as pointed out above, these arguments are not there in Qur'an or sunnah of the Prophet (PBUH). These arguments have been invented by some '*Ulama* to justify polygamy. Apart from these arguments, they also argue that there are more women than men and hence polygamy ensures dignified life for women rather than life of infamy and breaching the limits set by Allah.

The modernists and those championing women's rights, on the other hand, rebut all these arguments. They argue that it is not at all biologically and scientifically proven that women's sexual needs are any less than that of man. It is her social conditioning, which makes her sexually less active. Given proper environment a woman will also be equally sexually active.

The champions of women's rights also maintain than man is not created a mere sexual animal that he cannot restrain his sexual activity during menstrual period of his wife or when she gives birth to a child. Thousands of men do so. All men are not prone to polygamous marriages. Most of them, on the contrary, are monogamous. They can restrain themselves from sexual activity even when their wives are ill for long time and cannot cohabit with them.

Even when they are terminally ill, they can go without sexual activity and this sacrifice is worth making for a life time partnership. One cannot sacrifice this companionship just because she is terminally ill or is not capable of cohabitation. Those upholding women's rights argue that marriage is not all about sexual gratification only. The institution of marriage is much more than that. It is for life long partnership between the two, besides creating children and ensuring continuity of human life on earth. This can be ensured with minimum sexual activity. In fact polygamy is a medieval institution which was invented by man to fulfil his sexual lust and to keep women under his authority.

As for barrenness there seems to be some weight in taking another wife to procreate, as procreation is one of the objectives of marriage. But, in our society often blame is foisted on woman for failing to give birth to child. Man can also be barren and man often is. Unless it is medically tested one should not rush to the conclusion that woman is barren and hence man should take another wife to have children. Only and only when it is proved that a wife has medical problem in giving birth to a child or is completely barren she could be responsible for the absence of children.

Perhaps then there could be some justification for taking second wife. But thanks to modern scientific advances there are other possibilities: test tube babies. May be there is no ijma' so far about Islamic validity of test tube baby. We will have to leave it to the conscience of the persons concerned whether they would like to have test tube bay or not. Similarly adoption is also not permissible in Shari'ah law. Here is some bind for a conscientious Muslim. One can say in such case (i.e. when it is medically certified that wife, and not husband, is barren) husband could be permitted to take second wife. The other alternative is to remain childless. Some might prefer that way. Only when a wife is proved to be medically unfit for conceiving the husband perhaps could seek her permission (without using coercion in any form) to take second wife and provided, he is capable of doing equal justice to both of them, as required by the Qur'an.

Another argument for polygamy is that rather than let women lead sinful life it is better that one takes them as co-wives. Firstly there are very few societies wherein there are many more women than men. Even if there are more women, it is marginally so. Only during world wars when millions of people were killed there were substantially more women, than men. But it was a temporary and not lasting period. Perhaps there could have been some justification for polygamy during that period. But it is not correct to say that prostitution is because of more women in society than men. There is prostitution even when there is excess of men over women.

In India, for example, there is excess of men over women there being 1000 men for every 930 women and yet there is widespread prostitution. There are other reasons for prostitution than excess of women over men in a society. Prostitution has been in the world throughout history. In fact it is known as one of the oldest institutions in the world. Uneven distribution of wealth, migration of men to other countries or to urban areas in search of livelihood and extreme poverty in women's families, lax morals and organised crime are some of the factors responsible for prostitution. Mere polygamy, as some knively believe, cannot eradicate prostitution from the society. Even stringent law drives it underground rather than abolish it.

Thus all these arguments in favour of polygamy are hardly valid. These arguments have been invented for justifying polygamy; they hardly explain its existence. There are reasons other than the ones advanced above for persistence of this institution for so long. One must understand those causes and try, as much as possible, to control and regulate the institution of polygamy.

The Qur'an and Polygamy

Then one can justifiably ask why Qur'an permits it? Or what view the Qur'an takes of polygamy? One must take up the verses on polygamy in the Qur'an and explain them not merely as isolated verses but in the total spirit of the Qur'an. No verse of the Qur'an can be explained as an isolated verse. It is the context (in the light of asbab al-nuzul i.e. occasions of revelation) and norms of the Qur'an which have to be taken into account in order to understand the real intention of the Qur'anic verses. Also, it is not enough to refer to one verse on the subject but all concerned verses should be taken into account. Often one verse is quoted to prove one's point of view. It is not proper.

There are two verses in the Qur'an as far as multiplicity of wives is concerned i.e. 4:3 and 4:129. However, to take an overall view of Qur'anic spirit we will have to take more verses into account besides these two. Those other verses are equally important to determine the Qur'an approach to the controversial issue of polygamy.

First, let us take the two verses which make direct pronouncement on polygamy i.e. 4:3 and 4:129. The first verse i.e. 4:3 appears to permit taking up to four wives while 4:129 seems to caution against hazards of multiplicity of wives. Needless to say both the verses must be read together in order to determine Allah's intention. While the first verse takes given context into account and seems to permit multiplicity of wives, the second one takes long term view and also the likely consequences of taking second wife and this verse tends to be more normative than the other.

The first verse says: "And if you have reason to fear that you might not act equitably towards orphans, then marry from among women such as are lawful to you - two or three, or four: but if you have reason to fear that you might not be able to treat them with equal fairness, then (only) one - or those whom you rightfully possess." (4:3). This verse could be interpreted differently. It is not very clear whether it means two or three or four at a time or during ones lifetime. If up to four was meant it could have said "upto four". But the Qur'an rather chooses more complex way of putting it.

Even if what is meant is two or three or four at a time, the Qur'an does not permit it according to the whims of a man. It lays down strict condition for treating all wives with equal fairness and if you have reason to fear that they cannot be treated with equal fairness then marry only one. Thus if one reads even this verse alone literally, it would be obvious that more emphasis is on equal and fair treatment rather than having more than one wife. And this should not be determined by husband alone whether he can treat his wives with equal fairness or not.

Here in this verse the words "if you have reason to fear that you might not be able to treat them with equal fairness" are addressed to whole Muslim society and hence society as represented by its judicial institutions ('adalah) will determine whether the person has capability to treat his second or third or fourth wife with equal fairness or not and also whether there is any need for it. Thus it is obvious that taking of more than one wife should be socially regulated and should not be an individual decision. Unfortunately often decision is made individually as if it is personal privilege and no social intervention can be tolerated. The Qur'anic spirit, on the other hand, does require social intervention as equitable and fair treatment of wives is very essential.

There is also debate whether equitable and fair treatment implies only equal maintenance and equal facilities to all the wives or it also includes equal love. Some commentators, especially of the *Mu'tazilah* persuasion insist that equal love is also a necessary condition for all wives. And they argue that since equal love is humanly impossible (a man will always tend to love one of his wives more than the other wife or wives) polygamy is as good as banned by the Qur'an. Justice in treating all the wives equally is so important that the verse ends with the words alla ta'ulu (this is more proper that you may not do injustice.

Thus in verse 4:3 fear of injustice is stressed twice. Thus this moral dimension of polygamy cannot be taken lightly. Therefore, either it should be banned or should be strictly regulated and taking of second wife should not be left entirely to an individual. Social intervention is needed.

Also, the verse 4:3 should be read in conjunction with another verse on polygamy i.e. 4:129. This verse states, among other things, "Ye are never able to be fair and just as between women even if it is your ardent desire. But turn not away (from a woman) altogether so as to leave her (as it were) hanging (in the air). If ye come to a friendly understanding, and practice self-restraint, Allah is oft-forgiving and Merciful."

This verse is so clear on the question of justice and fair treatment with all wives that polygamy is almost impossible to practise. The words that you cannot do justice "even if it is your ardent desire" are so clear that there is no need for any further discussion. It is humanly impossible to treat all wives equitably (especially in matters of love) and one should not leave one woman hanging in the air and incline totally towards the other.

Here it is important to point out the Qur'anic methodology in social matters like slavery, polygamy and similar other matters. At the first stage the Qur'an permits an existing practice with proviso for reforms and improvement so as to lessen its negative impact but subsequently it points out in no uncertain language that it is best be abolished. A good example in this respect is of slavery. The Qur'an first requires Muslims to treat slaves in a humane way and also encourages their manumission as compensation for not able to keep obligatory fast or for expiation of sins etc. Bu subsequently it says that "All children of Adam have been honoured equally (laqad karramna *bani* Adam) (17:70). Thus all children of Adam deserve equal dignity and some cannot be slaves and others master. This makes institution of slavery totally redundant. But the Qur'an first accepts institution of slavery with necessary reforms and subsequently makes it clear that it is against human dignity.

Similarly approach has been adopted for the institution of polygamy. First it is permitted with strict proviso for fair and equal treatment and cautioning against injustice against any of the wives. It is also important to note that this verse (i.e. 4:3) has been revealed along with the verse pertaining to the problems of widows and orphans (*yatam*). This verse on polygamy begins with the words "If you fear that you shall not be able to deal justly with the orphans, marry women of your choice, two or three or four?."

Thus polygamy was permitted by the Qur'an to do away injustice to orphans and widows (actually the Arabic word yatama includes widows also). The Arabs, as per *'Zamakhshari of Al-Kasshshaf'* (Vol. I, Beirut, 1977, p. 496), would marry orphans and widows with beauty and wealth (far in excess of four women) and then try to usurp their wealth and do injustice to them in treatment. The Qur'an, in order to save these orphans from such injustices (and hence it begins with the words (If you fear that you shall not be able to deal justly with orphans?) those Arabs were permitted to marry up to four (thus reducing the number of wives one could take drastically) to avoid injustice to the orphans.

Thus polygamy (without any restriction as to the number of wives) already existed in the society and also injustices to the orphans. Thus with this verse (4:3) the Qur'an, which considers justice as most fundamental moral category, tried to stop abuse of orphan girls' properties (and this was vitally necessary) on one hand, and injustices to the women who were taken as wives without restriction to any number, and not treated fairly and equitably. This verse thus accomplished two objectives in one stroke - justice to orphans and justice to helpless wives by restricting their numbers to four and requiring oral responsibility of equal and fair treatment.

But, the Qur'an was aware that this is not the ideal solution as far as women were concerned. Thus in the second verse on polygamy (4:129) it was made clear that it is not possible to do equal justice to all wives even if one ardently desired and so the men were cautioned not to leave the first wife hanging in the air (fatazaruha kal *mu'allaqatin*). Thus, if both the verses are read together - and one must - monogamy would be the norm and polygamy a merely permitted measure to meet the given situation.

Thus the real intention of the Qur'an, is to ultimately abolish polygamy albeit gradually. It is also to be noted that marrying orphans to misappropriate their properties was peculiarly an Arab phenomenon, not a universal one. And polygamy was permitted by the Qur'an only in that context. It has also been pointed out by some commentators that the verse 4:3 was revealed after the battle of Uhud when more than 10% of Muslim men population was killed and there were many orphans and widows in the society and they had to be taken care of. Perpetuation of polygamy forever was far from the Qur'anic intention.

Thus the noted translator of the Qur'an Abdullah Yusuf Ali also says in the footnote to the above verse (4:3), "The unrestricted number of wives of the 'times of ignorance' was now strictly limited to a maximum of four, provided you could treat them with perfect equality, in material things as well as in affection and immaterial things. As this condition is most difficult to fulfil, I understand recommendation to be towards monogamy." (The Holy Qur'an, Abdullah Yusuf Ali, Vol. I, Hyderabad, India, n.d. p. 131)

More arguments can be advanced from other verses of the Qur'an if one takes the Qur'anic verses in totality as one must. The Qur'an uses the word zawj for husband and wife and zawj implies couple. So basically there should be one husband and wife - a couple - and not one husband and several wives. Adam, the first Prophet had one wife hawwa'. The Qur'an also describes husband and wife as each other's garment (2:187). Also the Qur'an says, "And the believers, men and women, are friends one of another. They enjoin good and forbid evil and keep up prayer and pay the poor-rate and obey Allah and His Messenger." (9:71)

Whole spirit of this verse is of equality and friendship between men and women. Thus this noble spirit of the Qur'an in respect of man and woman does not admit of four women being lorded over by one man. Also the verse 33:35 which makes men and women equal in every respect hardly can admit the institution of polygamy. Also, 2:228 establishes equality between men and women and can hardly admit of the polygamous marriages. Thus it will be seen that all these verses militate against polygamy. Polygamy can at best be an exception rather than a rule.

As for the Holy Prophet's *sunnah* is also concerned he preferred monogamy over polygamy. He remained highly faithful to his first wife Khadija as long as she lived though she was much senior (by fifteen years) to him. He never took second wife in her lifetime. He was a very loyal and devoted husband. He married A'ishah only after the death of his first wife Khadijah. And A'ishah was the only virgin wife he took. All other wives were either divorcees or widows and were more in the nature of political and tribal alliances than marriages for fulfilling sexual needs. Had he so desired he could have taken young women as his wives. But he never did after A'ishah.

He also strongly disapproved of Hazrat Ali, husband of his daughter Fatima, taking second wife during her lifetime. He was very angry when he learnt that Ali wanted to take second wife when Fatima was around. All this goes to show that the Prophet (PBUH) also stressed monogamy and one must follow his sunnah in this respect also.

Today's Qur'anic approach to justice and equality is much more relevant than before. Women's rights are being greatly stressed and if their rights to equality are to be respected, and one must, polygamy should be permitted only in highly exceptional circumstances. Actually monogamy should be the rule. The Qur'an foresaw this 1400 years ago and stressed concept of justice in sexual relations also and never accepted woman to be subordinated to man. The Qur'an, in fact gave dignity to woman by accepting her legal entity. However, through the ages she lost out to man in sexual politics. There is great need to restore dignity to her which is fundamental requirement of the Qur'an. She is equal partner to man in every respect.

In our attempt to codify Islamic law in India which is today quite loosely applied causing lot of problems to Muslim women, we interviewed number of prominent '*ulama*. One of our questions was should polygamy be regulated? With few exceptions most of them said 'no'. Polygamy is needed and some even said it is exclusive preserve of man and he can take second wife even without any reason or permission of first wife.

They also maintained that polygamy is needed to prevent prostitution in the society. To check sexual corruption polygamy is a must. This raises a fundamental question: Does Qur'an prescribe polygamy to check sexual corruption or prostitution. There are two verses in Qur'an on this subject 4:3 and 4:129. In both these verses there is no even indirect hint of any kind of sexual corruption.

The First verse 4:3 was revealed, we are told by earliest commentators on the Qur'an, after the battle of Uhud in which large number of Muslim men, in fact 10 per cent of Muslim male population, was killed. This led to creation of many widows and orphans which were to be taken care of. Many of these widows had their own land and property left behind by their husbands.

Who would look after the widows and their properties.? Some relatives or guardians. So Qur'an advises these guardians to be honest and not to change their bad property (*khabis*) with the good (*tayyib*) properties of orphans. And if one goes by the words of Qur'an it advises these guardians to marry one or two or three or four of these widows (not any women) children of whom they are in charge of.

And this verse ends by saying "If you fear you cannot do justice, then marry one (*wahidatan*). Thus we see two things clearly: one, Qur'an has clearly stated the reason for permitting multiple marriages and two, it is conditional that justice be done and gives strict warning. This conditionality becomes clearer in verse 4:129 where it is said "And you cannot do justice between wives, even though you wish (it), but be not disinclined (from one) with total disinclination, so that you leave her in suspense..."

If both verses on polygamy 4:3 and 4: 129 are read together (and they should be read together) The Qur'an's intention becomes clear. Qur'an's emphasis is not on number but on justice. In our male dominated societies emphasis unfortunately is on number, not on justice. Both verses read together make it absolutely clear that Qur'an has permitted polygamy most reluctantly in certain conditions like that of war and has made it conditional on justice.

Our '*ulama* and jurists unfortunately have ignored both the conditions (that of war and of justice) and give reasons for polygamy, not stated in Qur'an at all. Sexual corruption is no where stated in Qur'an for justifying polygamy as our '*ulama* are doing today. Many of them are not even aware of verse 4:129 which says it is so difficult to do justice between all the wives or if they are aware explain it away in some ways belittling its emphasis on justice.

Some of the '*ulama* even denied that this verse was revealed after the battle of Uhud and also maintained that the verse 4:3 does not require that one should marry widows or orphans only citing a *hadith* from Muslim which says Hadrat 'Aisha understood by that 'any women', not widows and orphans. If the Qur'an had meant any women it would require insertion of certain words which are not there.

And even if this report of Sahih Muslim be correct, how can one ignore the conditionality of justice which is stated so clearly and with so much emphasis? One Muslim scientist wrote to me that Qur'an prescribes polygamy because man is polygamous by nature. He, in his letter, argued elaborately but without substantiating his argument with any scientific evidence.

The Qur'an, on the other hand, clearly says that We have created everything in pairs (*wa khalaqnakum azwajan*) and it includes human beings too. Also, Qur'an lays emphasis on chastity ('*iffat*) and says, "And let those who cannot find a match keep chaste, until Allah makes them free from want..." (24:33). Thus Qur'an says if you have no means to marry one wife be chaste and our '*ulama* want men to marry more than one to refrain from sexual corruption. Who should we listen to? To Allah or these '*ulama*? We can draw our own conclusion.

No Sanction for Wife-beating

When the Indian parliament recently passed a law prescribing punishment for men beating up their women, the secretary of the Muslim Personal Law Board objected, saying parliament cannot take away a man's right to beat up his wife when the Quran allows him to do so. It was a shocking statement, indeed.

Verse 4:34 is often quoted by traditional jurists to say that the Quran allows the beating of one's wife as a last resort. The verse has been variously interpreted and those sensitive to women's dignity interpret it very differently. But before we discuss the verse and its different interpretations we should know the context in which it was revealed.

The earliest commentators have discussed the occasion of the revelation of every verse. Both Tabari and Kasshaf tell us that a woman complained to the Holy Prophet (PBUH) that her husband slapped her without any fault. "What should I do?" she asked. The Prophet said "Go and retaliate". The woman was happy but it cast a gloom over the men. They came to the Prophet, asking him how could they exercise control over their families if their wives were allowed to retaliate against them. The Prophet said the ruling he gave was his opinion but that he would wait for Allah's revelation regarding the matter.

Thus the verse 4:34 was revealed which reads as follows (usual translation): 'Men are the maintainers of women, with that Allah has made some of them to excel others and with what they spend out of their wealth. So the good women are obedient (to Allah), guarding the unseen as Allah has guarded. And (as to) those on whose part you fear desertion, admonish them, and leave them alone in the beds and chastise them. So if they obey you do not seek a way against them.'

The word qawwam also has been variously translated: authority, ruler, etc. But it means one who maintains or looks after. It's a functional term, not a term of superiority as usually made out by orthodox ulema.

Thus a wife who maintains her husband or runs the household can also be called qawwam. If both spouses earn and run the household together both will be qawwam. Nushuz (rebellion, desertion, misconduct) is also used in the Quran for men and women alike. Here it refers to women.

The word daraba has several meanings. It can mean to beat, chastise, strike off and, according to Imam Raghib in 'Mufradat al-Quran', '*daraba* '*ala*' means when a camel goes near the she camel. But what exactly does it mean in this verse is the real question. If we interpret wadribuhunna in the light of *hadith* it means striking lightly.

Tabari maintains that when the Prophet was asked how much to beat one's wife (if one must), he struck lightly with his kerchief and said no more than this, or that he was brushing his teeth and struck with the brush and said like this and no more. But if we try to understand this verse in the light of other verses about treatment of women, it is certainly not for beating them.

The Quran repeatedly tells men to treat wives with ma'ruf or ihsan (kindly or in a good manner). 'Even when retaining her or divorcing her, treat her kindly' (2:229). A woman enjoys equal rights and dignity with men and hence she cannot be treated in a manner which will hurt her self-esteem. Striking her, howsoever lightly, will also hurt her dignity and imply authority of men over women. It is un-Quranic in spirit.

The Quran frequently uses the word zawj for both husband and wife, implying one partner in a marriage and clearly indicating that the husband is just one partner in a marriage, not an authority figure. The Messenger of Allah (PBUH) never physically or mentally harmed his wives, let alone beat them.

We find this in the verses 33:28-29 and 66:3, that when his wives made demands on him he simply remained aloof, yet he always allowed them to argue with him. Thus we come to know how the Prophet treated his wives with dignity and never even implied that they should not argue with him.

One must reflect on the meaning of '*wadribuhunna*' and accept it in the sense of 'separating' or 'removing' or in the sense in which Imam Raghib tells us. In that case it would mean that if a woman rebels, deserts or misbehaves then first persuade her; after that leave her alone; even then if she is not persuaded strike her off (divorce her). Or go near her (if we accept Imam Raghib's meaning) after she has been persuaded to change her behaviour.

There is a great need today to read the Quranic verses from women's standpoint if we have to restore to them the rights the Quran has given them.

Islam and Family Planning

It is highly controversial issue among Muslims. Some maintain that Islam has no place for family planning and others, on the other hand, say it is not at all against the tenets of Islam. Generally, our *mullahs* who preach at mosque level sternly oppose it and maintain that our Prophet (PBUH) has asked us to increase the number of *ummah.* Muslims should, therefore, multiply their number.

They also quote a verse from the Qur'an, "And kill not your children for fear of poverty – We provide for them and for you. Surely the killing of them is a great wrong." (17:31). Here in this verse what is being said is not related to family planning for following reasons: One, this verse speaks of children born and not which have not even been conceived. (2) No one would ever advocate killing children already borne or even conceived and in advanced stage of pregnancy. It would certainly amount to killing.

And according to Imam Raghib in *Mufradat* (which is dictionary of Qur'an), here killing of children means *not giving them proper education* as ignorance is intellectual death and intellectual death is worse than physical death, in a sense. If what Imam Raghib says is taken as real meaning of the above verse, it strengthens position of those who advocate family planning. More children means parents will not be able to properly educate them.

Mot only that but parents will not even be able to feed them and give them nourishing food necessary for good health and healthy upbringing. This will be possible if number of children is less. Interestingly, this was the position of Imam Shafi'I which explaining the verse 4:3 The last words of this verse which is mainly on polygamy are *dhalika adna alla ta'ulu* which is normally rendered as "This is more proper so that you may not do injustice" but Imam Shafi'I translates it "so that you may not increase your progeny" (Arabic '*ayal*).

Thus Imam Shafi'I says the meaning of the verse would be if you fear you cannot do justice better marry one or prisoners of war so that you may not have more children. If Imam Shafi'I's translation is accepted then Qur'an itself advocates having few children or spacing children in such a way that you may not feel burdened and may educate them properly and nourish them properly as Imam Raghib also says.

Some other commentators maintain this verse i.e. 17:31 relates to the tradition of Arabs killing their daughters and used to give argument that we are poor and cannot provide for them. Therefore, Allah says, We provide for them and for you. In any case there is no question of killing children already borne. The family planning is certainly not about killing children already borne but spacing children and restricting their number to ones affordable income.

Imam Ghazali also quotes number of traditions from the Prophet (PBUH) to show that prevention of unwanted birth is permissible, especially if mother's health is in danger. According to the Imam both husband and wife can prevent birth of a child with mutual consent. Ghazali goes even one step further and says conception can be prevented even if mother's beauty is likely to be affected.

He even shows various ways of aborting a child up to third month of pregnancy if mother's health is in danger and shows ways of abortion. Many jurists maintain that abortion on grounds of mothers life is permissible up to third month of pregnancy as according to the Qur'an Allah infuses life in the 4th stage of conception. Hazrat Ali is also reported to have approved of abortion upto third month in case of danger to mother's life on the basis of this Qur'anic verse.

Also, the Prophet had permitted '*azl* (coitus interruptus) if one goes with one's wife on a long journey and does not want his wife to bear child during journey. Some scholars argue that 'azl should be taken in much wider meaning and can justify today use of contraceptive as 'azl was the only known contraceptive in those days.

Also, family planning was not a necessity in those days and this question did not arise as in our own times. In those days question arose only on grounds of mother's life or health. Thus we need to answer this question ourselves and our Islamic jurists today. One can also use the doctrine of *zarrorah* (necessity) which makes even haram as halal if there is pressing necessity.

In any case it would not be correct to denounce family planning as a sin as it basically involves prevention of unwanted pregnancy, nothing more and nothing less.

Muslim Women's Maintenance - Some New Judgements

Who is not aware of the Shah Bano controversy of the mid-eighties of the last century? It shook the whole country. Shah Bano, an elderly woman from Indore in Madhya Pradesh was divorced at the age of seventy by her husband who was an advocate. She sued him for maintenance under Criminal Procedure Code (Cr. P.C.), section 125 according to which the former husband of the divorced woman has to maintain her, if she is destitute and has no means of her own for her survival and he has to maintain her until she remarries or she dies. However, Shah Bano's husband refused to pay her maintenance beyond the period of *iddah* (i.e. three month's waiting period after divorce before which she cannot remarry). He maintained that according to the Muslim Personal Law he is obliged to pay her maintenance for the iddah period only and nothing beyond that. However, the Indore High Court and later the Supreme Court decided in her favour granting her (i.e. Shah Bano) maintenance for life under section 125 of Cr. P.C. The Supreme court argued that since Cr. P.C. is common for all citizens she can claim maintenance under Cr. P.C. and that Muslim Personal Law will not be applicable in this matter.

The Muslim leaders, particularly the *Ulama*, took great offence and opposed the Supreme court Judgement tooth and nail and maintained that it is blatant interference in the Muslim Personal Law. According to them the Shari'ah law is divine and cannot be interfered with. The Supreme Court, however, in its support had quoted Abdullah Yusuf Ali's translation of the Qur'anic verse 2:241 "For divorced women maintenance (should be provided) on a reasonable (scale). This is a duty on the righteous." The Supreme court argued that the provision of Cr. P.C. section 125 is supported even by the Holy Scripture of Islam. However, the *ulama* maintained that the Supreme court has no right to interpret the holy scripture.

The controversy snowballed into a major political problem as thousands of Muslims took to street and demonstrated against the Supreme court decision. Ultimately the Rajiv Gandhi Government bowed down to the pressure and enacted a law exempting the Muslim women from application of Cr. P.C. section 125. The new law enacted was known as The Muslim Women (Protection of Rights on Divorce) Law. It was enacted in 1986. The progressive Muslims and others dubbed this enactment as a great set back for Muslim women. They felt that the provision of Cr. P.C., section 125 was not essentially un-Islamic. This Act, as against section 125 of Cr. P.C., provides for one time payment as the Muslim theologians argued that the Qur'anic verse 2:241 uses the word mata' which means (one time) provision at the time of divorce.

Hence the Muslim Women's Act makes one time provision only as against recurring payment until she remarries or dies as provided for in Cr. P.C. According to the Muslim Women Act, the husband, at the time of divorce, should pay the mehr amount (if not already paid), should make one time provision for her as provided for in the Qur'an and should give three months' maintenance. Thus a Muslim divorcee will get a lump sum amount at the time of divorce. The very first judgement under this Act was given by the District Magistrate of Lucknow Rekha Dixit who awarded Rs. 80,000 to a Muslim divorcee. Rs. 60,000 were awarded as one time provision and remaining amount was for mehr as well as for three months' maintenance. The amount awarded was not so bad after all. But it seems Muslim women were not satisfied and number of cases continued to be filed in various courts for maintenance under section 125 of Cr. P.C. despite the enactment to the contrary.

However, many women's organisations challenged the Muslim Women's Act in the Supreme court after its enactment but the Supreme court is yet to take up those petitions. In the meanwhile some high courts have already pronounced their judgements on various petitions for maintenance. A couple of years ago the Bombay High court had awarded the Muslim divorcee maintenance for life under the provisions of the Muslim Women's Act. The Honourable Judge of the Bombay High court so interpreted the Act that he felt a Muslim divorcee should be given enough within the iddah period to maintain herself for life.

Similarly the Calcutta High court too while deciding Ms. Shakila Pervin's case opined that she should be given within the iddah period sufficient amount to last her for life. This judgement was given by Justice Basudev Panigrahi of Calcutta High court on the petition for maintenance by Shakila Pervin against her husband Haider Ali.. However, Haider Ali did not contest the case and remained absent from the court. The District Magistrate, however, had in its judgement, awarded her, besides her mehr amount of Rs. 2500 a maintenance of Rs. 800 per month until the iddah period. This judgement was given in 1993. Ms. Pervin, however, was not happy with this judgement and she filed an appeal against the lower court's judgement. The Judge tried to interpret section 3 of the Muslim Women's Act very broadly which says, "a reasonable and fair provision and maintenance to be made and paid to her within the iddah period by her former husband."

Justice Panigrahi maintained that the Supreme court had unequivocally held that the provisions of section 125 of the Cr.PC procedure override the personal law and it necessitated the enactment of the Act in Parliament in 1986. The judge said that "A divorced Muslim woman is entitled to maintenance after contemplating her future needs and the maintenance is not limited only up to the iddat period. The phrase used in Section 3 (I) (A) of the Act, 1986 is reasonable and fair provision and maintenance to be made to see that the divorced woman get sufficient means of livelihood after divorce and that she does not become destitute or is not thrown out on the street."

Now the full Bench of the Bombay High court has given similar judgement on 11th of July 2000. The full Bench of the Bombay High court also held that a Muslim husband must make a "fair and reasonable provision" for his divorced wife within the 'iddat' period to last her for her life time or till such time that she remarries or incurs any other disability under the Muslim Women (Protection of Rights on Divorce) Act, 1986. As Muslim husband's liability to pay maintenance to his divorced wife ceases the moment the 'iddat' period gets over, the court said he has to provide within that period a reasonable amount to her which should take care of her beyond the iddat period. The Bench came to this conclusion after debating whether a Muslim woman is entitled to get maintenance after the iddat period. The court also had to resolve the controversy about the scope and effect of the provisions of section 125 to 128 of Cr. P.C. The question before the court was whether the Muslim husband's liability under Section 3(A) of the MWA to make a reasonable and fair provision and pay maintenance is only restricted to the 'iddat' period or whether it extends beyond the iddat period. The court also held that while deciding the amount of the provision, several factors including the standard of life enjoyed by the divorced woman during her marriage and the means of income of her former husband will have to be taken into account. If the husband, the court said, is unable to arrange such a lump sum amount he can ask for instalments and the court shall consider granting him instalments.

Thus it will be seen that all courts now have been interpreting the Section 3 (a) of MWA, 1986 such as to give benefit of maintenance to Muslim divorcees beyond the iddah period which is in fact the intention of the section 125 of the Cr. P.C. Instead of giving maintenance every month as provided for in Cr. P.C the husband under the MWA, 1986 will have to pay lumpsum within the iddah period so as to benefit the divorcee beyond iddah period. The Muslim theologians too were insisting during the Shah Bano agitation that the Qur'an provides for one time provision only as in the verse 2:241. There were of course different interpretations of 2:241 by the companions of the holy Prophet. But some companions like Abdullah bin Abbas did hold that the provision (*mata*') has to be substantial and not merely symbolic.

Seen in this light the Calcutta and Bombay High Courts judgement is quite in keeping with the spirit of the provision of the Holy Qur'an. In fact it is the Qur'an which made this provision for divorcees much before any modern enactment. It is regrettable that this was not projected by the leaders of the Shah Bano movement. Instead they gave impression as if they are against the just rights of women. The Shah Bano movement has to be seen in the backdrop of eighties when Muslims, like the Christians today, were facing major threat to their security. Many major riots had taken place during that period in which hundreds of people were killed. The Shah Bano movement could gather such momentum only because of feeling of acute insecurity among the Muslims. Today, despite these landmark judgements by two leading high courts of India there is no sign of protest from Muslim leaders. The Supreme court judgement in case of the Shah Bano case of 1986 also would not have evoked much protest had there been not much feeling of insecurity due to major riots. The Shah Bano movement was basically a political movement in response to the prevailing political situation in the country.

The Muslim women had feared that the enactment of the MWA, 1986 has taken away their right of maintenance beyond the period of iddah. But these court judgements have given them the benefit which perhaps they did not expect. The Muslim leaders are not likely to protest against these judgements as they did after the Supreme court judgement and even if they do, they will not get the kind of response from Muslims as they did in mid eighties. Muslims are not in a mood for confrontation at all. They want to give priority to their basic economic and educational needs rather than take up emotional issues which take them no where. And with the increased awareness among Muslim women of their rights, they will not succeed even if they protested against such judgements. After all it is Muslim women who have gone to the courts for these benefits.

Model *Nikahnama* - A Hope or a Disappointment?

The electronic and print media have shown tremendous interest in the model *nikahnama* approved by the Muslim Personal Law Board, which is being referred to as the Bhopal Declaration. This Bhopal Declaration was issued by the MPLB after its session in Bhopal from 30 April to 1 May 2005.

Does it give hope or evokes disappointment. It depends how you look at it? If you are among the hopefuls you can say it is a step forward and that future will bring more relief. However, if you are pessimistic you can say it is too little too late and that much more was expected from the board.

In fact there is an element of truth in both the positions. For years the Board sat tight and did nothing in the matter. Now at least, one can argue, the Board realised the urgency of the matter and issued this declaration, which, if not revolutionary, is, at least, one step forward and it should be welcome as such. The Muslim community is also divided on this issue. While many have welcomed this declaration others have dismissed it as amounting to nothing.

It would be better if we understand the background of the Muslim Personal Law Board and the purpose for which it was formed. Before that we would like to point out that there is debate about the representative nature of the Board. Is it representative of all Muslims and shades of opinion or not? Obviously it is self-constituted and hence does not have representative character.

It was formed in 1972 in Mumbai by some '*ulama* who gathered there in response to the campaign for uniform civil code by some people. The fear was that as a result of this campaign Muslim personal law will be abolished and uniform civil code (UCC) will come into existence. Thus most orthodox '*ulama* came together to 'protect' the Shari'ah law. In fact in Indian context it is misnomer to call it Shari'ah law as in fact it was Anglo-Mohammedan Law, which we inherited from the British period and it was enacted as such by the British rulers.

The Muslim Personal Law Board so constituted by a section of the orthodox '*ulama* co-opted '*ulama* and others like advocates, academics and others from all sections of Muslims like Sunnis, Shi'ahs, Deobandis, Barelvis, Ahl-e-Hadith, Bohras etc. to make it as representative of Muslim opinion as possible though basically it remained self-constituted.

Thus the basic task of the Board was to 'protect' the Muslim personal law than to reform it or to change it in keeping with the demands of time. This continued for more than two decades but with the spread of education and awareness among Muslim women pressures began to be built up for necessary changes. It is important to note that more and more Muslim women are opting for modern education, which in turn makes them aware of their rights and they begin to campaign for the same.

In sixties and seventies, even up to eighties, there were no Muslim women NGOs but now several of them are functioning and campaigning for change in Muslim personal law, as it exists today. Not only this now Muslim women have even formed their own boards and one of them led by Shaista

Khan has even declared that since Bhopal declaration is not satisfactory they will frame their own *nikahnama* and make it enforceable.

It is important to note that what the MPLB has issues as declaration is only advisory in character and has no legal value and hence cannot be enforced. It being mere advice Muslims may or may not follow. Its effect, therefore, will be quite limited. A Muslim might well choose to ignore the advice and still pronounce triple divorce in a state of anger or drunkenness. One may, therefore, argue what good is this declaration issued after years of struggle and therefore could at best be characterised too little too late.

All '*ulama* agree that triple divorce is sinful form of divorce (talaq-e-bid'ah) and should be avoided. They question arises why the '*ulama* took so long to tender this advice to avoid this sinful form of divorce? They never tire of saying that divorce is most hated thing in the eyes of Allah and still keep on enforcing most accursed form of divorce. And it took decades of struggle on the part of Muslim women's organisations to issue this advice. Was it not their religious duty all these years to keep on campaigning against this sinful form of divorce? Have they not failed in their duty so far? And what after all have they achieved with this declaration?

This form of divorce has been banned in all Muslim countries including Pakistan and Bangladesh. It is only Indian '*ulama* who refuse to ban it and ironically enforce it in the name of divine law. How can a sinful form of divorce be divine, one would like to ask. Not only that it is not permitted by the Qur'an but not even by *hadith*. On the contrary the Prophet (PBUH) strongly condemned it. According to one *hadith*, when it was reported to the Prophet (PBUH) that someone had divorced his wife thrice in one sitting his face turned red with anger and he is reported to have said he is playing with Allah's laws in my own life time.

With Qur'an not allowing it and the Prophet so strongly condemning it why Indian '*ulama* are hesitating to ban it? Also, there is no unanimity among Muslims on this form of divorce. The *Ahl-e-Hadith*, the Shi'ahs and the Bohras do not accept it and among Sunnis too Hanbalis and *Malikis* generally do not permit it. Imam Ibn Taymiyyah, a great 14th century jurist vehemently argued against it and also it is quite unjust form of *talaq* whereas justice is very central to Islamic jurisprudence.

The Qur'an while disapproving *talaq* as it breaks husband-wife relations and Allah has created love and compassion between them (30:21) has shown very just method of divorcing (see verses 4:35 and 2:229) and also requires witnesses for divorce (see 65:2) and triple divorce violates all these Qur'anic injunctions. How can then it be validated and whether one should follow the Qur'an with such clear injunctions on divorce or some controversial *hadith*? It is for '*ulama* to answer.

It is high time therefore, to abolish triple divorce and if it is not possible to do so right away due to internal differences they should strongly campaign against it and also penalize those Muslims who resort to it. It was suggested by some women groups from Hyderabad that those men who resort to this *un-Qur'anic* form of divorce should be made to pay one lakh rupees by way of penalty. If the *'ulama* argue that they are not in a position to abolish triple divorce right away, let them penalise those who resort to it. But it seems they do not want to hurt the domination of men over women.

The least the MPLB can do is to take initiative to codify the Muslim personal law which will be quite in the spirit of the Islamic Shari'ah. Yes, *talaq* is permitted, polygamy is permitted in certain circumstances but in the absence of any codification unscrupulous use is made of these provisions. Maulana Ashraf Thanavi did so in 1939 by codifying the law on dissolution of Muslim marriage and asking the British Government to enact it and has shown way to us to stop abuse of certain provisions in Islamic law.

The *'ulama* themselves did it in 1986 when they drafted Muslim Women (on divorce) law in 1986 in the wake of the Shah Bano controversy. They did so readily since they thought it will benefit men (though it did not due to different interpretations but by the courts). But when it comes to protecting rights of women they show no initiative. Today in the absence of codification man's right to divorce his wife has become absolute. The Qur'an does not give such absolute right to man. Similarly in the absence of codification any Muslim man can take second or third or fourth wife.

In the process of codification one can clearly define the grounds on which divorce would be admissible and it should be justiciable. If *talaq* is hateful in the eyes of Allah how could then it be given so arbitrarily. No civilised community can allow such arbitrariness in divorcing ones wife. It must be made justiciable in the courts of law or at least in the Shari'ah courts (though secular courts are much more preferable) on well defined grounds.

Similarly, for polygamy too there should be well-defined procedure and just grounds as it has been done in almost all Muslim countries. The *'ulama* and well-known Muslim lawyers should draft a comprehensible bill in this respect within the Shari'ah framework and give it to the government to enact it through parliament. Thus there will be no interference in the Shari'ah law by any external agency and also it will achieve the purpose of doing justice to Muslim women.

Of course this will not come about without struggle on the part of Muslim women and men who stand by women's rights. Islam was most fair to women and gave them concretely defined rights but men through medieval ages found ways to deprive women of their Islamic rights. Now time has come to restore these Islamic rights back to women. It would be better if, like model *nikahnama*, some Muslim intellectuals, legal experts and activists draft such a bill and struggle for getting it accepted over period of time.

Only such comprehensive codification will ultimately help the cause of Muslim women. One can draw from Muslim countries in drafting such a bill.

Women's Discourse in Qur'an - Rights-based or Duty-based?

The Muslim women's issue has become quite important in the contemporary world for number of reasons. Women today are much more educated than ever before and this education is modern secular education, not only religious one. Also, many of them are working independently and many are even financial experts in their own rights. Thus they are no more dependent on parents or husbands or other male relatives. This dependence makes them more assertive of their rights.

Also, unlike in the past, media plays big role in reporting cases of gender discrimination or gender empowerment. Now besides print media there is also electronic media, which has much greater impact than print media. For example, when the Shahbano case for maintenance took place in mid-eighties, electronic media was not so much in vogue and case was reported only in newspapers and magazines. But recently when Gudia case or Imrana case of rape took place, it was widely covered by electronic media and there were discussions on various channels.

All this has increased awareness among Muslim women of their plight and so are putting pressure for change in laws pertaining to marriage, divorce, inheritance, rape and so on. There is one more factor, which plays important role. It is formation of women's NGOs. These NGOs are educating women for their rights and also organising them and fighting cases on their behalf. Muslim women are no exception to this rule.

Recently some women formed their own personal law board and are challenging decisions taken by All India Muslim personal Law Board, largely a man-dominated body of conservative *'Ulama* who base all their opinions on the medieval texts evolved by mainly male-interpreters of the Qur'an and *hadith*. Women had little role to play in formulation of these Shari'ah laws.

The medieval text cannot be enforced mechanically today. It has to be thoroughly re-thought in modern context. Women's rights are very crucial today and the way women's rights are violated in Islamic society is attracting wide criticism in media and also in scholarly circles. Many modern Islamic scholars are minutely studying various Islamic texts in relation to women's rights including the Qur'an and are trying to re-interpret them.

A careful study of the Qur'anic text would show that entire discourse on women in Qur'an is right-based and about men duty-based. But in Shari'ah laws this was reversed, partly, if not wholly and wholly, in customs and traditions. In this paper we will throw detailed light on Qur'anic text both in relation to women and men and see how far it is true. In fact the main source of Islamic legislation should be Qur'an and those *ahadith* which are in conformity with the Qur'anic teachings and not any *hadith*. Any *hadith* which contradicts the Qur'an, should be rejected howsoever authentic its narrators might be. Unfortunately today *hadith* prevails over the Qur'an, even if it contradicts the Qur'an.

The Qur'anic Discourse on Women

All the verses about women in Qur'an are right based except two or two i.e. 4:34, 24:31 which appear to be prescription of conduct for them. But even these verses need to be carefully read and on carefully reading them, as we will see, they too are very carefully worded as not to go against women so as to make them subservient to men as often Shari'ah texts of various schools tend to portray them. These verses have been much abused by orthodox '*Ulama* to portray women as 'subordinate sex'. However, a careful reading of these verses does not indicate, in any way, that women are subordinate sex. It should be noted that women became a subordinate sex in Muslim society in spite of the Qur'anic text.

The Qur'anic teachings are basically normative and transcendent and hence all prescriptions about women are right-based, transcending all constraints of time and space. However, when concrete laws were made during *Umayyad* rule, Muslims had already come in contact with Byzantine and Sassanid cultures, which were based on feudal values and the eminent jurists of Islam living during those times were influenced in their outlook by these feudal and patriarchal values.

Before we discuss this let us take a view of Quran's verses pertaining to women. I would like to refer to the verse 2:228, which is declaration of equality of sexes and intention of the Qur'an to project a right-based discourse for women. Needless to say in pre-Islamic Arabia too, with few exceptions, women were a subordinate sex and entire discourse was duty-based for women and right-based for men.

The Qur'an, which made human dignity (17:70), its fundamental approach, could not have accepted this situation. Men and women enjoyed equal dignity and since society accepted only male superiority, the Qur'an reversed its priority and made its discourse on women entirely right-based and about men duty-based. But unfortunately the society under feudal influences again reversed this and made substantial part of discourse on women in Shari'ah laws duty-based and that of men right-based.

Thus the Qur'an begins by declaration of equality of sexes and then goes on to prescribe rights for women. Women had no part in choosing her marital mate. Qur'an not only made marriage a contract (4:21) but allowed women to stipulate her own conditions and determine the mehr (dower) amount. She could demand as much as heap of gold (qintar), if she likes and in pre-Islamic society mehr belonged to father but Qur'an said it will belong to her and even her husband cannot take it away from her. If she wants she can give part or whole of it to her husband. Even Shari'ah had to concede that she could stipulate whatever conditions she like in her marriage contract and marriage will be valid only if those conditions are accepted by the husband to be.

One can of course say that polygamy goes against her right in marriage and she has to live with co-wives. The Qur'an created wives' rights even in polygamous marriage. First, the verse on polygamy is recommendatory in view of the situation arose as a result of battle of Uhud in which large number of men were killed and number of widows and orphans were to be taken care of and men were allowed up to four wives from amongst these orphans and widows (see 4:3). But the verse on polygamy also is right based rather than duty-based for women and duty-based for men. Men are strictly warned to do equal justice else they better marry one (4:3) and further warned in 4:129 that they cannot do justice even if they so desire and that they should not leave first wife hanging in the air. The very tenor of these verses shows that they are right based for women and duty based for men. The Mu'tazila theologians insisted on reading both verses on polygamy 4:3 and 4:129 together and insisted Qur'an recommends monogamy emphasising rigorous justice for co-wives in case of polygamy which is humanly impossible. Thus this verse is also clearly right based for women.

Divorce in pre-Islamic society was exclusive privilege enjoyed by man. Women had no right to divorce her husband and divorce was quite arbitrary. The Qur'an corrected this one-sided practice and allowed women too, to liberate herself from her husband, if she felt she could not fulfil the hudud (limits) of Allah, see verse 2:229. This right of women to obtain khula' from her husband is absolute and this is further confirmed by the *hadith* according to which the Prophet (PBUH) allowed Jamila Kula', though her husband Qais bin Thabit loved her and gave her maintenance generously. But Jamila did not approve of her husband's looks and hence she approached the Prophet (PBUH) and he granted her *khula*'. (see Bukhari, *Hadith* 197-199, Vl. 7 Book 63)

Thus in Arab society where no right existed for women to divorce, she was granted one and made it absolute. However, in a feudal social milieu where she was confined to home and did not play an active role in public life, her right to *khula*' was subjected to husband's consent which is not Qur'anic requirement. Today, according to the Shari'ah law, she has to beg her husband for his consent for *khula*' and husband often harasses her by refusing to give consent or demanding heavy price in terms of money for the same.

Even where husband divorces her, she has certain rights. The Qur'an clearly safeguards her right when husband decides to divorce her. According to the Qur'an, husband cannot take back meher amount, even if he has given her heap of gold. Secondly, she cannot be driven away from husband's house until she observes *'iddah* (three month's period after pronouncement of divorce).

Also, after completion of period of *'iddah* husband is required to either retain her in good fellowship or leave her with kindness (2:229). The same verse clearly says that you cannot take anything back from her whatever has been given to her. She has right to retain everything given her at the time of marriage.

Where husband intends to divorce his wife, he cannot do so arbitrarily, as it often happens in Muslim societies. The Qur'an requires process of arbitration before divorce in which wife has right to nominate one arbitrator along with husband who can nominate one from his people. (See 4:35). In this arbitration wife cannot go un-represented. And divorce has to be given in presence of two witnesses (65:2). Thus the Qur'an lays down proper procedure for divorce so that women do not become victim of arbitrariness. Unfortunately, all this was lost in Shari'ah laws and man retains the right to divorce his wife as and when he likes. It is totally un-Qur'anic.

The Qur'an takes into account other possibilities of divorce i.e. divorce before her husband touches her and before he fixes her dower. In that case he has to pay her some compensation rich according to his capacity and poor according to his capacity (2:236) and if he divorces her before touching her but after fixing dower amount, she has right to half that amount (2:237). She cannot just be thrown out.

Even after divorce she has right to maintenance (2:241) and if one goes by the literal meaning of the verse, she will be entitled to maintenance until she remains a divorcee since Qur'an does not prescribe any time period. The Qur'an says in verse 2:241 that make provision for divorcees in kindness, it is duty of the husband. Once she remarries she will not be entitled to it and if she dies this right ceases.

And when her husband dies she cannot be removed from her husband's house at least for one year and it is his duty to make a will to that effect. But if she leaves of her own will, she can (2:240). She will also be entitled to inherit one eighth of her husband's property as per verses on will.

Thus it will be seen that entire discourse about marriage and divorce of women is right-based in Qur'an. Her rights in all these respects have been clearly spelled out without any ambiguity. Yet, in practice these rights are not available to her due to patriarchal social ethos. She enjoys these rights both as married and as divorcee. She is entitled to maintenance when married, even if she has her own income, more than her husband's. Husband is required to maintain her in any case.

Even in orthodox Shari'ah law maintenance has been well-defined. According to a *fatwa* given by '*Ulama* during Aurangzeb Alamgir's time and copied under *Fatwa*' Alamgiri maintenance is defined as to include (1) food; (2) clothes; (3) house and (4) other requirements like maintaining her health and beauty.

Under food it is clearly led down that wife is not obliged to cook and husband has to arrange cooked food for wife. Similarly he has to give her stitched clothes and a separate house to live in and if not possible to arrange separate house, he has to arrange a separate room for her privacy with separate access so as not to be obliged to share it with other members of husband's family. He also has to arrange for medicines and other items of toiletry so that she can maintain her health and beauty.

If husband does not arrange for all these things and also does not pay her reasonable amount in cash for her maintenance, Shari'ah gives her right to remove an equivalent amount from her husband's pocket without being charged with theft. If this is also not possible and husband deprives her of maintenance for long, she can initiate divorce procedure.

The Qur'an gives her right to property, which she enjoys untrammelled (4:32). Her father or husband cannot force her to share with them unless she does it of her own will. She was also given right to inheritance as daughter, as wife and as mother though her share is half that of her brother, her husband and her father (4:11-12). The Qur'an created her right in inheritance where none existed before. The objection that she was given half may be justified in today's context but not in 7th century context. Also, her right to maintenance both as wife and as mother offsets to some extent her deprivation in share. Nevertheless, she got right to inherit when it was unthinkable in any system of law. The Qur'an also gave father right to will before his death and he can will more to his daughters. (4:11-12)

The Qur'an gave her equal dignity as pointed out above and protected it by banning certain practices prevalent in pre-Islamic society. The step - sons could marry their fathers' wives. Qur'an strictly banned such practice (see 4:22) and also there was practice in pre-Islamic society of Arabs that elder son could marry after death of his father to possess his widows, marrying themselves if they pleased without settling dowry on them or marrying them to others or prohibiting them to marry altogether (Bukhari, 65: iv, 6). Qur'an banned all these practices see 4:19 and 4:22.

Also, to consolidate her dignity Qur'an made it clear that Allah has created both men and women from a single being (4:1) and thus refuted the earlier belief that Adam was created first and then Eve. Both were created for each other's company (9:71). The story of adam and eve has been narrated in Qur'an in a way that does not hold eve responsible for inducing Adam to eat fruit of the banned tree but both are held responsible and Satan leads them astray together (2:35).

And all this dignity and rights were given her hundreds of years ago when there was absolutely no concept of women's rights, only of duties. No where Qur'an prescribes duties for her, but only rights. There are two verses, as pointed out above, which are quoted by the orthodox *'ulama* to establish her secondary status as compared to man i.e. the verse 4:34.

This verse is much debated as to whether it establishes superiority of men over women. In fact, the word *qawwam* (maintainer, manager of affairs or one who looks after etc.) is a functional term and does not ensure biological superiority in any sense of the word. Also, man is not maintainer for ever and in all societies. He was so in the Arab society of the time the Qur'an was being revealed. Today women also earn and hence they also become maintainers and managers (*qawwam*). there is no question of establishing men's superiority over women and this is further confirmed by following words that We have given more merit to some over some others, it does not say We have given more merit to men over women. The words used are very important to note. Still this verse is often quoted to prove male superiority.

The last portion of this verse, it is maintained by the *'Ulama*, allows men to beat their women (fadribuhunna) which again is questionable. The word daraba has several meanings in Arabic language and even in medieval ages, Imam Raghib Asfahani, an eminent Qur'anic lexicographer, has pointed out that *daraba 'ala* means she camel going near he camel. In this verse it would mean if women is persuaded after her revolt, you go near her, and not that you beat her.

Women were active participants in all debates relating to their rights and when this verse was revealed and was being debated they went to the prophet and asked whether it implies they are inferior to men in any way. In response to their poser the verse 33; 35 was revealed which classical statement of equality of men and women. This verse is almost suppressed by the orthodox jurists in all their discourse on women's rights. This verse further proves that Qur'anic discourse women is right-based and not duty-based. This verse should be given top priority in discussing gender question in the Qur'an.

Another important proof of gender equality in Qur'an is that all religious obligations are same both for men and women. Men and women both are required to pray five times, fast during the month of Ramadan, both should perform haj, if they have means to do so and both have to pay zakat based on ones income. Women have not been exempted from any of these duties.

Also, both women and men have to enforce what is good and contain what is evil and it is on this basis that Imam Abu Hanifa, Tabari and Imam Malik maintain that woman can become head of the state and qadi. However, many jurists and *'ulama*, despite all this maintain that a woman cannot become head of the state though some of them concede she can become *qadi* (judge).

Why this negative attitude towards women? It is obviously social, not Qur'anic. As pointed out before, human behaviour and opinion is moulded by several factors, social, economic, cultural and political, simply not by scriptural. The whole understanding of scripture undergoes drastic change or other texts are created (such as *hadith*) to bring about change I understanding of scriptural authority.

Islamic values and theology underwent radical change in patriarchal and feudal social structure. Instead of changing or transforming patriarchal, feudal social structure, the whole scriptural understanding was transformed to suit the patriarchal feudal society. Thus right-based discourse of the Qur'an for women was changed entirely into duty based one and duty based discourse for men became right based.

It because of this transformation from right based to duty based discourse that women are suffering in modern society. There is stranglehold of *Ulama* on the community and the *'Ulama* are under the stranglehold of medieval text. They have neither ability to creatively think in the new context nor have they any such training. For any problem that arises they consult the medieval text and opinions of classical jurists and based on that text they issue their fatwa.

As a result of such attitude Muslims in general and women in particular continue to suffer. The Shari'ah has totally become stagnant and has lost its earlier dyamism. There is urgent need today to make it dynamic again by revisiting the Qur'anic text and again restoring right based discourse. This will greatly help Muslim women who also depend on text and cannot do otherwise. It will be much better if women themselves develop expertise to interpret the Qur'anic text. We need more and ore Islamic feminist theologians than ever before.

Triple Divorce - Need to be Changed

Recently several cases of on the spot triple divorce have been reported in the press. In Bihar, just because wife of a person did not vote for the candidate of his choice in the Lok sabha election he pronounced triple divorce and threw out his wife. Again just a few days ago, a husband came drunk in Bhadrak, Orissa on 3rd June, and had a tiff with his wife and pronounced *talaq* thrice but in the morning he realised his mistake and wanted to take back his wife but leaders of the Muslim community separated them insisting that it is irrevocable divorce and they cannot live together as husband and wife. Besides this many cases just go unreported.

There is now report from Kerala that members of orthodox Sunni organisations have threatened to agitate if women are allowed to pray on Friday in the mosque. In the girls college in Manjeri, students have been praying on Friday in the mosque on college premises. But the Samastha Kerala Sunni Students Federation (SKSSF) has launched a public agitation against women being allowed to pray on Friday in the mosque.

What such acts of triple divorce or agitations against women praying on Friday in the mosque convey to the world? Do women have secondary status in Islam? Is it sin to pray to Allah in mosque on Friday? What sort of Islam is this? How can Islam banish women from praying on Friday inside the mosque? For these orthodox Muslims customs and traditions are more important than the Qur'anic injunctions.

They do not know that Islam was the first religion in the world to empower women and giver them equal legal status. The Qur'an clearly pronounces equality of sexes see verses 2:228 and 33:35. Commenting on the verse 2:228 Maulana Azad in his 'Tarjuman al-Qur'an' says that it is revolutionary declaration of equality of sexes 1300 years ago. But the Muslim society under the influence of feudal social ethos never realised this revolutionary potential of Qur'anic teachings.

However, these old institutions developed under different social ethos cannot work today. The women are making fast strides in different fields of life. The extent of education and consciousness of their rights is far more widespread today than ever before. Even in conservative Saudi society the women are no more prepared to accept their traditional role. Only last week i.e. beginning 12 June 2004, seventy Saudi Arabian scholars and intellectuals participated in the first day of third national dialogue forum in Madina to address the rights of women in particular prompt and full delivery of justice to women.

The overall theme of this three-day forum is women's rights and duties and their relation to education. Many women scholars read out papers in this forum to discuss ways to eliminate religious extremism in the Saudi Kingdom. In Madina the organisers hope to create an environment conducive for Saudi intellectuals and scholars to discuss the position of women in Saudi society and to find out the best ways to develop their status in line with Islamic teachings.

This clearly shows there is great deal of ferment among women even in the Saudi society. Women cannot be treated in the old ways any more. In India also Muslim women have become more conscious about their Islamic rights and are demanding changes in the Personal Law in keeping with the Qur'anic teachings. As pointed out the Islamic laws in relation to women are most modern in their approach but Muslim societies have preferred traditional interpretations by imams in pre-modern feudal society to the clearly worded Qur'anic injunctions.

Talaq is a highly sensitive issue as it can break years of marital relations between husband and wife. Thus the Holy Qur'an is also very cautious in matters of divorce. Firstly, it has adopted most modern approach to this sensitive issue. It requires arbitration before any breach of relations. The Qur'an says, "And if you fear a breach between the two, appoint an arbiter from his people and an arbiter from her people. If they both desire agreement, Allah will effect harmony between them." (4:35)

Thus through arbitration the breach should be prevented and attempt should be made to bring them together again as Allah desires harmony. Despite such clear Qur'anic injunction we approve of triple divorce in one sitting and destroy marital life in one breath. How such an act be Islamic? It is greatest injustice, specially with women. Again justice ('adl) is so central to Qur'anic teaching. And to throw ones wife but by pronouncing three words of *talaq* is most unjust act. There are three four key words in Qur'an ? *'adl*, *ihsan*, *rahmah* and *hikmah* (i.e. justice, benevolence, compassion and wisdom) and triple *talaq* is against all these key words. Neither it is justice, nor it is benevolence (*ihsan*), nor is it compassion (*rahmah*) nor is it an act of wisdom (*hikmah*).

All Muslims are also not unanimous on this form of divorce. Ahle-Hadith, Hanbalis and Shi?ahs reject this form of talaq. Even Hanafi Muslim countries like Jordan have reformed this practice and enforced the Qur'anic injunction of arbitration. Arbitration can and does save many marriages. The Qur'an does not permit triple divorce at all. Three talaqs has to be spaced over a period of three months so that husband and wife get enough time for reconciliation through intervention of relatives and friends. Moreover *talaq* can be given only when wife is in a state of tuhur i.e. purity after menstruation. If *talaq* is pronounced during the period of menstruation it will not be valid. The Prophet has ordered wife to be taken back if the *talaq* is pronounced during menstrual period. Triple divorce disregards all this completely.

Some Muslim women have devised a standard *nikahnama* (marriage contract) strictly within the Shari?ah framework and given to the Muslim Personal Law Board a couple of years ago so that Muslim women do not face such situations. Since marriage in Islam is a contract such nikahnama is perfectly valid and was approved by a great *'alim* like Maulana Ashraf Thanavi. But the personal board is hesitating to implement it. If implemented, it can give lot of relief to Muslim women. This is very modest piece of reform (in fact it is really not any reform or change but only a modicum of relief to suffering women) but the personal board is hesitating in implementing even this.

All *'ulama* agree that pronouncing triple *talaq* in one sitting is *bid'ah* (innovation) and that *bid'ah* is sin and yet this sinful practice is enforced in the name of divine law. In fact tripe divorce indeed is great sin as it so unjust and oppressive for women. Every possible attempt should be made to eradicate this sinful practice from our society. The *'ulama* who are guardians of Islamic law should play a leading role in this matter. I have had discussion with many *'ulama* who privately agree that this form of divorce should be abolished but do not have courage to say so publicly.

The personal law board should at least launch an awareness movement educating Muslim men about desisting from this sinful form of divorce and resort to the Qur'anic form of divorce as clearly spelled out. I am not aware of any such awareness movement. The Muslim men are Islamically illiterate and do not even know that triple divorce is a sinful form of divorce and Holy Prophet has strongly disapproved of this form of divorce. If the members of personal law board do not have courage to abolish this form of divorce they should at least have courage to launch an awareness movement among Muslim men and appeal to them not to resort to such form of divorce.

Maulana Ashraf Thanvi and others had taken a bold step in 1939 and drafted the Dissolution of Muslim Marriage Act, which gave great relief to suffering women. Can the members of Muslim personal law board not show such wisdom and draft a comprehensive law codifying the Muslim personal Law on the lines of the 1939 Act. It will give great and much needed relief to Muslim women.

However, there is no such sign of codifying the Muslim personal law and suffering of Muslim women continues. If Maulana Ashraf Thanvi and others could take such bold step way back in 1939 why can't our *'ulama* in 21st century take such step? This will be not only in keeping with the true spirit of Islam but will also go a long way in improving the image of Islam in India. It is due to such un-Qur'anic practices that image of Islam has suffered and the demand for Uniform Civil Code surfaces.

The Islamic law is most progressive and in fact should become a model law for all others if our orthodox *'ulama* care to understand and implement it in its true spirit. Maulavi Mumtaz Ali Khan, Maulavi Chiragh Ali, Justice Ameer Ali and others pleaded for reforms in late Nineteenth and early twentieth century but nothing has happened so far.

Now it is for Muslim women to acquaint themselves thoroughly with Islamic law and launch a movement for reform and change. Women in all Muslim countries have struggled for change and succeeded. Now, as referred to above, even women in the most conservative Saudi society have begun to assert themselves. It is therefore, high time that Muslim women in democratic society like that of India struggle for reform within the Qur'anic frame-work and win their rights guaranteed by the scripture.

That seems to be the only way left for them. Progressive and believing Muslim men should also come forward and support such movement for reform.

6

Politics Over Islam

Gujarat Carnage and Muslim Women

The Gujarat Carnage after the Godhra train burning incident in early 2002 brought disgrace to India. Such brutal communal carnage had never taken place before in the post-independent India. It attracted world-wide attention and number of countries including the European Union and the United States sent its official representatives to find out what went wrong and why such carnage took place at all.

From within India also several human rights groups, women's groups and human rights activists rushed to Gujarat to express their sympathy and solidarity with the victims of Hindutva aggression against helpless minority victims. Never before so many activists had rushed to any communal violence scene in India. So many reports were prepared of the ghastly crime against humanity and still that work is going on. There are several aspects to be probed and every probe raises cries of shame.

The crimes against women were really unspeakable. The women particularly those who are working for women's rights and empowerment were greatly perturbed at what happened with them in Gujarat. Many women activists went and interviewed the victims in refugee camps. Yet so much needs to be explored. The wounds inflicted on minority women can hardly heal especially when they were subjected to such unspeakable crimes. Still they are living with sense of shame and agony.

Recently, a team of women activists from different countries like France, Germany, U.K., The Netherlands, Sri Lanka and India visited Gujarat and wrote a report 'Threatened Existence-A Feminist Analysis, of the Genocide in Gujarat.' This report comprising 244 pages is a must for all those who want to know of festering wounds two years after the carnage. The report has been written after months of pains-taking research.

In the introduction to the report these anguished women say, "The specific targeting of women, as part of a conscious strategy to terrorise the Muslim population of Gujarat, also particularly concerned the panellists (of women)". According to Rhonda (one of the panellists), sexual violence played a fundamental role and was used 'as an engine of the mobilisation of hatred and destruction.' It further says, "The scale and brutality of the sexual violence unleashed upon women was new, or felt as it was new, to the panellists who could not be prepared for the testimonies they heard even though they were aware of the centrality of this method in the violence of 2002."

Meera, who lives in Gujarat and was acutely conscious of what had happened in Gujarat in February-March 2002 described it as follows:

"Many doubts arise in your mind [about the erosion of citizenship] particularly when you come face to face with women who have undergone brutal sexual attacks and mass rape. For first time married women broke their silence on the sexual attacks they suffered. A mother spoke of her two daughters but did not say that she herself was a victim. Testimonies were often given with young children looking on, punctuated with long silences. None of us could sleep that night; a community was being held to ransom accept your citizenship or. We exchanged experiences of Bosnia, Palestine and Israel but the extent, brutality and the varied methods of Gujarat were unheard of."

Thus these women panellists Sunila Abeyeskera of Sri Lanka, Rhonda Copelon of City University of New York, Anissa Helie of France, Gabriela Mischkowski of U.K., Uma Chakravarti of Delhi University and Wahida Nainar of the Netherlands, Farah Naqvi of Delhi and Meera Velaydan came to conclusion that sexual violence that took place in Gujarat was really unheard of and such things were not to be found even in places like Bosnia, Palestine and Israel.

On their Gujarat tour these women heard stones of sexual crimes at the hands of supporters of Hindutva. Yasmin, a woman survivor from Panchmahal district told the panellists "They cut off breasts of her neighbour's daughter, it is difficult to forget, it still swims in my vision. I have lost my mental peace."

Another woman survivor Sabah from the same district said, What had those kids done to them? I cannot forget those girls [who were raped]. We have to try and arrest them [the rapists]. Quoting Sabah's testimony the report says, "We ran in different directions and hid in the field. But the mob found some of us and started attacking. I recognised two people from my village Gano Baria and Sunil pulling away my daughter. She screamed, telling the men to get off her and leave her alone. The screams and cries of

Ruqayya, Suhana, Shabana, begging for their *izzat* [honour] could clearly be heard. I could do nothing to help my daughter from being assaulted sexually and tortured to death."

In Tanika Sarkar's words, "The pattern of cruelty suggests three things. One, the woman's body was a site of almost inexhaustible violence, with infinitely plural and innovative forms of torture. Secondly, their sexual and reproductive organs were attacked with a special savagery. Third, their children, born and unborn, shared the attacks and were killed before their eyes."

And despite such sexual savagery perpetrated against Muslim women in Gujarat, the NDA government at the centre, not to speak of Narendra Modi Government in Gujarat not only remained silent spectator but occasionally justified it. Remember Defence Minister George Fernandese justifying this in a debate in parliament on Gujarat said that this is nothing new, it has been happening in India for ages. Even the Prime Minister, though a poet and claiming poetic sensitivity remained silent, if not justified it a-la Fernandese.

The panellists in the report make one very pertinent point about Muslim women being sexually assaulted to such a degree as in Gujarat. The report says, "The women of the community suffer attacks in two ways. In the first case they are members of the collective, like any other, and are liable to be attacked. At the same time, they are the biological and cultural reproducers of the community and their bodies symbolize the body of the community and its boundaries. In the Hindutva project, the control of the Muslim other through gender and sexual domination is at the forefront of the political strategy in Gujarat and elsewhere."

Thus it would be seen that sexual assault is not simply fulfilment of ones lust; it is much more than that in such cases. By sexually violating the women of the 'other' you are destroying their honour and humiliating them as a community and treating body of women as body of the community. Woman's honour must be destroyed to destroy the honour of the community.

Thus supporting this view the report says that the sexual assault incidents were not just random or isolated incidents. They were widespread and pre-planned. For many cases ? Gujarat, Rawanda, the former Yugoslavia such wide scale violence could not have been conducted without a significant measure of complicity, if not participation, by the State. In Gujarat, it is clear that all events, including the mass use of rape and sexual assault, occurred with the knowledge of highly placed State actors, and in many instances, were carried out with full participation and support of the police.

There are many witnesses to the fact that the police often hit the stomachs of pregnant women in so called combing operations. A police officer of the rank of DCP himself entered the house and beat up small girls and women. One woman who was six month pregnant had an abortion. He said to these women "We will keep all your men and make you prostitutes." Besides this there was lot of suggestive sexual violence, hitting women on breasts, targeting private parts and targeting pregnant women.

Unfortunately, the RSS and the VHP women themselves were participating in this violence against Muslim women. Safia, a woman from Ahmedabad testified that the daughter of a Bajrang Dal leader was pulling women by hair and throwing them in fire. Other eyewitnesses also alleged that another woman was catching Muslim women and passing them on to the VHP and Bajrang Dal men to be raped.

This writer has also visited Gujarat number of times and heard similar testimonies which, are indeed hair raisanmg. The idea of recounting these stories is not to ignite fire of revenge but to understand what the *Hindutva* agenda is and what counter measures to fight this menace are required. India is a secular nation and it is duty of all of us to keep it secular and to promote peace and harmony.

The secular forces have to draw up their own strategies so that Gujarat like events do not repeat and we are able to keep violence away from our secular democracy. We will have to remember Gujarat to ward off fascism from our land. Unfortunately, the communal forces are united and secular forces are divided thus giving enough opportunities to communal forces to play havoc with our secular system. It is for the secular forces to keep Gujarat violence before their eyes so that the consequences of allowing political space to communal forces remains before them.

All of us who believe in secularism and humanism should spare no efforts to unite secular forces in the country.

Muslim Women in Indian Society

8th March, observed as the women's day, a day which women celebrate as a day of their empowerment and a day of their rights. As I read in newspapers about achievements of women I painfully remember the plight of Muslim women in India, their lack of empowerment, their grinding poverty, their illiteracy and various restrictions imposed on them by their parents and husbands in every day life.

When I deliver lectures on rights of women in Islam, participants invariably ask me about actual plight of women in Muslim society today. I have to do lot of explaining the reasons of their sad plight. There are certain factors for which Muslims cannot be blamed like poverty. But there are certain factors for which Muslims have to own responsibility like imposing restrictions, which have nothing to do with Islam. These restrictions are rooted more in social customs and traditions of the past but legitimised in the name of Shari'ah.

Muslim women are suffering both from internal and external oppression. Muslim men practise what they themselves believe is Islamic and oppress their women and refuse to entertain any thought of change. Many educated Muslim women thus start believing there can be no liberation within Islam and seek their freedom through secular laws. I conduct workshops for rights of Muslim women and when they listen to what is written in Qur'an, they say they never thought Qur'an liberates them. They thought Islam enslaves them. Thus those who attend our workshops become activists for their Islamic rights.

Some problems, Muslim women face are of social nature and are common to women of all religions in India. All women face problem of social conservatism as they are reduced to secondary to men. Men are thought to be bread winner and decision maker across religions in India. But only difference is that among Hindus this situation is fast changing at least in urban areas. Women are becoming self-sufficient and, in some cases, also decision makers. But situation is not so bright as far as Muslim women are concerned.

Non-Muslims generally think Muslim women are oppressed and face many restrictions. This is largely true but matter is much more complex. There are reasons for Muslim women facing such odds in India. Mostly Muslims are artisans and self -employed and sociologically speaking they have restricted world -view and live in their own universe. Then there are those Muslims who live in rural areas and are engaged as agricultural labourers and related operations. They tend to be even more conservative.

These sections of society do not know what is written in Qur'an or *hadith*, much less what are problems with *hadith* or different schools of law. For them what imam of their masjid says is Allah's hukm (injunction) and must be followed else, they will be confined to jahannam (hell). The imam of the mosque also comes from poor family and has, in most cases, very limited knowledge of theology and Islamic Shari'ah. His '*fatwas*' are based on ignorance. The '*fatwa*' issued by the imam of village mosque in case of Imrana (that she should marry her father-in-law who raped her) had absolutely no basis in Shari'ah. The media also tends to give undue publicity to such matters.

Thus it is important to understand role of society as much as that of religion. Women are oppressed not so much by religion as by society. In order to bring about change in the plight of Muslim women it would be equally necessary to bring about change in socio-economic conditions of Muslims in India. If Muslims remain poor and illiterate, it will be very difficult to improve conditions of Muslim women.

Awareness for Change

It is also necessary to understand that things are not totally stagnant on Muslim women's front. An educated middle class is emerging among Indian Muslims - though still small - which is well aware of changing society and need for change among Muslim women. The educated Muslim women exposed to democratic politics, electronic and print media, are becoming aware of their rights and no longer prepared to accept what is being imposed on them in the name of religion.

In last one decade there have been many positive indications of change. A group of Muslim women developed a standard *nikahnama* (marriage contract) and forced the Muslim personal Board to adopt it. Though the Board did not adopt it as it is, it did respond to this demand and developed its own *nikahnama*. Is not very satisfactory to women but nevertheless the process of change has started.

It must be said that Board's entire functioning is reactive rather than proactive. I must say it is incapable of being pro-active as it is busy defending medieval inheritance rather than re-think Islam like Muhammad Abduh, Fazlur Rehman, Ali Shariati and many others. They defend *riwayat* (tradition) rather than use *ijtihad* (assert intellectual capacity to reinterpret and re-think issues). Today when world is undergoing drastic changes, simply repeating, defending and stagnating will create discord between Qur'anic Islam and Shari'ah Islam on one hand, and Islamic Shari'ah and modern world, on the other.

Anyway, Muslim Personal Law Board changes or not, women are not going to wait indefinitely. They are already on the move. Some Muslim women got together and formed their own board called Muslim women's personal law board. This board is asking its own stand favouring women on the basis of Qur'an and *hadith*. Though Islamic feminism has not emerged in India, it is on its way.

Some Muslim women NGOs have come together and formed *Bhartiya Muslim Mahila Morcha*. They have decided to operate within Islamic framework on one hand, and Indian Constitutional framework, on the other. It held its first convention in Delhi, in early December. This is certainly a hopeful sign. Yet it is far from sufficient. It is just the beginning.

There is great need for Qur'anic literacy among Muslim women. Unfortunately the modern secular educated women know neither Arabic nor are aware of Qur'anic teachings. In order to bring real change in the Muslim women's condition, there is great need to have encounter with traditional *Ulama* on the basis of Qur'anic injunctions in respect of women. Needless to say the Qur'an accords equal rights to men and women and exhorts Muslim men of their obligations towards women. However, many of these

Qur'anic rights were lost in the Shari'ah formulations in a conservative traditional feudal society. It is for Islamic feminist to revisit Qur'an and develop Qur'anic discourse of women's rights.

Most of the Muslim countries have abolished triple divorce also known as oral divorce. India is the only country with second largest population of Muslims, which still upholds validity of oral divorce and orthodox *Ulama* even uphold divorce given through SMS flying in the face of Qur'an. It is totally unjust to women and Qur'an whose most fundamental value is justice (*'adl* can never permit such unjust form of divorce. Qur'an has laid down proper procedure for divorce, which unfortunately is not followed by Muslims though they swear by divinity of the Qur'an.

India being a secular democratic country there is much more political and social space available to Muslim women in India compared to their sisters in many other Muslim countries. To avail of this social and political space increased awareness among women is needed. The greatest stumbling block is poverty. One finds even great urge for modern education among women but poverty pulls them down.

Firoz Ashraf, an activist from Mumbai for women's education, told me there is unbelievable poverty among Muslims in Mumbai. There is great urge for education, he tells me yet they have no resources and hence drop out rate remains high. He and his wife work hard to coach these very poor girl children to prepare them for the SSC examination free of charge. Even then it is so difficult to sustain them on account of grinding poverty.

Another healthy change is that parents' resistance for girl's education is far less today compared to say 25 years ago. In many cases, Muslim women are far greater achievers in education field than boys. In Kolhapur, an industrial town in Maharashtra, I was told by Muslim leaders that there are twice as many Muslim girl post-graduates as boys.

Though one cannot expect drastic changes in the plight of Muslim women in India in near future but one can certainly hope for incremental changes. The number of Muslim women activists is on the increase as pointed out above. This will further increase with the passage of time. If Sachar Committee Report is implemented in right earnest, it will accelerate the pace of change in women's condition too But what is most unfortunate is that those who taunt Muslims about plight of Muslim women are today greatest opponent of implementation of Sachar Committee Report calling it 'blatant appeasement' of Muslims. One can very well see whether they are concerned with the plight of Muslim women or really trying to communalise Muslim women's issues.

To empower Muslim women, to reduce rate of child birth, to usher in religious and social reforms, there is great need to improve general economic condition which in turn will improve educational status of Muslim women and that in turn will bring in greater awareness for change. There is also great need for internal critique and at least educated Muslim men should attempt an honest criticism of condition of women in their community and consolidate efforts for change and reform. They also tend to be defensive and reactive. Time has certainly come to be proactive for improving Muslim women's status in India.

Muslim Women on South Asia

Muslim women, like other women, have been suffering for long for lack of empowerment in the male dominated society. Pakistan and Bangladesh, once part of India, have been no different in this respect. The women there suffered as much as in India for lack of rights. However, some changes were enacted in the Muslim personal law in Pakistan in 1961 during Ayub Khan's regime under intense pressure from women's organisations.

Triple divorce in one sitting was abolished and the Qur'anic concept of arbitration as indicated in the verse 4:35 which is quite fair to woman as she too has right to appoint an arbitrator to take care of her interests in the matter of divorce. Also, for polygamy the Muslim family ordinance promulgated by Ayub Khan in 1961 made it obligatory on the husband taking second wife to notify the first wife, obtain her approval and also to convince the court of law as to why second wife is needed. This was a great relief for Muslim women of Pakistan. That time Bangladesh was an integral part of Pakistan and had not seceded from it.

This amended law continued in Bangladesh even after it seceded from Pakistan. Even in Pakistan during hey day of Islamisation during Zia-ul-Haq's regime, despite pressures from the orthodox, these amendments to the Muslim personal Law in Pakistan could not be withdrawn. They are still valid in both the countries.

The case of Bangladesh is quite interesting. It is, for many reasons not to be discussed in detail here. There are strong secular and progressive trends as well as ultra-orthodox ones. Both have strong presence. The Bangladesh culture is a strong influence in contending orthodoxy but the semi-literate imams on the one hand, and ideologically oriented Jamat-e-Islami elements, on the other, dominate the orthodox trends. The secular and liberal elements strongly contend with the orthodoxy. A couple of months ago the Dacca High Court gave a ruling against triple divorce and also said in its judgement that any imam of the mosque giving *fatwa* in favour of triple divorce is liable to be prosecuted.

This ruling by the court caused a great stir in the orthodox circles and a call for strike was given by the Jamat-e-Islami and other orthodox elements which virtually turned into a battle between the secular and progressive elements and the orthodox elements resulting in loss of several lives. Similarly the Dacca High Court had ruled in 1999 that a divorcee is entitled for maintenance for life or until she remarries and this ruling was based on interpretation of the Qur'anic verse 2:241. The judges ruled interestingly that since maintenance is meant for a divorcee, she shall be entitled to it as long as she remains divorcee. This progressive judgement was unfortunately overturned by the Supreme Court of Bangla Desh.

Thus we see that the progressive and orthodox forces keep strongly contending against each other in Bnagla Desh. The secular forces in that country have been demanding further changes in the Muslim personal law. It is, however, interesting to note that like the Muslim minority in India the Hindu minority in Bangladesh resists any change in their personal law. Thus the Hindu women in Bangladesh are still governed by their age-old traditions and laws.

Now the Government of Bangladesh have prepared draft laws for enactment which go much further than the Muslim family ordinance of 1961. This draft has been approved by the opposition leaders like Khalida Ziya also. Khalida has an alliance with the conservative Jamat-e-Islami. Hasina Wajed, of course, has full support of the liberals and progressive elements. The proposed laws are going to be uniform in nature and will apply to all. This uniform family code to be enacted will offer women greater control over their lives. Divorce, according to the sources, may no longer be a traumatic experience for women in Bangladesh.

The main purpose of enacting the uniform family code seems to reform existing family laws to make them more humane and beneficial for women. These laws will end discrimination against women and will give them equal status in the society whatever religion they belong to. This uniform family code (UFC), under active consideration of the Government has been prepared by the Bangladesh Mahila Parishad. This women's organisation has been pressing for women's rights for last thirty years.

According to Ayesha Khan, General Secretary of Bangladesh Mahila Parishad (BMP), we realised that women are subject to oppression and discrimination in matters relating to personal rights. They are also denied access to opportunities for development, despite the Constitution guaranteeing equality to men and women." Ayesha Khan also said that though certain laws for women do exist like Cruelty to Women Ordinance, Dowry Prohibition Act and the Family Court Ordinance, structurally. Ayesha Khan also maintained that though 85% population in the country was of Muslims UFC cuts across all religions.

The first part of the UFC deals with marriage and divorce. According to this new Code it will be obligatory to register marriage and divorce. This part also lays down that the age of marriage for the boys shall be 22 and that of girls 18. In Bangladesh many girls, especially in rural areas, are married off as soon as they reach age of puberty and sometimes even earlier. These marriages, needless to say, are hardly ever registered.

These girls, married at an early age suffer greatly when either they are abandoned or divorced by pronouncing triple divorce. If marriages and divorces are registered, it will give women legal grounds to get what is rightfully theirs, points out Tania Amir, a prominent lawyer. In India too the National Women's Commission had recommended compulsory registration of marriages but the orthodox religious persons opposed it vehemently and this recommendation was never considered by the government. In India too. It will do great service to women's cause if compulsory registration of marriages is made into a law. But such a measure will be strongly resisted by the orthodox elements of all the communities.

The proposed UFC also outlines grounds for divorce both for men as well as women. While there are eight grounds on which men can obtain divorce, women have ten. Besides the usual grounds like immorality, impotency, and physical and mental torture for which women can claim divorce, the UFC also puts down dowry demands as a valid ground. Of course dowry has no Islamic sanction but to make it a ground for divorce would be a new concept. Dowry is not practised in other Islamic countries but is unfortunately quite common among Muslims of the Indian sub-continent. In the recent seminar of Muslim women held in Delhi on 7-8 April 2001 the *Ulama* themselves agreed that dowry is an anti-Islamic practice and a campaign should be launched against it

Desertion and impotency have clear sanction for divorce in Islamic shari'ah. The Dissolution of Muslim Marriage Act of 1939 gives a Muslim women right to divorce if husband deserts her for more than four years. The UFC, however, lays down that if husband does not pay maintenance for two years or is unheard of for the same period, a woman shall be entitled to demand divorce. In fact, even if the husband is addicted to drugs of any sort, divorce claim would be valid. A husband also could demand divorce if the wife is a drug addict.

It is, however, interesting to note that a husband, according to the draft UFC of Bangla Desh, will be entitled to divorce if wife is lesbian, a wife cannot claim divorce if husband is gay. These are also new grounds for divorce which do not exist in the traditional Islamic shari'ah. As impotency entitles a woman for divorce since she is deprived of her right to sex within marital frame-work, one can argue, through analogical reasoning (called qiyas in shari'ah terminology) a woman is deprived of sex if husband is gay (of course if he neglects her sexually) she could be entitled to divorce on that ground.

In the second part of the UFC , maintenance is to be made compulsory and uniform transcending religious customs and traditional laws. While laying down the grounds for maintenance, it also lays down the course of action that should be taken if maintenance is not paid. Farida Arif, a woman activist from Bangladesh says that the number of abandoned women is on the rise. Some trusts and NGOs look after the distressed women. Hence a clear line of action for maintenance is very necessary.

The other parts of theUFC provide for appointment of guardians for minors, adoption etc. The UFC provides for uniform law of adoption. It simplifies procedure for adoption for married couples but does not make provision for adoption for single man or woman. One of the aspects of the UFC is provision for uniform law of inheritance. Property rights are most contentious. According to UFC women, married or un-married, shall have equal rights to property. And for children born out of wedlock it gives them right in the maternal property. This will of course be most contentious part of the UFC as in shari'ah law equal rights in property to women does not exist.

Of course the draft UFC will be opposed by the orthodox section but women organisations will put pressure for its enactment. The Muslim women in India are also now pressing for change if one goes by the proceedings of the April seminar in Delhi where a number of women critiqued the legality of triple divorce and polygamy and wanted the Muslim personal law board to de-legislate triple divorce and regulate polygamy. One woman from West Bengal even pointed out that 75% prostitutes in Calcutta from amongst Muslims are those who have been divorced by their husbands arbitrarily. It is high time for Muslim Personal Law Board to approve the *Nikahnama* prepared by some Muslim women. It will give great relief to thousands of Muslim women in India. The Board cannot resist certain legitimate changes within the Shari'ah framework for long.

Women Reservation Bill

After 14 years of women's struggle, Rajya Sabha passed a women's Reservation Bill last week with two-third majority for constitutional amendment. The OBC satraps did their best to forestall the bill but did not succeed. Their argument that the bill will benefit only upper caste Hindu women at the cost of OBCs and minority women is only superficial and would hardly bears scrutiny. Truth is more complex and has to be examined with all its complexity.

In fact dalits and OBCs have already been given reservation and that reservation is fully justified. But by giving them reservation within reservation can make them even more dependants on reservation. Also, when the OBC men can fight elections and all of them are not highly educated, in fact many men are not literate beyond reading or writing their names why can't women, even if not highly literate, can go to state assembly or parliament. And this is also not true that all the OBC women are illiterate and all upper caste women are highly literate. Many upper caste women are also not highly literate.

Today female education is spreading fast and let alone the OBC women even dalit women are also getting better educated than their mothers. Truth is much more complex. The OBC men are not willing to allow their women folk to go to state assemblies or parliament. They do not want to part with their share of power. If women start representing in assemblies and parliament they will become dominant and assertive of their power. It hurts their male ego.

Also, if they are really concerned about their women getting reservation why can't they give 33% reservation to their women in party nomination. Why do they want quota within quota? They want extra reservation so that they do not want to cut down their own representation in parliament or assembly. And again who can say that the benefit will not go only to creamy layer among the OBC. So far all the benefits of reservation have gone to creamy layers among the OBCs and dalits. There is no reason to believe that political reservation will benefit all. The dalits and the OBCs as a whole have remained extremely poor and illiterate.

But the OBC satraps due to their numbers in Parliament are able to dictate terms and specially for passing the Finance Bill and without their cooperation Finance Bill can be stalled. That is the Government changed its strategy and postponed presenting Women's Reservation Bill in Lok Sabha until May so that it can seek cooperation of the OBC satraps in passing the Finance Bill.

But even in May these OBC leaders in Lok Sabha can succeed in stalling the Women's Reservation Bill and Mulayam Singh Yadav is talking of compromising by conceding twenty per cent seats for women in parliament and state assemblies. And government also may compromise to ensure smooth passage of bill. This would certainly be at the cost of justice to women. But in politics of vote bank who cares for justice. And it seems government may accept 20% reservation for women. The bill could have been passed 14 years ago with these amendments. Why then government waited for 14 long years if it had to accept such a compromise. I wish the government does not give in to such pressures. It will be gross injustice to cause of women. And that too those OBC leaders who are crying foul for non representation of the OBC women did not hesitate to make their wives even chief minister of the state. Laloo Prasad's wife Rabri Devi was made chief minister of Bihar who did not have any experience in politics, much less administering a huge state like Bihar. Similarly, BJP Uma Bharti, another OBC woman, chief minister of another big state like Madhya Pradesh. She too had hardly any experience except being mass agitator and a demagogue.

Reservation for Muslim Women Mulayam Singh Yadav and Laloo Prasad Yadav also are saying, to strengthen their position that a sub-quota be given to Muslim women. This has no iota of sincerity. Had they been sincere, they would have given tickets to Muslim women of their respective parties either for parliamentary elections or to say the least, assembly elections. As far as we know, these leaders did not give tickets even to Muslim men, in proportion to their population, let alone to Muslim women. Now to demand sub-quota for Muslim women is nothing more than politicking for winning support of Muslims. It is nothing more than mere politicking. It is this kind of politicking which denies justice to minorities and others. And as pointed out above, this is not even doing justice to the OBC but only to creamy layer.

Much greater irony is Muslim community does not speak in one voice even for its own benefit. While political minded Muslims are demanding sub-quota for Muslims the conservative Ulema are banning Muslim women from the arena of representational politics. A few years ago when women were given 33% and in some states even 50% representation in panchayats, zilla parishad and municipal elections, a Muslim woman from Deoband filed her nomination for municipal board election. A *fatwa* was issued by muftis of Deoband that it is haram for Muslim women to fight elections and campaign among men. However, the Muslim woman showed determination and refused to withdraw her nomination. The muftis then relaxed and asked her to wear hijab for campaigning among men. The woman again refused to bow down to wishes of muftis and campaigned and even won the election. Now we have news from Nadwatul Ulema, Lucknow that women should sit at home and perform her domestic chores than enter into public arena.

Our Ulema from India do not even know that Pakistan, the so called Islamic State has already given 22% reservation to women in National Assembly. Either this news has not reached Indian Ulema or they consider reservation for women in Pakistan "un Islamic". The Indian Ulema unfortunately are totally cut off from the modern world. They are still living the medieval Islam which they study in the books written by Islamic jurists and scholars of medieval era. It appears they consider medieval Islam as the only Islam they know. For them women have been created to serve their husbands and any other role for women as "un-Islamic". They even refuse to take cognizance of what is going on in other Islamic countries like Iran, Saudi Arabia, Kuwait, Indonesia and Malaysia. In Saudi Arabia, which is considered strictest regime for women, King Abdullah has nominated a woman as a cabinet minister. In Iran, women freely contest parliamentary elections and have become achievers in various fields of life. In Kuwait women fought their case up to Supreme Court to go to parliament without wearing hijab. In Malaysia, women have been appointed to naval ships and in Indonesia a Muslim woman Megawati Sukarnoputri became president of the country. And of course in Pakistan Benazir Bhutto was elected as Prime Minister. In Bangladesh power rotates between Khaleda Zia and Haseena Wajed.

In our opinion it is government's duty to ensure justice to women of all castes and communities and to refuse to slash 33% quota under pressure and there should not be sub-quotas for castes and communities. The democratic ideal requires that justice be done to women as a whole and all women to whatever castes and communities they belong to should have fair representation without taking resort to quota and suppose quota is agreed to how long will it last? Will it not become a permanent feature of Indian politics? Justice requires that only creamy layers and close relatives of regional satraps like Mulayam Singh Yadav and Laloo Prasad Yadav and the other OBC leaders could not be the only beneficiaries of reservations.

Women who Dared

Women generally are considered weak in our patriarchal society and men feel they need to be protected. Is it true? Well it may be true in some contexts but there are instances where women have dared where men chicken out or 'weaker' women have proved to be morally much stronger. Here it also needs to be stressed that only physical strength or strength of arms is not real strength, it is moral values which make really strong. Those who have moral superiority need not fear anyone and cannot be defeated.

Though no one can say women are inherently morally stronger but women tend to have better morals than men. There are number of reasons for that. Men aspire more for power and domination than women and hence resort to more morally unsound practices. They are involved more in crime than women and women tend to be more ethical in their behavior.

With very few exceptions women have not waged wars. Most of the ferocious and highly destructive wars in which millions of innocent human beings were killed were launched by men. In the last century two world wars were launched and fought by men, women only suffered. Women are far more sensitive to human life than men. It is women who give birth to life and sustain it. She carries human life for nine long months in her womb and than, after giving birth, nurtures it for years before child becomes self sufficient.

Men, on the other hand, to realize their own ambitions or wealth or power, would kill thousands of human beings within few seconds by dropping bombs or launching deadly missiles. Who caused atom bomb to be dropped on Nagasaki and Hiroshima killing more than two lakh people at a time? Not a woman. For men, power and authority are far more important than sensitivity to human life.

In communal riots in India too men have been real culprits than women. In my 40 years of investigating and monitoring communal riots in India I have not find a single instance in which any woman plotted and executed riots, much less killed any Hindu or Muslim. It was only in Gujarat that one Maya Kodnani is alleged to have instigated men to kill innocent human beings in Narodia Patia. I have found no other instance.

However, I have come across several instances in which women have saved the lives of innocent people. These women are real inspiration for peace loving people. I would like to throw some light here on the role of these women. Some I discovered while investigating riots and some I read about in newspapers and subsequently met them and some we had occasion to felicitate them on behalf of Women for Secularism, an organisation working for rights of women at grassroots.

I came first such instance during investigation of communal riots in Ahmedabad in 1969. Now I do not remember her name but she was a vegetable vendor living in Jalimsingh Ni Chawl in Ahmedabad where there were two Muslim families as her neighbours. During the riots of 1969 a mob surrounded the Chawl and demanded that the Muslims be handed over to them to be killed and their household looted.

This woman, a vegetable vendor, heard this and came out of her room with her sickle with which she used to cut her vegetables, came down the stairs and stood at the entrance challenging the mob to step forward to kill Muslims. I will cut the head of anyone stepping forward with this sickle, then you can kill me and walk over my dead body to kill the Muslims. None came forward and the mob of 500 dispersed.

I met this lady during my investigation and asked her why did you risk your life to save Muslims? She said first of all they were my neighbors and it was my duty to save their lives or die before they were killed. Secondly, they were from my own village in Rajasthan. What face I would have shown to my villagers if they were killed. Thirdly, it was my duty to save human lives. They were innocent and had nothing to do with the ongoing violence.

But there were men in the chawl, they could have come forward to save their neighbours' lives. If these men had no courage, what could I do? I did what I could to save my Muslim neighbours. She was indeed an inspiration for hundreds of men. These men hid inside their homes while this woman alone took the challenge.

Another instance I know of was of one Yadav from Aligarh when communal riots broke out there in 1994. A bus carrying *baraat* (marriage party) going towards Lucknow was parked in the bazaar and driver had gone for some work. A Hindu mob came to set fire to the bus. They were mostly women and children going for the marriage. Yadav was passing from there along with her son.

She saw that bus will be set afire killing 40 women and children. She looked around for something with which she could ward off the mob. She found an iron rod, picked it up and charged the mob with it. The mob ran away and she asked her son to drive the bus towards their house. Fortunately the driver had left the ignition key in the bus itself enabling her son to drive the bus off to their compound thus saving 40 lives single-handedly.

The Chief Minister Mulayam Singh Yadav himself met the lady and rewarded her with 1 lakh of rupees for her courage. I also met her when I went to Aligarh for investigation. She told me she was not sure whether she would be able to save their lives but I considered it my duty to at least make an attempt. More than courage, she said, it was my duty to save innocent lives, especially women and children. They all would have been reduced to ashes. I am fortunate to save their lives.

In this case too there were many men around but none showed courage or interest to save these innocent lives where a woman alone could pick courage and wielded rod and saved these lives. More than any thing else women after all are more sensitive to human life. She became talk of the town in Aligarh for her unusual feat.

In 2008, riots broke out in Bhainsa in Adilabad district of Andhra Pradesh. A house of Muslim Syed Osman was set afire on October 10 in which whole family including women and children would have been burnt alive but for the courage of Tuljabai 61 and her son and other women members of her family who saved their lives. Others looked on. Again a woman came forward showing extra-ordinary courage and others showed no concern. Communal minded men were busy killing and destroying.

Communal riots broke out in Sangli, Miraj, Ichalkaranji and Kolhapur district in early September 2009 on the eve of Ganesh festival 7-9 September 2009. During these riots 60 mosques and dargahs (mausoleums) were destroyed or damaged. But several Hindu women from these villages not only saved Muslim lives but also repaired these mosques and dargahs. For example the Gram Panchayat of Kavthepiran, which is run by women, decided to repair the damaged Muslim religious places and try to get life back to normal. These Hindu women said, Our Muslim sisters played an equal role in getting the award for our village. There are over 100 Muslim houses in the village and some had started leaving the village after the riots. But we stopped them. All women from the village visited the Muslim houses and assured to protect them? Thus they prevented Muslims from migrating from villages and assured them of security to their lives and properties. This sanity in the midst of communal frenzy by men was shown by illiterate rural women.

Some of these women were Hasubai Buchare, Rekha Chanade, Vandana Gaikwad and Nisha Butade, all grassroot workers. I met them in Icchalkaranji where we felicitated them on behalf of Women for Secularism in a convention held on 13th November 2009. I found them very courageous and though some of them illiterate or with very little education, spoke with great verve against those who organise communal violence to serve their political ends and vowed never to allow such violence in their village.

The communal violence in Kandhmal district wherein about 40 Christians were killed by some Hindu fanatics, also saw many Hindu courageous women who came forward to save lives of Christians fellow villagers in 2008. Some of these women were Ranchi Pradhan, Suruchi Pradhan of Rudenia village, Satyabhama Nayak and Nabojini Pradhan who showed exceptional courage in saving lives of many Christians or protect their houses. We felicitated all of them in the convention of All India Secular Forum. (Pradhan is the title used by Hindu tribals of Kandhmal)

These women are also all illiterate and grass root workers. Their humanism is very much alive and are free of communal prejudices. They proved to be more of human being than the Hindu, Christian or Muslim. It gives us great hope and proves two things: one, that women are far more compassionate than men and two, illiterate women are far more free of communal prejudices than highly educated urban people.

The Women for Secularism is, therefore, concentrating on these grass root women and mainly working among them. These women suffer much more at the hands of tradition bound men, especially those men who are votaries of communal ideologies and yet these women are far less prejudiced and are more humane. They are our asset and we must see that they get their Constitutional rights. They need to be better organised than they are today. There is also great need to build awareness of their rights.

Sir Syed Ahmad Khan and the Concept of Women's Rights

Sir Syed Ahmad Khan was a modernist and championed the cause of modern education among Indian Muslims. He was not only a scholar and educationist but also a man of future vision. He did everything possible to popularise modern scientific outlook among Indians in general, and, among Indian Muslims in particular. He got many scientific works translated into Indian languages so as to make them available to Indian people.

It is well known that he founded the Anglo-Oriental Mohammedan College in Aligarh which became the Aligarh Muslim University in 1920 much after the death of its founder. However, very few people know that

Sir Syed was not only a modern educationist but also was a profound scholar of Islam. His Islamic learning was second to none. He knew Arabic well and had great knowledge of the Holy Qur'an so much so that he undertook to write commentary on Qur'an (*tafsir*). A glance through his commentary on the holy Book shows that he had mastery over the Qur'anic knowledge (*Qur'ani 'ulum*). However, his approach was modern and the orthodox '*ulama* would not agree with him. He was close to M'utazalites (Islamic rationalists) in understanding Qur'an. In a sense he was also very close to Shah Waliyullah, the great 'alim and prolific Islamic writer of 18th century India. He approvingly quotes him while commenting on various Qur'anic verses. But he also quotes Tafsir-e-Kabir of Imam Fakhr al-Din Razi approvingly for explaining number of Qur'anic verses. Thus it will be seen that Sir Syed is quite versatile and has profound knowledge of the Qur'anic exegesis.

Sir Syed sets out the methodology of his *tafsir* right in the beginning. He has evolved 15 principles on which he bases his commentary in the introductory part of his commentary *Tahrir fi' Usul al –Tafsir.* In the very beginning he says that the main motive of writing this exegesis is to attempt secular and religious reforms. Secular reforms could be undertaken on their own grounds but for religious reforms it was necessary to explain the Qur'anic positions on the concerned issues. His main concern was that the modern knowledge (*'ulum-e-jadidah)* is apparently in conflict with the Islamic beliefs (*'aqa'id).* Sir Syed Ahmad Khan went through various classical commentaries and was not satisfied. He found nothing but stories in the exegetic literature most of which have been taken from Israeli sources. They are hardly in conformity withy the Qur'anic spirit. He then began to reflect on the contents of the Qur'an himself and evolved his own 15 principles of Qur'anic exegesis.

We are not concerned here with al the 15 principles which Sir Syed evolved after great deal of reflection. One of the principles of his exegetic methodology is that the contents of the Qur'an are quite true and it contains nothing which is wrong or contrary to observable facts. Thus in principle 9th of his exegesis Sir Syed rejects the belief in miracles. He maintains the there is nothing in the Qur'an which is not in conformity with the laws of nature. He quotes Shah Waliyullah whom he describes as *hujjatullah* and *hujjatul Islam* (i.e. proof of *Allah* and proof of Islam) to prove his point that there is no concept of miracle in Qur'an. Shah Waliyullah says in his *Tafhimat al-Ilahiyah* that *Allah* has not mentioned any miracle in His Book, nor indicated anything of the sort. Sir Syed further clarifies this by maintaining that it is not only during the life-time of the Prophet of Islam that miracles did not occur but during earlier prophets' time also. Thus according to him there is no place for anything which contradicts the law of nature *sunnat*

Allah. He also maintains that in the Qur'an there are no verses which have been abrogated. Thus Sir Syed negates the very concept of abrogating and abrogated verses (i.e. *nasikh-o-mansukh*). Sir Syed also maintains that the word of God cannot contradict the work of God and hence according to him the Qur'anic contents are quite in conformity with nature which is the work of God. In his fifteenth principle Sir Syed maintains that though the Qur'an is the word of God but like in any other language there are similes. Metaphors, symbols etc. in the Qur'anic language also. It also follows the way of Arabic rhetorics. All this has its won implications which cannot be avoided. In understanding of the Qur'an all this is necessary i.e. one cannot understand it in mere literal sense.

From all this, it is clear that Sir Syed had his own way of understanding the Qur'an. He neither completely rejects the classical exegesis nor imitates it mechanically. He brings to bear his own understanding in developing the Qur'anic exegeses. This applies not only to understanding of the Qur'anic verses in face of development of natural sciences but also with respect to development of natural sciences but also with respect to developments in the field of social ethics, economic morality, human dignity, sexual equations etc. This included issues of women's rights also. Though Sir Syed was not exactly the champion of sexual equality but he profoundly differs from many classical commentators on issues like divorce, marriage etc. it is pity that Sir Syed could not complete his commentary on the Qur'an and thus some of the vital issues pertaining to women's rights remained untouched in his commentary. It is also a pity that no one else later completed it following the principles laid down by the Syed as Shibli Nu'mani's *iratun Nabi* was completed by his disciple Syed Sulaiman Nadvi. Could have completed his commentary but he had to stay his project on account of intense pressure mounted on him by the Orthodox '*ulama*. He had to choose between popularising his religious views or founding the Anglo-Oriental Mohammedan College. He chose the later as he thought dissemination of modern education will make his religious views more acceptable.

Here in this article we would like to examine the Sir Syed's views on the question of women. He has written a commentary on the verses pertaining to women in the Qur'an but, it is regrettable that he has not commented on many important verses about women though we would have very much like to know his views about these verses. We will, in course of time refer to these verses. One of the important verses on women he has not commented upon is 2:228. Most of the modern commentators take this important verse to be the declaration of equality of sexes. Maulana Azad in his *'Tarjuman al-Qur'an'* also comments on this verse and concludes that it heralds equality of both the sexes fourteen hundred years ago. Sir Syed, who is Maulana Azad's mentor in a way simply translates it without any comment.

He translates it as *women have rights on men as men have on women.* His translation clearly indicates equality of rights of both sexes but, as pointed out, he refrains from commenting on it as their modern exegetes do. Perhaps Sir Syed thought his comments will infuriate the conservatives as he was already facing their fire and perhaps he did not want to further anger them. Whatever the reason, his translation; is also quite indicative of his inclination to uphold women's rights.

Similarly Sir Syed refrains from commenting on the verse 4:1. This verse also has been widely commented upon by the modernists as the one heralding equality of sexes. The verse says that *Allah* has created all of you from a single being (*nafs*) and created its mate (*zawjaha)* and spread from these two many men and women. Thus commenting on this verse Maulana Muhammad Ali of Lahore says in his Holy *Qur'an,* "The words occurring here – *Who created you from a single being and created its mate of same* – only declare the unity of the human race and the equality of the male and female." (p. 186). But again, perhaps for the reasons explained above, Sir Syed simply translates the verse without commenting over it.

However, more glaring is the case of verse 4:35 (4:38 in Sir Syed's translation) Sir Syed's translation of this verse is also close to conservative point of view. He translated the word *qawwam as tasallut i.e.* domination of man over woman. This rendition of the word *qawwam* has been rejected by all modernists and upholders of women's rights. For example Abdullah Yusuf Ali translates it as "protectors of women" and Muhammad Asad translates it as "taking care of women". Maulana Muhammad Ali, on the other hand, renders it as "maintainer". Thus according to these renderings man is protector or maintainer or care taker of woman, not one who dominates over her. Sir Syed's views are otherwise quite progressive about women too as we will show presently but he has adopted quite a conservative viewpoint in rendering this verse. This verse has been quite crucial in determining women's position in Islam. Conservatives and orthodox '*Ulama* have used it to prove that *Allah* has subordinated woman to man. The modernists have, therefore, tried to put the verse in proper perspective. They have specially challenged the rendering of the word *qawwam.*

What could be the reason for Sir Syed's acceptance of traditional concept of *qawwam* 1as one who dominates. On the question of polygamy and divorce Sir Syed takes, as we will see, a view quite acceptable to those who uphold women's rights. We will shortly throw light on these aspects. What could be the reason? May be Sir Syed did not believe in sexual equality as is borne out from the fact that he rebuked Maulvi Mumtaz Ali Khan for writing a book on women's rights on Islam. But when it came to polygamy and divorce he had to defend the Qur'anic positions vis-à-vis the west and he look quite progressive positions on these matters. His using the word *tasallut* for *qawwam* makes us think this way. Sir Syed who has deeply thought out meanings of Qur'anic words and argued vehemently in favour of rational positions would not have accepted, in passing, the conservative position on *qawwam.* He simply translates it and offers no comment on this important verse about women in Qur'an. It is difficult to gauge the real views of Sir Syed about position of women vis-a-vis men. In this respect perhaps he was product of his time and thought that women should be subordinated to men. It is difficult to say something categorically.

Sir Syed writes a detailed note on the verse 2:227 which is on divorce. We are presenting here a brief summary of Sir Syed's views on divorce which he gives on pp.212-216 of his *Tafsir.* He says that the opponents of Islam attack Islam on account of their obstinacy or misunderstanding on various counts one of which is divorce. The Jews cannot accuse Islam in this respect as Moses has instructed his followers to divorce their wives whenever they like. But some idolaters and the Christians who do not have custom of divorce or do not approve of divorce except in case of adultery can accuse Islam in this respect. They accuse Islam on the basis that this problem (divorce) is against mercy, love and sympathy (for the spouse). But John Milton has disagreed with this view and has proved with good (*umdah*) arguments that when husband and wife find it difficult to live in a way which is in keeping with civilised and cultured way, the bible does not prohibit divorce.

Then Sir Syed draws out attention to the fact that at present there are three codes (*shari'aten*) before us regarding divorce. First is of Jews which allow divorce without any strong reason. Sir Syed disapproves of absolute power for divorce and calls such shari'at as unlikeable and is against compassion, love and civilised way of living. Such unilateral divorce reduces the importance of marriage. Also, if man can pronounce such unilateral divorce man's love for woman and woman's loyalty to man has no meaning at all. The second shari'at is of idol-worshipers and the Christians among them there is no concept of divorce except in case of adultery. It no doubt, holds the sacred custom of marriage in great esteem but takes an extreme position in the matter of divorce. Such extremes are against the nature of human beings. If marriage develops unsurmountable problems and it becomes impossible to live together the only available remedy is divorce. The third shari'at is that of Islam which deals with the problem of divorce in this and the verses following this and in the guidance provided by the Holy Prophet (PBUH). This truthful shari'at has dealt with this problem in such moderate way (*i'tidal)* that one can think of no better way. No other shari'at can deal with this problem in such civilised manner. The Mohammad's Shari'at has allowed divorced only when it becomes impossible to save the marriage and except divorce no other way is available.........

……… Men have been exhorted to love their wives and should treat them with goodness and respect and should put up with their strong manners and tantrums. Women have been exhorted to be obedient men, should love them and be loyal to them. Then it was said about divorce that nothing on earth enrages *Allah* than divorce. Then I was said about women that those of them who ask for divorce without any strong reason and without trying all possible remedies, they shall not enter paradise. The holy Prophet (PUBH) used to be so angry with the news of any divorce that his companions often thought that as if business of divorcing needs to be punished by putting a person to death.

…….Then along with more exhortations against divorce, the Prophet found other ways of sustaining marriage. He required that effecting a divorce should be spread over three stages. After first divorce if the couple reconciles they can again live together as husband and wife. After second divorce too, they can effect reconciliation again and live as husband and wife. But if divorce is given third time again then it becomes evident that this marriage cannot be sustained and it is better that there is complete separation….. All these injunctions that these are Allah's limits and one should not transcend these limits. And if those people who object to the concept of divorce in Islam, if they try to understand it in a proper way, they would realise that this injunction is from one who has created human nature. (translated from Urdu into English by the author)

Sir Syed does not comment on other verses on divorce. He gives only this general comment. He does not comment on triple divorce in one sitting which has been prevalent among the Indian Muslims for centuries. He also does not give his comment on the question of women's right to divorce. It is either because such controversy about triple divorce did not exist in his time or he deliberately avoided commenting on such a sensitive problem.

Next important is polygamy. Sir Syed has written a long commentary on the verse 4:3 on the question of polygamy. The verse says: "And if you fear that you cannot do justice to orphans, marry such women as seem good to you, two, or three, or four; but if you fear that you will not do justice, then (marry) only one or that which your right hands possess." First of all Sir Syed explains the meaning of the term *yatim* i.e. orphan. Here by this word, he opines, are those girls 'unmarried women whose fathers have died. He says that in this verse and the verse preceding it (4:2) any injustice with orphan girls and women has been strictly prohibited. In this verse men have been exhorted that if you fear that you cannot do justice to orphan girls in matters of wealth and their rights, then marry other women. This is because of extreme caution in protecting the rights and wealth or orphan girls and women.

Then he explains the verse further by quoting a *hadith* from A 'Ishah, wife of the Holy Prophet, which has been narrated in *Tafsir-e-Kabir.* This makes it further clear that the verse permits men to marry upto four wives from amongst other women in order to protect orphan girls' and women's rights and interests. He also explains by throwing light on grammatical structure of the sentence that here there is no total prohibition for marrying orphans but only to protect their rights and interests. One can marry orphans provided one can do justice to them. Initially Sir Syed justices polygamy. He says that woman, on account of certain constraints, cannot enter into marriage contract before cancelling the earlier marriage contract whereas man can do and, he says, it is for this reason that Islam did not permit women to marry more than one man at a time. But man's condition is quite different. And besides this, man is concerned with different kinds of civilisational matters with which woman is not concerned. However, he does not explain what are those civilisational matters. But he also says that men have been permitted to take more than one wife only in certain circumstances and, according to him, to do so, is quite in keeping with nature. But the Muslims have very badly used this provision.

Then he says that original nature requires, if there are no other problems, that man take only one wife. But in certain exceptional circumstances he has to deviate from this natural rule. He also points out that absolute restriction on polygamy would have resulted in pitiable situation for women. Therefore, Sir Syed says, polygamy in certain circumstances must be permitted. He gives some examples: if a woman is suffering from terminable disease and is not fit for cohabitation, to desert her would be against the concept of justice, he argues. If a woman is barren and man intensely desires child will it not be proper for him to take another wife? He asks. And if you put absolute restriction on man not to marry another woman, it will lead to moral degeneration.

Sir Syed while justifving polygamy also says very clearly that it should not be for fulfilling ones sexual lust. He feels the Muslims have done so. That is why, he feels, Islam has put restriction for unrestrained practice of polygamy. He also draws our attention to the Qur'anic words *"if you fear you cannot do justice" (in khiftum alla t'adilu)* and says that these words are worth reflecting as there is no person who does not fear lack of justice. The Qur'an permits polygamy only when one can fulfill the condition of justice and even if one fulfills this condition it is only permissive and not imperative. Then he goes on to say that in this verse on polygamy the key word which is debatable is 'justice'. The '*ulama*, according to Sir Syed has restricted justice in matters of going to the wives turn by turn and in matters of maintenance and they have not made it conditional to love (inclination of heart) which is highly essential to sustenance of marital relationship.

The *'ulama* have drawn this inference of justice in going near the wives turn by turn and in maintenance only from one *hadith* which says that the Prophet (PBUH) used to divide his time between his wives in judicious manner and used to say O'*Allah* this is my [judicious] division of time in which I have control. Do not blame me in matters in which I have no control (i.e. equal love) and you have control. However, Sir Syed does not agree with this approach to justice between wives. Firstly, he does not accept the authenticity of this *hadith* and gives reasons for that. Then he goes on to say that even if we accept the *hadith* as correct then how one will explain the fact that the prophets who are normally not led by their selfish desires would pray to *Allah* that do not blame me if I incline towards particular women for reasons of lust. It is just not possible as it is against the noble character of the Prophet. He, therefore, concludes that the words 'if you fear you cannot do justice' refers to a great task which cannot be ordinarily fulfilled except by those who are great and pious souls. Such souls are never misguided by their lust. Secondly, Sir Syed says that to exclude equality of love from the concept of justice towards wives is a big mistake. In fact in marital relations love is most fundamental. Love, therefore, is most important as far as equal justice is concerned and it cannot be excluded from the concept of justice towards all wives. Then he quotes a verse 30:21 from the Qur'an to prove his point. The verse lays stress on quiet of mind and love and compassion between husband and wife. Sir Syed, therefore, thinks that love must be included in the concept of justice. Then referring to the verse 4:29 he says that this verse also makes it clear that love must be included in the concept of marital justice. The verse says that you cannot do justice even if you want. Had justice referred to maintenance only then it was not difficult even for ordinary souls. They can arrange for equal maintenance but what is impossible to achieve is equal love for all wives. As, equal justice towards all wives is not possible for ordinary mortals, the norm should be one wife only but in special circumstances one can take more than one. This is the conclusion arrived at by Sir Syed.

Similarly, Sir Syed discusses at length the institution of *muta* marriage (temporary marriage which is referred to in the verse 4:24 according to some exegetes). But he refers to the words of this verse which emphasise chastity and taking in marriage (*muhsinina)* and not for committing fornication (*musafihin)*. And muta' marriage according to him is like paying money for fornication and Qur'an can never permit such a thing. He, therefore, thinks that muta' marriage is prohibited by Qur'an which was prevale in the pre-Islamic period in Arabia.

Thus it will be seen that Sir Syed's position has been quite progressive in respect of women though at times he makes certain concession to conservatives. Or may be he himself held such views sincerely.

Islam in the West

As the population of Muslims is increasing in western countries like the U.K., the USA, Canada etc. the demand for applying Shari'ah law to Muslims is being voiced. The government of Canada was toying with the idea of enforcing Shari'ah law in the state of Toronto but none other than progressive Muslim women and men themselves opposed government's intention to apply Shari'ah law and in view of stiff opposition by these Muslims, government gave up the idea'

Now comes the news that the U.K. government may also think of applying Shari'ah law to Muslims of the U.K. the Archbishop of Canterbury has also favoured this measure. Rowan Williams, the Archbishop is reported to have said that the adoption of some aspects of Shari'ah law in the UK seems unavoidable. May be Archbishop is extending hand of friendship towards the Muslim minority which is of considerable size by now and is seeking some kind of accommodation with Muslim leaders. Or, may be he is under pressure to approve of application of Muslim law.

The BJP in this country wants Muslim law to be abolished although Muslim majority in India is much greater in size than in the UK. At one time it was unthinkable for Muslims of the UK to have Islamic law applied to them but fast increasing population is creating pressure on the government. Though as yet we have not heard any opposing voice from progressive Muslims of the UK, it may be matter of time before it is heard.

If Islamic law as codified by Muslim jurists of medieval ages is applied, it will create more problems for Muslim women. Our *'Ulama* voice stiff opposition to any change in the law in keeping with the Qur'anic spirit, it can certainly better the modern laws pertaining to marriage, divorce and property rights. But problem is our jurists and *'ulama* are too rigid to agree for any re-thinking even in the sprit of Qur'an.

Also, as rightly pointed out by some commentators there is no single law. Islamic law is different for Muslims of different sects. Even Sunni Muslims are divided into various legal schools like *Shafi'I, Hanafi, Maliki* and *Hanbali* and in the U.K. there are Muslims, following all these schools besides Shi'ah Ithna 'Asharis and Isma'ilis. Though marriage may not be much of a problem but divorce and inheritance laws can cause major problems in these different schools of law.

Though men will certainly gain but Muslim women will be great loosers, if one goes by traditional Shari'ah laws. The Qur'anic provisions were interpreted in medieval cultural ethos and women, in that cultural milieu was far from equal. In western countries discrimination on the basis of gender is a major issue and educated Muslim women mainly complain against discriminatory practices in the extant Shari'ah laws.

In all Muslim countries there is movement for change in existing Shari'ah laws and particularly women are demanding change and progressive men conscious of gender equality support them. If Shari'ah law is applied in countries like the UK, will it be applied as it exists, say in Sunni schools or it will be reformed? If it is reformed who will bring about reforms? In India Muslim women are against oral divorce pronounced in one breath and '*Ulama* oppose any such change. It is ultimately secular courts, which are rejecting triple divorce insisting on proof for divorce.

The Muslim women in India are also pressing for standard *nikahnama* which is perfectly Islamic as marriage is contract in Islam and yet '*Ulama* are not agreeing to nikah contract favouring women in Iran too, there is women's movement and many women have been condemned to death by stoning on charges of adultery and the Islamic jurists are not prepared to effect any change in traditional Ithna Ashari law prevalent in Iran. Those women demanding reforms have been sent to jail. There is also muta' marriage in force in Iran which again favours men.

In Saudi Arabia there are much severer problems and women cannot even enter into business deal directly without a male member apart from being forbidden to drive vehicles. They cannot vote in elections also. Recently municipal elections were introduced in Saudi Arabia but women were not allowed to vote despite demand from women.

I have met many '*ulama* in UK. They are as conservative as in Islamic countries, perhaps even more in the alien environment of the UK and other Western countries. If any attempt is made to apply Islamic law in the UK it will trigger off bitter controversy between Muslims and non-Muslims, on one hand, and between Muslims and Muslims, on the other. The Muslim women are bound to protest.

Large number of Muslims is from various Arab and African countries with extremely conservative background and if '*ulama* oppose any change in Muslim law or its selective application and these conservative Muslims will fully back up these '*ulama*. Obviously, progressive Muslims wanting change in Shari'ah law will be outnumbered and the Government will have to listen to the conservatives.

Though there is provision for re-thinking in Islamic law called ijtihad, to this day '*ulama* never allowed any one including one of their own tribe, to resort to ijtihad. An '*alim* of standing of Muhammad 'Abduh in Egypt in late nineteenth century and early twentieth century had to face stiff opposition for his advocacy of change and re-thinking of Islamic laws. Though he rose to the high status of grand mufti of Egypt, yet he could not bring any change.

When the then President Sadat's wife Jehan Sadat used her influence to introduce a law by interpreting a verse of the Qur'an that a marriage would be registered only if husband bought a house in the name of his wife, it was removed immediately after the assassination of Sadat. Hosni Mubarak, the present president of Egypt also faced stiff opposition from the '*ulama* of al-Azhar when he introduced a bill empowering women to obtain *khula*' (women's right to obtain divorce without husband's consent). He had to agree to a compromise formula before he could get the law passed.

This is the state of affairs in Islamic countries where reform should have been easier in totally Islamic milieu. How difficult it would be in non-Islamic countries, one can well imagine. In India where there are largest number of Muslims next only to Indonesia, *ulama* have opposed any change saying it is Muslim minority country and non-Muslim government has not right to interfere in Islamic laws.

When the Supreme Court of India granted maintenance to an aged woman beyond iddah period, the '*ulama*, as well as Muslim political leaders, raised storm of protest and ultimately Government of India reversed the judgment of the highest court by enacting a law restricting maintenance within the iddah period. Thus the UK Muslims will also face these dilemmas once Islamic law is introduced in the UK or for that matter in any European and other western countries like the USA or Canada.

The '*ulama* consider formulations of medieval ages sacred divine. For them the Qur'anic concept of justice is secondary to men's authority over women. Men's right to divorce is considered as absolute whereas women's right is constrained by men's consent. Thus it is men who has authority to divorce although there is no such authority given by the Qur'an to men.

The '*ulama* consider women as weak and emotional and incapable of taking proper decision and hence only men should take crucial decisions though women could be consulted. By the same reason they also think that a woman should not become head of state as it would be disaster for the state. This view is supposedly based on one *hadith* authenticity of which has been questioned.

Today, there is great need for re-codification of Islamic laws and if Qur'anic spirit is followed in re-codification of Islamic laws in the areas of marriage, divorce and inheritance, these laws will be as good as modern laws based on the concept of gender equality and also much of the differences between various madhahib (schools of law) can be minimised.

These differences between various schools of law are precisely because of differences of opinion between jurists as also due to impact of local conditions, customs and traditions. Despite these differences all the jurists of the time were agreed on one thing: women are sinferior to men in every respect though there is no such assumption in Qur'an at all. This assumption of inferiority of female sex was introduced by the '*ulama* and jurists who were themselves product of patriarchal ethos.

The Qur'anic injunctions on personal laws have no such direct or even indirect assumption and hence these injunctions prioritize women's rights. However, the right-based discourse for women could not be accepted by patriarchs of the time even though it was divine and hence Shari'ah laws were based more on patriarchal opinions and divinity was subjected to patriarchy.

Gender equality, originally found in Qur'an and lost in medieval patriarchal ethos has to be rediscovered buried in Qur'anic revelation and then only gender justice can be restored.

Women and Personal Law in Iran

Women had played very active role in Islamic revolution in Iran right from beginning. Before the revolution the Shah had imposed modern secular reforms and had abolished veil and Western dress was encouraged. However, these reforms were quite superficial as women had no freedom to participate in political activities and held no political office. She hardly enjoyed much freedom. It was again more an imitation of western culture than true freedom for women.

Women too, therefore, joined Islamic revolutionary movement in late seventies with great enthusiasm as they too were feeling constrained under Shah's regime. They freely chose, without any compulsion whatsoever, to give up their mini skirts and took to chador. One more reason why women voluntarily took to chador was that the Shah was accusing the revolutionaries as communist agents. They tried to prove their authentic Islamic character. Ayatollah Khomeini had also assured them of full political, cultural and social freedom after the revolution.

However, Khomeini did not fulfil his promise and women were to some extent disappointed as more restrictions were sought to be placed on them after revolution took place. But as the women had played very dynamic role in the revolution they did not give up fighting for their rights. Number of papers and magazines were being published before the revolution and more such magazines and journals. These were indeed years of struggle for women in Iran. Afsaneh Najmabadi, a woman activist, described post revolutionary years in Iran as "Years of hardship, years of growth."

Women issues have always remained quite sensitive issues in the third world society in general, and in Muslim societies, in particular. As a weekly women's journal 'Zan-I-Ruz' (Today's Woman) pointed out in its editorial, "colonialism was fully aware of the sensitive and vital role of woman in the formation of the individual and of human society. They considered her the best tool for subjugation of the nations?.women serve as the unconscious accomplices of the powers-to-be in the destruction of indigenous culture to the benefit of imperialists."

The editorial went on to conclude, that "the glory and depth of Iran's Islamic revolution to occur woman must be transformed. The centrality of gender to the construction of an Islamic political discourse thus changed that which had been marginal, secondary, postponed, illegitimate, and discredited into which was to central, primary, immediate and authentic. However, what is authentic remains highly controversial. Does it mean women's role should be restricted as against what is prevalent in the West? This is considered authentic role for women in many Muslim societies. Afghanistan is its best example. However, it was, though a prevalent view among conservative *ulama* in Iran too, could not go unchallenged. In countries like Afghaistan there is no, and possibly could not be, any contesting voice as women in that primarily a tribal society, had not played any role in bringing about Islamic revolution."

However, it was not so in case of Iran, as pointed out above. Iranian revolution, because of active role played in it by women, have opened new vistas and possibilities for growth of all kinds of feminisms - including secular. New configurations of Islam, revolution, and feminism, are now emerging. It is very difficult for conservative clergy in Iran to ignore women's demands. Of that there are no attempts to suppress women's movements. Like the reform movement in Iran - which is gaining ground and hence conservative clergy is trying to suppress it with all its might - women's movements also face their ire. But it is beyond the clergy's might to do away with these movements. Initially women in Iran did feel betrayed by the clergy but did not lose courage, and continued its struggle - and with good result.

The acts of defiance and resistance by women, as pointed out by Afsaneh Najmabadi, became instantly named as counter-revolutionary, a label that not only made these women easy targets of repression, but also cut off any possibilty of building alliances with Islamic women activists of the Revolution, many of whom were shocked into silence, frozen in disbelief at this unforseen turn of events. Islamic women activists had been political supporters and active organisers of the mass Islamic movement that overthrew the old regime. Many of these Islamic activists had been inspired by the Islamic womanhood as expounded, for example, in the writings of Ali Shari'ati who played very vital role in building up the Islamic consciousness, specially among the university students, both male and female and these students, in turn, played great role in bringing about Islamic revolution in Iran.

However, the post-revolutionary regime took measures promoting some of the most misogynous policies. Mihrangiz Kar, a noted feminist activist says:

"Iranian women have gone through a difficult test. During the past decade, they have experienced difficulties and dangers that were unprecedented in their individual and social lives?..Women have come out of these testing times, without owing any debt to any one's propaganda machinery, registering themselves from the margins to the centre of social text? Now women, who have fulfilled their obligation, demand, not beg, their rights."

It can be said without fear of any contradiction that despite all these problems the Iranian women today are in far better position than in many other Arab countries. The Iranian women have won, through sheer grit of their struggle, which is many women's envy in Islamic countries. In Kuwait women are struggling even for voting rights. In Iran, on the other hand, they not only have voting rights but can be, and are, elected to parliament and to high elective offices like vice president.

Not only this, women in Iran have won many concessions for themselves as far as personal laws are concerned. Today in Iran, if divorce takes place for no fault on the part of women or on account of her misconduct, she can claim from her divorcing husband half the property acquired during the married years or its equivalent. Such a provision does not exist in any other Muslim country. In Egypt a law was passed during Anwar Sadat's time, due to efforts of his wife Jahan Sadat that husband had to provide house in her name at the time of marriage. However, after Sadat's assassination, this law was reversed, under pressure from the conservative *ulama* of al-Azhar, the premier Islamic University in the Islamic world. Egypt is another Islamic country where women have been able to win some rights and affect change in their status.

Another important right which the Iranian women have won is of divorce on the following counts: (1) if the husband does not pay her maintenance for more than six mnths and if there is no possibility that he will pay and similarly his inability to fulfil the obligations of married life and ensuring the rights of his wife for that period; (2) misbehaviour and mistreating wife and if wife is unable to bear this misbehaviour she can claim divorce; (3) if the husband is suffering from addiction to alcohol or drugs; (4) if the husband neglects wife or family life without any reasonable ground continuously for more than six months; (5) and if the husband takes another wife without permission of first wife or unjust behaviour towards her.

These are far reaching concessions as far as conventional personal law is concerned. The women, as pointed out before, have not been able to win such rights. It is undoubtedly a great advance over the existing situation in other Muslim countries. Not only this an Iranian woman can also now claim compensation for all the house-keeping work she did for the number of years of married life if it is proved that wife is not be blamed for divorce. This is quite revolutionary provision in the law.

These provisions considerably restrict the rights and privileges of man available to him in other Muslim societies. This is the demand by women's organisations in many countries including Western countries. This has been possible in Iran because the whole Iranian society is in the throes of change and people are engaged in continuous struggle and the struggle creates sharp consciousness for ones rights.

In Iran women's press is also quite strong. As pointed out before number of magazines and journals are published by various women's organisations and it is very difficult for the regime to suppress these publications. Afsaneh Najmabadi points out, "Out of these early years of Islamic women's activism emerged the drive toward rethinking gender in Islam in more radical ways. A number of women's organisations and institutes, as well as variety of women's journals now published in Iran, attest to the significance of this rethinking. These journals are distinct in their respective constructions of womanhood, ranging from Nida' (The Call), a rather ideologically rigid organ of quasi-governmental organisation to '*Zanan*' (Women), a journal that explicitly defends itself as feminist."

This has been possible, as female literacy rate in Iran is quite high. In post-revolutionary period there has been special attention on female literacy. Female literacy, needless to say, plays very crucial role in bringing change in women's status. Even family planning consciousness increases sharply with the increase in rate of literacy. Increased rate of female literacy has been a great contribution of revolutionary regime and all the changes in the status of women in Iran have been possible because of increased literacy rate on one hand, and, continuous struggle on the part of women, on the other. Women's participation in Iranian revolution has played very vital role in this respect. Still the Iranian women have to go a long way in achieving equal status with men. But eventually they will, given the consciousness of Iranian women and continuous struggle on their part.

Women and Peace

Can women play better role for peace? Many feminists think women are much better suited for peace than men. If so why? What are those factors which make women play better role for peace. Does she not have same weaknesses as man? Has she proved better ruler than man? What do we find in history? We will try to answer some of these questions in this article.

If a woman is better suited for peace what are the primary factors which make her play peace better than man. Ours is a patriarchal society and we all know how women are dominated in a patriarchal society. In most of the cases she internalises this oppression and accepts it as her fate. She reconciles to playing a role of house maker and serves her husband and children after marriage. And in modern society she is even content playing double role i.e. as an earner as well as house maker. Some men who are against women working outside home never tire of pointing out that women have to bear double burden.

Anyway these are problems of a patriarchal society and women all over the world suffer from patriarchal cultural values, even in advanced democratic societies of western countries despite gender parity laws made in western countries. Thus women are oppressed and oppressed know the value of peace better than the oppressors. This is one important reason why women can prove to be better peace-makers.

We will throw more light on that aspect later. But more primary factor is woman as mother i.e. one who gives birth to life, nurtures and sustains it. As a mother her role is bringing life into existence is most fundamental. She conceives the baby, nurtures it in her womb for nine months and then bears it at the risk of her own life and after giving birth she has again to nurture it for several months, even years.

Thus who knows value of life more than a mother? Man, always arrogant about power often behaves as an ego-centric agent and does not hesitate to take life to fulfill his power-centric ambitions. A life which comes into existence after months of labour and pain, can be wiped out in less than a second with disastrous weapons made through modern technology. Not one but lakhs of human beings can be killed by simply pressing a button.

A woman who bears, nurtures and sustains life would hesitate to promote conflict which may result in such mass murder in far off places just by press of a button. Moreover, in a patriarchal society woman does not share power too and her behaviour is much less power centric than that of man. Also, as man does not have to bear pains of carrying baby, delivering and nurturing it he lacks compassion for life which a woman is gifted with. It is a natural quality which woman needs to sustain life.

Love and compassion are needed in abundance for life to flourish. It is hatred which destroys life and love that makes life richer and worth living for. And hatred is borne more often as a result of struggle for power. Power becomes a burning ambition and human life can be sacrificed at its altar. Man kills ruthlessly, women very hesitantly. Her orientation to life is very different and this difference is gendered one.

Even if a woman is involved in power struggle, except for very few exceptions, she would not kill as man does. She, by nature is more compassionate. In extremes of persecution she does become revengeful but only in extremes. It is her psyche. Also she is more patient than man. Her patience, in fact, is far more enduring as well as her tolerance. These are sterling qualities nature has gifted her for her motherhood.

Except in certain cases she is much less in crime. She does not have much presence in armed forces. It is true in these days of gender parity many women are seeking entry into armed forces, not only in non-combative but combative services. But it is more for gender parity than her feminine qualities. In fact it goes against her primordial nature. Here it must be borne in mind that gender parity too has its limits. Gender, as we all know, is a social construct whereas natural qualities are with ones birth.

I don't say that women should not take part in combat situations; she should but only for defense situations as by nature she has been programmed for love and compassion. Man should learn from her rather than woman, in order to pursue gender parity should trudge his path of aggression and ruthlessness. It is very delicate matter. Some feminists may argue why woman should not be as combative as men yes logically this argument is quite sound. If she is equal to man in all respects, why not in matters of combat. She should also participate equally ruthlessly and aggressively in combat roles.

But there is a difference in logical arguments and natural gifts or the way she has been gifted with for her motherhood which requires life affirmative and life promoting gifts. I am also aware of the fact that upholders of patriarchal values are likely to misuse this argument in favour of denying equality to women. But we have to face dilemma of one kind or the other. I believe this is not going to go too far.

Ultimately, what we need is life affirmative values. Patriarchy has not only deprived us of life affirmative values but has brought great disasters for humanity. In hundreds and thousands of battles and wars fought millions of lives have been lost and all that for patriarchal assertion, power struggles, domination of one patriarchal group over the other. Had matriarchal values prevailed world would have been very different.

It is also important to note that matriarchy changes entire perspective on life. Everywhere and in all fields it is life promoting perspective which matters and peace is one among them. When war or any kind of conflict is going on it is not only human lives which are at stake but also destruction of life facilitating factors. As now it is not only gross product which matters in capitalism but the very quality of life which prioritises health services and all other facilities which are needed to make life more worth living which matter.

Similarly, it is feminine concerns for making life richer in every possible manner which makes life worth its price. A feminine perspective should not be equated merely with domestic chores. A feminine perspective on life is basically concerned with richer and fuller life and that is possible only when peace prevails and for peace to prevail we need not patriarchal but matriarchal perspective on life which is life affirmative.

The peace pacts drawn up by men are more often of temporary nature as both sides want breathing period for preparing for 'winning war'. However, for women next war would not be a priority but a permanent peace which is life enriching. Generally, peace treaties drawn up by the UNO have predominant role by men as most of the top officers are men have very restrictive clauses and slightly violation leads to fresh breakout of wars.

In these treaties consideration is not life enriching possibilities but vaguely defined 'patriotism' which is all about possession of land rather than potentialities of peace. Peace goes much beyond possession of land and is more concerned with people and their lives. Women's very instinct is life affirming and hence women drawing up peace treaty would insert such clauses which would minimize chances of fresh outbreak of violence as violence is life negative.

Women for permanent peace, for example, would insert clauses which would make treaty more inclusive of other ethnic and identity groups, especially belonging to minorities and weaker sections transcending political ideologies and religious persuasions to save peace. Peace cannot prevail unless divisive clauses are minimised and inclusive clauses are given greater space in these treaties.

In most of the peace treaties drawn up by men land has priority, even land where even single blade of grass does not grow or be it mere desert. A lasting peace is not possible if one has obsession with land and no concern with human lives at all. People keep on dying for the sake of a piece of land. Land-oriented patriotism is part of our emotionally charged language too. In this orientation even mothers are honoured only for producing sons to defend land. Women are valued only for producing sons to sacrifice their lives for the sake of land.

This is not women's perspective for peace. Peace needs consolidation of life, not sacrificing it for saving piece of land. This was feudal patriarchal orientation. For peace we need patience, tolerance, democratic and inclusive perspective so that people of all ethnic, linguistic and racial groups are included. Only women are capable of bringing such perspective for peace as women care more for life. Life is beginning and end of their perspective.

Western Feminism and Islam

There is strong criticism of those who work for rights of women by conservative Islamists and they are accused of imitating western feminism.

It is debatable whether it is so but even if it is what is wrong with it? Western feminism is based on secular ideology but upholds dignity of women and their rights. If secularism is not always negation of religion (only atheistic secularism negates it, not other forms of secularism) and in most cases it is not, there is no objection to feminism. The Holy Prophet says acquire wisdom (*hikmah*) wherever it is found as it is believer's (*m'umin's*) property.

It is well known that until 1960s even Western societies - despite their secularism - had not accorded equal rights (sexual equality is still not meticulously practised in Western societies) to women. In fact even right to inheritance and property was given to women in Western countries in thirties. In some countries women got right to vote only during the decade of thirties. The women had to struggle, a lot in the West for acquiring these rights, which Islam had given to them centuries ago.

Even in western countries the debates go on many issues and many women's organisations are not fully satisfied about the women issues. Man's domination continues in most of the spheres including the domestic sphere. Man certainly enjoys more privileges, if not rights, in those western countries. Man still resists performing domestic chores and even wife beating is not unknown.

The fact is that patriarchal structure of society is still going strong and one does not know whether it will disappear in the foreseeable future. It is for this reason that with few exceptions political power rests with man in most of the countries. Again, in most of the western countries representation of women in legislative bodies hardly exceeds 10 per cent though their population is close to fifty per cent in all societies. It is for this reason that the feminists are struggling for equal rights in western countries too. All one can say is that the condition of women is somewhat better compared to third world countries or Islamic countries. Though in western countries equality of sexes has been established theoretically it is far from having been achieved in practice.

And those struggling for women's rights in third world countries in general and, in the Islamic countries in particular have to struggle against much greater odds. These odds remain insurmountable even if these women work within the framework of Islam. Many Muslim countries like Kuwait even refuse to give its women right to vote. The Saudi Government does not allow its women even to drive even when accompanied by their husbands, let alone go out alone in public.

We have such primitive conditions in several Islamic countries and if women protest against such intolerable restrictions they are dubbed as 'western feminists'. The real thing is that such demands of equal rights hurt male ego. Male domination is not at all Islamic, though it is justified in its name. Men use some selective verses from the Qur'an, ignore their social context and use them to perpetuate their domination. They conveniently ignore the verses empowering women or laying down equality of both the sexes. In fact in verses like 2:219, 2:228 and 33:35 there is clear statement about equality of both the sexes and yet they are totally ignored and instead they quote verses like 4:34 to establish their domination. They even distort the meaning of words like *qawwam* used in above verse to retain their hegemony.

They also use several *ahadith* (Prophet's sayings) to put undue restrictions on women. It is forgotten that thousands of *ahadith* cannot be even authenticated as many of them were forged by those who had anti-women attitude and these *ahadith* are used as authentic source for legislation about women even when they contradict clear Qur'anic assertions. Thus the Saudi law not allowing women to venture out alone is not Qur'anic but based on a *hadith* which prohibits women going out alone.

Even if the *hadith* is authentic one totally ignores the social conditions then and now. In those days there was conflict between the Jews and Muslims and the Jews used to tease Muslim women and so in view of this the Prophet might have cautioned women not to venture out alone. Most of the *ahadith* are narrated without mentioning any context or reason and these are followed by the orthodox *'ulama* mechanically. And practices like prohibiting to drive does not even have any base in *hadith*. There were no automobiles in those days.

One cannot even derive it by inference or *qiyas* (analogy) as women were not prohibited by the Holy Prophet from riding camels or horses. The women did ride camels and horses and they even drove them by themselves. Such prohibition is nothing more than extreme conservatism of the Saudi *'ulama* and their stubborn refusal to concede rights to women. It is interesting to note that while the Saudi government does not allow women to drive cars the Iranian government has started exclusive taxi service to be run by women. Thus Iranian women can not only drive private cars but can also be a taxi driver.

Similarly, while the Kuwait Government refuses its women to vote other Muslim countries like Pakistan, Bangladesh, Egypt and other countries allow them to vote. How does one explain these contradictory practices? Are their different Islams or there are differing attitudes towards women? Thus it is not Islamic sources but men's attitude which matters.

And when Muslim women demand their rights - and Islamic rights at that - they are denounced as western feminists. It is a fact that Muslim women enjoy differing degree of rights in different Islamic countries. While in Turkey Mustafa Kemal Pasha introduced secular Swiss code thus according equal rights to both men and women on one hand, and, the total restrictions in Saudi on the other hand. In other Muslim countries like Egypt, Morocco, Algeria, Jordan etc. there is comparatively greater latitude of freedom for women. It is because the rulers in these countries are more liberal towards women.

Thus it is not Islam, which comes in the way but man's attitude which determine the laws of Muslim countries regarding women. But these men in various Muslim countries invoke name of Islam to stem the tide of women's movement for better rights dubbing it as western feminism.

Some Muslim countries like Pakistan and Bangladesh had or have women prime minister and some Muslim countries like Kuwait do not accord women right to vote. Such gross contradictions are really difficult to gloss over in the name of Islam. It all depends either on social conditions of that country or even on political exigencies.

When Fatima Jinnah tried to contest for the office of President in early 1960s against Ayuub Khan, the latter wangled a *fatwa* from the conservative *'ulama* that a woman cannot become head of the state. They quoted a *hadith* from the Holy Prophet that if a woman becomes head of a nation that nation will face disaster. However, the supporters of Fatima which included head of Jama'at-e-Islami Maulana Maududi approved of her contesting the President's election. They also managed to obtain a *fatwa* to this effect from a prominent *'alim* like Maulana Ashraf Ali Thanvi who justified on grounds that in democracy the head of a state does not have absolute powers but depends on votes of members of parliament whose majority is of men.

All these political games are unfortunately played in the name of Islam rather than giving women rights due to them in a modern democratic society and which are not contrary to the teachings of the Qur'an. Most of the Muslim women in Islamic countries are not guilty of following 'western feminism' but are agitating for their Islamic rights. The Taliban regime was the worst offenders in this respect. They not only followed the rigid Saudi laws but put more restriction than the Saudis do.

The *Taliban* who were essentially following tribal norms justified all that in the name of Islam. They did not even allow women to go out for schools and madrasas totally ignoring the famous *hadith* of the Prophet that seeking knowledge is obligatory both for Muslim men and Muslim women (muslimah). The prophet separately mentioned Muslimah keeping in mind that soon after him the Muslim men would restrict women from acquiring knowledge. The Prophet used the word *'ilm* which includes both religious as well as secular knowledge.

However, with few exceptions throughout medieval ages Muslim women were not allowed to acquire literary skills and reason was cited that learning reading and writing would corrupt them and they might write 'love letters' to strangers which is sin. Today, no one argues on these lines and of course Muslim women are acquiring secular as well as religious knowledge in public institutions. And this is no more considered as un-Islamic.

Thus what was considered un-Islamic until yesterday has become perfectly Islamic today and is accepted with good Islamic conscience by men in all Islamic countries. Many Muslim countries even permit co-education, which was great 'sin' until recently. Thus it can be seen that much depends not on Islam but on social dynamics, on medievalism or modernity, on orthodoxy or liberalism.

The man in male-dominated society in Muslim countries forgets that Islam ushered in its days a great revolution, which can be called feminist revolution today. It accorded equality to both man and women in various ways sometimes saying that "women have rights similar to those against them" (2:228) and sometimes saying for everything men and women will be equally rewarded (33:35).

But except for initial period of few decades Muslim women never enjoyed equality in the Islamic world. Soon, for various reasons, more and more restrictions were imposed on them. Though there was absolutely no place for monarchy in Islam, the institution of monarchy developed in the Muslim world within 30 years of the death of the Prophet and all feudal customs and traditions associated with monarchy came to be adopted by Muslim monarchs (though continued to be called *caliphs* for religious reasons) including severe restrictions on Muslim women. In other words all feudal practices were imposed on women in the Muslim world which continue until today.

Within hundred years after the beginning of the Islamic calendar she almost lost all her Qur'aic rights. Qur'an recognised her as legal entity and gave her all rights including contracting marriage, divorce, right to inherit, to have her own property, to earn and have her own income and to own her own business. But by the time the Umayyads consolidated their rule, all pre-Islamic traditions and customs were revised and also feudal traditions added to them thus completely subjugating women.

The Qur'an had required her to dress in dignified manner and conceal her sexual charms, the Muslim society put her under veil requiring to conceal her face completely. She could only peep though her two holes provided in the veil. This is no where the intention of the Qur'an yet this form of veiling is practised in many Islamic countries today.

She was confined to her house whereas during the Prophet's time and for quite some time thereafter she even took part in battles fought against non-Muslims. It is said that it was Umm Ammarah who saved the Prophet's life in the battle of Uhud. However, from Umayyad period onwards she was not even allowed to go out of home without her husband's permission after marriage and with father's permission before that and that too accompanied by some male relative called mahram (a blood relation with whom marriage is not permissible like brother, uncle etc.)

A *hadith* was also invented requiring her to be totally obedient to her husband and that sajda before husband would have been ordered had it not been prohibited for anyone except Allah. This *hadith* is reflective of the feudalisation of Islamic ethos. In other words women by then had lost her autonomy and what revolutionary changes and empowerment of women effected by the Qur'an were totally lost.

It would be interesting to quote here from a medieval text to show the concept of an ideal woman prevailing in that society. "An ideal women", according to this medieval writer, "speaks and laughs rarely and never without a reason. She never leaves the hose, even to see neighbours or her acquaintance. She has no women friends, gives her confidence to nobody, and her husband is her sole reliance. She accepts nothing from anyone, excepting her husband and her parents. If she sees her relatives she does not meddle in their affairs. She is not treacherous and has no faults to hide, nor bad reasons to proffer. She does not try to entice people. If her husband shows his intention to performing the conjugal rites, she agrees to satisfy his desire and occasionally provokes it. She assists him always in his affairs, and is sparing in complaints and tears; she does not laugh or rejoice when she sees her husband moody or sorrowful but shares his troubles, and wheedles him into good humour till he is quite content again. She does not surrender herself to anybody but her husband, even if abstinence would kill her. Such a woman is cherished by everyone." (See Shaykh Nefzawi, The Perfumed Garden. Tr. Richard F. Burton, New York, 1964), p. 97). This is how a Muslim woman was pictured in medieval ages.

It is these feudal restrictions that we have inherited from our past and we glorify them as 'Islamic' and any deviation from it is condemned as western feminism. These restrictions are still practised in most of the Muslim countries because they still have not been democratised and women have no access to modern education. There is hardly any Muslim country, which has democratic governance. Either there is monarchy or military dictatorship or controlled democracy.

However, modernisation is also going apace and it is difficult for the rulers in Muslim countries to resist spread of modern education among women. More modern education spread among women and society becomes increasingly democratised, awareness for rights grows among them and they demand their rights either on Islamic or secular grounds.

It is interesting to note that while in several Muslim countries like Saudi Arabia and Kuwait women are demanding modernisation and political and social rights some women in Turkey are keen to go into *hijab*. In many non-Muslim countries also a section of Muslim women are taking to *hijab*. It is important to note the reasons for the same.

Though in general women are demanding their rights in all countries some Muslim women feel proud to observe Islamic dress code. It is more for reasons of identity. Westernisation (which is not necessarily modernisation and one must distinguish between the two) has led to certain excesses in manner of dressing which violate sexual modesty as the whole emphasis is on displaying feminine charms and body line rather than conceal them.

Today, there is feeling among the people in developing countries of western culture assuming hegemonising role, which creates resentment. Globalisation has further strengthened the hegemony of western culture and the people of developing countries have become quite conscious of their own culture and cultural practices. The Muslim women are also taking to their own cultural way of dressing to assert their cultural identity. *Hijab* should thus be seen as part of this process rather than a way of restricting women. Thus hijab today is part of visible cultural identity than anything else. However, this *hijab* should not be imposed and should not cover face to become restrictive. Wearing scarf or chador as Iranians call it, should suffice.

Such way of dressing should neither be imposed nor should it be opposed. In Turkey, the Member of Parliament was also not allowed to attend the House wearing *hijab*. She was disqualified from membership fearing she represents fundamentalists in Turkey. Such compulsion to wear only western dress is as condemnable as making it compulsory to wear *hijab*. A woman should be free to wear dress the way she likes though within the limits of modesty.

One should not condemn any movement for empowerment of women as western feminism. Women are as much human beings as men and today women's rights are part of human rights. Women have every right to take part in all social, cultural and political movements. They should not be debarred from any arena. There is no sphere of activity in which women have not excelled men. It is only in Muslim countries that she is still restricted from taking part in public sphere.

It is unfortunate that there is even debate whether a woman could pray in the mosque or not. Many Muslim communities still do not permit women to pray inside mosques let alone allow them to take part in public activities. In countries like India now there is reservation in jobs and even in political bodies like panchayats and municipalities and municipal corporations. There is reservation for women for posts of sarpanch and mayors. Some conservative `*ulama* gave *fatwa* that a woman cannot contest elections. Muslim women in India rightly defied such *fatwas* and contested elections.

Such *fatwas* are given more out of ignorance of Islamic jurisprudence. The past traditions should alone cannot be the guide for issuing such *fatwas*. As society is changing social legislation should also change in a healthy way. Such change does not necessarily amount to imitating the west. While we should condemn globalisation in as much as it imposes western hegemony we should not reject modernity per se.

Islamic legislation should be dynamic and the concept of *ijtihad* does provide spirit of dynamism to Islamic shari`ah. It is unfortunate that our *ulama* are quite incompetent to understand modern society. They are totally past oriented and they think everything past is in keeping with Islamic practices. Time has come to critically evaluate all past practices and legislate afresh in many areas in keeping with the Qur'anic values on one hand, and modern spirit on the other.

Our '*ulama* laid more emphasis on *hadith* literature than on the Qur'an, particularly, when it came to legislating about women and the *hadith* literature reflects medieval feudal ethos than the real Qur'anic spirit. There is, therefore, great need today for women theologian who could properly interpret and appreciate the Qur'anic verses concerning women's rights.

This writer has no hesitation in asserting that Qur'an is very assertive of women's rights and, if read carefully, it accords equal dignity and equal rights to both the sexes. However, this spirit of the Qur'an could be appreciated either by women theologians or men committed to women's rights.

Index

N